Choosing Contemporary Music

Seasonal, Topical, Lectionary Indexes

Compiled by Terri Bocklund McLean and Rob Glover

Augsburg Fortress | Minneapolis

Choosing Contemporary Music
Seasonal, Topical, Lectionary Indexes

Compiled by Terri Bocklund McLean and Rob Glover
Edited by Norma Aamodt-Nelson, Suzanne Burke, Martin A. Seltz, and Eric Vollen

Art by Markell Studios
Designed by The Kantor Group

The paper used in this publication meets the minimum requirements of American National Standard for Information Sciences—Permanence of Paper for Printed Library Materials, ANSI Z329.48-1984.
Manufactured in the U.S.A.

ISBN 0-8066-3874-5
AF 3-450

02 03 02 01 00 1 2 3 4 5

Contents

Introduction

Imagine you are at the mall, and staring at the lighted directory board. Three floors of shops appear on three different diagrams in an array of colors, and the one thing you need to get started is the little arrow that says, "You are here." *Choosing Contemporary Music* is a starting point, a guide into the exciting but sometimes overwhelming task of selecting songs for the worshiping congregation from the praise and worship as well as contemporary liturgical and folk repertoires. You are here!

The rapidly expanding array of musical resources for worship creates a delightful problem for those who go about this choosing. Are you new to this process, asking questions like these: Where do we begin? How do we determine what music will fit? Which songs will best support the readings and images of each day and season? What song resources are worth the investment to place on the planning shelf and the music stand? You are here! This book is for you.

Or, have you been at this a while, asking questions like these: How can we branch out from the "favorites" to expand the worship repertoire? How can we do better long-term worship planning? Is there a single resource that pulls information from many places so our planning can go more quickly? You are here! This book is for you, too.

What's in this book?

The first and largest section of the book presents *songs for the Christian church year.* Many of the churches that follow the Christian year (Advent, Christmas, and so on) also use a three-year cycle of Bible readings, a lectionary. Through the use of this pattern, worshipers are able to hear and take to heart over time a rich selection of passages from the Scriptures. On the pages that follow, these readings are noted, along with a brief summary of their content and an introduction to the themes and images of each set of readings. Although the readings listed here are those of the Revised Common Lectionary in use by many churches, they are similar to the readings chosen in other three-year lectionaries, especially in the choice of the gospel reading.

Then, for each week and festival, worship songs are listed that paraphrase, reflect, or support the biblical texts. References include the title or first line of the song, composer name(s), and a source reference. Some songs in this index can be found in more than one resource. In an effort to streamline this listing, we've listed songs available in Augsburg Fortress resources along with at least one additional collection where the song can be found.

Whether or not your worship planning always includes coordinating with a lectionary system, this book has other useful features for you. A *scripture index* lists chapter and verse from the books of the Bible and songs that connect to them through direct quote, paraphrase, or theme. There's also a *topical and seasonal index*. With this you can look up a word such as *joy* and find a list of songs that support this theme or include this word. This index also collects in one place a list of songs to support each festival and season. Finally, there is an alphabetical *title index* of all the songs included in this book, and where you can find each song's source information.

The *index of publishers and collections* is your key to the abbreviations used in this book, and it will help you track down anything referenced here. For most of the songs in these indexes, we've pointed you to larger collections in which they are found, rather than individual sheet music. These major resources are more readily available at Christian bookstores, or through a variety of catalogs. Be sure to check also www.augsburgfortress.org and other publisher's websites. Some of the best songs listed are available only in small collections, new collections, or through off-the-beaten-path publishers. If you have the budget for it and are looking for "jewels," these resources may be worth the extra effort and expense to obtain.

What do we mean by "contemporary"?

The "contemporary" in *Choosing Contemporary Music* is one of those words that means different things to different people. For the purposes of these indexes, we've chosen to include under this term worship songs that are set to music in a wide variety of popular musical styles: folk, ballad, gospel, country, rock, blues, and so on. Songwriters cover the spectrum from evangelical Protestants to contemporary liturgical Lutherans and Roman Catholics. Songs listed here range from the folk tunes of John Ylvisaker to the justice-oriented ballads of Marty Haugen to the hand-clapping songs of Darrell Evans. Most of these songs have been written in the last third of the twentieth century but are still alive and well moving into the twenty-first.

Depending on the musical resources and the context of your congregation, you'll want to choose carefully the song styles you use in your worship. Remember that the most important instrument for leading worship is the human voice, used in a way that doesn't dominate but helps the congregation find their voice. The songs and song collections listed in this book all present at least the melody in musical notation. However, when it comes to accompaniments, you'll find everything from fully arranged piano accompaniments to arrangements comprised of melody line and guitar chords only. For further help with leading and accompanying the various song styles, check out the helpful *additional resources* listed on page 167.

A caution to keep in mind: although these songs are "contemporary," you'll find that the words don't always reflect contemporary usage. For example, many popular worship songs contain some examples of exclusive or archaic language and a piling up of male images and pronouns for God. And, while we've tried to select the best examples of textual content and music within these repertoires, nothing can substitute for your own review and careful consideration of the words and music of each song and whether it's appropriate for your church setting.

Those who choose contemporary music know that new songs are being composed all the time. We realize that this resource will be incomplete the day it is released. You'll notice blank spaces following sections of an index and at other places in this book. Please feel free to customize this index for your own use. Remember, this index contains only a sampling of the contemporary worship repertoire; two folks picked the best of what's available at the beginning of 2000. We encourage you to become a co-author of this book. Keep it current, and make it your own. We hope this guide will become your companion and friend as you choose music for your community of faith!

—The Compilers

Abbreviations

AFP	Augsburg Fortress octavos
BC	Borning Cry
BL	Bread of Life: Mass and Songs for the Assembly
CC	Come Celebrate! Songbook 1
CCJ	Come Celebrate! Jesus
CCP	Come Celebrate! Praise & Worship
CEL	The Celebration Hymnal
CGA	Choristers Guild octavos
CMH	Change My Heart, Oh God Songbook, vols. 1–2
COK	Cokesbury Chorus Book, Expanded Edition
CPH	Concordia Publishing House octavos
DH	Dancing at the Harvest Songbook
G	GIA octavos and collections
GC	Gather Comprehensive
G&P	Glory & Praise, 2nd ed.
HCW	Hosanna! Music Come & Worship
HMS	Hosanna! Music Songbook vols. 10–14
LBG	Lord Be Glorified Songbook
MAR	Maranatha! Music Praise Hymns and Choruses
MAR2	Maranatha! Music Praise Chorus Book, 2nd ed.
OCP	Oregon Catholic Press octavos
PCY	Psalms for the Church Year, vols. 1–10
PS	Psalm Songs, vols. 1–3
REN	Renew!
RS	RitualSong
SCR	Spirit Calls, Rejoice!
SCS	Spirit Calls, Rejoice! Supplemental Songbook
SFL	Songs of the First Light
SPW	Songs for Praise & Worship
STP	Singing the Psalms, vol. 1–4
S&S	Spirit & Song
TFF	This Far by Faith
UMH	United Methodist Hymnal
UMP	Unity Music Press octavos
VIN	Worship Songs of the Vineyard, Songbooks 6–8
VO	Voices as One
WIS	Write It on My Heart Songbook
WLP	World Library Press octavos
WOV	With One Voice
W&P	Worship & Praise Songbook

Publishers

AFP **Augsburg Fortress**
Octavos
PO Box 1209
Minneapolis MN 55440-1209
800.328.4648
www.augsburgfortress.org

BC **Borning Cry**
Worship for a New Generation
New Generation Publishers
PO Box 321
Waverly IA 50677
319.352.4396
www.ylvisaker.com

BL **Bread of Life**
Mass and Songs for the Assembly
Augsburg Fortress
PO Box 1209
Minneapolis MN 55440-1209
800.328.4648
www.augsburgfortress.org

CC **Come Celebrate! Songbook 1**
Music for Contemporary Worship
© 1995 Abingdon Press
201 Eighth Avenue South
Nashville TN 37203
800.672.1789
www.cokesbury.org

CCJ **Come Celebrate! Jesus**
Music for Contemporary Worship
© 1997 Abingdon Press
201 Eighth Avenue South
Nashville TN 37203
800.672.1789
www.cokesbury.org

CCP **Come Celebrate! Praise & Worship**
Music for Contemporary Worship
© 1997 Abingdon Press
201 Eighth Avenue South
Nashville TN 37203
800.672.1789
www.cokesbury.org

CEL **The Celebration Hymnal**
Songs and Hymns for Worship
Word Music/Integrity Music
3319 West End Ave
Suite 200
Nashville TN 37203
www.celebrationhymnal.com

CGA **Choristers Guild**
Octavos
Lorenz Corporation
PO Box 802
Dayton OH 45401-0802
800.444.1144
www.lorenz.com/unity/index.html

CMH **Change My Heart, Oh God Songbook, vols. 1–2**
Vineyard Music Group U.S.
PO Box 68025
Anaheim, CA 92817-0825
800.852.VINE
www.vineyardmusic.com

COK **Cokesbury Chorus Book, Expanded Edition**
© 1999 Abingdon Press
201 Eighth Avenue South
Nashville TN 37203
800.672.1789
www.cokesbury.org

CPH **Concordia Publishing House octavos**
Concordia Publishing House
3558 S. Jefferson Avenue
St Louis MO 63118-3968
800.325.3040
www.cphmall.com

DH **Dancing at the Harvest Songs by Ray Makeever**
© 1997 Augsburg Fortress
PO Box 1209
Minneapolis, MN 55440-1209
800.328.4648
www.augsburgfortress.org

G **GIA Publications**
Octavos
7404 South Mason Ave
Chicago IL 60638
800.442.1358
www.giamusic.com

GC **Gather Comprehensive**
© 1994 GIA Publications
7404 South Mason Ave
Chicago IL 60638
800.442.1358
www.giamusic.com

G&P **Glory & Praise, 2nd ed.**
© 1997 OCP Publications
5536 NE Hassalo
Portland OR 97213
503.281.1191 or 800.547.8992
www.ocp.org

HCW **Hosanna! Music Come & Worship A Collection of 200 Popular Songs for Praise & Worship**
© 1994 Integrity Music, Inc.
1000 Cody Road
Mobile AL 36695
800.238.7000
www.integritymusic.com

HMS **Hosanna! Music Songbooks, vols. 10–14**
© 1996 Integrity Music, Inc.
1000 Cody Road
Mobile AL 36695
800.238.7000
www.integritymusic.com

LBG **Lord Be Glorified Companion Hymnal for Blended Worship**
© 1999 OCP Publications
5536 NE Hassalo
Portland OR 97213
503.281.1191 or 800.547.8992
www.ocp.org

MAR **Maranatha! Music Praise Hymns and Choruses, 4th ed.**
Word, Inc.
3319 West End Avenue
Nashville TN 37203
www.worshipmusic.com
888.324.9673

MAR2 **Maranatha! Music Praise Chorus Book, 2nd ed.**
© 1990 The Benson Company
365 Great Circle Road
Nashville TN 37228
800.846.7664
www.worshipmusic.com

OCP **Oregon Catholic Press**
Octavos
4435 NE Hassalo
Portland OR 972133
800.548.8749
www.ocp.org

PCY **Psalms for the Church Year, vols. 1–10**
GIA Publications
7404 South Mason Ave
Chicago IL 60638
800.442.1358
www.giamusic.com

PS **Psalm Songs, vols. 1–3**
Ed. David Ogden & Alan Smith
Augsburg Fortress Publishers
PO Box 1209
Minneapolis, MN 55440-1209
800.328.4648
www.augsburgfortress.org

REN **Renew! Songs & Hymns for Blended Worship**
© 1995 Hope Publishing Company
380 South Main Place
Carol Stream IL 60188
800.323.1049
www.hopepublishing.com

RS **RitualSong**
© 1996 GIA Publications
7404 South Mason Ave
Chicago IL 60638
800.442.1358
www.giamusic.com

SCR **Spirit Calls, Rejoice! A Collection of Songs for Worship**
© 1991 Prince of Peace Publishing
Changing Church Forum
200 E. Nicollet Boulevard
Burnsville MN 55337
800.874.2044
www.changingchurch.org

SCS **Spirit Calls, Rejoice! Supplemental Songbook**
© Changing Church Forum
200 E. Nicollet Boulevard
Burnsville MN 55337
800.874.2044
www.changingchurch.org

SFL **Songs of the First Light**
© 1996 Changing Church Forum
Changing Church Forum
200 E. Nicollet Boulevard
Burnsville MN 55337
800.874.2044
www.changingchurch.org

SPW **Songs for Praise & Worship Worship Planner Edition**
Word Music
3319 West End Ave
Suite 200
Nashville TN 37203
888.324.9673
www.celebrationhymnal.com

STP **Singing the Psalms, vols. 1–4**
OCP Publications
4435 NE Hassalo
Portland OR 972133
800.548.8749
www.ocp.org

S&S **Spirit & Song A Seeker's Guide for Liturgy and Prayer**
© Oregon Catholic Press
4435 NE Hassalo
Portland OR 972133
800.548.8749
www.ocp.org

TFF **This Far by Faith**
An African American Resource for Worship
© 1999 Augsburg Fortress
PO Box 1209
Minneapolis, MN 55440-1209
800.328.4648
www.augsburgfortress.org

UMH **United Methodist Hymnal**
© 1989 The United Methodist Publishing House
Abingdon Press
201 Eighth Avenue South
Nashville TN 37202
800.672.1789
www.cokesbury.org

UMP **Unity Music Press**
Octavos
Lorenz Corporation
501 E. Third Street
PO Box 802
Dayton OH 45401-0802
800.444.1144
www.lorenz.com/unity/index.html

VIN **Worship Songs of the Vineyard Songbooks 6–8**
Vineyard Music Group U.S.
PO Box 68025
Anaheim CA 92817-0825
800.852.VINE
www.vineyardmusic.com

VO **Voices as One**
Contemporary Hymnal
World Library Publications
3825 N. Willow Rd
Schiller Park IL 60176
800.566.6150
www.wlp.jspaluch.com

WIS **Write It on My Heart Songbook**
The Worship Songs of Terri McLean
© 1999 PrairieSoul Music, Inc.
8775 M Centre Park Drive, PMB 27
Columbia MD 21045
e-mail | prairiesoul@juno.com

WLP **World Library Publications**
Octavos
3825 N. Willow Rd
Schiller Park IL 60176
800.566.6150
www.wlp.jspaluch.com

WOV **With One Voice**
A Lutheran Resource for Worship
© 1995 Augsburg Fortress
PO Box 1209
Minneapolis MN 55440-1209
800.328.4648
www.augsburgfortress.org

W&P **Worship & Praise Songbook**
© 1999 Augsburg Fortress
PO Box 1209
Minneapolis MN 55440-1209
800.328.4648
www.augsburgfortress.org

Songs for the Church Year

Sundays and Principal Festivals

First Sunday of Advent

Year A

Of one thing we can be certain: our fragile, mortal lives will come to an end. We know neither the day nor the hour. Yet with our hearts enlightened by faith, we know that Christ—our life and our resurrection—is already with us in his word, his baptismal promise, his body and blood, his community of faith. We have been grasped and held for all time with Christ's steadfast love. In these gifts of grace, the people of God rejoice. Indeed, if there is any urgency, it concerns our mission in this fragile, broken world that yearns for light, life, and salvation.

ISAIAH 2:1-5
Weapons of war transformed into instruments of peace

All around your throne *DeShazo/Kerr* **HMS10 808**
How good it is *American* **GC 727**
Let peace fill the earth *Makeever* **DH 90**
Lord, my strength *Krippaehne* **W&P 93**
On that holy mountain *Mattingly* **VO 68**
Show me your ways *Fragar* **HMS11 949**

PSALM 122
I was glad when they said to me, "Let us go to the house of the LORD."

I love to be in your presence *Baloche/Kerr* **HCW 75**
I rejoiced *Farrell* **PS1**
I rejoiced *Walker* **PS2**
I rejoiced when I heard them say *Warner* **VO 41**
I was glad *Beech* **W&P 68**
I was glad *Haas* **GC 121**
Let us go rejoicing *Harbor* **TFF 17**
Let us go rejoicing *Joncas* **GC 120**
Let us go rejoicing *Roberts* **G-4606**
Once again *Hanson* **SCS 18**
Stand in the congregation *Batstone* **W&P 131, MAR 149**

ROMANS 13:11-14
Salvation is near; time to wake from sleep

Awake! Awake, and greet the new morn *Haugen* **WOV 633, GC 346, RS 494**
Put on love *Makeever* **DH 78**
Wake up *Hanson* **SCR 13**

MATTHEW 24:36-44
The sudden coming of the Son of Man

Arise *Barnett* **VIN7 33**
I'll be waitin' *Ylvisaker* **BC**
My Lord will come again *Haas* **GC 769**
When the Lord in glory comes *Moore* **GC 765**

ADDITIONAL SONGS FOR THE DAY/SEASON

A story for all people *Collins* **W&P 2**
Come to set us free *Farrell* **GC 338, G&P 298**
I want to be ready *Spiritual* **TFF 41**
Soon and very soon *Crouch* **W&P 128, TFF 38, WOV 744, CEL 757**
Wake up, sleeper *Ylvisaker* **BC**

Year B

The days of Advent point the people of God toward the three comings of the Lord Jesus. He came among us at Bethlehem. He comes among us now in the scriptures, the waters of baptism, the eucharistic meal, and the community of faith. He will come again in glory to judge the living and the dead. Keep awake, for his coming is certain and his day draws near.

ISAIAH 64:1-9
Prayer that God would come with power and compassion

Change my heart, O God *Wimber* **CMH 4, W&P 28**
Have thine own way, Lord *Pollard* **TFF 152**
I bend my knees again *Butler/Butler* **VIN8 85**
Now God our Father *Mills/Dearman* **W&P 103, CEL 654**

PSALM 80:1-7, 16-18
Show us the light of your countenance, and we shall be saved.

God of hosts, bring us back *Furlong* **PS1**
Lord, come and save us *Kendzia* **G&P 308**
Lord, make us turn to you *Haugen* **GC 75**
Lord, make us turn to you *Smith* **PS1**
Shine, Jesus, shine *Kendrick* **W&P 123, WOV 651**
Turn my heart *DeShazo* **HCW 179**

1 CORINTHIANS 1:3-9

Gifts of grace sustain those who wait for the end

- Everlasting grace *Carpenter* **VIN6 58**
- Faithful Father *Doerksen* **VIN7 72**
- Thank you for the gift *Hanson* **SCR 144**
- Thank you, Lord *Park* **VIN8 242**
- You are holy *Brown* **HMS10 884**

MARK 13:24-37

The sudden coming of the Son of Man

- Eternity *Doerksen* **CMH 28**
- Heaven and earth *DeShazo/Harville* **HMS10 829**
- My heart yearns for thee *Baroni* **HMS12 1022**
- The wondrous day of our God *Haugen* **G-4416**
- When the Lord in glory comes *Moore* **GC 765**

ADDITIONAL SONGS FOR THE DAY/SEASON

- Emmanuel *McGee* **SPW**
- Look to the one *Bolduc* **VO 57**
- My Lord will come again *Haas* **GC 769**
- Save us, O Lord *Dufford* **G&P 301**
- While we are waiting, come *Cason* **SPW**
- You are the potter *Ylvisaker* **BC**

Year C

In prayer and song, the liturgy of Advent announces God's vision of a world transformed by grace: justice will triumph, love will abound, the earth will be a place of safety. The power of evil, sin, and death will be utterly vanquished in the dawning light of redemption. Yet already the church experiences this vision in word and sacrament, in the communion of believers, in every gesture and word of justice and peace. A righteous branch springs up from David: in baptism we have been grafted into Christ's life and mission.

JEREMIAH 33:14-16

A righteous branch springs from David

- Arise, O Lord *Carpenter* **VIN6 16**
- Faithful Father *Doerksen* **VIN7 72**
- My soul in stillness waits *Haugen* **GC 328, RS 495**
- We bring the sacrifice of praise *Dearman* **W&P 150, CEL 213**

PSALM 25:1-9

To you, I lift up my soul

- Lead me, oh lead me *Smith* **HMS13 1085**
- Lift up my soul *Hurd* **G&P 302**
- O Lord to you *Sadler* **HMS11 937**
- Psalm 25 *Balhoff/Daigle/Ducote* **PCY6**
- Psalm 25: Remember *Cooney* **G-3972**
- Remember your love *Ducote/Daigle* **G&P 474**
- Remember your mercies *Haas* **GC 35, RS 54**
- Remember your mercy, Lord *Inwood* **G&P 476**
- Show me your ways *Fragar* **HMS11 949**
- To you, O God, I lift up my soul *Hurd* **G&P 302**
- To you, O Lord *Haas* **PCY9**
- To you, O Lord *Haugen* **GC 36, RS 53**
- To you, O Lord *Soper* **PS1**
- To you, O Lord *Thompson* **RS 50**
- To you, O Lord, I lift my soul *Roberts* **G-4601**

1 THESSALONIANS 3:9-13

Strengthen hearts of holiness

- All through the night *Ylvisaker* **BC**
- Awake, O sleeper *Haugen* **GC 803**
- I'll belong to you *Hanson* **SCR 126**
- Only you *Baloche/Kerr* **HMS13 1092**
- Turn our hearts *Kendrick* **HMS10 43**
- What shall I render *Douroux* **TFF 239**

LUKE 21:25-36

Watch for the coming of the Son of Man

- Eternity *Doerksen* **CMH 28**
- Heaven and earth *DeShazo/Harvill* **HMS10 829**
- My heart yearns for thee *Baroni* **HMS12 1022**
- My Lord will come again *Haas* **GC 769**
- The kingdom song *Evans* **HMS12 1040**
- This kingdom *Bullock* **HMS11 962**
- When the Lord in glory comes *Moore* **GC 765**

ADDITIONAL SONGS FOR THE DAY/SEASON

- Stand firm *Glover* **G-4593**
- Stir up *Makeever* **DH 51**
- The wondrous day of our God *Haugen* **G-4416**
- Unto thee, O Lord *Monroe* **CEL 531**
- Who will stand up *Soper* **G-4626**

Second Sunday of Advent

Year A

In the scripture, prayers, and hymns of Advent, John the Baptist brings us to the Jordan River and the waters of baptism. He calls us to repent, for the reign of God is near. He calls us to the font of new birth where we have been grafted into God's branch, the root of Jesse. He calls us to the holy supper where we receive forgiveness in the life-giving fruit of Christ's body and blood. From our Sunday assemblies we are called to go forth as a people whose mission is the proclamation of God's mercy for our suffering world.

ISAIAH 11:1-10
From David's line, a ruler bringing justice and peace

Carol of the child *Haas*	**G-4344**
Glorious *Daniels*	**VIN7 82**
He shall reign *Chopinsky*	**HMS12 999**
How good it is *American*	**GC 72**
On that holy mountain *Mattingly*	**VO 68**
The Lord of glory *O'Brien*	**G-3778**
Walk in the reign *Cooney*	**GC 319**
Wonderful Counselor *Yeager*	**MAR2**

PSALM 72:1-7, 18-19
In his time the righteous shall flourish.

Glorious God *Baroni/Fitts/Smith/Cloninger*	**HMS10 823**
In his days justice will flourish *Joncas*	**GC 72**
In his days *Ogden*	**PS1**
Justice shall flourish *Cooney*	**G&P 220**
Send out your grace abundantly *Ylvisaker/Ernest*	**BC**

ROMANS 15:4-13
Live in harmony, welcoming one another

Be near us *Hanson/Murakami*	**SCR 4**
In unity and peace *Chepponis*	**G-4452**
Meet us *Rethmeier*	**VIN8 136**
Reach out and take a hand *Kendrick*	**HMS12 1029**
People of the Word *Makeever*	**DH 1**

MATTHEW 3:1-2
A voice cries: Prepare the way of the Lord

Give us your vision *Hanson/Murakami*	**SCR 85**
He came to be baptized *Ylvisaker*	**BC**
He shall reign *Chopinsky*	**HMS12 999**
Look to the one *Bolduc*	**VO 57**
Prepare the way of the Lord *Taizé*	**GC 336, RS 491**
Refiner's fire *Doerksen*	**CMH 10**

ADDITIONAL SONGS FOR THE DAY/SEASON

A voice cries out *Joncas*	**G&P 294, RS 485**
O how I long to see *Hurd*	**G&P 306**
The King of glory *Jabusch/Israeli*	**W&P 136**

Year B

John, the Advent prophet, stands by the waters of baptism and calls the church to see that "our God is here." In baptism God has made us sisters and brothers of the Lord Jesus. God has clothed us with the Holy Spirit, a fire to warm what is cold within us and to kindle our hearts with love. Fed by word and meal, we go forth ourselves to prepare the way of the Lord by proclaiming the good tidings that Christ is coming.

ISAIAH 40:1-11
Good news of God's coming to a people in exile

Every valley *Dufford*	**G&P 297**
I see you *Mullins*	**CC 90**
Let the valleys be raised *Schutte*	**G&P 310**
Like a shepherd *Dufford*	**GC 325, G&P 708**
Spirit song *Wimber*	**W&P 130**
We will rise again *Haas*	**G&P 603**
You are I Am *Evans*	**HMS12 1051**

PSALM 85:1-2, 8-13
Righteousness and peace shall go before the LORD.

Come, O Lord, and set us free *Balhoff/Daigle/Ducote*	**GC 80, RS 114**
Let us see, O Lord, your mercy *Smith*	**PS1**
Lord, let us see your kindness *Haugen*	**GC 79, RS 112**
Lord, make us turn to you *Haugen*	**GC 7**
Your constant love *Hanson*	**SCR 100**
Your mercy like rain *Cooney*	**GC 330**
O Lord, let us see your kindness *Harbor*	**TFF 8**

2 PETER 3:8-15A

Waiting for and hastening the day of God

Let the peace of God reign *Zschech* **HMS11 926**

Wait for the Lord *Taizé* **GC 332**

MARK 1:1-8

John appears from the wilderness

He shall reign *Chopinsky* **HMS12 999**

Here begins the good news *Haugen* **G-4416, SCR 129**

The advent herald *Cooney* **G-4972**

Waterlife *Hanson* **W&P 145**

ADDITIONAL SONGS FOR THE DAY/SEASON

A voice cries out *Joncas* **G&P 294, RS 485**

Give us your vision *Hanson/Murakami* **SCR**

Maranatha *Schoenbachler* **G&P 29**

Year C

During this second week of Advent, John the Baptist walks onto the stage and calls people to a new beginning. Our baptism is also a new beginning. Day after day, as we are renewed in our baptism, God who began a good work in us continues to prepare us for the day of Jesus Christ.

MALACHAI 3:1-4

My messenger is a refiner and purifier

Purify my heart *Greco* **HCW 148**

Refiner's fire *Doerksen* **CMH 10**

The fire of your love *Baloche/Kerr* **HMS12 1037**

BARUCH 5:1-9

The return of scattered Israel

LUKE 1:68-79

In the tender compassion of our God, the dawn from high shall break upon us

Benedictus *Jones* **PS1**

Blessed be the Lord *Daigle/Ducote* **G&P 442**

Blessed be the Lord God of Israel *Sappington* **W&P 20**

Blessed be the name *Park* **VIN7 48**

Holy love, holy light *Batstone* **MAR 118**

PHILIPPIANS 1:3-11

A harvest of righteousness on the day of Jesus Christ

He who began a good work *Mohr* **HCW 60, W&P 56**

Over and over *Baloche* **HMS13 1096**

The harvest of justice *Haas* **GC 711**

When the Lord comes *Flowers* **VIN6 262**

LUKE 3:1-6

Prepare the way of the Lord

A voice cries out *Joncas* **G&P 294, RS 485**

Every valley *Dufford* **G&P 297**

Give us your vision *Hanson/Murakami* **SCR 85**

He shall reign *Chopinsky* **HMS12 999**

My heart yearns for thee *Baroni* **HMS12 1022**

On Jordan's bank *Miles* **GC 322**

ADDITIONAL SONGS FOR THE DAY/SEASON

Let the King of glory come *Joncas* **G&P 299**

Look to the one *Bolduc* **VO 57**

Open our eyes *Keil* **UMP 10/1737U-8**

Third Sunday of Advent

Year A

In today's gospel reading, Jesus points to signs of God's reign: the blind see, the lame walk, lepers are cleansed, the deaf hear. Those who thought themselves ignored by God now discover the merciful and healing presence of God's anointed servant. Echoing these words of Jesus, we ask God to open our eyes and ears so that we might see and hear God's strong and saving presence among us today: in word and holy supper, in the church and in our homes, in the silence of prayer and in the events of daily life. Strengthen your hearts, the Lord is near.

ISAIAH 35:1-10
The desert blooms as God's people return from exile
- Flow river flow *Hurd* **G&P 455**
- Glorious *Daniels* **VIN7 82**
- God is here *Moen/Overstreet* **HMS12 995**
- Lord of glory *Manion* **G&P 707**
- Open our eyes *Cull* **TFF 98, W&P 113**
- You've delivered me again *Ylvisaker* **BC**

PSALM 146:4-9
The Lord lifts up those who are bowed down.
- As long as I live *Haas* **G-4681**
- Lord, I lift your name on high *Founds* **W&P 90**
- Maranatha, alleluia! *Wellicome* **PS1**
- Sing unto the Lord *Makeever* **DH 47**

LUKE 1:47-55
My spirit rejoices in God my Savior
- Faithful One *Doerksen* **CMH2 60**
- Mary's song *Rethmeier* **VIN6 160**

JAMES 5:7-10
Patience until the coming of the Lord
- I will never be *Bullock* **HMS11 920**
- I'll be waitin' *Ylvisaker* **BC**
- Patience, people *Foley* **G&P 303**

MATTHEW 11:2-11
The forerunner of Christ
- For all people Christ was born *Makeever* **DH 52**
- Hold me in life *Huijbers* **GC 599**
- Let the river flow *Evans* **HMS12 1015**
- On Jordan's bank *Miles* **GC 322**
- We will draw near *Nystrom/Harris* **HMS11 966**

ADDITIONAL SONGS FOR THE DAY/SEASON
- All earth is hopeful *Taulé/Keesecker* **AFP 11-10877**
- The Lord of glory *O'Brien* **G-3778**
- Walk in the reign *Cooney* **GC 319**
- We will draw near *Nystrom/Harris* **HMS13**

Year B

The ancient name for this day is Gaudete, or "Rejoice Sunday," inspired by the opening words of the second reading, "Rejoice always." In the midst of our preparations and longings we rejoice that the faithful one who brings good news to the oppressed and brokenhearted is already in our midst, helping us hold fast to what is good. With John the Baptist we point the way to the coming light that brings great joy to all the world.

ISAIAH 61:1-4, 8-11
Righteousness and praise flourish like a garden
- Good news *Ethiopian/Olson* **GC 679**
- He is Lord *Smith* **HMS12 998**
- I Am *Hanson* **SFL**
- The kingdom song *Evans* **HMS12 1040**
- You have anointed me *Balhoff/Ducote/Daigle* **G&P 555, GC 676**

PSALM 126
The LORD has done great things for us
- Give thanks *Smith* **W&P 41, TFF 292, HCW 46**
- God has done great things for us *Haugen* **GC 124**
- My God reigns *Evans* **HMS12 1021**
- Reason to celebrate *Chumchal* **VIN8 165**
- The Lord has done great things *Cortez* **G&P 271**
- The Lord has done great things *Guimont* **RS 169**
- The Lord has done great things *Smith* **PS1**
- The Lord has done great things *Stewart* **RS 170**

LUKE 1:47-55
The Lord has lifted up the lowly
Faithful One *Doerksen* **CMH2 60**
Magnificat *Smith* **PS1**
Mary's song *Rethmeier* **VIN6 160**
My soul does magnify the Lord *Brown* **TFF 168**
Sanctuary *Thompson/Scruggs* **HCW 154**

1 THESSALONIANS 5:16-24
Kept in faith until the coming of Christ
I will rejoice *Brown* **G&P 674**
My Lord will come again *Haas* **GC 769**
Purify my heart *Greco* **HCW 148**
Sanctuary *Thompson/Scruggs* **HCW 154**

JOHN 1:6-8, 19-28
A witness to the light
Christ, be our light *Farrell* **G&P 656**
City of God *Schutte* **GC 678**
He came down *Cameroon/Bell* **TFF 37**
Jesus, lead on *Helming* **VIN8 114**
Shine on us *Glover* **G-4583**
The Holy Lamb of God *Ylvisaker* **BC**

ADDITIONAL SONGS FOR THE DAY/SEASON
Each winter as year grows older *Gay/Haugen* **GC 339, RS 481**
Lift up your heads *Kendrick* **W&P 88**
Look to the one *Bolduc* **VO 57**

Year C

The arrival is fast approaching; the light from the Advent wreath is growing. How shall we prepare for God's coming among us? With joy! With resolute action! With prayer and thanksgiving! The Lord is near.

ZEPHANIAH 3:14-20
Rejoice, the LORD *is in your midst*
Be my home *Hanson/Murakami* **W&P 16**
He brings peace *Hanson* **SCR 217**
Lift up your hearts *O'Connor* **G&P 676, SCR 45**
Whom shall I fear? *Evans* **HMS13 1115**

ISAIAH 12:2-6
In your midst is the Holy One of Israel
Cry out with joy and gladness *Haugen* **GC 148**
Lord, my strength *Krippaehne* **W&P 93**
Sing a song to the Lord *Rushbridge* **PS1**
The first song of Isaiah *White* **REN 122**

PHILIPPIANS 4:4-7
Rejoice, the Lord is near
Awake! Awake, and greet the new morn *Haugen* **WOV 633, GC 346**
Closer *Butler* **VIN6 36**
Give thanks *Smith* **W&P 41, TFF 292, HCW 46**
Let the peace of God reign *Zschech* **HMS11 926**
Meet us *Rethmeier* **VIN8 136**
Rejoice in the mission *Collins* **W&P 120**
Teach me how to pray *Hanson/Murakami* **SCR 25**

LUKE 3:7-18
One more powerful is coming, baptizing with fire
All the power you need *Fragar* **HMS11 888**
I will never be *Bullock* **HMS11 920**
On Jordan's bank *Miles* **GC 322**
The Advent herald *Cooney* **G-4972**
The fire of your love *Baloche/Kerr* **HMS12 1037**

ADDITIONAL SONGS FOR THE DAY/SEASON
A story for all people *Collins* **W&P 2**
Advent song: Lead us from darkness *Clarke* **G-3902**
Cry out with joy and gladness *Haugen* **GC 148**
Eat this bread, drink this cup *Young* **BL, AFP 11-10651, WOV 706**

Fourth Sunday of Advent

Year A

We do well to acknowledge that one of the reasons we celebrate the festivals and seasons of the year is our tendency to forget God's merciful presence. In the words of scripture, in baptism and holy communion, we are reminded of God's promises and encounter the very presence of Jesus Christ. Advent names him Emmanuel, "God is with us." God comes to us in ordinary ways, offering extraordinary gifts: new life in baptism, gracious words to guide us on life's path, welcome food for the journey of faith. With Mary and Joseph and all the angels, we offer thanks to God for the one who was born to save us from the power of sin. Let us not forget: God is with us now.

ISAIAH 7:10-16
The sign of Immanuel

- Emmanuel *Manion* **G&P 329**
- Emmanuel *McGee* **TFF 45, W&P 36**
- God with us *Kendrick* **HMS**

PSALM 80:1-7, 16-18
Show us the light of your countenance and we shall be saved.

- God of hosts, bring us back *Furlong* **PS1**
- Holy is your name *Haas* **GC 147**
- Jesus lead on *Helming* **VIN8 114**

ROMANS 1:1-7
Paul's greeting to the church at Rome

- God sent his Son *Gaither/Gaither* **TFF 93**
- Jesus, child of God *Makeever* **DH 53**
- Peace child *Glover* **G-4339**

MATTHEW 1:18-25
A God near at hand

- All earth is hopeful *Taulé* **TFF 47, AFP 11-10877, WOV 629**
- Be near us, Lord Jesus *Hanson/Murakami* **SCR 4**
- For all you've done *Moen* **HMS12 992**
- Lift up your heads *Fry* **HCW 111**
- Meet us *Rethmeier* **VIN8 136**
- No wind at the window *Gaelic/Bell* **RS 876**
- Praise we the Lord this day *Swabia* **GC 777**

ADDITIONAL SONGS FOR THE DAY/SEASON

- Let the King of glory come *Joncas* **G&P 299**
- Maranatha, come *O'Brien* **G-4526**
- Take of the wonder *Wetzler* **AFP 11-10647**
- Who has known *Foley* **G&P 327**

Year B

With Mary, the church hears these words: Do not be afraid, you have found favor with God. You, the people of God. You, the baptized Christian. In an anxious and uncertain world, you need not be fearful, the Lord is with you. With these words of consolation, we also hear Mary's response: I am the servant of the Lord. Baptized into the Lord's death and resurrection, and strengthened by his body and blood, we are sent into the world to witness to God's favor for all creation.

2 SAMUEL 7:1-11, 16
The LORD's promise to David

- Like a shepherd *Dufford* **GC 325, G&P 708**
- You are mine *Haas* **W&P 158**

LUKE 1:47-55
The Lord has lifted up the lowly

- Faithful One *Doerksen* **CMH2 60**
- Magnificat *Smith* **PS1**
- Magnificat *Ylvisaker* **BC**
- Mary's song *Rethmeier* **VIN6 160**

PSALM 89:1-4,19-26
Your love, O LORD, forever will I sing.

- I could sing of your love forever *Smith* **HMS13 1075**
- I will sing *Ogden* **PS1**
- Magnificat *Chepponis* **GC 146**
- Lord, with grateful hearts *Ylvisaker* **BC**
- You have been good *Paris* **HCW 198**

ROMANS 16:25-27
The mystery of God revealed in Jesus Christ

- I can do all things *Baloche/Harris* **HMS11 913**
- I can do all things *Smith* **HMS13 1074**

Look to the one *Bolduc* **VO 57**
Lord, my strength *Krippaehne* **W&P 93**

LUKE 1:26-38
The angel appears to Mary
A message came to maiden young *Dutch* **RS 478**
Here I am *Batstone* **MAR 115**
Here is my heart *Nystrom* **HMS13 1070**
I belong to a mighty God *DeShazo* **MHS 8**
Magnificat *Smith* **PS1**

No wind at the window *Gaelic/Bell* **RS 876**
The angel Gabriel from heaven came *Basque* **G&P 441, RS**

ADDITIONAL SONGS FOR THE DAY/SEASON
Awake! Awake, and greet the new morn *Haugen* **WOV 633, GC 346, RS 494**
He is Jesus *Bolduc* **VO 34**
Let the King of glory come *Joncas* **G&P 299, OCP**

Year C

We come to the threshold of the celebration. The time is right; the place, Bethlehem of Judah, is identified; Mary's song announces the great things God is doing. A new day is being birthed into existence and we are meant to be a part of it. This final Sunday of preparation leads to the darkness of Christmas Eve and the dawn of Christmas Day, where the mystery unfolds again.

MICAH 5:2-5A
From Bethlehem comes a ruler
Like a shepherd *Dufford* **GC 325, G&P 708**
Peace child *Glover* **G-4339**
Peace *Hanson* **SCS 20**
Star of David *Murakami* **SCR 206**

LUKE 1:47-55
The Lord has lifted up the lowly
Canticle of the turning *Irish/Cooney* **W&P 26**
Faithful One *Doerksen* **CMH2 60**
Magnificat *Ylvisaker* **BC**
Mary's song *Rethmeier* **VIN6 160**

PSALM 80:1-7
Show the light of your countenance and we shall be saved.
Holy is your name *Haas* **GC 147**
Jesus lead on *Helming* **VIN8 114**
Magnificat *Cherepponis* **GC 146**

HEBREWS 10:5-10
I have come to do your will
For me *Hanson* **SCR 176**
God, beyond all names *Farrell* **G&P 667, GC 491**
In Christ a new creation *Ylvisaker* **BC**

LUKE 39-45 [46-55]
Blessed are you among women/My soul magnifies the Lord
Ave Maria *Kantor* **GC 785, RS 896**
Faithful One *Doerksen* **CMH2 60**
Magnificat *Ylvisaker* **BC**
Mary's song *Rethmeier* **VIN6 160**
No wind at the window *Gaelic/Bell* **RS 876**

ADDITIONAL SONGS FOR THE DAY/SEASON
Awake! Awake, and greet the new morn *Haugen* **WOV 633, GC 346, RS 494**
Emmanuel *McGee* **W&P 36**
Oh, come, oh, come, Emmanuel *Young* **AFP 11-10891**
What feast of love *Barber* **AFP 11-10674**
Who has known *Foley* **G&P 32**
Within our hearts be born *Joncas* **GC 329**

Nativity of the Lord

Years A, B, C

Christmas Eve (I)

Tonight we join with Christians throughout the world to celebrate the great mystery of our faith: God speaks to us in our words so that we might know God's mercy; God comes to us in human flesh—in Christ's body and blood—so that we might share in God's unfailing love. It is not a baby's birth we celebrate, but the light of redemption. As Paul reminds us, the grace of God has appeared bringing salvation to all. Christ unites himself to our fragile, mortal lives so that we might know he is with us, always offering us life, health, and salvation. With the heavenly host we sing, "Glory to God in the highest heaven."

ISAIAH 9:2-7
Light shines: a child is born for us

- Child of mercy *Haas* **GC 357, RS 506**
- City of God *Schutte* **GC 678**
- He is Jesus *Bolduc* **VO 34**
- Jehovah *Springer* **VIN6 124**
- King of kings *Batya/Conty* **W&P 80**
- Who has known *Foley* **G&P 327**
- Wonderful Counselor *Yeager* **MAR2 35**

PSALM 96
Let the heavens rejoice and the earth be glad.

- Great is the Lord *Smith/Smith* **W&P 53**
- Let the heavens rejoice *Harbor* **TFF 10**
- Proclaim to all the nations *Haas/Haugen* **GC 93**
- Rise up and praise him *Baloche/Sadler* **HMS13 1098**
- Shout to the Lord *Zschech* **W&P 124, HMS10 862**
- Today a Saviour has been born *Ollis* **PS1**
- Today is born our Savior *Haugen* **GC 91**
- Today our Savior is born *Cortez* **G&P 238**
- We declare your name *Baloche/Baloche* **HMS10 874**

TITUS 2:11-14
The grace of God has appeared

- Everlasting grace *Carpenter* **VIN6 58**
- Night of silence *Kantor* **GC 342, RS 523, W&P 101**
- Peace child *Glover* **G-4339**

LUKE 2:1-14 [15-20]
God with us

- A stable lamp is lighted *Haugen* **GC 356**
- Emmanuel *Manion* **G&P 329**
- Hear the angels *Cain/Kadidlo* **W&P 57**
- Jesus, child of God *Ylvisaker* **BC**
- Nativity carol *O'Brien* **GC 365, RS 521**
- On Christmas night *Hanson/Murakami* **SCR 210**
- Star of David *Murakami* **SCR 206**
- That boy-child of Mary *Colvin* **TFF 54**
- Welcome the child *Haugen* **G-3803**

ADDITIONAL SONGS FOR THE DAY/SEASON

- Gentle night *Manion* **G&P 323**
- People of the night *Haas* **GC 340**
- Song of the stable *Haas* **GC 364, RS 364**
- The Lord of glory *O'Brien* **G-3778**
- The tiny child to Bethlehem came *Haugen* **GC 355**
- The virgin Mary had a baby boy *West Indian* **TFF 53, GC 345, RS 501**
- Within our hearts be born *Joncas* **GC 329**

Christmas Dawn (II)

The angels proclaim, "To you is born this day a Savior!" The scriptures announce the presence of God among the people of the earth. At the table we meet the child born of Mary, our crucified and risen Lord. Through holy baptism we have become children of the true Light. We go forth to proclaim this news of great joy: God is with us.

ISAIAH 62:6-12
God comes to restore the people

- Faithful One *Doerksen* **CMH2 60**
- He came down *Cameroon/Bell* **GC 370, RS 519**
- You are mine *Haas* **W&P 158**
- You have called us *DeShazo/Nystrom* **HCW 199**

PSALM 97
Light has sprung up for the righteous.

- Be glad in the Lord *Manalo* **G-4363**
- Lord most high *Harris/Sadler* **HMS11 930**
- Our God is here *Haas* **G-5041**
- This day new light will shine *Beckett* **PS1**

TITUS 3:4-7

Saved through water and the Spirit

- He is Jesus *Bolduc* **VO 34**
- Saved by the grace of a miracle *Ylvisaker* **BC**
- The Spirit is singing *Hanson/Murakami* **SCR 72**

LUKE 2:[1-7] 8-20

The birth of the Messiah revealed to shepherds

- All is Christmas *Hanson/Murakami* **SCR 193**
- Hear the angels *Cain/Kadidlo* **W&P 57**
- Jesus, child of God *Ylvisaker* **BC**
- Nativity carol *O'Brien* **GC 365, RS 521**
- Night of silence *Kantor* **W&P 101**
- On Christmas day *Ylvisaker* **BC**
- On Christmas night *Hanson/Murakami* **SCR 210**
- Ring the chimes, ring the Christmas bells *Ylvisaker* **BC**
- Star of David *Murakami* **SCR 206**
- That boy-child of Mary *Colvin* **TFF 54**
- The virgin Mary had a baby boy *West Indian* **TFF 53, GC 345, RS 501**
- Wake from your sleep *Schutte* **G&P 328**

ADDITIONAL SONGS FOR THE DAY/SEASON

- Awake! Awake, and greet the new morn *Haugen* **WOV 633, GC 346**
- Carol at the manger *Haugen* **WOV 638, GC 369**
- Rise up, shepherd, and follow *Spiritual* **WOV 645, GC 360, RS 505**
- Within our hearts be born *Joncas* **GC 329**

Christmas Day (III)

Since the beginning of time, the coming of light has been a sign of life and hope. The sun and the stars transform the darkness into an inhabitable space. On the festival of the Lord's nativity, the church gathers to celebrate the light of God's grace present in Christ. In the holy bath of baptism, he enlightens and claims us as brothers and sisters. In the holy word of scripture, he speaks to us of God's love for each human being. In the holy meal of communion, he gives us the bread of eternal life. From this celebration we go forth to be light-bearers in the ordinary rhythms of daily life.

ISAIAH 52:7-10

Heralds announce God's salvation

- Lord most high *Harris/Sadler* **HMS11 930**
- Our God reigns *Smith* **VO 73**
- The King of glory *Israeli* **W&P 136**

PSALM 98

All the ends of the earth have seen the victory of our God.

- All the ends of the earth *Johnson* **PS1**
- Celebrate love *Hanson* **SCR 16**
- Our God reigns *Smith* **VO 73**
- The kingdom song *Evans* **HMS12 1040**

HEBREWS 1:1-4 [5-12]

God has spoken by a Son

- Like a rose in winter *Hanson/Murakami* **SCR 204**
- Majesty *Hayford* **W&P 94**

JOHN 1:1-14

The Word became flesh

- All is Christmas *Hanson/Murakami* **SCR 193**
- Child of mercy *Haas* **GC 357, RS 506**
- Child of the poor/What child is this *Soper* **G&P 336/337**
- Jesus, child of God *Ylvisaker* **BC**
- Make my life a candle *Hanson* **SCR 163**
- That boy-child of Mary *Colvin* **TFF 54**
- There was the Word *Makeever* **DH 55**

ADDITIONAL SONGS FOR THE DAY/SEASON

- Carol at the manger *Haugen* **GC 369, RS 516**
- Gloria, gloria, gloria *Sosa* **WOV 637**
- He came down *Cameroon/Bell* **GC 370, RS 519, TFF 37**

First Sunday after Christmas

Year A

The gospel reading for this day juxtaposes the birth of Christ with the death of innocent children. Indeed, whenever we sentimentalize the nativity of the Lord, we need to hear this story of the slaughter of the holy innocents. Christian faith does not lead us out of the world of evil rulers, injustice, and death. Rather, the gift of faith strengthens us to contend with any force that threatens the life God has created. Here is this potent sign: in the holy supper we receive the body and blood of the one who accompanies us in this broken and fragile world.

ISAIAH 63:7-9
Israel saved by God's own presence
He came down *Cameroon/Bell* **GC 370, RS 519, TFF 37**
I could sing of your love forever *Smith* **HMS13 1075**
The King of glory *Israeli* **W&P 136**

PSALM 148
The splendor of the LORD is over heaven and earth.
Ancient of days *Sadler/Harvill* **HCW 11**
He is exalted *Paris* **W&P 55**
Heaven and earth *DeShazo/Harvill* **HMS10 829**
Let all creation sing *Ogden* **PS1**
Praise in the heights *Haas* **G-5041**
Shout to the Lord *Zschech* **W&P 124, HMS10 862**
We've come to praise you *Grant/Darnall* **MAR 80**
You alone *Hanson/Murakami* **SCR 36**

HEBREWS 2:10-18
Christ shares flesh and blood to free humankind
A stable lamp is lighted *Haugen* **GC 356**
Come to me today *Hanson* **SCR 174**
Everlasting grace *Carpenter* **VIN6 58**
For all people Christ was born *Makeever* **DH 52**
God with us *Kendrick* **HMS5 392**

MATTHEW 2:13-23
The slaughter of innocent children
All is Christmas *Hanson/Murakami* **SCR 193**
Carol at the manger *Haugen* **GC 369, RS 516**
Faithful Father *Doerksen* **VIN7 72**
Holy child *Makeever* **DH 54**
On Christmas day *Ylvisaker* **BC**
The aye carol *Bell* **GC 371, RS 525**

ADDITIONAL SONGS FOR THE DAY/SEASON
Child of mercy *Haas* **GC 357, RS 506**
Child of the poor/What child is this *Soper* **G&P 336/337**
I wonder as I wander *Appalachian/Niles* **WOV 642**

Year B

With Simeon and Anna, the church proclaims that salvation has come to the people of God in Christ Jesus. "The splendor of the Lord is over heaven and earth"—Christ is present in the world for all people in all conditions of life. In, with, and through Jesus, the Christian community welcomes all people to the scriptures, the baptismal bath, and the holy supper.

ISAIAH 61:10-62:3
Clothed in garments of salvation
Beauty for brokenness *Kendrick* **W&P 17**
Before you now *Butler/Osbrink* **VIN7 44**
City of God *Schutte* **GC 678**
He is Jesus *Bolduc* **VO 34**
Jesus, Jesus *Bullock* **HMS11 923**

PSALM 148
The splendor of the LORD is over heaven and earth.
Ancient of days *Sadler/Harvill* **HCW 11**
He is exalted *Paris* **W&P 55**
Heaven and earth *DeShazo/Harvill* **HMS10 829**
Let all creation sing *Ogden* **PS1**
Praise in the heights *Haas* **G-5041**
Shout to the Lord *Zschech* **W&P 124, HMS11 947**
We've come to praise you *Grant/Darnall* **MAR 80**
You alone *Hanson/Murakami* **SCR 36**

GALATIANS 4:4-7

Children and heirs of God

- Faithful Father *Doerksen* **VIN7 72**
- I belong to a mighty God *DeShazo* **HMS8 654**
- Let the peace of God reign *Zschech* **HMS11 926**
- Saved by the grace of a miracle *Ylvisaker* **BC**
- Welcome the child *Haugen* **G-3803**

LUKE 2:22-40

The presentation of the child

- I wonder if he knew *Hanson/Murakami* **SCR 196**
- Like a rose in winter *Hanson/Murakami* **SCR 204**
- Lord, bid your servant go in peace *Wyeth* **RS 874**
- Now let your servant go *Chant* **GC 776**
- Shalom, my good friends *Traditional* **BC**
- Shine on us/Now let your servant *Glover* **G-4583**

ADDITIONAL SONGS FOR THE DAY/SEASON

- Arise and sing *Ray* **SPW**
- Child of mercy *Haas* **GC 357, RS 506**

Year C

During Christmastide, our attention is drawn to the holy family: Jesus, Mary, and Joseph. We, too, are God's children and part of a holy family, set apart through the baptismal waters in which we have been washed. As we end one year and begin another, we ask how God's likeness in Christ may become more visible in us, God's new offspring.

1 SAMUEL 2:18-20, 26

The boy Samuel grew in favor with the LORD and the people

- Lift up your hearts *O'Connor* **G&P 676**
- Lord of glory *Manion* **G&P 707**
- Open our lives to the Word *Makeever* **DH 8**

PSALM 148

The splendor of the LORD is over earth and heaven.

- Ancient of days *Sadler/Harvill* **HCW 11**
- He is exalted *Paris* **W&P 55**
- Heaven and earth *DeShazo/Harvill* **HMS10 829**
- Let all creation sing *Ogden* **PS1**
- Praise and exalt God *Makeever* **DH 48**
- Praise in the heights *Haas* **G-5041**
- Shout to the Lord *Zschech* **HMS10 862, W&P 124**
- We've come to praise you *Grant/Darnall* **MAR 80**
- You alone *Hanson/Murakami* **SCR 36**

COLOSSIANS 3:12-17

Clothe yourselves in love; let the peace of Christ rule your hearts

- Forever grateful *Altrogge* **HCW 44**
- Give thanks *Smith* **W&P 41, TFF 292, HCW 46**
- Let the peace of God reign *Zschech* **HMS11 926**
- Put on love *Makeever* **DH 78**
- Put on love *Powell* **G-4078**
- Someone in need of your love *Makeever* **DH 94**
- Turn our hearts *Kendrick* **HMS12 1043**

LUKE 2:41-52

The boy Jesus increased in wisdom, and in divine and human favor

- Jesus, lead on *Helming* **VIN8 114**
- Lord, listen to your children praying *Medema* **W&P 92, TFF 247**
- Sing of Mary, pure and lowly *Traditional* **WOV 634**
- The Aye Carol *Bell* **GC 371, RS 525**

ADDITIONAL SONGS FOR THE DAY/SEASON

- Children, go where I send thee *Haugen* **G-3814**
- Give thanks *Smith* **W&P 41, TFF 292, HCW 46**
- Carol at the manger *Haugen* **WOV 638, RS 516**

Second Sunday after Christmas

Years A, B, C

Today, in the concluding days of the Christmas season, we reflect more deeply on the significance of the Christ who was born at Bethlehem. Our minds not be unable to comprehend just how Jesus existed with God from the very beginning of time, as the first chapter from the gospel of John proclaims today. What we do know is this: God comes into our presence today through Jesus Christ. Indeed it happens each Sunday and every other time that the church gathers. Through the scriptures as they are read and preached, through the bread and the wine as it is offered to the baptized, God is made flesh among us. The real miracle of Christmas is that God is here now with us—always.

JEREMIAH 31:7-14

Joy at the gathering of God's scattered flock

- Carol at the manger *Haugen* **GC 369, WOV 638**
- Mourning into dancing *Walker* **W&P 99, HCW 125**
- We declare your name *Baloche/Cloninger* **HMS10 874**

SIRACH 24:1-12

Wisdom lives among God's people

PSALM 147:13-21

Worship the LORD*, O Jerusalem; praise your God, O Zion.*

- Praise the Lord *Polyblank* **PS3**

WISDOM OF SOLOMON 10:15-21

We sing, O LORD*, to your holy name; we praise with one accord your defending hand.*

- All around your throne *DeShazo/Kerr* **HMS10 808**
- Bless the Lord, my soul *Haugen* **GC 141**
- Come, let us worship God *Makeever* **DH 2**
- I will bow down and worship *Chambers/Brewster* **HMS13 1081**
- We've come to worship you *Kerr* **HMS10 878**

EPHESIANS 1:3-14

The will of God made known in Christ

- Freely, given freely *Hanson/Murakami* **SCR 74**
- Holy love, holy light *Batstone* **MAR 118**
- It has always been you *Butler/Butler* **VIN6 120**
- Song of the chosen *Cooney* **GC 813**

JOHN 1:[1-9] 10-18

God with us: the incarnation of the Word

- City of God *Schutte* **G&P 548, GC 678**
- Emmanuel *McGee* **W&P 36, TFF 45**
- God with us *Kendrick* **HMS5 392**
- It has always been you *Butler/Butler* **VIN6 120**
- O star of beauty *Glover* **G-4585**
- Once and for all time *Hanson/Murakami* **SCR 200**
- There was the Word *Makeever* **DH 55**

ADDITIONAL SONGS FOR THE DAY/SEASON

- All the earth, proclaim God's glory *Fisher* **GC 552**
- He came down *Haugen* **G-3808**
- Peace child *Glover* **G-4339**

Epiphany of the Lord

Years A, B, C

On this day the church celebrates its universal nature and mission. In worship we pray that the Holy Spirit would make our lives radiant with the brightness of Christ. From the Lord's table the church goes forth into the world as a witness to Christ's merciful presence. As the stars light up the darkness of night, so the baptized are called to be light in the world.

ISAIAH 60:1-6
Nations come to the light

- Arise, shine out *Haas* **G-4868**
- Arise, shine! *Urspringer/Robinson* **HCW 14**
- Arise, shine! *Haugen* **G-3266**
- Here I am, Lord *Schutte* **WOV 752, BC, TFF 230**
- Shine, Jesus, shine *Kendrick* **WOV 651, W&P 123, TFF 64, HCW 155**

PSALM 72:1-7, 10-14
All kings shall bow before him.

- Every nation on earth *Joncas* **GC 72**
- Lord, every nation *Cooney* **G&P 220**
- O Lord, be my help *Ogden* **PS3**
- The kingdom song *Evans* **HMS12 1040**
- This kingdom *Bullock* **HMS11 962**
- We bow down *Paris* **W&P 149, HCW 183**

EPHESIANS 3:1-12
The gospel's promise extends to all

- Come to me *Ylvisaker* **BC**
- Dwelling place *Foley* **G&P 591**
- Into the life *McLean* **WIS 11**
- Life in his hands *Hanson* **SCR**
- The least of all the saints *Ylvisaker* **BC**
- Who has known *Foley* **G&P 327**

MATTHEW 2:1-12
Revelation of Christ to the nations of the earth

- Alleluia *Sinclair* **HMS11 889, W&P 6**
- Child of the poor/What child is this *Soper* **G&P 336/337**
- I will bow down and worship *Chambers/Brewster* **HMS13 1081**
- Shine on us/What star is this *Glover* **G-4596, GC 378**

ADDITIONAL SONGS FOR THE DAY/SEASON

- Hear the angels *Cain/Kadidlo* **W&P 57**
- Lord today *Ducote* **G&P 338, GC 375**
- O star of beauty *Glover* **G-4585**

Baptism of the Lord

First Sunday after the Epiphany

Year A

In the waters of the Jordan, Jesus is baptized by John. The Spirit descends on him and a voice from heaven says, "You are my beloved." Here is the pattern for our entrance into Christ's community and mission: we come to the waters of the font, our Jordan; we are washed by the Word and anointed by the Spirit; we are named God's beloved children. With Christ we are chosen to proclaim God's mercy in a suffering world. With Christ we are made public witnesses to God's justice. With Christ we are called to do good and relieve the suffering of the oppressed.

ISAIAH 42:1-9
The servant of the Lord *brings justice*
- All the earth, proclaim God's glory *Fisher* **GC 552**
- I Am *Hanson* **SFL**
- Make me a servant *Willard* **W&P 96**
- Open the eyes of my heart *Baloche* **HMS12 1027, HMS13 1093**

PSALM 29
The voice of the Lord *is upon the waters.*
- Give strength to your people, Lord *Smith* **PS1**
- God of glory *Hanson* **SCR 89**
- Lord, bless your people *Warner* **VO 59**
- Only for your glory *Hanson* **SCR 34**
- Singing through the water *Hanson/Murakami* **SCR 32**
- Song over the waters *Haugen* **W&P 127**
- The Lord will bless all people *Haas* **G-4579**
- The Lord will bless his people *Guimont* **GC 40**

ACTS 10:34-43
Jesus' ministry after his baptism
- Good news *Ethiopian/Olson* **GC 679**
- He is Lord *Smith* **HMS12 998**
- Singing through the water *Hanson/Murakami* **SCR 132**

MATTHEW 3:13-17
Revelation of Christ as God's servant
- He came to be baptized *Ylvisaker* **BC**
- O'er the river Jordan *Haas* **G-4689**
- Wade in the water *Spiritual* **TFF 114**

ADDITIONAL SONGS FOR THE DAY/SEASON
- Glory be! *Ylvisaker* **BC**
- I saw water *Young* **BL**
- King of kings *Batya/Conty* **W&P 80**
- The God of all grace *Manalo* **OCP 10510**
- You have anointed me *Balhoff/Ducote/Daigle* **G&P 555, GC 676**

Year B

In the waters of baptism, we have been joined to the Son in whom the Father is well pleased. The baptismal font or pool is our Jordan where the Holy Spirit comes to us, strengthening and enlightening us for service in the world. On this great baptismal day, the church prays that all who are reborn as daughters and sons of God will continue to grow in faith, hope, and love.

GENESIS 1:1-5
God creates light
- Arise, shine! *Haugen* **G-3266**
- Morning has broken *Traditional* **W&P 98**
- Singing through the water *Hanson/Murakami* **SCR 132**
- Song over the waters *Haugen* **W&P 127**
- Wind of the spirit *Hanson/Murakami* **W&P 157, SCR 18**

PSALM 29
The voice of the Lord *is upon the waters.*
- God of glory *Hanson* **SCR 89**
- The Lord will bless all people *Haas* **G-4579**
- The Lord will bless his people *Guimont* **GC 40**
- Lord, bless your people *Warner* **VO 59**
- Only for your glory *Hanson* **SCR 34**
- Singing through the water *Hanson/Murakami* **SCR 132**
- Song over the waters *Haugen* **W&P 127**

ACTS 19:1-7

Baptized in the name of the Lord Jesus

- I don't belong to me *Hanson* **SCR 152**
- Oh, let the Son of God enfold you *Wimber* **TFF 105**
- Spirit song *Wimber* **W&P 130, CMH 6**
- You have anointed me *Balhoff/Ducote/Daigle* **G&P 555, GC 676**

MARK 1:4-11

Revelation of Christ as God's servant

- He came to be baptized *Ylvisaker* **BC**
- King of kings *Batya/Conty* **W&P 80**
- O star of beauty *Glover* **G-4585**
- Singing through the water *Hanson/Murakami* **SCR 132**
- Waterlife *Hanson* **W&P 145, SCR 129**

ADDITIONAL SONGS FOR THE DAY/SEASON

- All the earth, proclaim God's glory *Fisher* **GC 552**
- Glory be! *Ylvisaker* **BC**
- Wade in the water *Spiritual* **TFF 114**

Year C

Baptism is the beginning of a new story. It was for Jesus; it is for us. God claims us as sons and daughters, fills us with the Holy Spirit, and promises to travel the path with us—a path that will bring us home.

ISAIAH 43:1-7

When you pass through the waters, do not fear, for I am with you

- Be not afraid *Dufford* **G&P 602, GC 608**
- Faithful One *Doerksen* **CMH2 60**
- Out in the wilderness *Beech* **W&P 115**
- You have been given *Kauflin* **HCW 197**

PSALM 29

The voice of the Lord *is upon the waters.*

- God of glory *Hanson* **SCR 89**
- Lord, bless your people *Warner* **VO 59**
- Only for your glory *Hanson* **SCR 34**
- Singing through the water *Hanson/Murakami* **SCR 132**
- Song over the waters *Haugen* **W&P 127**
- The Lord will bless all people *Haas* **G-4579**
- The Lord will bless his people *Guimont* **GC 40**

ACTS 8:14-17

Prayer and laying on of hands for the Holy Spirit

- The Spirit is singing *Hanson/Murakami* **SCR 72**
- We receive power *Marchonda* **VO 101**

LUKE 3:15-17, 21-22

The baptism of Jesus with the descent of the Holy Spirit

- He came to be baptized *Ylvisaker* **BC**
- Holy love *Park* **VIN7 107**
- O star of beauty *Rob Glover* **G-4585**
- Singing through the water *Hanson/Murakami* **SCR 132**
- Waterlife *Hanson* **W&P 145, SCR 129**
- You have anointed me *Balhoff/Ducote/Daigle* **G&P 555, GC 676**

ADDITIONAL SONGS FOR THE DAY/SEASON

- Glory be! *Ylvisaker* **BC**
- King of kings *Batya/Conty* **W&P 80**
- Lay down that spirit *Mattingly* **VO 52**
- Let the fire fall *Misulia* **VO 53**
- Shine on us, Lord *Mattingly* **VO 82**
- You are mine *Haas* **W&P 158**

Second Sunday after the Epiphany

Year A

Here is a simple pattern for the church's celebration during Epiphany: Christ is revealed as the servant of all people; Christ is baptized for his mission; Christ proclaims his message in word and deed until he goes up to Jerusalem. Here the season and the readings set forth a pattern for the community of faith: we enter this church, shaped and sustained by holy baptism and holy communion, with a mission to serve the world. We are called to invite others to come and see the Lord. Come and touch the waters of new life, we say. Come and hear the words of good news. Come and taste the bread of life and the cup of mercy. Let your lives be shaped and sustained by these good things of God's grace.

ISAIAH 49:1-7
The servant brings light to the nations
- Make my life a candle *Hanson* **SCR 163**
- Speak now, O Lord *Mattingly* **VO 86**
- The spirit of God *Deiss* **GC 458, WLP**
- You are my hiding place *Ledner* **W&P 160, MAR 167**
- You have anointed me *Balhoff/Ducote/Daigle* **G&P 555, GC 676**

PSALM 40:1-12
I love to do your will, O my God.
- Here I am *Batstone* **MAR 115**
- Here I am *Cooney* **GC 49, G&P 204, RS 74**
- Here I am, O God *Warner* **VO 36**
- Make me a servant *Willard* **W&P 96**
- Now God our Father *Dearman/Mills* **W&P 103**

1 CORINTHIANS 1:1-9
Paul's greeting to the church at Corinth
- Faithful Father *Doerksen* **VIN7 72**
- You are holy *Brown* **HMS10 884**

JOHN 1:29-42
Revelation of Christ as the Lamb of God
- Behold the Lamb of God *Bell* **SPW, G-4391**
- Lamb of God *Beech* **WOV 622**
- Lamb of God *Paris* **HCW 100**
- You are my all in all *Jernigan* **HMS11 976**

ADDITIONAL SONGS FOR THE DAY/SEASON
- Behold the Lamb of God *Willet* **GC 823**
- Jesus, come to us *Haas* **G&P 304**
- Lamb of God *Park* **W&P 83**
- Lamb of God, come take away *Makeever* **DH 25**

Year B

In the weeks of Epiphany, the church focuses on its mission in the world. Like Samuel we seek to hear God's voice as we pray: "Speak, your servant is listening." In baptism God calls us to be servants who go forth with a simple mission: invite others to come and see. Having seen God's great epiphany in Christ Jesus, we now graciously invite others to see Christ who is with us in the word, the waters of rebirth, and the holy supper.

1 SAMUEL 3:1-10 [11-20]
The calling of Samuel
- Here I am *Batstone* **MAR 115**
- Here I am, Lord *Schutte* **WOV 752, BC, TFF 230**
- Speak now, O Lord *Mattingly* **VO 86**
- When you call *Makeever* **DH 100**

PSALM 139:1-5, 12-17
You have searched me out and known me.
- I was there to hear your borning cry *Ylvisaker* **WOV 770, W&P 69, BC**
- Filling me with joy *Lisicky* **GC 135**
- Guide me, Lord *Hughes* **RS 186**
- Step by step *Beaker* **W&P 132, HMS13 1103**

1 CORINTHIANS 6:12-20
Glorify God in your body
- I belong to a mighty God *DeShazo* **HMS8 654**
- I don't belong to me *Hanson* **SCR 152**
- Let the peace of God reign *Zschech* **HMS11 926**

JOHN 1:43-51
The calling of the first disciples
- Come and see *LeBlanc* **W&P 29**
- Come and see *Makeever* **DH 56**
- Jesus, lead on *Helming* **VIN8 114**
- Lead me, oh lead me *Smith* **HMS13 1085**
- The summons *Scottish/Bell* **W&P 137, GC 700**
- Two fishermen *Toolan* **RS 812, GC 688**
- Where you lead me *DeShetler/Craig* **HMS13 1113**

ADDITIONAL SONGS FOR THE DAY/SEASON

Cry of my heart *Butler* **MAR**
In the morning *Houge* **W&P 75**
Kyrie eleison *Olson* **W&P 81**

Year C

Scenes from familiar life and landscapes of disappointment become the setting where God intends to perform miracles. A wedding is about to happen between God and people, joining the predictable with the extraordinary.

ISAIAH 62:1-5

As bridegroom and bride rejoice, so shall God rejoice over you

My God reigns *Evans* **HMS12 1021**
Zion sing *Deiss* **WLP**

PSALM 36:5-10

We feast on the abundance of your house, O Lord.

The fountain of all life *Haas* **G-5041**
The river is here *Park* **VIN6 232, HMS11 958**
These things are true of you *Walker* **MAR 248**
Your constant love *Hanson* **SCR 100**
Your steadfast love *Sandquist* **HCW 200**

1 CORINTHIANS 12:1-11

There are a variety of gifts but the same Spirit

One bread, one body *Foley* **W&P 111, TFF 122, WOV 710**
They'll know we are Christians *Traditional* **COK 74**
We are many parts *Haugen* **GC 733, RS 840**

JOHN 2:1-11

The wedding at Cana

Bridegroom and bride *Irish* **RS 944, GC 868**
The kingdom song *Evans* **HMS12 1040**
The trumpets sound, the angels sing *Kendrick* **W&P 139**
This kingdom *Bullock* **HMS11 962**

ADDITIONAL SONGS FOR THE DAY/SEASON

Bind us together *Gillman* **W&P 18, WOV 748**
God be with you *Edwards* **W&P 50**
Let there be praise *Tunney* **HCW 211**
This is the feast of victory *Young* **W&P 142, BL**

Third Sunday after the Epiphany

Year A

Today's gospel reading narrates a strange fishing expedition. Jesus utters simple words that change human lives: "Follow me and I will make you fish for people." There is no glitz, no slick marketing, no extravagant claim; only these words: "Follow me." Here is the mission that flows from the watery pool of our baptism into Christ. The Christian community goes forth and invites others to see what good things God offers in the waters of rebirth, in the scriptures, in the holy supper, in the community of faith. People can be "caught" in many things. What happens when they are caught in the net of God's mercy?

ISAIAH 9:1-4
Light shines for those in darkness
- City of God *Schutte* **G&P 548, GC 678**
- God will make a way *Moen* **HCW 52**
- Lord, my strength *Krippaehne* **W&P 93**
- Shine, Jesus, shine *Kendrick* **WOV 651, W&P 123, TFF 64, HCW 155**

PSALM 27:1, 4-9
The Lord is my light and my salvation.
- Holy love, holy light *Batstone* **MAR 118**
- Lead me, guide me *Akers* **TFF 70**
- Make my life a candle *Hanson* **SCR 163**
- The Lord is my life and my light *Leftley* **PS2**
- The Lord is my light *Haas* **GC 39, RS 57**

1 CORINTHIANS 1:10-18
Appeal for unity in the gospel
- In unity and peace *Chepponis* **G-4452**
- O, mighty cross *Baroni/Chisum* **HCW 136**
- Only for your glory *Hanson* **SCR 34**

MATTHEW 4:12-23
Revelation of Christ as a prophet
- I'll belong to you *Hanson* **SCR 126**
- Jesus, lead on *Helming* **VIN8 114**
- The stranger and the nets *Cooney/Cooney* **VO 92**
- Two fishermen *Toolan* **RS 812, GC 688**

ADDITIONAL SONGS FOR THE DAY/SEASON
- Go, make disciples *Hanson* **W&P 47**
- You have come down to the lakeshore *Gabaraín* **WOV 784, RS 817, G&P 580, GC 696**
- The summons *Bell* **W&P 137, GC 700**

Year B

In today's gospel reading, Jesus uses the common experience of fishing and turns it upside down. Each baptized Christian, born in God's gracious sea, is called to fish for people. We are given the net of God's mercy and the gift of the Holy Spirit's presence as we go forth and invite others to join us in our communal journey of discipleship.

JONAH 3:1-5, 10
Repentance at Nineveh
- Rain down on us *Butler/Butler/Butler* **VIN8 160**
- Turn my heart *DeShazo* **HCW 179**
- Turn our hearts *Kendrick* **HMS12 1043**

PSALM 62:6-14
In God is my safety and my honor.
- In God alone *Haas* **GC 59, RS 88**
- Rest in God alone *Makeever* **DH 37**
- Rock of ages *Baloche* **HMS13 1099**
- You are my rock *Carpenter* **VIN6 278**

1 CORINTHIANS 7:29-31
Living in the end times
- Ancient of days *Sadler/Harvill* **HCW 11**
- Heaven and earth *DeShazo/Harvill* **HMS10 829**
- Jesus, Jesus *Bullock* **HMS11 923**

MARK 1:14-20
The calling of the disciples at the sea
- Follow me *Haugen* **G-4416**
- Jesus, lead on *Helming* **VIN8 114**
- Two fishermen *Toolan* **RS 812, GC 688**
- Where you lead me *DeShetler/Craig* **HMS13 1113**

ADDITIONAL SONGS FOR THE DAY/SEASON
- Embrace my way and cross *Glover* **G-4594**
- I will follow *Barbour/Barbour* **MAR**
- The summons *Bell* **W&P 137, GC 700**

Year C

Preaching is powerful, and the power is in the word. That word can convict us of sin and raise us to new life. That word can heal divisions in Christ's body and help us appreciate the gifts of others. And that Word has become flesh in Jesus of Nazareth. Let us join with other Christians to pray that we can come together in Christ.

NEHEMIAH 8:1-3, 5-6, 8-10
Ezra reads the law of Moses before the people
- Freely, given freely *Hanson/Murakami* **SCR 74**
- I will celebrate *Baloche* **MAR 43**
- Lord, my strength *Krippaehne* **W&P 93**
- Open our lives to the Word *Makeever* **DH 8**

PSALM 19
The law of the LORD revives the soul.
- Lord, you have the words *Bolduc* **VO 61**
- Lord, you have the words *Haas* **GC 27, RS 40**
- More precious than silver *DeShazo* **HCW 122**
- Psalm 19 *Butler* **VIN7**
- You, Lord, have the message of eternal life *Ogden* **PS2**

1 CORINTHIANS 12:12-13A
You are the body of Christ
- As bread that is broken *Baloche/Cloninger* **HMS10 811**
- One bread we bless and share *Manalo* **G-4362**
- One bread, one body *Foley* **W&P 111, TFF 122**
- Table song *Haas* **GC 849**
- The wise may bring their learning *Ylvisaker* **BC**
- We are many parts *Haugen* **GC 733, RS 840**
- We are members of each other *McLean* **WIS 37**

LUKE 4:14-21
Jesus reads from the scroll of the prophet Isaiah
- Good news *Ethiopian/Olson* **GC 679**
- It has always been you *Butler/Butler* **VIN6 120**
- Let the river flow *Evans* **HMS12 1015**
- The spirit of God *Deiss* **GC 458, WLP**
- Thy word *Smith/Grant* **TFF 132, W&P 144**
- Thy word *Webb* **W&P 143**

ADDITIONAL SONGS FOR THE DAY/SEASON
- Life-giving bread *Manalo* **G-3911**
- O love of God/Amor de Dios *Hurd* **G&P 541**
- You have anointed me *Balhoff/Ducote/Daigle* **G&P 555, GC 676**

Fourth Sunday after the Epiphany

Year A

What does the Lord ask of us? To do justice, to love kindness, and to walk humbly with God. These are simple words from today's first reading that, nonetheless, remain a challenge for anyone who recognizes the injustice and suffering that mark and mar much of human existence. In the gospel reading, Jesus teaches his disciples a way of seeing those who are blessed in God's sight: the poor, mourners, the meek, those who hunger for righteousness, the merciful, the pure in heart, the peacemaker. These are the people to whom Jesus has constant recourse in his ministry. How does this congregation serve them?

MICAH 6:1-8
The offering of justice, kindness, humility
- I want Jesus to walk with me *Traditional* **TFF 66**
- Just a closer walk with thee *Traditional* **TFF 253**
- We are called *Haas* **GC 718, RS 820**
- When Jesus came preaching *Southern Harmony* **RS 773**

PSALM 15
LORD, who may abide upon your holy hill?
- Sanctuary *Thompson/Scruggs* **HCW 154**
- The just will live *Batastini* **RS 33**
- They who do justice *Haas* **GC 22**

1 CORINTHIANS 1:18-31
Christ crucified, the wisdom and power of God
- O, mighty cross *Baroni/Chisum* **HCW 136**
- Sanctuary *Thompson/Scruggs* **HCW 154**
- The cross of Jesus *O'Brien* **G-4517**
- We love you *Hanson* **SCR 147**
- Worthy the Lamb that was slain *Moen* **HCW 192**

MATTHEW 5:1-12
The teaching of Christ: Beatitudes
- Blessed are you *Makeever* **DH 86**
- Blest are they *Haas* **WOV 764, GC 659, RS 774**
- Give thanks *Evans* **VIN6 128**
- Give thanks *Smith* **W&P 41, TFF 292, HCW 46**
- Let the river flow *Evans* **HMS12 1015**

ADDITIONAL SONGS FOR THE DAY/SEASON
- He came down *Haugen* **G-3808**
- O loving God *Makeever* **DH 82**

Year B

In the scriptures the word is announced through prophets who speak for God, and later through Jesus who teaches with authority. The church continues to proclaim the gospel of God's great love for humankind. We gather around Christ, the Word made flesh, to hear that God is gracious and full of compassion. It is the authority of the gospel that enables us to announce a prophetic word of judgment and mercy to the world in which we live.

DEUTERONOMY 18:15-20
The prophet speaks with God's authority
- Thy word *Smith/Grant* **W&P 144, TFF 132**
- Thy word *Webb* **W&P 143**

PSALM 111
The fear of the LORD is the beginning of wisdom.
- With all my heart *Avery* **CC 11**

1 CORINTHIANS 8:1-13
Limits to liberty: the case of food offered to idols
- Faithful Father *Doerksen* **VIN7 72**
- One *Hanson/Murakami* **SCR 160**

MARK 1:21-28
The healing of one with an unclean spirit
- Heal me, O Lord *Moen* **HMS10 828**
- Healing word *McCoy* **VIN6 82**
- Jesus, Jesus *Bullock* **HMS11 923**
- Let your healing love *Butler* **VIN6 144**
- You have anointed me *Balhoff/Ducote/Daigle* **G&P 555, GC 676**

ADDITIONAL SONGS FOR THE DAY/SEASON
- God has spoken, bread is broken *Young* **BL, AFP 11-10733**
- Good news *Olson/Ethiopia* **GC 679, RS 797**

Praise to you, O Christ *Farrell* **G&P 662, GC 515, RS 652**
The battle belongs to the Lord *Owens/Collins* **SPW**
The heavens are telling *Ylvisaker* **BC**
There is a balm in Gilead *Spiritual* **WOV 737, TFF 185, RS 764**

Year C

An epiphany ought to be a surprise. The prophet Jeremiah is surprised that God would call a youth, but Jeremiah has been in God's sight for a long, long time. Jesus is popular in many places but maybe not at home. And love, which seems so familiar, is really a radical invitation to care for others on their terms. How will love surprise us this day?

JEREMIAH 1:4-10
I appointed you a prophet to the nations
Awaken the song *Rethmeier* **VIN6 22**
Before the sun burned bright *Schutte* **G&P 577**
Teach me how to pray *Hanson/Murakami* **SCR 25**

PSALM 71:1-6
From my mother's womb you have been my strength.
I was there to hear your borning cry *Ylvisaker* **WOV 770, W&P 69, BC**
I will sing *Haas* **GC 71, RS 99**
My life is in you, Lord *Gardner* **HCW 128**
O Lord, be my help *Ogden* **PS3**
Since my mother's womb *Guimont* **RS 100**

1 CORINTHIANS 13:1-13
If I speak without love, I am a noisy gong
In love we choose to live *Cotter* **GC 873**
No greater love *Walker* **MAR 54**
Put on love *Makeever* **DH 78**
Set your heart on the higher gifts *Warner* **VO 80**
The greatest is love *Pote* **CGA 781**

LUKE 4:21-30
Jesus says a prophet is not accepted in his hometown
Good news *Ethiopian/Olson* **GC 679, RS 797**
I believe in Jesus *Nelson* **HCW 71**
I do believe *Ylvisaker* **BC**
Jesus, I believe *Batstone* **MAR 130**
O Lord to you *Sadler* **HMS11 937**

ADDITIONAL SONGS FOR THE DAY/SEASON
I will sing, I will sing *Dyer* **W&P 73**
Praise to you, O Christ *Farrell* **G&P 662, GC 515, RS 652**
You are the rock of my salvation *Muller* **W&P 161**

Fifth Sunday after the Epiphany

Year A

Diverse yet complementary actions take place in holy baptism: the forgiveness of sins, entrance into a community of disciples, rebirth as children of God, anointing as servants and heralds, union with Christ, receiving the promise of eternal life. The ancient practice of baptism included two rituals inspired by today's gospel reading. Salt was placed in the mouth and a burning candle was held next to the newly baptized. Baptism is a moment of enlightenment concerning our truest identity. We are scattered in the world as salt is shaken; we are sent into the world as lights who point to the greater light of God's grace.

ISAIAH 58:1-9A [9B-12]
The fast God chooses
- Arise *Barnett* **VIN7 33**
- Arise, oh Lord *Carpenter* **VIN6 16**
- Arise, shine *Urspringer/Robinson* **HCW 14**
- Faithful One *Doerksen* **CMH2 60**
- Rise up and praise him *Baloche/Sadler* **HMS13 1098**
- Share your bread with the hungry *Haas* **G-4734**

PSALM 112:1-9 [10]
Light shines in the darkness for the upright.
- A light rises in the darkness *Guimont* **GC 104, RS 149**
- Good people are a light *Inwood* **PS3**
- You're a child of God *Ylvisaker* **BC**

1 CORINTHIANS 2:1-12 [13-16]
God's wisdom revealed through the Spirit
- Eye has not seen *Haugen* **GC 638, RS 758**
- Glorious God *Baroni/Fitts/Smith/Cloninger* **HMS10 823**
- Jesus, help me see *Ylvisaker* **BC**
- Spirit of the living God *Iverson* **W&P 129, TFF 101**
- Spirit of the living God *Sanchez* **HCW 158**

MATTHEW 5:13-20
The teaching of Christ: salt and light
- Bring forth the kingdom *Haugen* **GC 658, RS 772**
- Go, make disciples *Hanson* **W&P 47**
- Make my life a candle *Hanson* **SCR 163**
- This little light of mine *Spiritual* **TFF 65**

ADDITIONAL SONGS FOR THE DAY/SEASON
- Arise, shine! *Haugen* **G-3266**
- Brighter than the sun *Makeever* **DH 64**
- I am the light of the world *Hayakawa* **G&P 658, GC 510**
- In your heart there is a voice *McLean* **CCJ**
- Shine on us *Glover* **G-4596**

Year B

In today's gospel Jesus cures the sick, proclaims the gospel, and casts out demons. His ministry reveals God's compassionate heart in which the lowly are lifted up and the brokenhearted are healed. As we gather around Christ present in word and meal, we are given strength to wait for the Lord in the midst of our suffering. Living as the body of Christ, our very lives are signs of God's gracious intent for humankind.

ISAIAH 40:21-31
The creator of all cares for the powerless
- Faithful One *Doerksen* **CMH2 60**
- I see you *Mullins* **CC 90**
- May you run and not be weary *Hanson* **W&P 97, SCR 116**
- We will rise again *Haas* **G&P 603**

PSALM 147:1-11, 20C
The Lord heals the brokenhearted.
- Beauty for brokenness *Kendrick* **W&P 17**
- Bless the Lord, my soul *Haugen* **GC 141**
- Healing word *McCoy* **VIN6 82**
- Let your healing love *Butler* **VIN6 144**
- Praise the Lord *Polyblank* **PS3**

1 CORINTHIANS 9:16-23
A servant for the sake of the gospel
- Go in peace and serve the Lord *Hanson* **W&P 46, SCR 120**
- Make me a servant *Willard* **W&P 96**
- This is the gospel of Christ *Brown* **HMS10 870**

MARK 1:29-39
The healing of Peter's mother-in-law
- Healer of our every ill *Haugen* **WOV 738, GC 882**

I'll belong to you *Hanson* **SCR 126**
Lay hands upon us *Glover* **G-4591**
Life in his hands *Hanson* **SCR**
Precious Lord, take my hand *Allen/Dorsey* **TFF 193**
Reach out and take a hand *Kendrick* **HMS12 1029**
When Jesus came preaching *Traditional* **RS 773**

ADDITIONAL SONGS FOR THE DAY/SEASON

All the power you need *Fragar* **HMS11**
Heal me, O Lord *Eulberg* **TFF 189**
On eagle's wings *Joncas* **WOV 779, W&P 110**
Shine on us *Glover* **G-4596**
You are mine *Haas* **GC 649**

Year C

We are part of God's epiphany. In baptism God calls us. In holy communion Christ feeds us and sends us to the world—just as God called Isaiah, and just as Jesus sent Simon, James, and John. The good news handed down to us is meant to be passed on to others.

ISAIAH 6:1-8 [9-13]

Isaiah says, Here am I; send me

Glorious God *Baroni/Fitts/Smith* **HMS10 823**
Here I am *Batstone* **MAR 115**
Here I am, Lord *Schutte* **WOV 752, BC 115, G&P 542, GC 686**
I see the Lord *Baloche* **HMS13 1079**
I see the Lord *Falson* **MAR 41**
Open the eyes of my heart, Lord *Baloche* **HMS12 1027, HMS13 1093**
Santo, santo, santo/Holy, holy, holy *Cuellar* **GC 563, RS 672**
Speak now, O Lord *Mattingly* **VO 86**
The summons *Bell* **W&P 137, GC 700**

PSALM 138

I bow down toward your holy temple.

For he alone is worthy *Traditional* **TFF 284**
I thank you, Lord *Ylvisaker* **BC**
I will bow down and worship *Chambers/Brewster* **HMS13 1081**
I will come and bow down *Nystrom* **HCW 87**
In the presence of the angels *Inwood* **PS3**
In the sight of the angels *Guimont* **RS 185**
Lord, your love is eternal *Stewart* **GC 133**
On the day I called *Cooney* **STP 4**
We bow down *Paris* **W&P 149, HCW 183**

1 CORINTHIANS 15:1-11

I am the least of the apostles

Because we believe *Gordon/Harvill* **HMS12 985**
Freely, given freely *Hanson/Murakami* **SCR 74**
That we may be filled *Hanson/Murakami* **W&P 134, SCR 182**

LUKE 5:1-11

Jesus calls the disciples to fish for people

I can do all things *Baloche/Harris* **HMS11 913**
I can do all things *Smith* **HMS13 1074**
You have come down to the lakeshore *Gabaraín* **WOV 784, RS 817, G&P 580, GC 696**
Spirit calls, rejoice! *Hanson/Murakami* **SCR 1**
The stranger and the nets *Cooney* **VO 92**
You have called us *DeShazo/Nystrom* **HCW 199**

ADDITIONAL SONGS FOR THE DAY/SEASON

We see the Lord *Pulkingham* **W&P 153**

Sixth Sunday after the Epiphany

Proper 1

Year A

Much of today's gospel reading echoes portions of the Ten Commandments. Jesus' instructions to the crowds reveal a pattern of behavior that honors both God and the neighbor, resulting in life and health for the whole community. We, too, are invited to embrace these commandments, not out of fear of retribution, but because God has promised that to do so means life for us.

DEUTERONOMY 30:15-20
Choose life
- Awesome power *Elliott* **CEL 150**
- I will not be shaken *Founds* **MAR 203**

SIRACH 15:15-20
Choose between life and death
- Abundant life *Glover* **G-3952**
- Life in his hands *Hanson* **SCR**
- With all my heart *Avery* **CC 11**

PSALM 119:1-8
Happy are they who walk in the law of the Lord.
- First love *Baloche/Sadler* **HMS13 1062**
- Happy are those who follow *Cooney* **GC 116**
- Hear me, O God *Tate* **VO 35**
- Seek ye first *Lafferty* **WOV 783, W&P 122, TFF 149**
- Step by step *Beaker* **W&P 132, HMS13 1103**
- Teach me, O God *Walker* **PS3**

1 CORINTHIANS 3:1-9
God gives the growth
- Come and grow *McLean* **CCJ, WIS 1**
- Open our lives to the Word *Makeever* **DH 8**

MATTHEW 5:21-37
The teaching of Christ: forgiveness
- In love we choose to live *Cotter* **GC 873**
- Let your healing love *Butler* **VIN6 144**
- Purify my heart *Greco* **HCW 148**
- Turn our hearts *Kendrick* **HMS12 1043**

ADDITIONAL SONGS FOR THE DAY/SEASON
- Lay hands upon us *Glover* **G-4591**
- Healer of our every ill *Haugen* **WOV 738, GC 882**
- You are mine *Haas* **GC 649**

Year B

Today's readings include two stories of lepers cleansed of their disease. Naaman washes in the Jordan River and Jesus stretches out his hand and touches a leper. In the waters of baptism we are cleansed of our sin and throughout our lives we continue to be nourished by the healing power of the eucharistic meal. With our words and deeds we touch others with God's compassion and love.

2 KINGS 5:1-14
Naaman is healed of leprosy
- Heal me, O Lord *Moen* **HMS10 828**
- In the light *Poirier* **VO 48**

PSALM 30
My God, I cried out to you, and you restored me to health.
- I will praise you *Smith* **PS2**
- I will praise you, Lord *Inwood* **GC 41, G&P 192**
- I will praise you, Lord *Ridge* **G&P 193**
- Let your healing love *Butler* **VIN6 144**
- Mourning into dancing *Walker* **W&P 99, HCW 125**

1 CORINTHIANS 9:24-27
Run the race for an imperishable prize
- I have kept the faith *Baloche* **HMS13 1076**
- May you run and not be weary *Hanson* **W&P 97, SCR 116**
- Only this I want *Schutte* **GC 695, G&P 575**

MARK 1:40-45
The healing of one with leprosy
- Forever grateful *Altrogge* **HCW 44**
- Healing word *McCoy* **VIN6 82**
- Jesus, Jesus *Bullock* **HMS11 923**
- When Jesus came preaching *Traditional* **RS 773**
- You are mine *Haas* **GC 645**

ADDITIONAL SONGS FOR THE DAY/SEASON

Create in me a clean heart, O God *Anonymous* **W&P 34**

I've just come from the fountain *Spiritual* **TFF 111, WOV 696**

Washed anew *Keesecker* **AFP 11-10676**

Year C

A fundamental decision is placed before us this day: Will we choose the way of blessing or the way of woe? The death and resurrection of Jesus is the pivot on which the decision turns. To be in Christ means that we get planted by streams of water and are rooted among those who thirst for God's reign. The mystery of our faith points the path to life: Christ has died. Christ is risen. Christ will come again.

JEREMIAH 17:5-10

Blessed are those who trust the LORD, they are like trees by water

Holy love *Park* **VIN7 107**

Water from heaven *Hanson/Murakami* **SCR 136**

PSALM 1

They are like trees planted by streams of water.

Happy are they who hope *Dufford* **G&P 167**

Happy are they *Haas* **GC 18, RS 28**

I will never be *Bullock* **HMS11 920**

In Christ, a new creation *Ylvisaker* **BC**

1 CORINTHIANS 15:12-20

Christ has been raised, the first fruits of those who have died

Be exalted *Butler/Butler/Park* **VIN8 10**

He is exalted *Paris* **W&P 55, HCW 57**

Lord, I lift your name on high *Founds* **W&P 90**

We can be lifted up *Hanson* **SCR 105**

LUKE 6:17-26

Jesus speaks blessings on the poor and hungry; woes on the rich and full

Cares chorus *Willard* **W&P 27**

Give thanks *Smith* **W&P 41, TFF 292, HCW 46**

The gift *Ylvisaker* **BC**

The people of God *O'Brien* **GC 653**

ADDITIONAL SONGS FOR THE DAY/SEASON

He is exalted *Pethel* **W&P 55**

Praise to you, O Christ *Farrell* **G&P 662, GC 515, RS 652**

Seventh Sunday after the Epiphany

Proper 2

Year A

Nobody's perfect!" we protest when our behavior disappoints us and others. Our attempts to love neighbors and even enemies as ourselves fall short of what God desires for us. We cannot achieve perfection. Indeed, the ultimate example of perfection and holiness is God alone. Yet in today's first reading we hear, "You shall be holy, for I the LORD your God am holy." We are made holy in baptism, and forgiven at the table of God's mercy. As a people made holy by God, we go in peace to love as we have been loved.

LEVITICUS 19:1-2, 9-18
Holiness revealed in acts of mercy and justice
- O God of matchless glory *Duck* **GC 546**
- Turn our hearts *Kendrick* **HMS12 1043**
- We've come to praise you *Grant/Darnall* **MAR 80**

PSALM 119:33-40
Teach me, O LORD, the way of your statutes.
- Happy are they who hope *Dufford* **G&P 167**
- Happy are they *Haas* **GC 18, RS 28**
- Show me your ways *Fragar* **HMS11 949**

1 CORINTHIANS 3:10-11, 16-23
Allegiance to Christ, not human leaders
- Firm foundation *Gordon/Harvill* **HCW 42**
- I don't belong to me *Hanson* **SCR 152**
- Sanctuary *Thompson/Scruggs* **HCW 154**

MATTHEW 5:38-48
The teaching of Christ: love
- Celebrate love *Hanson* **SCR 16**
- First love *Baloche/Sadler* **HMS13 1062**
- No greater love *Walker* **MAR 54**

ADDITIONAL SONGS FOR THE DAY/SEASON
- 'Round the table *Glover* **G-4590**
- The God of all grace *Manalo* **OCP 10510**

Year B

Though we often proclaim God's faithfulness in ages past, God continues to do new things in our midst. In baptism God provides water in the wilderness, and in the Lord's supper God gives us food and drink for sustenance. The crosses placed on our brows in baptism are the seal of the Spirit's presence in our lives, and by Christ's authority we are forgiven. Healed and restored, we pray that God's healing and forgiveness would be made known in our daily lives.

ISAIAH 43:18-25
Like rivers in the desert, God makes new
- God will make a way *Moen* **HCW 52**
- In the wilderness *Ylvisaker* **BC**
- The river is here *Park* **VIN6 232, HMS11 958**

PSALM 41
Heal me, for I have sinned against you.
- Heal me, oh Lord *Moen* **HMS10 828**
- Lord, heal my soul *Guimont* **GC 50**
- Song of longing *Cooney* **GC 51**

2 CORINTHIANS 1:18-22
Every promise of God is a "Yes"
- Amen *Fitts* **HMS12 982**
- Every time I feel the spirit *Spiritual* **TFF 241**
- Give us your vision *Hanson/Murakami* **SCR 85**

MARK 2:1-12
The healing of a paralyzed man
- Healer of our every ill *Haugen* **WOV 738, GC 882**
- Jesus, amazing *Hanson/Murakami* **SCR 79**
- Stand up and give him the praise *DeShazo* **HMS10 867**
- Thank you for the gift *Hanson* **SCR 144**

When Jesus came preaching *Traditional* **RS 773**
You are mine *Haas* **GC 649**

ADDITIONAL SONGS FOR THE DAY/SEASON
Behold I make all things new *Bell* **G-4391**
Lay hands upon us *Glover* **G-4591**
Your mercy flows *Sutton* **SPW**

Year C

The promise and its fulfillment may not look at all alike, even though they are intimately connected. Paul speaks about seeds and plants as he tries to picture resurrection life. Joseph's brothers never thought they would see him alive again, so how shocking he must have appeared to them as an Egyptian leader! Jesus invites us to sow seeds of new life by loving enemies.

GENESIS 45:3-11, 15
Joseph forgives his brothers
God of love, have mercy *Makeever* **DH 10**
Heavenly Father *Park* **VIN7 92**
Mercy *DeShazo/Sadler* **HMS14**
Praise to you, O Christ *Farrell* **G&P 662, GC 515, RS 652**

PSALM 37:1-11, 39-40
The lowly shall possess the land; they will delight in abundance of peace.
Don't be worried *Brown* **TFF 212**
I love to be in your presence *Baloche/Kerr* **HCW 75**
I see you *Mullins* **CC 90**

1 CORINTHIANS 15:35-38, 42-50
The mystery of the resurrection of the body
My life is in you, Lord *Gardner* **HCW 128**
We can be lifted up *Hanson* **SCR 105**

LUKE 6:27-38
Love your enemies
Change my heart, O God *Espinosa* **SPW**
Give us your vision *Hanson/Murakami* **SCR 85**
Our hope is alive *Ylvisaker* **BC**
Stir up the love *Ylvisaker* **BC**
Turn our hearts *Kendrick* **HMS12 1043**

ADDITIONAL SONGS FOR THE DAY/SEASON
Good soil *Hanson* **WOV 713, W&P 50, SCR**
In love we choose to live *Cotter* **GC 873**
The God of all grace *Manalo* **OCP 10510**

Eighth Sunday after the Epiphany

Proper 3

Year A

Christians recognize that the source of all good things is the God who feeds the birds and clothes the grass of the field. We rejoice that we are held in the palm of God's hand. Gathered at Christ's supper, we offer thanksgiving for the bread of life and the cup of blessing. And here, as we share these gifts, we are knit together into a community whose mission is among those who are poor and in need.

ISAIAH 49:8-16A
God's motherly compassion for the people
- All around your throne *DeShazo/Kerr* **HMS10 808**
- God beyond all names *Farrell* **GC 491, RS 634, G&P 66**
- Isaiah 49 *Landry* **G&P 711**
- You've delivered me again *Ylvisaker* **BC**

PSALM 131
Like a child upon its mother's breast, my soul is quieted within me.
- Cares chorus *Willard* **W&P 27**
- Guard my soul *Smith* **PS3**
- Leave your heart with me *Hanson* **SCR 150**
- Like a little child *Haas* **G-3956**
- Lord, listen to your children *Hanson* **W&P 91, SCR 23**
- My soul is still *Haas* **GC 129**
- O Lord, my heart is not proud *Rizza* **W&P 109**
- You, Lord *Hanson* **W&P 162, SCR 42**

1 CORINTHIANS 4:1-5
Servants accountable to God for their stewardship
- Change my heart, oh God *Espinoza* **W&P 28, HCW 28**
- When the Lord comes *Flowers* **VIN6 262**

MATTHEW 6:24-34
The teaching of Christ: trust in God
- Don't be anxious *Hanson* **SCR 141**
- His eye is on the sparrow *Gabriel* **TFF 252**
- Leave your heart with me *Hanson* **SCR 150**
- My heart will trust *Morgan* **HMS14**
- Nothing is as wonderful *Underwood* **VIN8 150**

ADDITIONAL SONGS FOR THE DAY/SEASON
- Age to age *Vogt* **OCP 10900**
- Seek first the kingdom *Haas* **G-3955**
- Seek ye first *Lafferty* **W&P 122, WOV 783**

Year B

Eating is one of the most intimate things that we do. Our divisions have often kept us apart from one another at the Lord's table, and disagreement regarding who is welcome to share the church's meal still festers among denominations. Jesus was criticized for eating with tax collectors and sinners, the outsiders of his day. We who follow Christ are called to invite all people to share the riches of God's faithful love. We share the new wine of the kingdom, that our lives will proclaim the justice and righteousness of God's ways.

HOSEA 2:14-20
The covenant renewed by God's persistent love
- Age to age, everlasting *Ylvisaker* **BC**
- Everlasting grace *Carpenter* **VIN6 58**
- Hosea *Norbet* **GC 386**
- Your everlasting love *Batstone* **MAR 85**

PSALM 103:1-13, 22
The Lord is full of compassion and mercy.
- Bless the Lord *Crouch* **W&P 19, TFF 273**
- Bless the Lord *Makeever* **DH 42**
- How blessed *Hampton* **VIN6 106**
- I'll bless the Lord for evermore *Traditional* **BC**
- Loving and forgiving *Soper* **G&P 251**
- The Lord is kind and merciful *Cotter* **GC 99**
- The Lord is kind and merciful *Haugen* **GC 100**

2 CORINTHIANS 3:1-6
Equipped as ministers of God's new covenant
- All the earth, proclaim God's glory *Fisher* **GC 552**
- Amen *Fitts* **HMS12 982**
- Spirit of the living God *Iverson* **W&P 129, TFF 101**
- Spirit of the living God *Sanchez* **HCW**
- Write it on my heart *McLean* **WIS 41**

MARK 2:13-22

Eating and drinking with tax collectors and prostitutes

Behold I make all things new *Bell* **G-4391**
For all people Christ was born *Makeever* **DH 52**
Mercy *DeShazo/Sadler* **HMS14**
Nothing at all but love *Ylvisaker* **BC**
Song about grace *Ylvisaker* **BC**

ADDITIONAL SONGS FOR THE DAY/SEASON

Praise to you, O Christ *Farrell* **WOV 614, GC 515, RS 652**
Thanks be to you *Haugen* **WOV 790, RS 708, GC 569**

Year C

Our firm roots in Christ, planted in us in our baptism, nourish and strengthen us in our lives of witness to God's sustaining love. This foundation cannot be uprooted or destroyed, even in the face of life's setbacks and catastrophes. Moved by the life-giving pulse of daily death and resurrection, we produce good and abundant fruit.

ISAIAH 55:10-13

The word goes forth from the mouth of God

He shall reign *Chopinsky* **HMS12 999**
Let it rain *Park* **VIN8 126**
Most holy one *Willard/Baloche* **MAR 223**
Sow the word *Zavelli/SJanco* **GC 516**

SIRACH 27:4-7

Wisdom rules both heaven and earth

PSALM 92:1-4, 12-15

The righteous shall flourish like a palm tree.

It is good to give thanks *Dean* **PS3**
It is good *Adler* **CCJ 16**
Lord, it is good *Guimont* **GC 86, RS 124**

1 CORINTHIANS 15:51-58

The mystery of the resurrection

Almighty *Watson* **HCW 8, HMS10 810**
God sent his Son *Gaither/Gaither* **TFF 93**
Ring all the living bells *Ylvisaker* **BC**
Thanks be to you *Haugen* **WOV 790, RS 708, GC 569**
When the Lord comes *Flowers* **VIN6 262**

LUKE 6:39-49

Take the speck from your eye; build your house on a firm foundation

Firm foundation *Gordon/Harvill* **HCW 42**
Jesus, help me see *Ylvisaker* **BC**
Open the eyes of my heart *Baloche* **HMS12 1027**
The word is in your heart *Moore* **GC 518**

ADDITIONAL SONGS FOR THE DAY/SEASON

How can I keep from singing *Shaker* **WOV 781, G&P 616, GC 603, RS 733**
On the wings of change *Galipeau* **WLP 5209**
Praise to you, O Christ *Farrell* **WOV 614, G&P 662, GC 515, RS 652**

Transfiguration Sunday

Last Sunday after the Epiphany

Year A

Today's gospel reading is the inspiration for the festival of the Transfiguration, which concludes the Christmas cycle that began in Advent. On one level it celebrates the manifestation of Jesus as God's beloved child and servant (an echo of the Christmas, Epiphany, and baptism festivals). At the same time, the church's calendar is influenced by the gospel story: after his transfiguration, Jesus announces his impending death in Jerusalem. From the festival of the Transfiguration, the church turns this week to Ash Wednesday and its baptismal journey to the celebration of Christ's death and resurrection.

EXODUS 24:12-18

Moses enters the cloud of God's glory on Mount Sinai

- Amen *Fitts* **HMS12 982**
- Joyfully singing *Balhoff/Ducotte/Daigle* **GC 548**
- Open our lives to the Word *Makeever* **DH 8**
- Shake up the morning *Bell* **GC 529**

PSALM 2

You are my son; this day have I begotten you.

- God sent his Son *Gaither/Gaither* **TFF 93**
- He is Lord *Smith* **HMS12 998**

PSALM 99

Proclaim the greatness of the LORD our God and worship upon God's holy hill.

- You are holy *Brown* **HMS10 884**

2 PETER 1:16-21

The apostle's message confirmed on the mount of transfiguration

- Come to the mountain *Tunseth* **W&P 32**
- Thy word *Smith/Grant* **W&P 144, TFF 132**
- Thy word *Webb* **W&P 143**

MATTHEW 17:1-9

Revelation of Christ as God's beloved Son

- Arise, shine *Urspringer/Robinson* **HCW 14**
- I believe in Jesus *Nelson* **MAR 121**
- Let your glory fill this place *Graves* **MAR 218**
- Open our eyes, Lord *Cull* **W&P 113, TFF 98, MAR 59**
- Shine, Jesus, shine *Kendrick* **W&P 123, TFF 64, WOV 651, HCW 155**
- 'Tis good, Lord, to be here *Speiss* **GC 778**
- Transfiguration *Landry* **G&P 443**

ADDITIONAL SONGS FOR THE DAY/SEASON

- Awesome God *Mullins* **W&P 13**
- Majesty *Hayford* **W&P 94**
- Shine on us *Glover* **G-4596**
- Transform us *Dunstan/Gerike* **RS 881**
- We are marching in the light of God *South African* **WOV 650**

Year B

This Epiphany festival concludes the cycle of the year that is suffused with the image of light. In Advent, the church prays for the light of God's justice in the world. At Christmas, we celebrate this light in Christ, and throughout the weeks of Epiphany, we welcome this gracious light in the diverse cultures of the world. From the mountain of transfiguring light, Christ goes forth to Jerusalem and leads us to the passover from death to life. Here we find the meaning of his birth and baptism: he was born to die, so that in our death, we might be born to eternal life.

2 KINGS 2:1-12
Elijah taken up to heaven and succeeded by Elisha
Glory *Bullock* **MAR 185**
I will be with you always *Hanson/Murakami* **SCR 118**
Swing low, sweet chariot *African American* **TFF 171**

PSALM 50:1-6
Out of Zion, perfect in beauty, God shines forth in glory.
Before you now *Butler/Osbrink* **VIN7 44**
From the sunrise *Walker* **MAR 184**
I will show God's salvation *Dean* **PS3**

2 CORINTHIANS 4:3-6
God's light seen clearly in the face of Christ
I heard the voice of Jesus say *Bonar/Traditional* **TFF 62**
Jesus, Jesus *Bullock* **HMS11 923**
Rejoice, the Lord is king *Wesley* **MAR 236**
Shine on us *Glover* **G-4596**
Shine, Jesus, shine *Kendrick* **W&P 123, TFF 64, HCW 155**
We cry out for grace again *Kerr* **HMS12 1045**

MARK 9:2-9
Revelation of Christ as God's beloved Son
Come to the mountain *Tunseth* **W&P 32**
Holy, you are holy *Hanson* **SFL**
I see you *Mullins* **CC 90**
Oh Lord, you're beautiful *Green* **MAR 231**
Transfiguration *Landry* **G&P 443**
White as snow *Olguin* **MAR 82**

ADDITIONAL SONGS FOR THE DAY/SEASON
Jesus, you reign over all *Cook* **MAR 208**
'Tis good, Lord, to be here *Speiss* **GC 778**

Year C

Things are not always what they seem! Bread and wine can become a place where we meet God. We, too, are changed in our encounter with grace. When Moses came back from speaking with God, no one could look at him the same. How are our lives a reflection of God's transfiguring love?

EXODUS 34:29-35

Coming down from Mount Sinai, Moses' face shone

- Holy ground *Davis* **HCW 65, COK 5**
- I will not die *Conry* **RS 771, GC 657**

PSALM 99

Proclaim the greatness of the LORD; worship upon God's holy hill.

- Commune with me *Dearman* **MAR 20**
- Great is the Lord *Smith/Smith* **W&P 53**
- I exalt thee *Sanchez* **MAR 123**
- You are holy *Brown* **HMS10 884**

2 CORINTHIANS 3:12—4:2

With unveiled faces we see the Lord's glory as we are transformed

- Jesus, Jesus *Bullock* **HMS11 923**
- Let it be said of us *Fry* **MAR 217**
- On the mountain top *Ylvisaker* **BC**
- Praise to you, O Christ *Farrell* **G&P 662, GC 515, RS 652**
- Spirit of the living God *Iverson* **W&P 129, TFF 101**
- Spirit of the living God *Sanchez* **HCW 158**
- There's a sweet, sweet Spirit in this place *Akers* **TFF 102**

LUKE 9:28-36 [37-43]

Jesus is transfigured on the mountain

- Before you now *Butler/Osbrink* **VIN7 44**
- On the mountain top *Ylvisaker* **BC**
- Shine, Jesus, shine *Kendrick* **W&P 123, TFF 64, HCW 155**
- Stand up *Carroll* **MAR 240**
- 'Tis good, Lord, to be here *Speiss* **GC 778**

ADDITIONAL SONGS FOR THE DAY/SEASON

- Come to the mountain *Tunseth* **W&P 32**
- I see you *Mullins* **CC 90**
- Jesus reigns *Compton* **MAR 207**
- My chosen one *Young* **BL, AFP 11-10753**
- Transfiguration *Landry* **G&P 443**

Ash Wednesday

Years A, B, C

Christians gather on this day to mark the beginning of Lent's baptismal preparation for Easter. On this day, the people of God may receive an ashen cross on the forehead (a gesture rooted in baptism), hear the solemn proclamation to keep a fast in preparation for Easter's feast, and contemplate anew the ongoing meaning of baptismal initiation into the Lord's death and resurrection. While marked with the ashes of human mortality, the church hears God's promise of forgiveness and tastes God's mercy in the bread of life and the cup of salvation. From this solemn liturgy, the church goes forth on its journey to the great baptismal feast of Easter.

JOEL 2:1-2,12-17
Return to the Lord, your God

God of love, have mercy *Makeever*	**DH 10**
Please have mercy on me *Ylvisaker*	**BC**
Return to God *Haugen*	**GC 389**
We cry out for grace again *Kerr*	**HMS12 1045**

ISAIAH 58:1-12
The fast that God chooses

Morning has broken *Farjeon/Traditional*	**W&P 98**

PSALM 51:1-17
Have mercy on me, O God, according to your loving-kindness.

Be merciful, O Lord *Haugen*	**GC 56, RS 83**
Change our hearts *Cooney*	**G&P 349, GC 394**
Create in me a clean heart *Anonymous*	**HCW 36**
Create in me a clean heart *Hopkins*	**W&P 35**
Create in me *Haas*	**GC 57, RS 85**
Create in me *Hurd*	**G&P 209**
Give me a new heart *Walker*	**G&P 210**
God of love, have mercy *Makeever*	**DH 10**

2 CORINTHIANS 5:20B—6:10
Now is the day of salvation

Give thanks *Smith*	**W&P 41, TFF 292, HCW 46**
Let the river flow *Evans*	**HMS12 1015, VIN6 128**
Now *Cooney*	**G-3974**
We can be lifted up *Hanson*	**SCR 105**

MATTHEW 6:1-6, 16-21
The practice of faith

First love *Baloche/Sadler*	**HMS13 1062**
Lord, listen to your children *Hanson*	**W&P 91, SCR 23**
O Lord to you *Sadler*	**HMS11 937**

ADDITIONAL SONGS FOR THE DAY/SEASON

Ashes *Conry*	**G&P 340, RS 957**
Beauty for ashes *Manzano*	**MAR**
Deep within *Haas*	**GC 399, RS 546**
Dust and ashes *Haas*	**GC 381, RS 539**
Mourning into dancing *Walker*	**MAR, W&P 99**
Seek the Lord *O'Connor*	**G&P 351, RS 540**
Share your bread with the hungry *Haas*	**G-4734**

First Sunday in Lent

Year A

In the early church, those to be baptized at Easter were given intense preparation in the preceding weeks. This is the origin and purpose of the Lenten season: a time for the church and its baptismal candidates to ponder the meaning of baptism into the death and resurrection of the Lord. The forty days—a scriptural image of testing and renewal—invite us to return to holy baptism. The weeks of Lent invite us to speak the truth about the keeping of our baptismal promises. The weeks of Lent invite us to hear and taste God's abundant forgiveness in word and sacrament.

GENESIS 2:15-17; 3:1-7
Eating of the tree of the knowledge of good and evil
- Leave your heart with me *Hanson* **SCR 150**

PSALM 32
Mercy embraces those who trust in the LORD.
- I turn to you *Cooney* **GC 44**
- I turn to you, Lord *Stewart* **RS 64**
- Lord, forgive the wrong *Guimont* **RS 65**
- Shout to God, O faithful people *Ylvisaker* **BC**
- You are my hiding place *Ledner* **W&P 160, MAR 167**

ROMANS 5:12-19
Death came through one; life comes through one
- King of life *Sadler* **HMS12 1014**
- Life in his hands *Hanson* **SCR 10**
- One *Hanson/Murakami* **SCR 160**

MATTHEW 4:1-11
The temptation of Jesus in the wilderness for forty days
- First love *Baloche/Sadler* **HMS13 1062**
- God with us *Kendrick* **HMS5 392**
- Jesus walked this lonesome valley *Ferguson* **G-3279**
- Jesus, tempted in the desert *Welsh* **RS 548**
- Lord, my strength *Krippaehne* **W&P 93**
- Seek ye first (without alleluia) *Lafferty* **W&P 122, TFF 149**

ADDITIONAL SONGS FOR THE DAY/SEASON
- Embrace my way and cross *Glover* **G-4594**
- Only by grace *Gustafson* **W&P 112**

Year B

Jesus joins the church in the wilderness for forty days as we contemplate the meaning of our baptism into his death and resurrection. We are with Noah in the ark, Israel in the desert, and Elijah on rocky Mount Horeb for a time of prayer, fasting, and preparation. We do this together as a people who have been brought into existence by God's mercy. We hear this covenant proclaimed in the word of God and share this promise in the body and blood of Christ.

GENESIS 9:8-17
The rainbow, sign of God's covenant
- I Am *Hanson* **SFL**
- We are faithful *Bolduc* **VO 96**
- You are my hiding place *Ledner* **W&P 160, MAR 167**

PSALM 25:1-10
Your paths are love and faithfulness to those who keep your covenant.
- Mercy *DeShazo/Sadler* **HMS14**
- Psalm 25: Remember *Cooney* **G-3972**
- Remember your love *Ducote/Daigle* **G&P 474**
- Remember your mercies *Haas* **GC 35, RS 54**
- Remember your mercy, Lord *Inwood* **G&P 476**
- Show me your ways *Fragar* **HMS11 949**
- To you, O God, I lift up my soul *Hurd* **G&P 302**
- To you, O Lord *Thompson* **RS 50**
- To you, O Lord *Haugen* **GC 36, RS 53**
- To you, O Lord I lift my soul *Roberts* **G-4601**

1 PETER 3:18-22
Saved through water
- In the water *McLean* **WIS 14**
- Let it rain *Park* **VIN8 126**
- Singing through the water *Hanson/Murakami* **SCR 132**
- Spirit calls, rejoice! *Hanson/Murakami* **SCR 1**
- Waterlife *Hanson* **W&P 145, SCR 129**

MARK 1:9-15

The temptation of Jesus in the wilderness for forty days

- Come to the river of life *Moen/Cloninger* **HMS10 818**
- First love *Baloche/Sadler* **HMS13 1062**
- God with us *Kendrick* **HMS5 392**
- Lord, my strength *Krippaehne* **W&P 93**
- Out in the wilderness *Beech* **W&P 115**
- The river is here *Park* **VIN6 232, HMS11 958, CMH 58**
- This is the time of fulfillment! *Chepponis* **RS 556**
- Tree of life *Haugen* **GC 397**

ADDITIONAL SONGS FOR THE DAY/SEASON

- All that is hidden *Farrell* **G&P 585**
- Revive us, oh Lord *Camp/Licciarello* **SPW**
- The cross of Jesus *O'Brien* **G-4517**

Year C

The Lenten discipline is a spiritual struggle. When we confess our sins we acknowledge that we struggle and seek God's strength. Jesus struggles with us, and so we are sustained. Help is as close as a prayer and a confession that we cannot do it on our own or by ourselves. God gives life and its fruit, and so all we offer in worship is giving back what was first given us by grace.

DEUTERONOMY 26:1-11

The L*ORD* *brought us out of Egypt with a mighty hand*

- Eternal Lord of love *Joncas* **RS 554, GC 385**
- King of life *Sadler* **HMS12 1014**

PSALM 91:1-2, 9-16

God shall charge the angels to keep you in all your ways.

- Be with me *Haugen* **RS 123, GC 85**
- Be with me, Lord *Mattingly* **VO 10**
- On eagle's wings *Joncas* **W&P 110, GC 611, G&P 598, RS 740**

ROMANS 10:8B-13

If you confess that Jesus is Lord, you will be saved

- Because we believe *Gordon/Harvill* **HMS12 985**
- Jesus, I believe *Batstone* **MAR 130**
- The word is in your heart *Moore* **GC 518**
- We know and believe *Glover* **GC 836**

LUKE 4:1-13

The temptation of Jesus in the wilderness for forty days

- First love *Baloche/Sadler* **HMS13 1062**
- God with us *Kendrick* **HMS5 392**
- Jesus walked this lonesome valley *Ferguson* **G-3279**
- Jesus, amazing *Hanson/Murakami* **SCR 79**
- Jesus, tempted in the desert *Welsh* **RS 548**
- Lord, my strength *Krippaehne* **W&P 93**
- Out in the wilderness *Beech* **W&P 115**

ADDITIONAL SONGS FOR THE DAY/SEASON

- I believe in Jesus *Nelson* **MAR**
- I will choose Christ *Booth* **G&P 459**

Second Sunday in Lent

Year A

In today's gospel, Jesus directs our attention to the waters of holy baptism. By water and the word, the Holy Spirit gives us new birth. We are made sons and daughters of God, brothers and sisters of the Lord Jesus, messengers of the Holy Spirit. God does all this for us, freely, out of love. From the waters of baptism we rise as a people blessed by God. We are sent forth into the world, not to condemn but to offer mercy.

GENESIS 12:1-4A
The blessing of God upon Abram
- Before the sun burned bright *Schutte* **G&P 577**
- I want Jesus to walk with me *Traditional* **TFF 66**
- Step by step *Beaker* **W&P 132, HMS13 1103**

PSALM 121
It is the L*ORD who watches over you.*
- God is ever wakeful *Haas* **G-4579**
- I lift up my eyes *Ogden* **PS3**
- I shall not be moved *Spiritual* **TFF 147**
- The Lord will keep me safe and holy *Ylvisaker* **BC**

ROMANS 4:1-5, 13-17
The promise to those who share Abraham's faith
- Everlasting grace *Carpenter* **VIN6 58**
- We walk by faith *Ylvisaker* **BC**
- Your everlasting love *Batstone* **MAR 85**

JOHN 3:1-17
The mission of Christ: to save the world
- Eternity *Doerksen* **CMH 28**
- God so loved the world *Hanson* **SCR 129**
- God so loved the world *Hanson/Murakami* **SCR 18**
- God so loved the world *Tate* **VO 27**
- Jesus, I believe *Batstone* **MAR 130**
- Singing through the water *Hanson/Murakami* **SCR 132**
- Spirit calls, rejoice! *Hanson/Murakami* **SCR 1**
- This is the gospel of Christ *Brown* **HMS10 870**
- Waterlife *Hanson* **W&P 145**
- Wind of the spirit *Hanson/Murakami* **W&P 157**

ADDITIONAL SONGS FOR THE DAY/SEASON
- All that is hidden *Farrell* **G&P 585**
- By grace we have been saved *Edwards* **W&P 25**
- The cross of Jesus *O'Brien* **G-4517**

Year B

The readiness of Abraham and Sarah, and the eagerness of Jesus to do God's will are models for contemporary disciples in the church. Baptized into Christ's death and resurrection, we are called to live a distinctive style of life shaped by faith in God's mercy. As followers of Christ, we take up our cross and stand with all those who suffer in our midst. Our Lenten journey always takes us to the cross, the heart of God's love for the world.

GENESIS 17:1-7, 15-16
God blesses Abraham and Sarah
- Faithful One *Doerksen* **CMH2 60, VIN7 72**
- Open our lives to the Word *Makeever* **DH 8**
- Step by step *Beaker* **W&P 132, HMS13 1103**
- Wonderful, merciful Savior *Rodgers/Wyse* **SPW**

PSALM 22:23-31
All the ends of the earth shall remember and turn to the L*ORD.*
- I will praise you Lord *Guimont* **GC 28, RS 41**
- I will praise you, Lord *Kogut* **G-4718**
- Lord, most high *Harris/Sadler* **HMS11 930**
- My God, my God *Haugen* **GC 29, RS 43**
- My God, my God *Smith* **PS2**
- Praises resound *Ylvisaker/Casabolt* **BC**
- We will glorify *Paris* **W&P 154, HCW 187, TFF 281**
- You are the Lord of me *Sims* **SCR 76**

ROMANS 4:13-25
The promise to those who share Abraham's faith
- Firm foundation *Gordon/Harvill* **HCW 42**
- I have kept the faith *Baloche* **HMS13 1076**
- We walk by faith *Ylvisaker* **BC**

MARK 8:31-38

The passion prediction

- Come and follow me *O'Brien* **G-3028**
- Come to me today *Hanson* **SCR 174**
- I come to the cross *Somma/Batstone* **MAR 122**
- I have decided to follow Jesus *Traditional* **MAR 198**
- I have decided *Liles* **HCW 182**
- My life is in you, Lord *Gardner* **HCW 128**
- We are an offering *Liles* **W&P 146**

ADDITIONAL SONGS FOR THE DAY/SEASON

- All that is hidden *Farrell* **G&P 585**
- Before the sun burned bright *Schutte* **G&P 577**
- God of Abraham *Farrell* **GC 391, G&P 450**

Year C

Baptism is the compass that guides our way through life. And Lent is a season for immersing ourselves in that new identity—reminding us who we are and calling us to what we are to be doing. All of it is a miracle of grace, as wonderful as starting a family in your old age, as Abraham and Sarah did, or being reminded that our true citizenship lies beyond this world.

GENESIS 15:1-12, 17-18

The covenant with Abram and his descendants

- El Shaddai *Mullins* **UM 123**
- Step by step *Beaker* **W&P 132, HMS13 1103**
- What you are *Harris* **HMS14 18**

PSALM 27

In the day of trouble, the LORD shall keep me safe.

- Holy love, holy light *Batstone* **MAR 118**
- In the land of the living *Johengen* **GC 38**
- Lead me, guide me *Akers* **TFF 70**
- Lead me, oh lead me *Smith* **HMS13 1085**

PHILIPPIANS 3:17-4:1

Our citizenship is in heaven from where we expect a Savior

- Ring all the living bells *Ylvisaker* **BC**
- Stand firm *Cameroon/Glover* **G-4593**
- We can be lifted up *Hanson* **SCR 105**

LUKE 13:31-35

I have desired to gather Jerusalem as a hen gathers her brood

- A song of unity *Jahn* **W&P 1**
- All around your throne *DeShazo/Kerr* **HMS10 808**
- Closer *Butler* **VIN6 36**
- Come and see *LeBlanc* **W&P 29**
- Come closer *Hanson* **SCR 47**

ADDITIONAL SONGS FOR THE DAY/SEASON

- By the waters of Babylon *Jamaican* **TFF 67**
- Embrace my way and cross *Glover* **G-4594**
- The cross of Jesus *O'Brien* **G-4517**
- You are my all in all *Jernigan* **SPW**

Third Sunday in Lent

Year A

In the early church, immediate preparation for baptism at Easter was heightened by the proclamation of gospel stories chosen especially for the last Sundays in Lent. In Year A, these readings are retained. Today's gospel is the story of the Samaritan woman asking Jesus for water. It is an image of our great thirst for God's mercy, grace, and forgiveness. It is an image of God's grace freely given to us in scripture, baptism, the Lord's supper, and the faith of our brothers and sisters. The church invites all who seek God to come to these good things where we encounter the one who gives us life-giving water.

EXODUS 17:1-7
Water from the rock in the wilderness
- Built on a rock *James* **G-3525**
- Eternal Lord of love *Joncas* **RS 554, GC 385**
- You are my rock *Carpenter* **VIN6 278**

PSALM 95
Let us shout for joy to the rock of our salvation.
- I will come and bow down *Nystrom* **HCW 87**
- If today you hear God's voice *Haas* **GC 89, RS 129**
- If today you hear his voice *Stewart* **RS 128**
- If today you hear the voice of God *Bolduc* **VO 45**
- Listen to the voice of God *Geary* **PS2**
- Shout to God, O faithful people *Ylvisaker* **BC**
- We bow down *Paris* **W&P 149, HCW 183**

ROMANS 5:1-11
Reconciled to God by Christ's death
- For all you've done *Moen* **HMS12 992**
- Lamb of God *Paris* **HCW 100**
- Saved by the grace of a miracle *Ylvisaker* **BC**
- Spirit calls, rejoice! *Hanson/Murakami* **SCR 1**

JOHN 4:5-42
Baptismal image: the woman at the well
- Flow like a river *Funk* **HMS13 1063**
- Flow river flow *Hurd* **G&P 455**
- Flowing river *Baloche* **HMS13 1064**
- God of all power *Haas* **RS 232**
- God provides a brand new heart *Ylvisaker* **BC**
- I heard the voice of Jesus say *Bonar* **TFF 62**
- I saw water *Young* **BL**
- Let it rain *Park* **VIN8 126**
- Singing through the water *Hanson/Murakami* **SCR 132**
- There's a sweet, sweet spirit in this place *Akers* **TFF 102**
- Water from heaven *Hanson/Murakami* **SCR 136**

ADDITIONAL SONGS FOR THE DAY/SEASON
- Amazing love *Kendrick* **W&P 8, HCW 10**
- Cup we bless *Young* **BL**
- Dust and ashes *Haas* **GC 381**
- The cross of Jesus *O'Brien* **G-4517**

Year B

In our society, even churches can become like marketplaces, and congregations can be characterized chiefly as consumers. The drive to satisfy every taste and opinion can distract the church from its center: Jesus Christ among us in the regular celebration of word and sacrament. In the word of God and the eucharistic meal, the temple of Christ's body is strengthened for its witness in daily life.

EXODUS 20:1-17
The commandments given at Sinai
- Eternal Lord of love *Joncas* **RS 554, GC 385**
- Thy word *Smith/Grant* **TFF 132, W&P 144**
- Thy word *Webb* **W&P 143**

PSALM 19
The commandment of the LORD gives light to the eyes.
- Lord, you have the words *Haas* **GC 27, RS 40**
- Lord, you have the words *Bolduc* **VO 61**
- More precious than silver *DeShazo* **HCW 122**
- Psalm 19 *Butler* **VIN7 190**
- You, Lord, have the message of eternal life *Ogden* **PS2**

1 CORINTHIANS 1:18-25
Christ crucified, the wisdom of God
- Cup we bless *Young* **BL**
- Hop on the bus *Underwood* **VIN7 120**
- I come to the cross *Somma/Batstone* **MAR 122**
- O, mighty cross *Baroni/Chisum* **HCW 136**
- Only God for me *Harris* **HMS14**

JOHN 2:13-22

The cleansing of the temple

- Arise, oh Lord *Carpenter* **VIN6 16**
- Closer *Butler* **VIN6 36**
- Stand up and give him the praise *DeShazo* **HMS10 867**

ADDITIONAL SONGS FOR THE DAY/SEASON

- All that is hidden *Farrell* **G&P 585**
- Come and taste *Hanson/Murakami* **W&P 30**
- Who will stand up? *Soper* **G-4626**

Year C

Can we take the news to heart? Each story we encounter is really about us. An ashen cross at the beginning of Lent reminded us that we do not have forever. The clock is ticking; the forty days are unwinding. We have now! If we take this day seriously, we may discover that our deepest hungers can be filled. And when we know that we are heading toward a forgiving God, the news becomes good news.

ISAIAH 55:1-9

Everyone who thirsts, come to the water; seek the LORD

- Come to the river of life *Moen/Cloninger* **HMS10 818**
- Come to the water *Foley* **G&P 706, GC 502**
- Let it rain *Park* **VIN8 126**
- Most holy one *Willard/Baloche* **MAR 223**
- Seek the Lord *O'Connor* **G&P 351, RS 540**

PSALM 63:1-8

O God, eagerly I seek you; my soul thirsts for you.

- I long for you *Balhoff/Daigle/Ducote* **GC 63**
- I love to be in your presence *Baloche/Kerr* **HCW 75**
- Make your presence known *Barbour* **MAR 221**
- My soul is thirsting *Joncas* **GC 61, RS 90**
- You are my God *Delavan* **HCW 196**
- You are my help *Ashton* **PS1**
- Your love is finer than life *Haugen* **GC 62**

1 CORINTHIANS 10:1-13

Israel, baptized in cloud and seas, ate the same spiritual food as Christians

- Freely, given freely *Hanson/Murakami* **SCR 74**
- Lord, my strength *Krippaehne* **W&P 93**
- You are holy *Brown* **HMS10 884**

LUKE 13:1-9

Unless you repent, you will perish: parable of the fig tree

- Change my heart, oh God *Espinoza* **W&P 28, HCW 28**
- Deep within *Haas* **GC 399, RS 546**
- Life in his hands *Hanson* **SCR 10**
- Turn my heart *DeShazo* **HCW 179**

ADDITIONAL SONGS FOR THE DAY/SEASON

- All that is hidden *Farrell* **G&P 585**
- Change our hearts *Cooney* **G&P 349, GC 394**
- Turn to me *Foley* **G&P 342**
- You are the rock of my salvation *Muller* **W&P 161**

Fourth Sunday in Lent

Year A

The gospel for this Sunday is the story of a man blind from birth healed by Christ. It is a profound image of our human condition: we seek after greater clarity and light. It is also a baptismal image of washing and receiving sight, of Christ's desire to enlighten us with the truth of who we are: God's beloved daughters and sons.

1 SAMUEL 16:1-13
David is chosen and anointed
God of glory *Hanson* **SCR 89**

PSALM 23
You have anointed my head with oil.
I am the Good Shepherd *Ylvisaker* **BC**
In the arms of the Shepherd *Weckler* **VO 47**
Like a shepherd *Moen/Simpson* **HCW 112**
My heart will trust *Morgan* **HMS14**
My shepherd is the Lord *Guiao* **UMP 10/1734U**
Shepherd me, O God *Haugen* **GC 31, RS 756**
The Lord is my shepherd *Ollis* **PS2**
You are my shepherd *Haas* **G-4994**

EPHESIANS 5:8-14
Awake from sleep, live as children of light
Awake, O sleeper *Haugen* **GC 803**
Now in this banquet *Haugen* **W&P 104**
Shine, Jesus, shine *Kendrick* **W&P 123, TFF 64, HCW 155**
Wake up, sleeper *Ylvisaker* **BC**
Wake up *Hanson* **SCR 13**

JOHN 9:1-41
Baptismal image: the man born blind
God of all mercy *Haas* **RS 232**
He healed the darkness *Haas* **GC 876**
I do believe *Ylvisaker* **BC**
Open our eyes, Lord *Cull* **W&P 113, TFF 98, MAR 59**
Open the eyes of my heart *Baloche* **HMS12 1027, HMS13 1093**

ADDITIONAL SONGS FOR THE DAY/SEASON
Lay hands upon us *Glover* **G-4591**
That priceless grace *Ghanaian* **TFF 68**

Year B

In today's gospel reading, Jesus compares himself to the serpent in the wilderness. He is lifted up on the cross so that all who hold to him will be healed. God sent the Son, not to condemn, but to save the world. We who have heard the words of love and mercy in today's scriptures go forth to speak with forgiveness rather than condemnation. Our baptism calls us to a life of good works, not to point to ourselves but to the immeasurable riches of God's grace made known to all the world in Christ our Lord.

NUMBERS 21:4-9
The lifting up of the serpent
God my refuge *Montemayer* **HCW 50**

PSALM 107:1-3, 17-22
The LORD delivered them from their distress.
Give thanks to the Lord *Carroll* **RS 147**
Give thanks to the Lord *Stewart* **GC 102**
Heal me, O Lord *Moen* **HMS10 828**
We cry out for grace again *Kerr* **HMS12 1045**

EPHESIANS 2:1-10
Saved by grace through faith for good works
All we like sheep *Moen* **HCW 7**
For by grace *Nicholas* **W&P 38**
Nothing at all but love *Ylvisaker* **BC**
Oh, how he loves you and me *Kaiser* **TFF 82**
Only by grace *Gustafson* **W&P 112, HCW 140**
Song about grace *Ylvisaker* **BC**
Thank you for the gift *Hanson* **SCR 144**

JOHN 3:14-21
The lifting up of the Son of Man
Eternity *Doerksen* **CMH 28**
For God so loved the world *Dauermann* **W&P 39**
God so loved the world *Tate* **VO 27**
Jesus, I believe *Batstone* **MAR 130**
John 3:16 *Lloyd* **MAR**
King of life *Sadler* **HMS12 1014**
Lord, I lift your name on high *Founds* **W&P 90**

ADDITIONAL SONGS FOR THE DAY/SEASON

- All that is hidden *Farrell* **G&P 585**
- Tree of life *Haugen* **GC 397, RS 541**
- You are my hiding place *Ledner* **W&P 160**

Year C

Lent is the time for coming home. In the ancient church it was the season for reconciling lapsed Christians to the community of the faithful. Today's readings provide images of homecoming—Israel's entry into the land of promise, a prodigal son who returned to his waiting father. In Jesus, God makes a home with us—a dwelling place of peace. Welcome home!

JOSHUA 5:9-12

Israel eats bread and grain, the produce of the land

- God is so good *Traditional* **TFF 275**

PSALM 32

Be glad, you righteous, and rejoice in the LORD.

- I turn to you *Cooney* **GC 44**
- I turn to you, Lord *Stewart* **RS 64**
- Lord, forgive the wrong *Guimont* **RS 65**
- Shout to God, O faithful people *Ylvisaker* **BC**
- You are my hiding place *Ledner* **W&P 160**

2 CORINTHIANS 5:16-21

The mystery and ministry of reconciliation

- Brighter than the sun *Makeever* **DH 64**
- In Christ, a new creation *Ylvisaker* **BC**
- Jesus, I believe *Batstone* **MAR 130**
- Jesus, Jesus *Bullock* **HMS11 923**

LUKE 15:1-3, 11B-32

The parable of the prodigal father and the repentant son

- Come closer *Hanson* **SCR 47**
- Come home *Landry* **G&P 46**
- Come home *Mattingly* **VO 16**
- Come to me today *Hanson* **SCR 174**
- God of love, have mercy *Makeever* **DH 10**
- Mercy *DeShazo/Sadler* **HMS14**
- We cry out for grace again *Kerr* **HMS12 1045**
- We love you *Hanson* **SCR 147**

ADDITIONAL SONGS FOR THE DAY/SEASON

- Jesus, keep me near the cross *Keesecker* **AFP 11-10744**
- Journey for home *Bolduc* **VO 50**

Fifth Sunday in Lent

Year A

Today's gospel is the story of Jesus raising Lazarus from the dead. With Martha and Mary we stand at the graves of our beloved dead and hear Jesus say, "I am the resurrection and the life." His words give hope to all who dwell in the shadows of death. But also they are words spoken next to the waters of holy baptism, where we die to death and rise to life in Christ. In the power and presence of the risen Christ, Christians prepare to renew their baptismal promises and welcome new brothers and sisters at Easter.

EZEKIEL 37:1-14
The dry bones of Israel brought to life
- All that is hidden *Farrell* **G&P 585**
- Wind of God *Sadler* **HMS13 1116**

PSALM 130
With the L*ORD there is mercy and plenteous redemption.*
- Bright and morning star *Makeever* **DH 50**
- De profundis blues *Wellicome* **PS3**
- From the depths *Smith* **PS2**
- Only by grace *Gustafson* **W&P 112, HCW 140**
- Out of the depths *Batastini* **RS 947**
- Out of the depths *Hay* **VO 74**
- With the Lord there is mercy *Haugen* **RS 176, GC 130**
- With the Lord there is mercy *Joncas* **RS 174**

ROMANS 8:6-11
Life in the Spirit
- Alive in Christ Jesus *Haas* **GC 803**
- Come share the spirit *Hanson/Murakami* **SCR 116**
- Life in his hands *Hanson* **SCR 10**
- My life is in you, Lord *Gardner* **HCW 128**
- Spirit of the living God *Iverson* **W&P 129, TFF 101**
- Spirit of the living God *Sanchez* **HCW 158**

JOHN 11:1-45
Baptismal image: the raising of Lazarus
- Because we believe *Gordon/Harvill* **HMS12 985**
- God of the living *Haas* **RS 232**
- I am the Bread of life *Toolan* **RS 931, GC 828**
- I am the resurrection *Ylvisaker* **BC**
- I do believe *Ylvisaker* **BC**
- Only God for me *Harris* **HMS14**
- Tree of life *Haugen* **GC 397, RS 541**
- Up from the earth *Cooney* **G&P 386, GC 452, RS 589**
- We shall rise again *Young* **RS 872**
- You only *McCoy* **VIN8 242**

ADDITIONAL SONGS FOR THE DAY/SEASON
- A story for all people *Collins* **W&P 2**
- Ashes *Conroy* **LBG 25**
- Awake, O sleeper *Haugen* **GC 803, RS 650**
- Taste and see *Young* **BL, AFP 11-10895**

Year B

In today's gospel reading, Jesus speaks of grain dying in the earth as an image of his death and resurrection. Christ is the seed fallen to earth that yields the harvest of life, health, and salvation. Christ is the one who accompanies us in our baptismal death and raises us to life with him. Christ is the grain of wheat that we share in the breaking of the bread. Christ's Spirit strengthens us in lives of fruitful service to those who hunger and thirst for life.

JEREMIAH 31:31-34
A new covenant written on the heart
- Change our hearts *Cooney* **G&P 349, GC 394**
- Deep within *Haas* **GC 399, RS 546**
- I want to know you *Evans* **HMS12 1008**
- Write it on my heart *McLean* **WIS 41**
- You are mine *Haas* **W&P 158**

PSALM 51:1-12
Create in me a clean heart, O God.
- Be merciful, O Lord *Haugen* **GC 56, RS 83**
- Create in me a clean heart *Anonymous* **HCW 36**
- Create in me a clean heart *Hopkins* **W&P 35**
- Create in me *Hurd* **G&P 209**
- Create in me *Haas* **GC 57, RS 85**
- Give me a new heart *Walker* **G&P 210**
- Mercy *DeShazo/Sadler* **HMS14**

PSALM 119:9-16

I treasure your promise in my heart.

- Closer *Butler* **VIN6 36**
- Teach me, O God *Walker* **PS3**
- Thy word *Webb* **W&P 143**
- Thy word *Smith/Grant* **TFF 132, W&P 144**

HEBREWS 5:5-10

Through suffering Christ becomes the source of salvation

- Broken hearts *Hanson/Murakami* **SCR 170**
- Lamb of God *Paris* **HCW 100**
- The love of the Lord *Joncas* **RS 814, GC 702**
- You, Lord *Hanson* **W&P 162, SCR 42**

JOHN 12:20-33

The grain of wheat dying in the earth

- All that is hidden (st. 4) *Farrell* **G&P 585**
- Be glorified *Funk* **HCW 19**
- Glorify thy name *Adkins* **W&P 42**
- Step by step *Beaker* **W&P 132, HMS13 1103**
- Unless a grain of wheat *Farrell* **G&P 579, GC 697**
- Up from the earth *Cooney* **G&P 386, GC 452, RS 589**

ADDITIONAL SONGS FOR THE DAY/SEASON

- Carol of the thorn tree *Haugen* **G-4416**
- Shout to the Lord *Zschech* **W&P 124**
- The cross of Jesus *O'Brien* **G-4517**

Year C

The Lenten preparation is almost at an end. Something new is about to happen! Mary's act of anointing Jesus is extravagant, but when we know that grace has come to us, it is time for lavishness. Our old values get rearranged when we realize how deeply we are loved.

ISAIAH 43:16-21

The L*ORD gives water in the wilderness to the chosen people*

- God will make a way *Moen* **HCW 52**
- Out in the wilderness *Beech* **W&P 115**
- You are mine *Haas* **W&P 158**

PSALM 126

Those who sowed with tears will reap with songs of joy.

- Give thanks *Smith* **HCW 46, TFF 292, W&P 41**
- God has done great things for us *Haugen* **GC 124**
- The Lord has done great things *Cortez* **G&P 271**
- The Lord has done great things *Guimont* **RS 169**
- The Lord has done great things *Stewart* **RS 170**
- Trading my sorrows *Evans* **HMS14**

PHILIPPIANS 3:4B-14

To know Christ and his resurrection, to share in his sufferings

- Amen *Fitts* **HMS12 982**
- Broken hearts *Hanson/Murakami* **SCR 170**
- Change my heart, oh God *Espinoza* **HCW 28, W&P 28**
- Hop on the bus *Underwood* **VIN7 120**
- I want to know you *Evans* **HMS12 1008**
- Only this I want *Schutte* **GC 695**

JOHN 12:1-8

Mary anoints Jesus for his burial

- All that is hidden (sts. 2, 3) *Farrell* **G&P 585**
- Be near us, Lord Jesus *Hanson/Murakami* **SCR 4**
- Closer *Butler* **VIN6 36**
- Come closer *Hanson* **SCR 47**
- We will draw near *Nystrom/Harris* **HMS11 966**

ADDITIONAL SONGS FOR THE DAY/SEASON

- Amazing love *Kendrick* **CEL 351**
- To know you more *Horness* **MAR**
- Tree of life *Haugen* **GC 397**

Passion Sunday

Palm Sunday

Year A

On this day Christians throughout the world begin the great and holy week that culminates in the central celebration of our faith: the Lord's passage from death to new life celebrated in the Three Days of Maundy Thursday, Good Friday, and the Resurrection of Our Lord. Today's reading of Christ's passion, or suffering, sets forth the central act of God's love for humankind. In the reception of the Lord's body and blood, the church receives this life-giving love. In prayer, hymns, and readings, we hear the great paradox of our faith: Christ is proclaimed the mighty one who reigns from the cross.

PROCESSION WITH PALMS
MATTHEW 21:1-11
Entrance into the final days

PSALM 118:1-2, 19-29
Blessed is he who comes in the name of the LORD.

SONGS AT THE PROCESSION

- Blessed be the name *Park* **VIN7 48**
- Blessings on the King *Lynch* **G&P 357**
- Holy! Holy! Holy Lord *Ylvisaker* **BC**
- Hosanna to the Son of David *Schutte* **G&P 358**
- I will enter his gates *Brethorst* **TFF 291**
- Lord of heaven *Ashwood* **CCP 23**
- Ride on Jesus ride *Spiritual* **RS 562, GC 405**
- Ride on, King Jesus *Spiritual* **G&P 359**
- Stand up and give him the praise *DeShazo* **HMS10 867**
- Welcome the King *Kendrick* **HMS12 1048**

LITURGY OF THE PASSION
ISAIAH 50:4-9A
The servant of the Lord submits to suffering

- Lord, my strength *Krippaehne* **W&P 93**

PSALM 31:9-16
Into your hands, O Lord, I commend my spirit.

- Father, I put my life in your hands *Hughes* **RS 62**
- Father, I put my life in your hands *Talbot* **G&P 195**
- Father, into your hands *Smith* **PS2**
- God of love, have mercy *Makeever* **DH 10**
- I place my life *Cooney* **G-3613**
- I put my life in your hands *Haas* **GC 42, RS 61**
- I put my life in your hands *Haugen* **GC 43**
- You are my God *Delavan* **HCW 196**

PHILIPPIANS 2:5-11
Humbled to the point of death on a cross

- At the name of Jesus *Bolduc* **VO 5**
- At the name of Jesus *Webb* **W&P 12**
- He is exalted *Paris* **HCW 57, W&P 55**
- He is Lord *Smith* **HMS12 998**
- I come to the cross *Somma/Batstone* **MAR 122**
- Jesus, name above all names *Cain* **W&P 77, TFF 268**
- Jesus, the Lord *O'Connor* **GC 418, RS 574, G&P 370**
- We bow before his holy name *Ylvisaker* **BC**
- You have been given *Kauflin* **HCW 197**

MATTHEW 26:14-27:66 *OR* MATTHEW 27:11-54
The passion of the Lord

- Bless the body broken for my sin *Ylvisaker* **BC**
- Broken in love *Hanson* **SCR 177, W&P 24**
- Come to me today *Hanson* **SCR 174**
- Poured out and broken *Hanson/Murakami* **SCR 184**
- Stay here *Taizé* **GC 411, RS 565**
- Strange King *Makeever* **DH 61**
- The cross of Jesus *O'Brien* **G-4517**
- The night of his betrayal *Ylvisaker* **BC**

ADDITIONAL SONGS FOR THE DAY/SEASON

- Now we remain *Haas* **GC 594, RS 813**
- Tree of life/Adoramus te *Haugen* **GC 396/397, RS 541/542**

Year B

On this day the church continues its procession with our crucified and risen Lord. He is in our midst as we hear of his life-giving death and as we share his body and blood. At the beginning of this great week, the passion gospel sets forth the central mystery of the Christian faith: Christ emptied himself in death so that we might know God's mercy and love for all creation.

PROCESSION WITH PALMS
MARK 11:1-11 *OR* JOHN 12:12-16
Entrance into the final days

PSALM 118:1-2, 19-29
Blessed is he who comes in the name of the LORD.

SONGS AT THE PROCESSION

Blessed be the name	*Park*	**VIN7 48**
Holy! Holy! Holy Lord	*Ylvisaker*	**BC**
I will enter his gates	*Brethorst*	**TFF 291**
King of life	*Sadler*	**HMS12 1014**
Lift up your heads	*Kendrick*	**W&P 88**
Mark's Sanctus	*Ylvisaker*	**BC**
Stand up and give him the praise	*DeShazo*	**HMS10 867**
The cross of Jesus	*O'Brien*	**G-4517**

LITURGY OF THE PASSION
ISAIAH 50:4-9A
The servant of the Lord submits to suffering

Lord, my strength	*Krippaehne*	**W&P 93**

PSALM 31:9-16
Into your hands, O Lord, I commend my spirit.

Father, I put my life in your hands	*Hughes*	**RS 62**
Father, I put my life in your hands	*Talbot*	**G&P 195**
God of love, have mercy	*Makeever*	**DH 10**
I put my life in your hands	*Haugen*	**GC 43**
I put my life in your hands/Pongo mi vida	*Haas*	**GC 42, RS 61**
You are my God	*Delavan*	**HCW 196**

PHILIPPIANS 2:5-11
Humbled to the point of death on a cross

At the name of Jesus	*Cain*	**TFF 268**
At the name of Jesus	*Bolduc*	**VO 5**
For the life of the world	*Haas*	**GC 801**
He is exalted	*Paris*	**W&P 55**
He is Lord	*Smith*	**HMS12 998**
I come to the cross	*Somma/Batstone*	**MAR 122**
Jesus, name above all names	*Cain*	**W&P 77**
Jesus, the Lord	*O'Connor*	**GC 418, RS 574, G&P 370**
Jesus, the Lord	*Paris*	**HCW 57**
We bow before his holy name	*Ylvisaker*	**BC**
You have been given	*Kauflin*	**HCW 197**

MARK 14:1-15:47 *OR* MARK 15:1-39 [40-47]
The passion of the Lord

Bless the body broken for my sin	*Ylvisaker*	**BC**
Carol of the thorn tree	*Haugen*	**G-4416**
Come to me today	*Hanson*	**SCR 174**
Crucifixion: Song of Mark	*Haugen*	**G-4416**
Poured out and broken	*Hanson/Murakami*	**SCR 184**
Strange King	*Makeever*	**DH 61**
The night of his betrayal	*Ylvisaker*	**BC**

ADDITIONAL SONGS FOR THE DAY/SEASON

Broken in love	*Hanson*	**SCR 177, W&P 24**
Calvary	*Spiritual*	**TFF 85**

Year C

The procession with palms brings us into Holy Week and the celebration of the mystery of our salvation. We enter the week by hearing the story of Jesus' passion—his suffering and death. In baptism we have been fused to this story; in Holy Week we make our way through it again because it brings us to life with Christ.

PROCESSION WITH PALMS
LUKE 19:28-40
Entrance into the final days

PSALM 118:1-2, 19-29
Blessed is he who comes in the name of the LORD.

SONGS AT THE PROCESSION

- Blessed be the name *Park* **VIN7 48**
- Holy! Holy! Holy Lord *Ylvisaker* **BC**
- Hosanna to the Son of David *Schutte* **G&P 358**
- Hosanna: Song of Mark *Haugen* **G-4416**
- I will enter his gates *Brethorst* **TFF 291**
- Palm Sunday processional *Cooney* **G-5012**
- Stand up and give him the praise *DeShazo* **HMS10 867**
- Welcome the King *Kendrick* **HMS12**

LITURGY OF THE PASSION
ISAIAH 50:4-9A
The servant of the Lord submits to suffering

- Lord, my strength *Krippaehne* **W&P 93**

PSALM 31:9-16
Into your hands, O Lord, I commend my spirit.

- Father, I put my life in your hands *Hughes* **RS 62**
- Father, I put my life in your hands *Talbott* **G&P 195**
- God of love, have mercy *Makeever* **DH 10**
- I put my life in your hands *Haas* **GC 42, RS 61**
- I put my life in your hands *Haugen* **GC 43**
- You are my God *Delavan* **HCW 196**

PHILIPPIANS 2:5-11
Humbled to the point of death on a cross

- At the name of Jesus *Bolduc* **VO 5**
- For the life of the world *Haas* **GC 801**
- He is exalted *Paris* **HCW 57, W&P 55**
- He is Lord *Smith* **HMS12 998**
- I come to the cross *Somma/Batstone* **MAR 122**
- Jesus, name above all names *Cain* **TFF 268, W&P 77**
- Jesus, the Lord *O'Connor* **GC 418, RS 574, G&P 370**
- We bow before his holy name *Ylvisaker* **BC**
- You have been given *Kauflin* **HCW 197**

LUKE 22:14—23:56 *OR* LUKE 23:1-49
The passion of the Lord

- Bless the body broken for my sin *Ylvisaker* **BC**
- Broken in love *Hanson* **SCR 177, W&P 24**
- Come to me today *Hanson* **SCR 174**
- For me *Hanson* **SCR 176**
- Here is bread *Kendrick* **W&P 58**
- Jesus, remember me *Berthier* **W&P 78, RS 770, GC 404**
- Open our eyes, Lord *Cull* **TFF 98, MAR 59, W&P 113**
- Poured out and broken *Hanson/Murakami* **SCR 184**
- Stay here *Taizé* **GC 411, RS 565**
- Strange King *Makeever* **DH 61**
- The cross of Jesus *O'Brien* **G-4517**
- The night of his betrayal *Ylvisaker* **BC**

ADDITIONAL SONGS FOR THE DAY/SEASON

- Carol of the thorn tree *Haugen* **G-4416**
- Ride on, Jesus, ride *Spiritual* **RS 562, GC 405**

Weekdays of Holy Week

Monday, Tuesday, and Wednesday in Holy Week focus on the events of the last week of Jesus' earthly life. Rather than trying to "walk where Jesus walked," the church uses these days to view Christ more particularly in our lives today. Jesus comes to us in our day through the reading of scripture, through preaching, through the water of baptism, through the bread and wine of communion, and through the prayers. Be open for the surprising ways in which Christ is made known to you this week. Also look for opportunities to share the gift of his life with others.

Monday

Years A, B, C

ISAIAH 42:1-9
The servant brings forth justice
Make me a servant *Willard* **W&P 96**
Open the eyes of my heart *Baloche* **HMS13 1093, HMS12 1027**

PSALM 36:5-11
Your people take refuge under the shadow of your wings.
These things are true of you *Walker* **MAR 248**
Your constant love *Hanson* **SCR 100**
Your everlasting love *Batstone* **MAR 85**
Your steadfast love *Sandquist* **HCW 200**

HEBREWS 9:11-15
The redeeming blood of Christ
O, mighty cross *Baroni/Chisum* **HCW 136**
Refiner's fire *Doerksen* **CMH 10**

JOHN 12:1-11
Mary anoints the feet of Jesus
There's a sweet, sweet spirit in this place *Akers* **TFF 102**
Ubi caritas et amor *Berthier* **WOV 665, REN**
We will draw near *Nystrom/Harris* **HMS11 966**

Tuesday

Years A, B, C

ISAIAH 49:1-7
The servant brings salvation to earth's ends
I come to the cross *Somma/Batstone* **MAR 122**

PSALM 71:1-14
From my mother's womb you have been my strength.
Lord, my strength *Krippaehne* **W&P 93**

1 CORINTHIANS 1:18-31
Christ crucified, the wisdom of God

JOHN 12:20-36
The hour has come
Be glorified *Funk* **HCW 19**
Glorify thy name *Adkins* **W&P 42**
Step by step *Beaker* **W&P 132, HMS13 1103**

Wednesday

Years A, B, C

ISAIAH 50:4-9A
The servant is vindicated by God
No greater love *Walker* **MAR 54**

PSALM 70
Be pleased, O God, to deliver me.
Be magnified *DeShazo* **HCW 20**

HEBREWS 12:1-3
Look to Jesus, who endured the cross
God provides a brand new heart *Ylvisaker* **BC**
May you run and not be weary *Hanson* **SCR 116, W&P 97**

JOHN 13:21-32
The departure of Jesus' betrayer
The night of his betrayal *Ylvisaker* **BC**

Holy Thursday

Maundy Thursday

Years A, B, C

On this day the Christian community gathers to share in the holy supper which Christ gave the church to reveal his unfailing love for the human family. In the gospel reading Christ demonstrates this love by speaking his faithful word, washing his disciples' feet, and giving his body and blood. From this gathering we are sent to continue these actions in daily life: to serve those in need, to offer mercy, to feed the hungry.

EXODUS 12:1-4 [5-10] 11-14
The passover of the Lord
- Lamb of God *Paris* **MAR**
- We bring the sacrifice of praise *Dearman* **W&P 150**
- You are my all in all *Jernigan* **HMS11 976**

PSALM 116:1-2, 12-19
I will take the cup of salvation and call on the name of the LORD.
- An offering of thanksgiving *Ylvisaker* **BC**
- I love you, Lord *Klein* **TFF 288, W&P 67**
- Our blessing-cup *Haugen* **RS 155, GC 107, G&P 257**
- The name of God *Haas* **RS 152, GC 110**

1 CORINTHIANS 11:23-26
Proclaim the Lord's death until he comes
- Bread of life *Fisher* **G&P 522**
- Broken in love *Hanson* **SCR 177, W&P**
- Here is bread *Kendrick* **W&P 58**
- That we may be filled *Hanson/Murakami* **SCR 182, W&P 134**
- This bread that we break *Makeever* **DH 30**
- When we eat this bread *Joncas* **G&P 510**

JOHN 13:1-17, 31B-35
The service of Christ: footwashing and meal
- A new commandment *Anonymous* **WOV 664**
- Amen *Fitts* **HMS12 982**
- As bread that is broken *Baloche/Cloninger* **HMS10 811**
- Here I am *Batstone* **MAR 115**
- Jesu, Jesu, fill us with your love *Johnston* **G-3000**
- Make me a servant *Willard* **W&P 96**
- No greater love *Joncas* **GC 628**
- Reach out and take a hand *Kendrick* **HMS12 1029**
- So you must do *Haugen* **G-4841**
- Song of the Lord's command *Haas* **G-4682**
- Take off your shoes *Makeever* **DH 62**

ADDITIONAL SONGS FOR THE DAY/SEASON
- No greater love *Schoenbahler* **G&P 362**
- O Jerusalem *Vogt* **LBG**
- One bread we bless and share *Mahalo* **G-4362**
- Remember *Keesecker* **AFP 11-10743**
- Stay here *Berthier* **WOV 667**
- The servant song *Gillard* **GC 669**
- Ubi caritas et amor *Berthier* **WOV 665, REN**

Good Friday

Years A, B, C

On this day the church gathers to hear the proclamation of Christ's suffering and death, to pray for the life of the world, and to meditate on the life-giving cross. The ancient title for this day—the triumph of the cross—reminds us that the church gathers to offer thanksgiving for the wood of the tree on which hung our salvation.

ISAIAH 52:13—53:12

The suffering servant

- All we like sheep *Moen* **HCW 7**
- Amazing love *Kendrick* **HCW 10, W&P 8**
- Behold the Lamb of God *Dufford* **G&P 360**
- How beautiful upon the mountains *Ylvisaker* **BC**
- Lamb of God *Paris* **SPW**

PSALM 22

My God, my God, why have you forsaken me?

- Broken hearts *Hanson/Murakami* **SCR 170**
- God is here *Moen/Overstreet* **HMS12 995**
- Lord most high *Harris/Sadler* **HMS11 930**
- My God, my God *Haugen* **GC 29, RS 43**
- My God, my God *Schiavone* **G&P 177**
- My God, my God *Smith* **PS2**
- My God, my God *Manion* **G&P 175**
- Praises resound *Ylvisaker/Casabolt* **BC**
- You are the Lord of me *Sims* **SCR 76**

HEBREWS 10:16-25

The way to God is opened by Jesus' death

- Our hope is alive *Ylvisaker* **BC**
- Stir up the love *Ylvisaker* **BC**
- We will draw near *Nystrom/Harris* **HMS11 966**
- We've come to worship you *Kerr* **HMS10 878**
- You are holy *Brown* **HMS10 884**

HEBREWS 4:14-16; 5:7-9

Jesus, the merciful high priest

- A taste of the joys of heaven *Ylvisaker* **BC**
- How blessed *Hampton* **VIN6 106**
- Only by grace *Gustafson* **W&P 112, HCW 140**

JOHN 18:1-19:42

The passion and death of Christ

- Behold the wood *Schutte* **G&P 369, GC 420**
- For me *Hanson* **SCR 176**
- Jesus, Lamb of God (All in all) *Jernigan* **W&P 76**
- Oh, how he loves you and me *Kaiser* **TFF 82**

ADDITIONAL SONGS FOR THE DAY/SEASON

- Abba, Father, we approach you *Batstone* **MAR**
- By grace we have been saved *Edwards* **W&P 25**
- In the cross of Christ *Haugen* **G-4838**
- Jesus, the Lord *O'Connor* **GC 418, RS 574, G&P 370**
- No greater love *Schoenbahler* **G&P 362**
- Our God reigns *Smith.* **VO 73**
- The cross of Jesus *O'Brien* **G-4517**
- Tree of life/Adoramus te *Haugen* **GC 396/397, RS 541/542**

Resurrection of the Lord

Easter Vigil

Year A, B, C

Tonight's Easter Proclamation announces, "This is the night in which all who believe in Christ are rescued from evil and the gloom of sin, are renewed in grace, and are restored to holiness." It is the very foundation of our Christian faith, and it is what makes this the crowning moment of the church's year. This night the church celebrates the presence of the risen Lord as he brings us to new life in baptism, gives us his body and blood, speaks his word of promise, and comes to us in the Christian community.

FIRST READING: GENESIS 1:1-2:4A
Creation

- A canticle of creation *Carmona* **OCP 9973**
- Morning has broken *Farjeon* **W&P 98**
- Song over the waters *Haugen* **W&P 127**
- Tales of wonder (Creation) *Haugen* **G-3320**
- Wind of the spirit *Hanson/Murakami* **SCR 18, W&P 157**

RESPONSE: PSALM 136:1-9, 23-36
God's mercy endures forever.

- Everlasting grace is yours *Haas* **G-4579**
- Everlasting grace *Carpenter* **VIN6 58**
- God's love is eternal *Tate* **VO 29**
- God's love is for ever! *Smith* **PS2**
- Love is never ending *Haugen* **GC 131**
- Your everlasting love *Batstone* **MAR 85**

SECOND READING:
GENESIS 7:1-5, 11-18, 8:6-18, 9:8-13
The flood

- I saw water *Young* **BL**
- In the water *Makeever* **DH 68**
- In the water *McLean* **WIS 14**
- Let it rain *Park* **VIN8 126**
- Streams of living water *Consiglio* **S&S**

RESPONSE: PSALM 46
The Lord of hosts is with us; the God of Jacob is our stronghold.

- Awesome God *Mullins* **W&P 13**
- God my refuge *Montemayer* **HCW 50**
- The Lord of hosts is with us *Harbor* **TFF 6**
- We are faithful *Bolduc* **VO 96**
- You are mine *Haas* **W&P 158**

THIRD READING: GENESIS 22:1-18
The testing of Abraham

- All around your throne *DeShazo/Kerr* **HMS10 808**
- I want Jesus to walk with me *Traditional* **WOV 660, TFF 66**

RESPONSE: PSALM 16
You will show me the path of life.

- Centre of my life *Inwood* **PS2**
- Harbor of my heart *Warner* **VO 31**
- I love to be in your presence *Baloche/Kerr* **HCW 75**
- Keep me safe, O God *Foley* **GC 23, RS 35**
- Show me the path *Haas* **G-4579**
- The Lord is my portion *Ylvisaker* **BC**
- You will show me the path of life *Haugen* **GC 24, RS 36**

FOURTH READING: EXODUS 14:10-31; 15:20-21
Israel's deliverance at the Red Sea

- Lord, my strength *Krippaehne* **W&P 93**
- Miriam's song *Barker* **CGA 740**
- Walk across the water *Makeever* **DH 69**
- You've delivered me again *Ylvisaker* **BC**

RESPONSE: EXODUS 15:1B-13, 17-18
I will sing to the Lord who has triumphed gloriously.

- Canticle of Moses *Inwood* **G&P 286**
- Go down, Moses *Spiritual* **TFF 87, WOV 670**
- Sing unto the Lord *Makeever* **DH 47**
- Song at the sea *O'Kelly-Fischer* **GC 143, RS 202**

FIFTH READING: ISAIAH 55:1-11
Salvation freely offered to all

- Come to the river of life *Moen/Cloninger* **HMS10 818**
- Come to the water *Foley* **G&P 706, GC 502**
- Seek the Lord *O'Connor* **G&P 351, RS 540**
- Send us flowing water *Mattingly* **VO 81**
- Streams of living water *Consiglio* **OCP 10898**
- Table of plenty *Schutte* **G&P 530**
- Wade in the water *Spiritual* **G&P 456, TFF 114**
- Waters of life *Kutscher* **VO 95**

RESPONSE: ISAIAH 12:2-6

With joy you will draw water from the wells of salvation.

- Rain down on us *Butler/Butler/Butler* **VIN8 160**
- Surely it is God who saves me *Chávez-Melo* **WOV 635**
- We can be lifted up *Hanson* **SCR 105**
- We shall draw water *Inwood* **G&P 288**
- With joy you shall draw water *Haugen* **GC 148**
- You will draw water *Guimont* **RS 204**

SIXTH READING: PROVERBS 8:1-8. 19-21; 9:4B-6 *OR* BARUCH 3:9-15, 32—4:4

The wisdom of God

- More precious than silver *DeShazo* **HCW 122**

RESPONSE: PSALM 19

The statutes of the LORD *are just and rejoice the heart.*

- Lord, you have the words *Haas* **GC 27, RS 40**
- Lord, you have the words *Bolduc* **VO 61**
- Psalm 19 *Butler* **VIN7 190**
- You, Lord, have the message of eternal life *Ogden* **PS2**

SEVENTH READING: EZEKIEL 36:24-28

A new heart and a new spirit

- Deep within *Haas* **GC 399, RS 546**
- God provides a brand new heart *Ylvisaker* **BC**
- Now in this banquet *Haugen* **W&P 104**

RESPONSE: PSALM 42 AND 43

My soul is athirst for the living God.

- As the deer longs *Hurd* **G&P 207**
- As the deer *Nystrom* **HMS11 892, W&P 9**
- Just like a deer *Joncas* **G&P 205**
- Like a deer that longs *Bauman* **RS 77**
- Like a deer that longs *Haugen* **G-3261**
- My heart yearns for thee *Baroni* **HMS12 1022**
- O God, for you I long *Farrell* **G&P 206**
- Song of longing *Cooney* **GC 51**
- Why so downcast? *Berrios/Brooks/Hamlin* **HCW 191**

EIGHTH READING: EZEKIEL 37:1-14

The valley of the dry bones

- Change our hearts *Cooney* **G&P 349, GC 394**
- Deep within *Haas* **GC 399, RS 546**
- Wind of God *Sadler* **HMS13 1116**

RESPONSE: PSALM 143

Revive me, O LORD, *for your name's sake.*

- Great is the Lord *Smith/Smith* **W&P 53**
- Show me the way *Makeever* **DH 45**

NINTH READING: ZEPHANIAH 3:14-20

The gathering of God's people

- Come, let us worship God *Makeever* **DH 2**
- Gather us in *Haugen* **WOV 718**

RESPONSE: PSALM 98

Lift up your voice, rejoice and sing.

- All the ends of the earth *Hurd* **G&P 241**
- All the ends of the earth *Haas/Haugen* **GC 95, RS 135**
- Let all the world sing praises *Falson* **MAR 216**

TENTH READING: JONAH 3:1-10

The call of Jonah

- Here I am *Batstone* **MAR 115**
- Here I am, Lord *Schutte* **WOV 752, GC 686, RS 802**

RESPONSE: JONAH 2:1-3 [4-6] 7-9

Deliverance belongs to the LORD.

- You've delivered me again *Ylvisaker* **BC**

ELEVENTH READING: DEUTERONOMY 31:19-30

The song of Moses

- El Shaddai *Card/Thompson* **UM 123**
- Faithful One *Doerksen* **CMH2 60**

RESPONSE: DEUTERONOMY 32:1-4, 7, 36A, 43A

The LORD *will give his people justice.*

- Arise, oh Lord *Carpenter* **VIN6 16**

TWELFTH READING: DANIEL 3:1-29

The fiery furnace

- All you works of God *Haugen* **GC 492**
- The fire of your love *Baloche/Kerr* **HMS12 1037**

RESPONSE:
SONG OF THE THREE YOUNG MEN 35-65

Sing praise to the LORD *and highly exalt him forever.*

- Be exalted *Butler/Butler/Park* **VIN8 10**
- Glory and praise for ever *Ash* **G&P 289**
- He is exalted *Paris* **HCW 57, W&P 55**
- Song of the three children *Proulx* **G-1863**
- Song of three children *Guimont* **GC 150**

NEW TESTAMENT READING: ROMANS 6:3-11

Dying and rising with Christ

- Arise, shine *Urspringer/Robinson* **HCW 14**
- Baptized in water *Bisbee* **WOV 693**
- Christ is alive! *Williams* **RS 601**
- For me *Hanson* **SCR 176**
- Put on love *Makeever* **DH 78**
- We were baptized in Christ Jesus *Ylvisaker* **WOV 698**
- You have put on Christ *Dean* **G&P 458**
- You have put on Christ *Hughes* **GC 245**

RESPONSE: PSALM 114

Tremble, O earth, at the presence of the LORD.

- Heaven and earth *DeShazo/Harvill* **HMS10 829**

GOSPEL: MATTHEW 28:1-10 (YEAR A)

Proclaim the resurrection

- Celebrate Jesus *Oliver* **HCW 27**
- Christ is risen *Hanson* **SCR 156**
- Ring all the living bells *Ylvisaker* **BC**
- That Easter day with joy *Praetorius* **GC 445, RS 599**

MARK 16:1-8 (YEAR B)

The resurrection of Jesus is announced

- Celebrate Jesus *Oliver* **HCW 27**
- Christ has arisen, alleluia *Tanzanian* **WOV 678**
- Ring all the living bells *Ylvisaker* **BC**
- Roll away the stone *Conry* **OCP 10054CC**

LUKE 24:1-12 (YEAR C)

The women proclaim the resurrection

- Alleluia! Jesus is risen! *Brokering/Johnson* **TFF 91, WOV 674**
- Arise, shine *Urspringer/Robinson* **HCW 14**
- Christ has arisen, alleluia *Tanzanian* **WOV 678**
- Christ is risen *Hanson* **SCR 156**
- That Easter day with joy *Praetorius* **GC 445, RS 599**

ADDITIONAL SONGS FOR THE DAY/SEASON

- Behold the glory of God *O'Connor* **G&P 385**
- Brighter than the sun *Makeever* **DH 64**
- Christ is risen! Shout hosanna *Haas* **GC 431**
- Come to the feast *Haugen* **GC 503, RS 642**
- Join in the dance *Schutte* **G&P 393**
- Up from the earth *Cooney* **G&P 386, GC 452, RS 589**

Resurrection of the Lord

Easter Day

Year A

Today is the day God began creation, transforming darkness into light. Today is the day Jesus Christ rose from the darkness of the grave to new life. Today is the day when the church celebrates its birth from the waters of baptism and its new life in the holy supper. Though suffering, injustice, and sin continue to mark the world in which we live, the Christian community goes forth from baptismal washing and communion table with Christ's mission to heal, liberate, and forgive. In these days of Easter rejoicing, the church asks the question: How does our baptism send us forth in joyful service to the world?

ACTS 10:34-43
God raised Jesus on the third day
- He is Lord *Smith* **HMS12 998**
- One *Hanson/Murakami* **SCR 160**
- Only God for me *Harris* **HMS14**

JEREMIAH 31:1-6
Joy at the restoration of God's people
- Almighty *Watson* **HCW 8, HMS10 810**
- Mourning into dancing *Walker* **HCW 125, W&P 99**
- Trading my sorrows *Evans* **HMS14**

PSALM 118:1-2, 14-24
On this day the LORD has acted; we will rejoice and be glad in it.
- Alleluia, alleluia *Haas* **GC 113**
- Blessed be the name *Park* **VIN7 48**
- Holy! Holy! Holy Lord *Ylvisaker* **BC**
- I will enter his gates *Brethorst* **TFF 291**
- Let us rejoice *Haugen* **GC 114, RS 158**
- Stand up and give him the praise *DeShazo* **HMS10 867**
- This day was made by the Lord *Walker* **G&P 383**
- This is the day *Garrett* **W&P 141, TFF 262**
- This is the day *Joncas* **RS 576, G&P**

COLOSSIANS 3:1-4
Raised with Christ to seek the higher things
- Alleluia, give thanks *Fishel* **GC 443, RS 581, G&P 389**
- Jesus, amazing *Hanson/Murakami* **SCR 79**
- My life is in you, Lord *Gardner* **HCW 128**

JOHN 20:1-18
Seeing the risen Christ
- Alleluia! Jesus is risen! *Brokering/Johnson* **WOV 674, TFF 91**
- Arise, shine *Urspringer/Robinson* **HCW 14**
- Celebrate Jesus *Oliver* **HCW 27**
- Christ is risen *Hanson* **SCR 156**
- Christ the Lord is risen *Ghanian* **GC 439, RS 600**
- Come away to the skies *American* **WOV 669, GC 440**
- Ring all the living bells *Ylvisaker* **BC**

MATTHEW 28:1-10
Proclaim the ressurection
- Alleluia *Sinclair* **HMS11 889, W&P 6**
- He is exalted *Paris* **HCW 57, W&P 55**
- Lord, I lift your name on high *Founds* **W&P 90**

ADDITIONAL SONGS FOR THE DAY/SEASON
- All things new *Cooney* **GC 427**
- Christ is risen! Shout hosanna *Haas* **GC 431**
- Eastertide carol *Ridge* **G&P 380**
- The Honduras alleluia *Honduran/Glover* **G-4588**
- The trumpets sound, the angels sing *Kendrick* **W&P 139**

Year B

The story of Mary Magdalene is the church's story. We hear the voice of the risen Lord in the scriptures. We receive his body and blood in the holy supper. We encounter him in our brothers and sisters and in all those in need who look for salvation. We are charged to go forth in daily life and proclaim with our words and deeds that we have seen the Lord. It is the day of resurrection, the day the Lord has made. Let us be glad and rejoice.

ACTS 10:34-43
God raised Jesus on the third day
- He is Lord *Smith* **HMS12 998**
- One *Hanson/Murakami* **SCR 160**
- Only God for me *Harris* **HMS14**

ISAIAH 25:6-9
The feast of victory
- Now in this banquet *Haugen* **W&P 104**
- Now the feast and celebration *Haugen* **WOV 789**
- On the mountain top *Ylvisaker* **BC**
- This is the feast of victory *Hillert* **REN 199**
- This is the feast of victory *Young* **W&P 142**
- We come to the hungry feast *Makeever* **DH 84, WOV 766**

PSALM 118:1-2, 14-24
On this day the LORD has acted; we will rejoice and be glad in it.
- Alleluia, alleluia *Haas* **GC 113**
- Let us rejoice *Haugen* **GC 114, RS 158**
- This day was made by the Lord *Walker* **G&P 383**
- This is the day *Joncas* **RS 576, G&P**

1 CORINTHIANS 15:1-11
Witnesses to the risen Christ
- Because we believe *Gordon/Harvill* **HMS12 985**
- Freely, given freely *Hanson/Murakami* **SCR 74**
- That we may be filled *Hanson/Murakami* **W&P 134, SCR 182**
- This joyful Eastertide *Dutch* **GC 434, WOV 676**

JOHN 20:1-18
Seeing the risen Christ
- Alleluia *Sinclair* **HMS11 889, W&P 6**
- Alleluia! Jesus is risen! *Brokering/Johnson* **TFF 91, WOV 674**
- Arise, shine *Urspringer/Robinson* **HCW 14**
- Celebrate Jesus *Oliver* **HCW 27**
- Christ is risen *Hanson* **SCR 156**
- Christ the Lord is risen *Ghanaian* **GC 439, RS 600**
- Come away to the skies *Traditional* **GC 440**
- He is exalted *Paris* **HCW 57, W&P 55**
- Lord, I lift your name on high *Founds* **W&P 90**
- Ring all the living bells *Ylvisaker* **BC**

MARK 16:1-8
The resurrection is announced
- Celebrate Jesus *Oliver* **HCW 27**
- Ring all the living bells *Ylvisaker* **BC**
- Roll away the stone *Conry* **OCP 10054CC**

ADDITIONAL SONGS FOR THE DAY/SEASON
- Glory to the Lamb *Batstone* **MAR**
- Good news, alleluia! *Makeever* **DH 65**
- I cannot tell it all *Spiritual* **G&P 390**
- Our God reigns *Smith* **VO 73**
- Shine on us/That Easter day *Glover* **G-4596**

Year C

The Lord is risen indeed! The open tomb of Jesus is the door to a new way of being in the world. Easter is not one day but fifty. For a week of weeks—fifty days—the church will explore the dimensions of this new life and raise a joyful Alleluia!

ACTS 10:34-43
God raised Jesus on the third day
He is Lord *Smith* **HMS12 998**
One *Hanson/Murakami* **SCR 160**
Only God for me *Harris* **HMS14**

ISAIAH 65:17-25
God promises a new heaven and a new earth
Heaven and earth *DeShazo/Harvill* **HMS10 829**

PSALM 118:1-2, 14-24
On this day the LORD has acted; we will rejoice and be glad in it.
Alleluia, alleluia *Haas* **GC 113**
Let us rejoice *Haugen* **GC 114, RS 158**
This day was made by the Lord *Walker* **G&P 383**
This is the day *Joncas* **RS 576, G&P**

1 CORINTHIANS 15: 19-26
Christ raised from the dead, the first fruits
Be exalted *Butler/Butler/Park* **VIN8 10**
He is exalted *Paris* **HCW 57, W&P 55**
Lord, I lift your name on high *Founds* **W&P 90**
Now the green blade rises *French carol* **GC 444, RS**
We can be lifted up *Hanson* **SCR 105**

ACTS 10:34-43
God raised Jesus on the third day
He is Lord *Smith* **HMS12 998**
One *Hanson/Murakami* **SCR 160**
Only God for me *Harris* **HMS14**

JOHN 20:1-18
Seeing the risen Christ
All things new *Cooney* **GC 427**
Alleluia *Sinclair* **HMS11 889, W&P 6**
Alleluia! Jesus is risen! *Brokering/Johnson* **WOV 674, TFF 91**
Arise, shine *Urspringer/Robinson* **HCW 14**
Celebrate Jesus *Oliver* **HCW 27**
Christ is risen *Hanson* **SCR 156**
He is exalted *Paris* **HCW 57, W&P 55**
Lord, I lift your name on high *Founds* **W&P 90**
Ring, ring all the living bells *Ylvisaker* **BC**
Shine on us/That Easter day *Glover* **G-4596**

LUKE 24:1-12
The women proclaim the resurrection
Alleluia! Jesus is risen! *Brokering/Johnson* **TFF 91, WOV 674**
Arise, shine *Urspringer/Robinson* **HCW 14**
Christ is risen *Hanson* **SCR 156**
That Easter day with joy *Praetorius* **GC 445, RS 599**

ADDITIONAL SONGS FOR THE DAY/SEASON
Christ is risen! Shout hosanna *Haas* **GC 431**
Eastertide carol *Ridge* **G&P 380**
I cannot tell it all *Spiritual/Booth* **G&P 390**
Our God reigns *Smith* **VO 73**
Sing to the mountains *Dufford* **RS 590, GC, G&P 673**
The Honduras alleluia *Honduran/Glover* **G-4588**
Up from the earth *Cooney* **G&P 386, GC 452, RS 589**

Resurrection of the Lord

Easter Evening

Years A, B, C

Easter is a feast. And what feasting there is in scriptures this evening! The news of God's salvation, brought to the world in the death and resurrection of Christ, is worthy of the grandest of celebrations. The gospel from Luke 24 may remind us that the meal we receive in holy communion is a share in Christ's death and resurrection. Like the disciples who met with the Lord on the evening of his resurrection, Christ's words and his supper burn in us as well.

ISAIAH 25:6-9
The feast of victory
- Now in this banquet *Haugen* **W&P 104**
- Now the feast and celebration *Haugen* **WOV 789**
- On the mountain top *Ylvisaker* **BC**
- This is the feast of victory *Young* **W&P 142**
- This is the feast of victory *Hillert* **REN 199**
- We come to the hungry feast *Makeever* **DH 84, WOV 766**

PSALM 114
Hallelujah.
- Alleluia *Sinclair* **HMS11 889, W&P 6**

1 CORINTHIANS 5:6B-8
Celebrating with sincerity and truth
- Celebrate love *Hanson* **SCR 16**
- I will celebrate *Baloche* **MAR 43**
- Reason to celebrate *Chumchal* **VIN8 165**
- We walk by faith *Ylvisaker* **BC**

LUKE 24:13-49
At evening, the risen Christ is revealed
- Don't you know where you are *Ylvisaker* **BC**
- Here is bread *Kendrick* **W&P 58**
- I see the Lord *Baloche* **HMS13 1079**
- I see the Lord *Falson* **MAR 41**
- Jesus, help me see *Ylvisaker* **BC**
- On the road to Emmaus *Ylvisaker* **BC**
- Open our eyes, Lord *Cull* **MAR 59, TFF 98, W&P 113**
- Open the eyes of my heart *Baloche* **HMS13 1093, HMS12 1027**
- Stay with us *Taizé* **WOV 743**

ADDITIONAL SONGS FOR THE DAY/SEASON
- In the breaking of the bread *Hurd* **GC 841**

Second Sunday of Easter

Year A

In today's gospel reading, the risen Christ appears to the disciples who have locked themselves into a house. In the midst of their fear he offers his peace so that they might go forth to proclaim God's victory over death. Christ offers us his peace anew each time we prepare to come to the table where he gives us his body and blood. As we receive bread and cup he says, Do not doubt but believe that I am with you. He sends us forth to be his peacemakers in a community and a world locked in by fear and injustice.

ACTS 2:14A, 22-32
Christ's resurrection: the fulfillment of God's promise to David
- Saved by the grace of a miracle *Ylvisaker* **BC**
- Show me your ways *Fragar* **HMS11 949**
- Spirit song *Wimber* **CMH 6, W&P 130, TFF 105**
- That Easter day with joy *Traditional* **GC 445, RS 599**

PSALM 16
In your presence there is fullness of joy.
- Before you now *Butler/Osbrink* **VIN7 44**
- Centre of my life *Inwood* **PS2**
- Harbor of my heart *Warner* **VO 31**
- I love to be in your presence *Baloche/Kerr* **HCW 75**
- Keep me safe, O God *Foley* **GC 23, RS 35**
- Show me the path *Haas* **G-4579**
- The Lord is my portion *Ylvisaker* **BC**
- You will show me the path of life *Haugen* **GC 24, RS 36**

1 PETER 1:3-9
New birth to a living hope through the resurrection
- Firm foundation *Gordon/Harvill* **HCW 42**
- My Lord, what a morning *Ylvisaker* **BC**
- Without seeing you *Haas* **GC 844**

JOHN 20:19-31
Beholding the wounds of the risen Christ
- Come to me today *Hanson* **SCR 174**
- Go in peace and serve the Lord *Hanson* **SCR 120, W&P 46**
- Halleluya! We sing your praises *South African* **GC 562, RS 692**
- Spirit of the living God *Iverson* **TFF 101, W&P 129**
- Spirit of the living God *Sanchez* **HCW 158**
- We walk by faith *Haugen* **GC 590, G-2841**

ADDITIONAL SONGS FOR THE DAY/SEASON
- Amazing love *Kendrick* **W&P 8, CEL 351**
- God has spoken, bread is broken *Young* **BL, AFP 11-10733**
- Shine on us/That Easter day *Glover* **G-4596**
- Shout to the Lord *Zschech* **W&P 124**
- We walk by faith *Haugen* **GC 590, RS 723**

Year B

In the waters of baptism, God raises us up in Jesus and gives us life that endures. Though we do not see him in the flesh, he continues to reveal himself to us in the breaking of the bread, our foretaste of the feast to come. Day by day, we pray that God would strengthen our faith, so that we who have not seen Christ Jesus may truly confess him as our Lord and God.

ACTS 4:32-25
The believers' common life
- Let all the world sing praises *Falson* **MAR 216**
- Meet us *Rethmeier* **VIN8 136**
- Our heart *Chisum/Searcy* **HMS13 1094, HCW 143**

PSALM 133
How good and pleasant it is to live together in unity.
- In unity and peace *Chepponis* **G-4452**
- Only for your glory *Hanson* **SCR 34**
- The family of the Lord *Hanson* **SCR 39**

1 JOHN 1:1—2:2
Walking in the light
God is love *Haas* **GC 629**
Jesus lead on *Helming* **VIN8 114**
Thy word *Smith/Grant* **W&P 144, TFF 132**
Thy word *Webb* **W&P 143**

JOHN 20:19-31
Beholding the wounds of the risen Christ
Amazing love *Kendrick* **HCW 10, W&P 8**
Come to me today *Hanson* **SCR 174**
Go in peace and serve the Lord *Hanson* **SCR 120, W&P 46**
Shine on us/That Easter day *Glover* **G-4596**
Spirit of the living God *Iverson* **W&P 129**
Spirit of the living God *Sanchez* **HCW 158**
We walk by faith *Haugen* **GC 590, G-2841**

ADDITIONAL SONGS FOR THE DAY/SEASON
Come and see *LeBlanc* **W&P 29**
Glory, glory, hallelujah! *Spiritual* **TFF 148**
I am the living bread *Keesecker* **AFP 11-10684**

Year C

These first weeks of Easter focus our attention on appearances of the risen Lord. It is not always easy to see Jesus after his resurrection. The gospel will remind us that Jesus has a new body in which he now lives. As we gather this day to greet each other and share the peace of the Lord, may our eyes be opened to discern that we are looking at the risen body of Christ!

ACTS 5:27-32
The God of our ancestors raised up Jesus
Be exalted *Butler/Butler/Park* **VIN8 10**
He is exalted *Paris* **HCW 57, W&P 55**

PSALM 118:14-29
This is the LORD's doing and it is marvelous in our eyes.
Alleluia, alleluia *Haas* **GC 113**
I will enter his gates *Brethorst* **TFF 291**
Let us rejoice *Haugen* **GC 114, RS 158**
This day was made by the Lord *Walker* **G&P 383**
This is the day *Ganett* **W&P 141**
This is the day *Joncas* **RS 576, G&P**

PSALM 150
Let everything that has breath praise the LORD.
Hallelujah! Praise the Lord *Post* **REN**
Let all the world sing praises *Falson* **MAR 216**
Praise God with the trumpet *Young* **BL, AFP 11-10893**
Praise we render *Ylvisaker* **BC**
Praises resound *Ylvisaker/Casabolt* **BC**
The Honduras alleluia *Honduran/Glover* **G-4588**
Rise up and praise him *Baloche/Sadler* **HMS13 1098**
Singing praise to God *Haas* **G-5041**

REVELATION 1:4-8
Jesus Christ, the firstborn of the dead, is coming
From A to O *Hanson* **SCR 56**
It has always been you *Butler/Butler* **VIN6 120**
Soon and very soon *Crouch* **W&P 128, WOV 744**

JOHN 20:19-31
Beholding the wounds of the risen Christ
Amazing love *Kendrick* **HCW 10**
Come to me today *Hanson* **SCR 174**
Go in peace and serve the Lord *Hanson* **SCR 120, W&P 46**
Shine on us/That Easter day *Glover* **G-4596**
Spirit of the living God *Iverson* **W&P 129**
Spirit of the living God *Sanchez* **HCW 158**
We walk by faith *Haugen* **GC 590, G-2841**

ADDITIONAL SONGS FOR THE DAY/SEASON
Join in the dance *Schutte* **G&P 393**
Let heaven rejoice *Dufford* **G&P 392**
Sing out, earth and skies *Haugen* **W&P 126**

Third Sunday of Easter

Year A

In this story from Luke's gospel, the risen Christ joins two disciples overcome by the apparent loss of one who was "a prophet mighty in deed and word" (Luke 24:19). Here Luke presents us with two things: our yearning to see the risen Christ and the Lord's response to that yearning. In word (interpreting the scriptures) and sacrament (breaking the bread) he reveals himself to them and to us. In these two central actions—readings with preaching and thanksgiving with communion—our eyes are opened to see the risen Lord in our midst.

ACTS 2:14A, 36-41
Receiving God's promise through baptism

- I want to be ready *Spiritual* **TFF 41**
- Saved by the grace of a miracle *Ylvisaker* **BC**
- Show me your ways *Fragar* **HMS11 949**
- Song of the chosen *Cooney* **GC 813**
- Spirit song *Wimber* **CMH 6**
- Turn my heart *DeShazo* **HCW 179**
- We are God's work of art *Haugen* **GC 808**
- You are God's work of art *Haas* **GC 810**

PSALM 116:1-4, 12-19
I will call upon the name of the LORD.

- An offering of thanksgiving *Ylvisaker* **BC**
- Our blessing cup *Joncas* **G&P 257**
- Our blessing-cup *Haugen* **RS 155, GC 107**
- The name of God *Haas* **RS 152, GC 110**
- We bring the sacrifice of praise *Dearman* **W&P 150**

1 PETER 1:17-23
Born anew through the living word of God

- All things new *Cooney* **GC 427**
- Lamb of God *Paris* **HCW 100**
- Open our lives to the Word *Makeever* **DH 8**
- The holy Lamb of God *Ylvisaker* **BC**
- The Lamb *Coleman* **TFF 89**
- You are my all in all *Jernigan* **HMS11 976**

LUKE 24:13-35
Eating with the risen Christ

- Alleluia! Jesus is risen! *Brokering/Johnson* **TFF 91, WOV 674**
- Don't you know where you are *Ylvisaker* **BC**
- Here is bread *Kendrick* **W&P 58**
- I see the Lord *Baloche* **HMS13 1079**
- I see the Lord *Falson* **MAR 41**
- In the breaking of the bread *Hurd* **G&P 508, GC 841, RS 932**
- Jesus, help me see *Ylvisaker* **BC**
- Journeysong *Hurd* **G&P 581**
- On the journey to Emmaus *Haugen* **RS 816, G-4278**
- On the road to Emmaus *Ylvisaker* **BC**
- Open our eyes, Lord *Cull* **MAR 59**
- Open the eyes of my heart *Baloche* **HMS12 1027, HMS13 1093**

ADDITIONAL SONGS FOR THE DAY/SEASON

- Good news, alleluia! *Makeever* **DH 65**
- I come with joy to meet my Lord *American* **GC 806**
- Shout to the Lord *Zschech* **W&P 124**
- We who once were dead *Haas* **G-3504**

Year B

The church gathers in the power of the risen Lord. Here in this assembly made holy by its consecration in baptism, Christ opens the scriptures and reveals himself to us. Gathered at his table as the bread is broken, we see that his life has been broken for us, so that our broken lives might be healed. From the table of the word and the table of the eucharist, Christ feeds us with his love and abundant mercy.

ACTS 3:12-19
Health and forgiveness through the risen Jesus

- Christ is risen! Shout hosanna *Haas* **GC 431**
- Jesus, Jesus *Bullock* **HMS11 923**
- King of life *Sadler* **HMS12 1014**
- Over and over *Baloche* **HMS13 1096**

PSALM 4
The LORD does wonders for the faithful.

- All through the night *Heber/Traditional* **BC**
- Let your face shine upon us *Haugen* **RS 30, GC 19**
- Rest in my love *Hanson/Swanson* **SCR 93**
- Rest in your love *Sadler* **HMS11 945**

1 JOHN 3:1-7
The revealing of the children of God

- Change my heart, oh God *Espinoza* **HCW 28, W&P 28**
- God is love *Haas* **GC 629**
- Make me a servant *Willard* **W&P 96**
- More like Jesus Christ *McLean* **WIS 28**
- Open our eyes, Lord *Cull* **MAR 59**

LUKE 24:36B-48
Eating with the risen Christ

- Christ is risen! Shout hosanna *Haas* **GC 431**
- Come touch *Hanson* **SCR 180**
- Don't you know where you are *Ylvisaker* **BC**
- Hallelujah! We sing your praises *South African* **WOV 722, GC 562, RS 692**
- On the road to Emmaus *Ylvisaker* **BC**
- We walk by faith *Haugen* **GC 590, G-2841**
- We who once were dead *Haas* **G-3504**

ADDITIONAL SONGS FOR THE DAY/SEASON

- Behold, what manner of love *vanTine* **TFF 218**
- Come and taste *Hanson/Murakami* **W&P 30**
- Come touch *Hanson* **SCR**
- Jesus, be with us now *Haas* **G-4732**
- Journeysong *Hurd* **G&P 581**

Year C

Resurrection also means reconciliation. In today's gospel, Peter's denials are trumped by a threefold commissioning from Jesus. We, too, are reconciled to each other and to God as we join in the hymn of all creation with angels and archangels and all the company of heaven: "Worthy is the Lamb who was slain!"

ACTS 9:1-6 [7-20]
Paul's conversion, baptism, and preaching

- Amazing love *Kendrick* **HCW 10, W&P 8**
- Before you now *Butler/Osbrink* **VIN7 44**
- In Christ, a new creation *Ylvisaker* **BC**
- Jesus, amazing *Hanson/Murakami* **SCR 79**
- Shout for joy *Traditional* **GC 559**

PSALM 30
You have turned my wailing into dancing.

- I will praise you, Lord *Inwood* **GC 41, G&P 192**
- I will praise you, Lord *Ridge* **G&P 193**
- Mourning into dancing *Walker* **HCW 125, W&P 99**
- Trading my sorrows *Evans* **HMS14**

REVELATION 5:11-14
The song of the living creatures to the Lamb

- Alabaré *Alonso/Pagán* **WOV 791**
- Glorify thy name *Adkins* **W&P 42**
- Now the feast and celebration *Haugen* **WOV 789**
- We will glorify *Paris* **HCW 187, W&P 154**
- Worthy the Lamb that was slain *Moen* **HCW 192**
- You are holy *Brown* **HMS10 884**
- You are the Lord of me *Sims* **SCR 76**

JOHN 21:1-19
Jesus appears to the disciples at the Sea of Tiberias

- Here in this place *Haas* **GC 839**
- Journeysong *Hurd* **G&P 581**
- Meet us *Rethmeier* **VIN8 136**
- Shine on us/That Easter day *Glover* **G-4596**
- Step by step *Beaker* **HMS13 1103, W&P 132**
- We love you *Hanson* **SCR 147**

ADDITIONAL SONGS FOR THE DAY/SEASON

- Alive in Christ Jesus *Haas* **GC 799**
- Blessing, honor and glory *Bullock/Reidy* **W&P 21**

Fourth Sunday of Easter

Year A

To some contemporary Christians, the image of Christ as shepherd appears outdated. Yet the continuing popularity of this "Good Shepherd Sunday" and the tender psalm appointed for today begs the question, Why are moderns attracted to a shepherd? Is it not that we yearn for guidance, protection, and strength in a world that is filled with much chaos, violence, and fast-paced change? The readings this day offer the image of our God as shepherd: the one who guides us—not out of this world, but in and through it with staff and overflowing cup, with word and holy supper.

ACTS 2:42-47
The believers' common life

- Alive in Christ Jesus *Haas* **GC 799**
- Meet us *Rethmeier* **VIN8 136**
- Open our lives to the word *Makeever* **DH 8**

PSALM 23
The LORD *is my shepherd; I shall not be in want.*

- I am the Good Shepherd *Ylvisaker* **BC**
- In the arms of the Shepherd *Weckler* **VO 47**
- Like a shepherd *Moen/Simpson* **HCW 112**
- My heart will trust *Morgan* **HMS14**
- My shepherd is the Lord *Glynn* **PS2**
- My shepherd is the Lord *Guiao* **UMP 10/1734U**
- Shepherd me, O God *Haugen* **GC 31, RS 756**
- The Lord is my shepherd *Ollis* **PS2**
- The Lord is my shepherd *Christopherson* **AFP 11-4691**
- The Lord's my shepherd *Archer* **G-4645**
- You are my shepherd *Haas* **G-4994**

1 PETER 2:19-25
Follow the shepherd, even in suffering

- I have decided to follow Jesus *Traditional* **MAR 198**
- Jesus lead on *Helming* **VIN8 114**
- Step by step *Beaker* **HMS13 1103, W&P 132**

JOHN 10:1-10
Christ the shepherd

- I am the Good Shepherd *Ylvisaker* **BC**
- I come to the cross *Somma/Batstone* **MAR 122**
- Life in his hands *Hanson* **SCR 10**
- With a shepherd's care *Chepponis* **GC 654, RS 738**

ADDITIONAL SONGS FOR THE DAY/SEASON

- I cannot tell it all *Spiritual/Booth* **G&P 390, OCP 10663**
- Shepherd of my soul *Nystrom* **MAR 65**

Year B

Like our Good Shepherd who holds all people in love, the church is called to lead those who thirst to living waters. At the banquet table set before us, the shepherd who lays down his life for the lost gives himself to us. Here is a great promise: Christ leads us through the shadows and valleys of life. He will neither abandon nor forget us. He is with us, now and forever.

ACTS 4:5-12
Salvation in the name of Jesus

- Jesus, name above all names *Cain* **W&P 77**
- Mighty is our God *Walker* **HCW 118**

PSALM 23
The LORD *is my shepherd; I shall not be in want.*
See Year A.

1 JOHN 3:16-24
Love in truth and action

- As bread that is broken *Baloche/Cloninger* **HMS10 811**
- Someone in need of your love *Makeever* **DH 94**
- Turn our hearts *Kendrick* **HMS12 1043**
- We love you *Hanson* **SCR 147**

JOHN 10:11-18
Christ the shepherd

- I am the Good Shepherd *Ylvisaker* **BC**
- I come with joy *Wren/Traditional* **BC**
- Spirit song *Wimber* **CMH 6, W&P 130**
- With a shepherd's care *Chepponis* **GC 654, RS 738**

ADDITIONAL SONGS FOR THE DAY/SEASON

- Greater love *Barbour/Barbour* **MAR 30**
- Shepherd of my soul *Nystrom* **MAR 65**

Year C

With the fourth Sunday of Easter the gospel readings turn away from resurrection appearances of Jesus and begin to focus on echoes of Jesus' earlier words that had pointed toward his death and resurrection during his ministry. He meant to go this path all along. As we listen to Jesus' words from the tenth chapter of John's gospel, we learn that Jesus is both shepherd as well as the victorious Lamb. Peter is a shepherd like Jesus as he leads one of Jesus' sheep from death to life.

ACTS 9:36-43

Peter raises Tabitha/Dorcas from the dead

- New life again and again *Hanson/Murakami* **SCR 102**
- We can be lifted up *Hanson* **SCR 105**

PSALM 23

The LORD is my shepherd; I shall not be in want.

See Year A.

REVELATION 7:9-17

A white-robed multitude sings before the Lamb

- All around your throne *DeShazo/Kerr* **HMS10 808**
- Eternity *Doerksen* **CMH 28**
- He is exalted *Paris* **W&P 55, HCW 57**
- Praise we render *Ylvisaker* **BC**
- Shall we gather at the river *Lowry* **WOV 690, TFF 179**
- Water from heaven *Hanson/Murakami* **SCR 136**
- Worthy the Lamb that was slain *Moen* **HCW 192**

JOHN 10:22-30

Jesus promises eternal life to his sheep

- All that is hidden *Farrell* **G&P 585**
- All we like sheep *Moen* **HCW 7**
- Forever my friend *Carpenter* **CMH2 51**
- I am the Good Shepherd *Ylvisaker* **BC**
- Like a shepherd *Moen/Simpson* **HCW 112**

ADDITIONAL SONGS FOR THE DAY/SEASON

- I'm so glad Jesus lifted me *Spiritual* **TFF 191, WOV 673**
- Streams of living water *Consiglio* **OCP 10898**
- Surely goodness and mercy *Peterson/Smith* **CEL 691**

Fifth Sunday of Easter

Year A

The gospel readings for the last Sundays of Easter shift the focus from Christ's presence among the disciples to his care for those who will continue his mission in the world. While the scriptural context is obvious, Christ addresses his contemporary disciples as well. To the community that bears his name he says, You will also do the works that I do. The church keeps these Easter days in order to discern anew its baptismal witness in the world. In our community, at this time, with these gifts, what witness can we offer to the one who is our way, our truth, and our life?

ACTS 7:55-60
The martyrdom of Stephen
Make my life a candle *Hanson* **SCR 163**

PSALM 31:1-5, 15-16
Into your hands, O Lord, I commend my spirit.
Father, I put my life in your hands *Hughes* **RS 62**
Father, I put my life in your hands *Talbot* **G&P 195**
God of love, have mercy *Makeever* **DH 10**
I put my life in your hands *Haas* **GC 42, RS 61**
I put my life in your hands *Haugen* **GC 43**
You are my God *Delavan* **HCW 196**

1 PETER 2:2-10
God's people chosen to proclaim God's mighty acts
Almighty *Watson* **HCW 8, HMS10 810**
I belong to a mighty God *DeShazo* **HMS8 654**
Mighty is our God *Walker* **HCW 118**
Out of darkness *Walker* **G&P 574, GC 689**
We bring the sacrifice of praise *Dearman* **W&P 150**
You alone *Hanson/Murakami* **SCR 36**
You have called us *DeShazo/Nystrom* **HCW 199**

JOHN 14:1-14
Christ the way, truth, and life
Be my home *Hanson/Murakami* **SCR 45, W&P 16**
Do not let your hearts be troubled *Haas* **G-349**
God without and within *Hanson/Murakami* **SCR 70**
I am the Bread of life *Toolan* **WOV 702**
I want to know you *Evans* **HMS12 1008**
Jesus is here right now *Roberts* **RS 930**
Soon and very soon *Crouch* **TFF 38, W&P 128, WOV 744**
Take and eat *Joncas* **GC 831, RS 910**
You only *McCoy* **VIN8 242**

ADDITIONAL SONGS FOR THE DAY/SEASON
Jesus is here right now *Roberts* **RS 930**
No greater love *Walker* **MAR**
You are the branches *Joncas* **CGA-755**

Year B

Like vines that grow from a single strong root, we are grafted into Christ at baptism and nourished on his life in communion. Christ feeds our hunger and satisfies our thirst with his word and sacraments and encourages us so that we might become fruitful in service to others. Today Christ calls the church to remember the source of our faith, hope, and love.

ACTS 8:26-40
Philip teaches and baptizes an Ethiopian
In the water *McLean* **WIS 14**
I've just come from the fountain *Traditional* **TFF 111, WOV 696**
Singing through the water *Hanson/Murakami* **SCR 132**
They'll know we are Christians *Traditional* **COK 74**

PSALM 22:25-31
All the ends of the earth shall remember and turn to the L*ORD.*
Lord most high *Harris/Sadler* **HMS11 930**
My God, my God *Haugen* **GC 29, RS 43**
My God, my God *Manion* **G&P 175**
My God, my God *Schiavone* **G&P 177**
Praises resound *Ylvisaker/Casabolt* **BC**

1 JOHN 4:7-21
God's love perfected in love for one another
- Come closer *Hanson* **SCR 47**
- Forever grateful *Altrogge* **HCW 44**
- God is love *Haas* **GC 629**
- I love you, Lord *Klein* **TFF 288, W&P 67**
- Jesus, I believe *Batstone* **MAR 130**
- O, mighty cross *Baroni/Chisum* **HCW 136**
- This kingdom *Bullock* **HMS11 962**
- Turn our hearts *Kendrick* **HMS12 1043**
- We love you *Hanson* **SCR 147**
- We will draw near *Nystrom/Harris* **HMS11 966**

JOHN 15:1-8
Christ the vine
- Amazing love *Kendrick* **HCW 10, W&P 8**
- Come and grow *McLean* **CCJ**
- Good soil *Hanson* **SCR 30, W&P 52, WOV 713**
- I am the vine *Bell* **G-4391**
- I am the vine *Hurd* **GC 672, G&P 545**
- Live in me *Bolduc* **VO 55**
- Rest in my love *Hanson/Swanson* **SCR 93**
- You are the branches *Joncas* **CGA-755**

ADDITIONAL SONGS FOR THE DAY/SEASON
- Life-giving bread *Manalo* **G-3911**
- We have been told *Haas* **GC 699**

Year C

Visions of the end time work their way into our Easter worship. A strange and wondrous vision from God instructs Peter about how wide the new fellowship in Christ might be. John's vision of a new Jerusalem suggests that beginnings and endings are tied to Jesus. And in the gospel, Jesus begins to prepare his disciples for his departure. We, too, gather this day as Jesus' end-time community, with one foot planted in this world and the other in the world to come.

ACTS 11:1-18
Peter's vision: God gives the Gentiles repentance that leads to life
- Building block *Stookey* **BC**

PSALM 148
The splendor of the LORD is over earth and heaven.
- He is exalted *Paris* **HCW 57, W&P 55**
- Let all praise the name of the Lord *Smith* **G-2989**
- Lord most high *Harris/Sadler* **HMS11 930**
- Praise in the heights *Haas* **G-5041**
- Shout to the Lord *Zschech* **HMS11 947, W&P 124**

REVELATION 21:1-6
New heaven, new earth: springs of living water in the new Jerusalem
- All things new *Cooney* **GC 427**
- Behold I make all things new *Bell* **G-4391**
- Come to the fount of creation *Ylvisaker* **BC**
- Heaven and earth *DeShazo/Harvill* **HMS10 829**
- Jehovah *Springer* **VIN6 124**
- Mourning into dancing *Walker* **HCW 125, W&P 99**
- Soon and very soon *Crouch* **W&P 128, TFF 38, WOV 744**

JOHN 13:31-35
Jesus gives a new commandment: Love one another as I have loved you
- Love is his word *Hutmacher* **RS 750**
- No greater love *Walker* **MAR**
- Reach out and take a hand *Kendrick* **HMS12 1029**
- They'll know we are Christians *Traditional* **CC 94, COK 74**

ADDITIONAL SONGS FOR THE DAY/SEASON
- Gather us in *Haugen* **WOV 718**
- Gathered in the love of Christ *Haugen* **G-5066**
- I want to be ready *Spiritual* **TFF 41**
- Jerusalem, my happy home *American* **RS 871, GC 771**
- What is this place *Huijbers* **G&P 538, RS 892, GC 748**

Sixth Sunday of Easter

Year A

In today's gospel reading, Jesus speaks clearly of the Spirit he will send to his disciples of every generation. Earlier in John's gospel, Jesus announces that a person comes to birth as a child of God through water and the Spirit. In this reading he calls the Spirit another advocate, the one who will speak to the heart of the baptized, who listen in silence for his voice. In their prayers, hymns, and preaching, Western Christians have tended to place greater emphasis on Christ than the Holy Spirit. In these Sundays, when the role of the Spirit in Christian life is highlighted, it may be appropriate to reflect on our understanding of this seemingly silent yet ever-present person of the Holy Trinity.

ACTS 17:22-31
Paul's message to the Athenians

- Alleluia, alleluia, give thanks *Fishel* **WOV 671, G&P 389, GC 443, RS 581**
- Awesome God *Mullins* **W&P 13**
- Heaven and earth *DeShazo/Harvill* **HMS10 829**
- Wind of God *Sadler* **HMS13 1116**

PSALM 66:7-18
Be joyful in God, all you lands.

- Cry out to the Lord *Warner* **G&P 217**
- Let all the earth cry out *Cooney* **G&P 216**
- Let all the earth *Haugen* **RS 93, GC 65**
- Purify my heart *Greco* **HCW 148**
- Shout to God, O faithful people *Ylvisaker* **BC**
- Shout with joy *Smith* **PS2**
- We bring the sacrifice of praise *Dearman* **W&P 150**

1 PETER 3:13-22
The days of Noah, a sign of baptism

- I saw water *Young* **BL**
- In the water *Makeever* **DH 68**
- In the water *McLean* **WIS 14**
- Singing through the water *Hanson/Murakami* **SCR 132**
- Waterlife *Hanson* **SCR 129, W&P 145**

JOHN 14:15-21
Christ our advocate

- Be my home *Hanson/Murakami* **SCR 45, W&P 16**
- Celebrate love *Hanson* **SCR 16**
- Faithful One *Doerksen* **CMH2 60**
- Forever my friend *Carpenter* **CMH2 51**
- I love you, Lord *Klein* **MAR, W&P 67**
- Love is his word *Hutmacher* **RS 750**
- No greater love *Joncas* **GC 628**
- We have been told *Haas* **GC 699**

ADDITIONAL SONGS FOR THE DAY/SEASON

- Glory and praise to our God *Schutte* **G&P 671, RS 696, GC 522**
- Lift up your hearts *O'Connor* **G&P 676, RS 691, GC 558**
- Who will stand up? *Soper* **G-4626**

Year B

The church is called to be an apostolic community that dwells in the new commandment of Christ. The challenge of the gospel is not to love others as others love us, but to love others as Jesus Christ loves us. He sees our failings and fears with utter clarity, yet offers us the gentle gifts of forgiveness and healing. Here we find ground for hope: we have been made friends of God in baptism.

ACTS 10:44-48

The Spirit poured out on the Gentiles

- Let it rain *Park* **VIN8 126**
- Rain down on us *Butler/Butler/Butler* **VIN8 160**
- Song over the waters *Haugen* **GC 585, RS 855**
- The river is here *Park* **CMH 58, VIN6 232**

PSALM 98

Shout with joy to the LORD, all you lands.

- All the ends of the earth *Haas/Haugen* **GC 95, RS 135**
- All the ends of the earth *Hurd* **G&P 241**
- Shout to God, O faithful people *Ylvisaker* **BC**
- Shout to the Lord *Zschech* **HMS10 862, HMS11 947, W&P 124**
- The kingdom song *Evans* **HMS12 1040**

1 JOHN 5:1-6

The victory of faith

- God is love *Haas* **GC 629**
- I have kept the faith *Baloche* **HMS13 1076**
- Rock of ages *Baloche* **HMS13 1099**
- You are my rock *Carpenter* **VIN6 278**

JOHN 15:9-17

Christ the friend and lover

- As the deer *Nystrom* **CEL 548**
- Forever my friend *Carpenter* **CMH2 51**
- Jesus, amazing *Hanson/Murakami* **SCR 79**
- Love is his word *Hutmacher* **RS 750**
- No greater love *Walker* **MAR 54**
- We have been told *Haas* **GC 699**
- You are I Am *Evans* **HMS12 1051**

ADDITIONAL SONGS FOR THE DAY/SEASON

- Great is our God *Ylvisaker* **BC**
- No greater love *Joncas* **GC 628**

Year C

Visions are the distinctive mark of this day. Paul receives a vision from God telling him that he needs to leap from one continent to another to take the good news abroad. John the Seer shares his vision of the new Jerusalem—an image of what it means to live with God. Jesus is the reflection of God's plan for the world and for our lives.

ACTS 16:9-15

Lydia and her household are baptized by Paul

Give us your vision *Hanson/Murakami* **SCR 85**

PSALM 67

Let the nations be glad and sing for joy.

God, be gracious *Kendrick* **HMS12 994**

Let all the people praise you *Makeever* **DH 38**

May God bless us in his mercy *Batastini* **RS 95**

May God bless us in his mercy *Guimont* **RS 94, GC 66**

May God bless us in his mercy *Kogut* **G-4718**

May we have peace *Ylvisaker* **BC**

Rise up and praise him *Baloche/Sadler* **HMS13 1098**

REVELATION 21:10, 22-22:5

The Lamb is the light of the city of God

All around your throne *DeShazo/Kerr* **HMS10 808**

Come to the river of life *Moen/Cloninger* **HMS10 818**

O holy city, seen of John *American* **GC 767**

JOHN 14:23-29

The Father will send the Holy Spirit

I will give you peace *Ylvisaker* **BC**

Peace I leave with you *Haas* **G-4869**

Teach me how to pray *Hanson/Murakami* **SCR 25**

You are mine *Haas* **W&P 158**

JOHN 5:1-9

Jesus heals on the Sabbath

In your heart there is a voice *McLean* **CCJ, WIS 17**

Peace *Hanson* **SCS 20**

You are mine *Haas* **W&P 158**

ADDITIONAL SONGS FOR THE DAY/SEASON

Jerusalem, my happy home *American* **RS 871, GC 771**

My peace *Routledge* **MAR**

What is this place *Huijbers* **G&P 538, RS 892, GC 748**

Ascension of the Lord

Years A, B, C

The risen Lord enters the invisible presence of God in order to be present in all times and in all places to the church and to the world. Where shall we find the risen and ascended Lord today? In his word and his bread, in his people and his washing with water and the Spirit, and in all who cry out for mercy.

ACTS 1:1-11
Jesus sends the apostles
- Go in peace and serve the Lord *Hanson* **SCR 120, W&P 46**
- Go, make disciples *Hanson* **W&P 47, SCR 114**

PSALM 47
God has gone up with a shout.
- Clap your hands *Hanson/Murakami* **SCR 32**
- Clap your hands *Owens* **MAR**
- God mounts his throne to shouts *Kogut* **G-4718**
- God mounts his throne *Haugen* **GC 53, RS 80**
- God mounts his throne *Inwood* **G&P 208**
- My God reigns *Evans* **HMS12 1021**
- Shout to the Lord *Zschech* **W&P 124, HMS10 862, HMS11 947**

PSALM 93
Ever since the world began, your throne has been established.
- Lord most high *Harris/Sadler* **HMS11 930**
- Majesty *Hayford* **W&P 94, MAR**
- Mighty is our God *Walker* **HCW 118**

EPHESIANS 1:15-23
Eyes to see the risen and ascended Christ
- I do believe *Ylvisaker* **BC**
- Open our eyes, Lord *Cull* **MAR 59, W&P 113**
- Open the eyes of my heart *Baloche* **HMS12 1027, HMS13 1093**
- The fullness of the Lord *Ylvisaker* **BC**

LUKE 24:44-53
Christ present in all times and places
- Age to age, everlasting *Ylvisaker* **BC**
- El Shaddai *Card/Thompson* **UM 123**
- God without and within *Hanson/Murakami* **SCR 70**
- I will be with you always *Hanson/Murakami* **SCR 118**
- It has always been you *Butler/Butler* **VIN6 120**
- Lord, I lift your name on high *Founds* **W&P 90**
- Soon and very soon *Crouch* **TFF 38, WOV 744**

ADDITIONAL SONGS FOR THE DAY/SEASON
- Go *Patillo* **GC 454, RS 604**
- Go to the world! *Johengen* **G-4395**
- I will be with you *Moore* **GC 455, RS 603**
- Our God is lifted up *Smith* **SPW**
- Who will stand up? *Soper* **G-4626**

Seventh Sunday of Easter

Year A

Holy Father, protect them in your name . . . so that they may be one" (John 17:11). With these words, Jesus prays for the unity of his disciples in every age, for their life and for their mission in the world. Throughout these last days of Easter leading to Pentecost, we could readily pray these words: Holy Father, protect us in your name so that we may be one. In the midst of much economic, ethnic, and cultural diversity, there is ample room for letting what is distinctive about us become divisive. Yet, as Christians, our deepest identity is discovered in baptism, proclaimed in the word, and nourished in the holy supper: we are one people who struggle for the unity that God intends for the entire human family.

ACTS 1:6-14
Jesus' companions at prayer after his departure
All the power you need *Fragar* **HMS11 888**

PSALM 68:1-10, 32-35
Sing to God, who rides upon the heavens.
You have made a home *Cooney* **GC 67**

1 PETER 4:12-14, 5:6-11
God will sustain and restore those who suffer
Cares chorus *Willard* **W&P 27**
Faithful One *Doerksen* **CMH2 60**
Leave your heart with me *Hanson* **SCR 150**

JOHN 17:1-11
Christ's prayer for his disciples
Be glorified *Funk* **HCW 19**
God of glory *Hanson* **SCR 89**
Thank you, Lord *Park* **VIN8 202**

ADDITIONAL SONGS FOR THE DAY/SEASON
Blessed be Yahweh *Young* **AFP 11-10669**
Go to the world! *Johengen* **G-4395**
God of glory *Hanson* **SCR**
Who will stand up? *Soper* **G-4626**

Year B

This past Thursday the church celebrated the Ascension of the Lord. Today's gospel includes the words of Jesus' high priestly prayer the night before his death. Though he is absent from us, Christ has given the church his word and sacraments so that we may be one in him, and united in his service to all who seek God. Even as Jesus' followers waited for the promised Holy Spirit, we pray during these days before Pentecost that the Spirit would renew the lives of all who profess faith in Christ.

ACTS 1:15-17. 21-26
Matthias added to the apostles
Lead me, guide me *Akers* **TFF 70**
Lead me, oh lead me *Smith* **HMS13 1085**

PSALM 1
The LORD knows the way of the righteous.
Happy are they who hope *Dufford* **G&P 167**
Happy are they *Haas* **GC 18, RS 28**
I will never be *Bullock* **HMS11 920**
In Christ, a new creation *Ylvisaker* **BC**

1 JOHN 5:9-13
Life in the Son of God
Life in his hands *Hanson* **SCR 10**
My life is in you, Lord *Gardner* **HCW 128**
New life again and again *Hanson/Murakami* **SCR 102**

JOHN 17:6-19
Christ's prayer for his disciples
I belong to a mighty God *DeShazo* **HMS8 654**
I'll belong to you *Hanson* **SCR 126**
Seed scattered and sown *Feiten* **GC 834**
You are mine *Haas* **W&P 158**

ADDITIONAL SONGS FOR THE DAY/SEASON
Bread for the world *Farrell* **G&P 528, GC 827**
With you by my side *Haas* **G-5008**

Year C

"Come, Lord Jesus!" John the Seer shares the ancient prayer of the early church in today's second reading. Echoes of the prayer occur as the church gathers for the Lord's supper, and some of us use those ancient words at our own dinner tables. The "threefold truth" propels us into this day: Christ has died. Christ is risen. Christ will come again.

ACTS 16:16-34

While in prison, Paul speaks to the jailer, who is then baptized

Bend my knees again *Butler/Butler* **VIN8 85**
I believe in Jesus *Nelson* **HCW 71**
Saved by the grace of a miracle *Ylvisaker* **BC**

PSALM 97

Rejoice in the Lord, you righteous.

Be glad in the Lord *Manalo* **G-4363**
He is exalted *Paris* **HCW 57, W&P 55**
Lord most high *Harris/Sadler* **HMS11 930**
Our God is here *Haas* **G-5041**
See also Christmas Dawn.

REVELATION 22:12-14. 16-17, 20-21

Blessed are those who wash their robes

Bright and morning star *Makeever* **DH 50**
From A to O *Hanson* **SCR 56**
Soon and very soon *Crouch* **W&P 128, WOV 744**
The Lord reigns *Stradwick* **MAR**

JOHN 17:20-26

Jesus prays that the disciples will be one and abide in his love

As the grains of wheat *Haas* **W&P 10**
As the grains of wheat *Haugen* **WOV 705**
Closer *Butler* **VIN6 36**
Come closer *Hanson* **SCR 47**
Many are the lightbeams *Haugen* **GC 841**
Rest in my love *Hanson/Swanson* **SCR 93**
Rest in your love *Sadler* **HMS11 945**

ADDITIONAL SONGS FOR THE DAY/SEASON

Bind us together *Gilman* **W&P 18, WOV 748**
Church of God *Denton* **GC 664, G&P 571, RS 783**
Praise to you, O Christ *Farrell* **WOV 614, G&P 662, RS 652, GC 515**

Vigil of Pentecost

Years A, B, C

Pentecost is one of the principal festivals of the church year. Several of the festivals have the tradition of night vigils preceding them. In this night of extended prayer and silence, we anticipate being filled with the power of the Spirit, perhaps as the believers were in the second chapter of Acts (an alternate first reading this night). The Spirit gathers the church together. It is the same Spirit that enlightens us by the word, calls us in baptism, and sanctifies us with the bread of life and the cup of salvation. Come, Holy Spirit!

EXODUS 19:1-9
The covenant at Sinai
- God my refuge *Montemayer* **HCW 50**
- You've delivered me again *Ylvisaker* **BC**

ACTS 2:1-11
Filled with the Spirit to tell God's deeds
- Breathe on me **HMS14**
- Every time I feel the Spirit *Spiritual/Ylvisaker* **BC**
- Let your fire fall *DeShazo/Sadler* **HMS12 1016**
- Spirit of the living God *Iverson* **TFF 101, W&P 129**
- Spirit of the living God *Sanchez* **HCW 158**
- Wind of the Spirit *Hanson/Murakami* **SCR 18, W&P 157**

PSALM 33:12-22
The Lord is our help and our shield.
- He is exalted *Paris* **W&P 55, HCW 57**

PSALM 130
There is forgiveness with you.
- Bright and morning star *Makeever* **DH 50**
- Only by grace *Gustafson* **HCW 140, W&P 112**
- Out of the depths *Batastini* **RS 947**
- Out of the depths *Hay* **VO 74**
- Rain down *Cortez* **G&P 713**
- With the Lord there is mercy *Haugen* **RS 176, GC 130**
- With the Lord there is mercy *Joncas* **RS 174**

ROMANS 8:14-17, 22-27
Praying with the Spirit
- Spirit of the living God *Iverson* **W&P 129**
- Spirit of the living God *Sanchez* **HCW 158**
- Teach me how to pray *Hanson/Murakami* **SCR 25**
- That we may be filled *Hanson/Murakami* **SCR 182, W&P 134**
- The people on your heart *DeShazo/Sadler* **HMS10 869**

JOHN 7:37-39A
Jesus is the true living water
- Come to me today *Hanson* **SCR 174**
- Fill us with your Spirit *Makeever* **DH 71**
- Let the river flow *Evans* **VIN6 128, HMS12 1015**
- Spirit song *Wimber* **CMH 6, W&P 130**
- The river is here *Park* **HMS11 958, CMH 58, VIN6 232**

Day of Pentecost

Year A

Today the church gathers to celebrate the ongoing life of the Holy Spirit who is its breath, vitality, and inspiration. Through the Holy Spirit, the good news unravels age-old divisions among peoples and nations. In the waters of baptism, the Spirit gives us birth as brothers and sisters of Christ and unites people of different races, tribes, and ethnic groups. In the bread and cup of the Lord's supper, the Spirit nourishes our unity in worship and witness. Far from celebrating its "birthday" on this day, the church offers thanksgiving to God for the very one who continues to sustain its life in each new generation and makes its prayer possible.

ACTS 2:1-21
Filled with the Spirit to tell God's deeds
- Every time I feel the Spirit *Spiritual/Ylvisaker* **BC**
- Everyone who calls upon the name *Makeever* **DH 17**
- I want to be ready *Spiritual* **TFF 41**
- Let your fire fall *DeShazo/Sadler* **HMS12 1016**
- Spirit calls, rejoice! *Hanson/Murakami* **SCR 1**
- Spirit of the living God *Iverson* **W&P 129**
- Spirit of the living God *Sanchez* **HCW 158**
- Wind of the Spirit *Hanson/Murakami* **SCR 18, W&P 157**

NUMBERS 11:24-30
The Spirit comes upon the elders of Israel
- Spirit song *Wimber* **W&P 130, CMH 6**

PSALM 104:24-34, 35B
Alleluia, OR Send forth your Spirit and renew the face of the earth.
- Life in his hands *Hanson* **SCR 10**
- Lord, send out your Spirit *Lisicky* **RS 146, GC 101**
- Lord, send out your Spirit *Zsigray* **G&P 253**
- Send forth your Spirit, O Lord *Warner* **VO 79, PS2**
- When you send forth your Spirit *Makeever* **DH 43**

1 CORINTHIANS 12:3B-13
Varieties of gifts from the same Spirit
- One bread, one body *Foley* **W&P 111, WOV 710**
- Revival fire, fall *Baloche* **HMS11 946**
- Thank you for the gift *Hanson* **SCR 144**
- They'll know we are Christians *Traditional* **COK 74**
- We are many parts *Haugen* **GC 733, RS 840**
- We know and believe *Glover* **GC 836**

JOHN 20:19-23
The Spirit poured out
- Let it rain *Park* **VIN8 126**
- Let the fire fall *Mattingly* **VO 53**
- Let the peace of God reign *Zschech* **HMS11 926**
- Rain down on us *Butler/Butler/Butler* **VIN8 160**

JOHN 7:37-39
Jesus is the true living water
- Come to me today *Hanson* **SCR 174**
- Let the river flow *Evans* **HMS12 1015**
- Shall we gather at the river *Lowry* **WOV 690, TFF 179**
- Spirit song *Wimber* **CMH 6, W&P 130**
- The river is here *Park* **VIN6 232**

ADDITIONAL SONGS FOR THE DAY/SEASON
- Send down the fire *Haugen* **GC 466**
- Send us your Spirit *Haas* **GC470, RS 612**
- Spirit-friend *Gonja/Glover* **GC 467, G-4589**

Year B

On Pentecost, the fiftieth day of Easter, the church prays that God would send forth the flame of the Holy Spirit and fill the church with an abundance of gifts needed to carry out its baptismal mission. We pray that the Holy Spirit would lend fire to our words and strength to our witness. We ask that God would send us forth to proclaim with boldness the wondrous work of raising Christ, who is our life and our hope.

ACTS 2:1-21
Filled with the Spirit to tell God's deeds
See Pentecost A.

EZEKIEL 37:1-14
Life to dry bones
Breathe on me **HMS14**
Wind of God *Sadler* **HMS13 1116**

PSALM 104:24-34, 35B
Alleluia, OR Send forth your Spirit, O Lord, and renew the face of the earth.
See Pentecost A.

ROMANS 8:22-27
Praying with the Spirit
Alive in Christ Jesus *Haas* **GC 799**
Spirit of the living God *Iverson* **W&P 129**
Spirit of the living God *Sanchez* **HCW 158**
Teach me how to pray *Hanson/Murakami* **SCR 25**
That we may be filled *Hanson/Murakami* **SCR 182, W&P 134**
The people on your heart *DeShazo/Sadler* **HMS10 869**

JOHN 15:26-27, 16:4B-15
Christ sends the Spirit of truth
Precious Lord, take my hand *Allen/Dorsey* **TFF 193, WOV 731**
Spirit blowing through creation *Haugen* **GC 462**
You are mine *Haas* **W&P 158**

ADDITIONAL SONGS FOR THE DAY/SEASON
Envia tu Espiritu *Hurd* **GC 459, G&P 407**
Go to the world! *Johengen* **G-4395**
Send down the fire *Haugen* **GC 466**
The Spirit of God *Deiss* **GC 458**

Year C

An ancient Hebrew harvest festival which came to be associated with the giving of God's law at Mount Sinai, Pentecost became for Christians the occasion for the gift of the Holy Spirit to the church. The Spirit is the power of the resurrected Jesus in our midst, claiming us in baptism, feeding us at the Lord's table, and sending us into the world to be bearers of that divine word that can raise the dead to new life.

ACTS 2:1-21
Filled with the Spirit to tell God's deeds
See Pentecost A.

GENESIS 11:1-9
God destroys the tower of Babel
Glorious God *Baroni/Fitts/Smith/Cloninger* **HMS10 823**

PSALM 104:25-35, 37
Send forth your Spirit and renew the face of the earth.
See Pentecost A

ROMANS 8:14-17
The Spirit makes us children of God
Everyone moved by the Spirit *Landry* **G&P 412**
Lord, listen to your chidren *Hanson* **SCR 23, W&P 91**
Lord, listen to your children praying *Medema* **W&P 92**
Whom shall I fear? *Evans* **HMS13 1115**

JOHN 14:8-17 [25-27]
The Father will give you another Advocate, the Spirit of truth
Come to me *Ylvisaker* **BC**
Deep is the prayer *Young* **BL**
I will give you peace *Ylvisaker* **BC**
If you believe and I believe *Bell* **GC 722, RS 825**
Peace I leave with you *Haas* **GC**
Teach me how to pray *Hanson/Murakami* **SCR 25**
The least of all the saints *Ylvisaker* **BC**
You are mine *Haas* **W&P 158**

ADDITIONAL SONGS FOR THE DAY/SEASON
Send down the fire *Haugen* **GC 466**
Spirit-friend *Gonja/Glover* **GC 467, G-4589**
Spirit of the living God *Makeever* **DH 72**

Trinity Sunday

First Sunday after Pentecost

Year A

Christians have held a festival in honor of the Holy Trinity since the ninth century, when it was celebrated in French monastic communities. In the fourteenth century, the festival was added to the calendar and has been celebrated throughout the world since that time. Every celebration of baptism and communion is a trinitarian celebration, just as every gathering "in the name of the Father, the Son, and the Holy Spirit" is done in union with the Sacred Three. In the power of the Holy Spirit, the church gathers on Sunday—the day of resurrection—to offer thanksgiving to the Father for Christ's saving life given to us in the word and in the meal. We are accompanied in life's journey by a community of persons. We are not alone. Indeed, the church is intended to be a sign in the world of the Holy Trinity's unity-in-diversity.

GENESIS 1:1-2:4A
The creation of the heavens and the earth
- God the sculptor of the mountains *Thornburg/Husberg* **TFF 222**
- Morning has broken *Farjeon/Traditional* **W&P 98**
- Singing through the water *Hanson/Murakami* **SCR 132**
- Song over the waters *Haugen* **W&P 127**
- Tales of wonder (Creation) *Haugen* **G**
- Wind of the Spirit *Hanson/Murakami* **SCR 18, W&P 157**

PSALM 8
How exalted is your name in all the world!
- All my days *Schutte* **G&P 701**
- Come and see *LeBlanc* **W&P 29**
- How glorious is your name *Cooney* **GC 20, RS 32, G-3412**
- How majestic is your name *Smith* **MAR, W&P 66**
- Many and great, O God, are your works *Dakota* **WOV 794**
- Who are we *Makeever* **DH 33**
- Your wonderful name *Haas* **G-5041**

2 CORINTHIANS 13:11-13
Paul's farewell to the church at Corinth
- As you go on your way *Ylvisaker* **BC**

MATTHEW 28:16-20
Living in the community of the Trinity
- Because we believe *Gordon/Harvill* **HMS12 985**
- Go *Patillo* **GC 454, RS 604**
- Go in peace and serve the Lord *Hanson* **SCR 120, W&P 46**
- Go, make disciples *Hanson* **SCR 114, W&P 47**
- Go to the world! *Johengen* **G-4395**
- Go ye therefore *Cain/Webb* **W&P 49**

ADDITIONAL SONGS FOR THE DAY/SEASON
- All the earth, proclaim God's glory *Fisher* **GC 552**
- Holy, holy *Owens* **W&P 60**
- In the name of the Father *Capers* **TFF 142**
- Stand up friends *Haas* **GC 478**

Year B

The festival of the Holy Trinity celebrates the mystery of God, both transcendent and immanent. Though the nature of God is beyond our rational explanation, we ascribe glory to the one who is holy, whose glory fills the whole earth. Christians are born of water and the Spirit, and when we make the sign of the cross, we remember our baptism in the name of the triune God. Born anew in baptism, and nourished at the Lord's table, we now live as witnesses to God's love for us and all the world.

ISAIAH 6:1-8
Isaiah's vision and call
- Glorious God *Baroni/Fitts/Smith* **HMS10 823**
- God we praise you *American* **RS 676**
- Here I am *Batstone* **MAR 115**
- Here I am, Lord *Schutte* **WOV 752, BC**
- I see the Lord *Baloche* **HMS13 1079**
- I see the Lord *Falson* **MAR 41**
- Open the eyes of my heart *Baloche* **HMS12 1027**
- Send me, Jesus *South African* **WOV 773**

PSALM 29

Worship the LORD in the beauty of holiness.

- Before you now *Butler/Osbrink* **VIN7 44**
- Give strength to your people, Lord *Smith* **PS1**
- God of glory *Hanson* **SCR 89**
- Lord, bless your people *Warner* **VO 59**
- Only for your glory *Hanson* **SCR 34**
- Singing through the water *Hanson/Murakami* **SCR 132**
- Song over the waters *Haugen* **W&P 127**
- The Lord will bless all people *Haas* **G-4579**
- The Lord will bless his people *Guimont* **GC 40**

ROMANS 8:12-17

Living by the Spirit

- Abba, Father *Landry* **G&P 696**
- Alive in Christ Jesus *Haas* **GC 799**
- Lord, listen to your children praying *Medema* **W&P 92**
- Lord, listen to your children *Hanson* **SCR 23, W&P 91**
- Whom shall I fear? *Evans* **HMS13 1115**

JOHN 3:1-17

Entering the reign of God through water and the Spirit

- Eternity *Doerksen* **CMH 28**
- For God so loved *Dauermann* **W&P 39**
- God so loved the world *Tate* **VO 27**
- Jesus, I believe *Batstone* **MAR 130**
- Singing through the water *Hanson/Murakami* **SCR 132**
- Spirit blowing through creation *Haugen* **GC 462**
- Spirit calls, rejoice! *Hanson/Murakami* **SCR 1**
- Stand up friends *Haas* **GC 478**
- Waterlife *Hanson* **SCR 129, W&P 145**
- Wind of the Spirit *Hanson/Murakami* **SCR 18, W&P 157**

ADDITIONAL SONGS FOR THE DAY/SEASON

- All the earth, proclaim God's glory *Fisher* **GC 552**
- Holy, holy, holy *Cuellar* **W&P 61**
- How wonderful the three in one *Haugen* **GC 472**
- Praise to the Trinity *Glover* **CGA 668**

Year C

Early Christians began to speak of the one God in three persons in order to fully describe the wonder of salvation. God is above us, beside us, within us. God is our loving Father, our friend Jesus, our companion Spirit. To be baptized in this name is to enter into God's community.

PROVERBS 8:1-4, 22-31

Wisdom rejoices in the creation

- Before the sun burned bright *Schutte* **G&P 577**
- You are I Am *Evans* **HMS12 1051**
- You are the Lord of me *Sims* **SCR 76**

PSALM 8

Your majesty is praised above the heavens.

See Holy Trinity A.

ROMANS 5:1-5

God's love poured into our hearts through the Holy Spirit

- Alive in Christ Jesus *Haas* **GC 799**
- Firm foundation *Gordon/Harvill* **HCW 42**
- For all you've done *Moen* **HMS12 992**
- Rain down on us *Butler/Butler/Butler* **VIN8 160**

JOHN 16:12-15

The Spirit will guide you into the truth

- Precious Lord, take my hand *Allen/Dorsey* **TFF 193, WOV 731**
- Spirit calls, rejoice! *Hanson/Murakami* **SCR 1**
- We walk by faith *Ylvisaker* **BC**

ADDITIONAL SONGS FOR THE DAY/SEASON

- All the earth, proclaim God's glory *Fisher* **GC 552**
- Alleluia, sing! *Haas* **GC 473**
- Great one in three *Tate/Berrell* **VO 30**

Proper 3

Sunday between May 24 and 28 Inclusive (If after Trinity Sunday)

Year A

Christians recognize that the source of all good things is the God who feeds the birds and clothes the grass of the field. We rejoice that we are held in the palm of God's hand. Gathered at Christ's supper, we offer thanksgiving for the bread of life and the cup of blessing. And here, as we share these gifts, we are knit together into a community whose mission is among those who are poor and in need.

ISAIAH 49:8-16A
God's motherly compassion for the people
- All around your throne *DeShazo/Kerr* **HMS10 808**
- Isaiah 49 *Landry* **G&P 711**
- You've delivered me again *Ylvisaker* **BC**

PSALM 131
Like a child upon its mother's breast, my soul is quieted within me.
- Cares chorus *Willard* **W&P 27**
- Guard my soul *Smith* **PS3**
- Leave your heart with me *Hanson* **SCR 150**
- Like a little child *Haas* **G-3956**
- Lord, listen to your children *Hanson* **SCR 23, W&P 91**
- My soul is still *Haas* **GC 129**
- O Lord, my heart is not proud *Rizza* **W&P 109**
- You, Lord *Hanson* **SCR 42, W&P 162**

1 CORINTHIANS 4:1-5
Servants accountable to God for their stewardship
- Change my heart, O God *Espinoza* **HCW 28, W&P 28**
- Show us the way *Light/Tate* **VO 83**
- When the Lord comes *Flowers* **VIN6 262**

MATTHEW 6:24-34
The teaching of Christ: trust in God
- Don't be anxious *Hanson* **SCR 141**
- Leave your heart with me *Hanson* **SCR 150**
- My heart will trust *Morgan* **HMS14**
- Nothing is as wonderful *Underwood* **VIN8 150**
- Seek first the kingdom *Haas* **G-3955**
- Seek ye first *Lafferty* **TFF 149, W&P 122**

ADDITIONAL SONGS FOR THE DAY/SEASON
- Age to age *Vogt* **OCP 10900**
- Church of God *Denton* **GC 664, G&P 571, RS 783**
- Everything I am *Dyer/Horness* **MAR**
- God beyond all names *Farrell* **GC 491**

Year B

Eating is one of the most intimate things that we do. Our divisions have often kept us apart from one another at the Lord's table, and disagreement regarding who is welcome to share the church's meal still festers among denominations. Jesus was criticized for eating with tax collectors and sinners, the outsiders of his day. We who follow Christ are called to invite all people to share the riches of God's faithful love. We share the new wine of the kingdom, that our lives will proclaim the justice and righteousness of God's ways.

HOSEA 2:14-20
The covenant renewed by God's persistent love
- Age to age, everlasting *Ylvisaker* **BC**
- Everlasting grace *Carpenter* **VIN6 58**
- Your everlasting love *Batstone* **MAR 85**

PSALM 103:1-13,22
The LORD is full of compassion and mercy.
- God of love, have mercy *Makeever* **DH 10**
- How blessed *Hampton* **VIN6 106**
- I'll bless the Lord for evermore *Traditional* **BC**
- The Lord is kind and merciful *Bolduc* **VO 90**
- The Lord is kind and merciful *Haugen* **GC 100**
- The Lord is kind and merciful *Cotter* **GC 99**

2 CORINTHIANS 3:1-6
Equipped as ministers of God's new covenant
- Amen *Fitts* **HMS12 982**
- Spirit of the living God *Iverson* **W&P 129**
- Spirit of the living God *Sanchez* **HCW**
- Write it on my heart *McLean* **WIS 41**

MARK 2:13-22

Eating and drinking with tax collectors and prostitutes

- Embrace my way and cross *Glover* **G-4594**
- For all people Christ was born *Makeever* **DH 52**
- Mercy *DeShazo/Sadler* **HMS14**
- Nothing at all but love *Ylvisaker* **BC**
- Song about grace *Ylvisaker* **BC**

ADDITIONAL SONGS FOR THE DAY/SEASON

- A story of unity *Jahn* **W&P 1**
- As the grains of wheat *Haas* **W&P 10**
- As the grains of wheat *Haugen* **WOV 705**
- Church of God *Denton* **GC 664, G&P 571, RS 783**
- Embrace my way and cross *Glover* **G-4594**
- Praise to you, O Christ *Farrell* **WOV 614, G&P 662, RS 652, GC 51**

Year C

Our firm roots in Christ, planted in us in our baptism, nourish and strengthen us in our lives of witness to God's sustaining love. This foundation cannot be uprooted or destroyed, even in the face of life's setbacks and catastrophes. Moved by the life-giving pulse of daily death and resurrection, we produce good and abundant fruit.

ISAIAH 55:10-13

The word goes forth from the mouth of God

- He shall reign *Chopinsky* **HMS12 999**
- Let it rain *Park* **VIN8 126**
- Most holy one *Willard/Baloche* **MAR 223**
- Thy kingdom come *Cooney* **RS 776, GC 656, G&P 710**

SIRACH 27:4-7

Wisdom rules both heaven and earth

PSALM 92:1-4, 12-15

The righteous shall flourish like a palm tree.

- It is good *Adler* **CCJ 16**
- Lord, it is good *Guimont* **GC 86, RS 124**

1 CORINTHIANS 15:51-58

The mystery of the resurrection

- Almighty *Watson* **HCW 8**
- God sent his son *Gaither/Gaither* **TFF 93**
- Praise to you, O Christ *Farrell* **WOV 614, G&P 662, RS 652, GC 515**
- Ring all the living bells *Ylvisaker* **BC**
- When the Lord comes *Flowers* **VIN6 262**

LUKE 6:39-49

Take the speck from your eye; build your house on a firm foundation

- Church of God *Denton* **GC 664, G&P 571, RS 783**
- Firm foundation *Gordon/Harvill* **HCW 42**
- Jesus, help me see *Ylvisaker* **BC**
- Jesus, you are my life *Fry* **MAR**
- Open the eyes of my heart *Baloche* **HMS12 1027**
- The word is in your heart *Moore* **GC 518**

ADDITIONAL SONGS FOR THE DAY/SEASON

- Cares chorus *Willard* **MAR**
- How can I keep from singing *Lowry* **WOV 781, RS 733, G&P 616, GC 603**
- Thy kingdom come *Cooney* **RS 776, GC 656, G&P 710**

Proper 4

Sunday between May 29 and June 4 Inclusive (If after Trinity Sunday)

Year A

The parable of the wise man who built his house on a rock so that it would withstand the force of the elements reminds us that a solid foundation is crucial to survival. Our baptism roots us firmly and unshakably in Christ. Steeped in God's word and nourished with Christ's life-giving supper, we are strengthened to withstand the temptation to place our trust in the shaky ground of false gods. Though our lives will not be free of adversity, God's word—written in our hearts and souls—will hold us fast.

DEUTERONOMY 11:18-21, 26-28
Keeping the words of God at the center of life
- Open our lives to the Word *Makeever* **DH 8**

PSALM 31:1-5, 19-24
Be my strong rock, a castle to keep me safe.
- Father, I put my life in your hands *Hughes* **RS 62**
- Father, I put my life in your hands *Talbot* **G&P 195**
- I put my life in your hands *Haas* **GC 42, RS 61**
- I put my life in your hands *Haugen* **GC 43**
- You are my rock *Carpenter* **VIN6 278**

GENESIS 6:9-22, 7:24, 8:14-19
The great flood
- I saw water *Young* **BL**
- Singing through the water *Hanson/Murakami* **SCR 132**

PSALM 46
The LORD of hosts is with us; the God of Jacob is our stronghold.
- Awesome God *Mullins* **W&P 13**
- God my refuge *Montemayer* **HCW 50**
- You are mine *Haas* **W&P 158**

ROMANS 1:16-17, 3:22B-28 [29-31]
Justified by God's grace as a gift
- Because we believe *Gordon/Harvill* **HMS12 985**
- For all you've done *Moen* **HMS12 992**
- Only by grace *Gustafson* **HCW 140, W&P 112**
- Thanksgiving to the living God *Makeever* **DH 3**
- We've come to praise you *Grant/Darnall* **MAR 80**

MATTHEW 7:21-29
The teaching of Christ: doing the works of God
- First love *Baloche/Sadler* **HMS13 1062**
- Heavenly Father *Park* **VIN7 92**

Year B

In today's gospel Jesus tells his critics, "The sabbath was made for humankind, and not humankind for the sabbath." We keep our weekly sabbath, gathering for prayer and Bible study, songs of praise and petition, and fellowship with others. Just as healing the man with the withered hand was work that could not wait, so is carrying the gospel into the whole world an activity that ought not be restricted to one day a week. Welcoming these elements of our weekly worship in our daily lives helps us to remember the sabbath and share the good news with others each and every day.

DEUTERONOMY 5:12-15
The commandment regarding the sabbath
- Rest in my love *Hanson/Swanson* **SCR 93**
- This is the day *Garrett* **W&P 141**

PSALM 81:1-10
Raise a loud shout to the God of Jacob.
- Shout to God, O faithful people *Ylvisaker* **BC**
- Shout to the Lord *Zschech* **HMS10 862, W&P 124**
- Sing with joy to God *Currie* **RS 109**
- Sing with joy to God *Guimont* **GC 76**

1 SAMUEL 3:1-10 [11-20]
The calling of Samuel
- Here I am *Batstone* **MAR 115**
- Here I am, Lord *Schutte* **WOV 718, BC**
- Make me a servant *Willard* **W&P 96**

PSALM 139:1-6, 13-18
You have searched me out and known me.
I was there to hear your borning cry *Ylvisaker* **W&P 69, WOV 770, BC**
O God, you search me *Farrell* **PS3**

2 CORINTHIANS 4:5-12
Treasure in clay jars
Earthen vessels *Foley* **G&P 584**
I heard the voice of Jesus say *Bonar/Traditional* **TFF 62**
Jesus, Jesus *Bullock* **HMS11 923**
Rain down on us *Butler/Butler/Butler* **VIN8 160**
Righteous one *Muller* **MAR 144**
Shine on us *Glover* **G-4596**
Shine, Jesus, shine *Kendrick* **WOV 651, MAR 238**
We cry out for grace again *Kerr* **HMS12 1045**

MARK 2:23—3:6
Doing the work of God on the sabbath
Gather us in *Haugen* **RS 850, GC 744**
Heal me, O Lord *Moen* **HMS10 828**
Healing word *McCoy* **VIN6 82**
Let your healing love *Butler* **VIN6 144**

ADDITIONAL SONGS FOR THE DAY/SEASON
In the presence of your people *Chambers* **WOV 720**
No higher calling *LeBlanc/Gulley* **MAR**

Year C

The centurion—a Roman official—in today's gospel reading believes that Jesus' ability and willingness to heal and cure extends beyond those of the house of Israel. Do we understand God's invitation to life and salvation in Christ as being for all—not just those who pray and worship like us? How might our communities of faith be places of welcome for all?

1 KINGS 8:22-23, 41-43
God's everlasting covenant is for all people
For all people Christ was born *Makeever* **DH 52**
Let all the world sing praises *Falson* **MAR 216**

PSALM 96:1-9
Declare the glory of the LORD among the nations.
Glory *Bullock* **MAR 185**
He is Lord *Smith* **HMS12 998**
Jesus reigns *Compton* **MAR 207**
Proclaim to all the nations *Haas/Haugen* **GC 93**
Rise up and praise him *Baloche/Sadler* **HMS13 1098**
We declare your name *Baloche/Baloche* **HMS10 874**

1 KINGS 18:20-21 [22-29] 30-39
Elijah and the prophets of Baal
Let your fire fall *DeShazo/Sadler* **HMS12 1016**
The fire of your love *Baloche/Kerr* **HMS12 1037**

PSALM 96
Ascribe to the LORD honor and power.
Great is the Lord *Smith/Smith* **W&P 53**
Let the heavens rejoice *Harbor* **TFF 10**
Sing unto the Lord *Makeever* **DH 47**

GALATIANS 1:1-12
Beware of contrary gospels
For he alone is worthy *Traditional/Wade* **TFF 284**
Glory be! *Ylvisaker* **BC**
Only God for me *Harris* **HMS14**

LUKE 7:1-10
Jesus heals the centurion's slave
Good news *Olson* **RS 797, GC 679**
King of life *Sadler* **HMS12 1014**
Let your healing love *Butler* **VIN6 144**
Life in his hands *Hanson* **SCR 10**

ADDITIONAL SONGS FOR THE DAY/SEASON
Church of God *Denton* **GC 664, G&P 571, RS 783**
Come as you are *Helming* **MAR 178**
Come just as you are *Sabolick* **MAR 179**

Proper 5

Sunday between June 5 and 11 Inclusive (If after Trinity Sunday)

Year A

The weeks of summer coincide with the beginning of the Pentecost season. Summer brings sunny warmth, growing crops, and the promise of harvest: images of the Holy Spirit's presence and activity in our lives, the church, and the world. Hosea speaks of God's presence as the dawn, as a gentle shower, as light. In our life together as a community of faith, what needs light, warmth, and watering to grow and flourish? How might we be attentive to others' needs to receive this nourishment through God's words of life and holy supper?

HOSEA 5:15-6:6
God desires steadfast love
- Hosea *Norbet* **G&P 471, GC 386**
- I want to know you *Evans* **HMS12 1008**
- Morning has broken *Farjeon/Traditional* **W&P 98**
- Rain down on us *Butler/Butler/Butler* **VIN8 160**

PSALM 50:7-15
To those who keep in my way will I show the salvation of God.
- I will show God's salvation *Dean* **PS3**
- Rain down *Cortez* **G&P 713**
- Thank you for the gift *Hanson* **SCR 144**
- Thank you, Lord *Park* **VIN8 202**

GENESIS 12:1-9
Abram's journey in the promise
- I want Jesus to walk with me *Traditional* **TFF 66, WOV 660**
- Step by step *Beaker* **HMS13 1103, W&P 132**

PSALM 33:1-12
Happy is the nation whose God is the LORD*!*
- He is exalted *Paris* **HCW 57, W&P 55**
- Rest your love *Ogden* **PS2**
- You are so faithful *LeBlanc/Gulley* **MAR 84**

ROMANS 4:13-25
The promise to those who share Abraham's faith
- Everlasting grace *Carpenter* **VIN6 58**
- We walk by faith *Ylvisaker* **BC**

MATTHEW 9:9-13, 18-26
Christ heals a woman and raises a synagogue leader's daughter
- Healer of our every ill *Haugen* **WOV 738, GC 882, RS 958**
- Healing word *McCoy* **VIN6 82**
- Jesus lead on *Helming* **VIN8 114**
- Let your healing love *Butler* **VIN6 144**
- There is a longing *Quigley* **G&P 620**
- We can be lifted up *Hanson* **SCR 105**
- We say yes *Walker* **MAR 164**
- Your song of love *Fabing* **G&P 583**

ADDITIONAL SONGS FOR THE DAY/SEASON
- Cup we bless *Young* **BL**
- From the sunrise *Walker* **MAR 184**

Year B

A house divided against itself cannot stand. Jesus makes this observation in light of charges that he is possessed. He *is* possessed, not by a demon, but by the Holy Spirit. We who have received the Holy Spirit through our baptism have been joined to Christ's death and resurrection and knit together in the body of Christ. Those with whom we sing and pray this day are sisters and brothers of the Lord. With them we go forth in peace to do the will of God.

GENESIS 3:8-15

God confronts Adam and Eve in the garden

We've come to praise you *Grant/Darnall* **MAR 80**

PSALM 130

With the Lord there is mercy and plenteous redemption.

Bright and morning star *Makeever* **DH 50**

Only by grace *Gustafson* **HCW 140, W&P 112**

With the Lord there is mercy *Haugen* **RS 176, GC 130**

With the Lord there is mercy *Joncas* **RS 174**

1 SAMUEL 8:4-11 [12-15] 16-20 [11:14-15]

Israel determined to have a king

King of kings *Batya/Conty* **W&P 80**

PSALM 138

Your love endures forever; do not abandon the work of your hands.

I praise your name *Ylvisaker* **BC**

I will bow down and worship *Chambers/Brewster* **HMS13 1081**

I will come and bow down *Nystrom* **HCW 87**

We bow before his holy name *Ylvisaker* **BC**

We bow down *Paris* **HCW 183, W&P 149**

2 CORINTHIANS 4:13-5:1

Renewed in the inner nature

I know that my redeemer lives *Haas* **GC 854**

In Christ, a new creation *Ylvisaker* **BC**

In the presence of the angels *Inwood* **PS2**

Let your healing love *Butler* **VIN6 144**

Nothing is as wonderful *Underwood* **VIN8 150**

Open the eyes of my heart *Baloche* **HMS12 1027**

MARK 3:20-35

Doing the work of God as brothers and sisters of Christ

Born from the gospel *Glover* **G-4587**

The family of the Lord *Hanson* **SCR 39**

The kingdom song *Evans* **HMS12 1040**

They'll know we are Christians *Traditional* **CC 94, COK 74**

ADDITIONAL SONGS FOR THE DAY/SEASON

Creating God *Haas* **GC 580**

Year C

From all appearances the young man from Nain was dead. The funeral procession moves along until Jesus stops it with a word—"Do not weep"—and a touch. Another word, "I say to you, rise!" and the dead man is restored to life; another touch and he is restored to his community. Jesus' powerful word and healing touch are for us, too, for God has looked favorably on we who are God's people.

1 KINGS 17:17-24
Elijah revives a widow's son
- Healing word *McCoy* **VIN6 82**
- Let your healing love *Butler* **VIN6 144**
- We can be lifted up *Hanson* **SCR 105**

PSALM 30
My God, I cried out to you, and you restored me to health.
- I will praise you, Lord *Inwood* **GC 41, G&P 192**
- I will praise you, Lord *Ridge* **G&P 193**
- Mourning into dancing *Walker* **HCW 125, W&P 99**

1 KINGS 17:8-16 [17-24]
A widow offers hospitality to Elijah
See 1 Kings 17:17-24.

PSALM 146
The LORD lifts up those who are bowed down.
- Awesome God *Mullins* **MAR 92**
- He shall reign *Chopinsky* **HMS12 999**
- Lord, I lift your name on high *Founds* **W&P 90**
- Maranatha, alleluia! *Wellicome* **PS1**
- Sing unto the Lord *Makeever* **DH 47**

GALATIANS 1:11-24
The gospel is received through a revelation of Jesus Christ
- Change my heart, O God *Espinoza* **HCW 28, W&P 28**
- This is the gospel of Christ *Brown* **HMS10 870**

LUKE 7:11-17
Jesus revives a widow's son
- Good news *Olson* **RS 797, GC 679**
- Into the life *McLean* **WIS 11**
- King of life *Sadler* **HMS12 1014**
- Life in his hands *Hanson* **SCR 10**
- My life is in you, Lord *Gardner* **HCW 128**
- New life again and again *Hanson/Murakami* **SCR 102**
- There is a longing *Quigley* **G&P 620**
- Your song of love *Fabing* **G&P 583**

ADDITIONAL SONGS FOR THE DAY/SEASON
- I will celebrate *Duvall* **MAR, CEL 66**
- Rise up and sing! *Makeever* **DH 7**

Proper 6

Sunday between June 12 and 18 Inclusive

(If after Trinity Sunday)

Year A

In today's gospel reading, Jesus speaks of the church's mission with images drawn from daily life. The harvest is already plentiful, he says, but laborers are needed for work in the fields of daily life. What are we to do? We are to do what our worship invites us to do: let our conversation be shaped by the good news, extend Christ's peace wherever we find ourselves, and share our bread with the hungry.

EXODUS 19:2-8A
The covenant with Israel at Sinai
- God my refuge *Montemayer* **HCW 50**
- On eagle's wings *Joncas* **WOV 779, RS 740, G&P 598, GC 611**
- You are mine *Haas* **COK 58, W&P 158**

PSALM 100
We are God's people and the sheep of God's pasture.
- Come with joy *Makeever* **DH 41**
- God is good (All the time) *Chapman* **MAR 186**
- He has made me glad *Brethorst* **COK 3**
- Indeed, how good is the Lord *Roberts* **TFF 12**
- Our blessing cup *Joncas* **G&P 257**
- Our blessing-cup *Haugen* **RS 155, GC 107**
- Shout to the Lord *Zschech* **HMS11 947, W&P 124**
- Thanksgiving to the living God *Makeever* **DH 3**
- The name of God *Haas* **RS 152, GC 110**
- You have been good *Paris* **HCW 198**

GENESIS 18:1-15 [21:1-7]
The LORD appears to Abraham and Sarah
- I can do all things *Baloche/Harris* **HMS11 913**
- I can do all things *Smith* **HMS13 1074**

PSALM 116:1-2, 12-19
I will call upon the name of the LORD.
- An offering of thanksgiving *Ylvisaker* **BC**
- Good people are a light *Inwood* **PS3**
- The blessing cup *Brown* **PS2**

ROMANS 5:1-8
While we were sinners, Christ died for us
- Amazing love *Kendrick* **HCW 10, W&P 8**
- For all you've done *Moen* **HMS12 992**
- Leave your heart with me *Hanson* **SCR 150**

MATTHEW 9:35-10:8 [9-23]
The sending of the Twelve
- Come with me into the fields *Schutte* **G&P 553**
- Freely, given freely *Hanson/Murakami* **SCR 74**
- Go in peace and serve the Lord *Hanson* **SCR 120, W&P 46**
- God will make a way *Moen* **HCW 52**
- God, here is my life and my will *Young* **BL, AFP 11-10786**

ADDITIONAL SONGS FOR THE DAY/SEASON
- Thy kingdom come *Cooney* **RS 776, GC 656, G&P 710**

Year B

The smallest seeds grow into a plant large enough to shelter birds and provide abundant shade. God can accomplish great things with meager resources and humble beginnings. Communities of faith begin with a few, then grow to sheltering homes for many. Claimed in baptism, shaped by the scriptures, and nourished with the holy meal, the people of God extend the branches of Christ's tree of life to all in need.

EZEKIEL 17:22-24
The sign of the cedar planted on the mountain of Israel
- Come and grow *McLean* **CCJ**
- Life in his hands *Hanson* **SCR 10**

PSALM 92:1-4, 11-14
The righteous shall spread abroad like a cedar of Lebanon.
- It is good to give thanks *Dean* **PS3**
- It is good *Adler* **CCJ 16**
- Lord, it is good *Guimont* **GC 86, RS 124**

1 SAMUEL 15:34—16:13
David anointed by Samuel
King of kings *Batya/Conty* **W&P 80**
King of life *Sadler* **HMS12 1014**
You are my God *Delavan* **HCW 196**

PSALM 20
The Lord gives victory to the anointed.
Awesome God *Mullins* **W&P 13**

2 CORINTHIANS 5:6-10 [11-13] 14-17
In Christ, a new creation
For me *Hanson* **SCR 176**
How can I keep from singing *Lowry* **WOV 781, RS 733, G&P 616, GC 603**
In Christ, a new creation *Ylvisaker* **BC**
Jesus, I believe *Batstone* **MAR 130**
Reason to celebrate *Chumchal* **VIN8 165**
Say to the mountain *Wilbur* **HMS12 1033**
We walk by faith *Ylvisaker* **BC**

MARK 4:26-34
The parable of the mustard seed
Good soil *Hanson* **SCR 30, W&P 52, WOV 713**
Open our lives to the word *Makeever* **DH 8**
Song of the mustard seed *Hopson* **G-2239**
This kingdom *Bullock* **HMS11 962**

ADDITIONAL SONGS FOR THE DAY/SEASON
Seek the Lord *O'Connor* **G&P 351**
Thy kingdom come *Cooney* **RS 776, GC 656, G&P 710**

Year C

Confession and forgiveness frequently serve as a doorway to worship. We come into God's presence not because we earn it but purely as an act of grace. Today's readings introduce us to some of the world's great sinners, and we take our place among them, hungry to taste the wonderful love of God.

2 SAMUEL 11:26-12:10, 13-15
Nathan tells the story of the lamb to David
God of love, have mercy *Makeever* **DH 10**

PSALM 32
Then you forgave me the guilt of my sin.
I turn to you *Cooney* **GC 44**
I turn to you, Lord *Stewart* **RS 64**
Lord, forgive the wrong *Guimont* **RS 65**
You are my hiding place *Ledner* **W&P 160, MAR 167**

1 KINGS 21:1-10 [11-14]
Ahab kills the owner of a vineyard
Closer *Butler* **VIN6 36**

PSALM 5:1-8
Lead me, O Lord, in your righteousness; make your way straight before me.
Lead me, oh lead me *Smith* **HMS13 1085**
Lord, my strength *Krippaehne* **W&P 93**
Lord, listen to your children praying *Medema* **TFF 247, W&P 92**
Lord, listen to your children *Hanson* **SCR 23, W&P 91**
Psalm 5 *Sprouse* **MAR 143**

GALATIANS 2:15-21
Crucified with Christ; justification through grace
Alleluia, alleluia, give thanks *Fishel* **WOV 671, GC 443, RS 581, G&P 389**
Celebrate love *Hanson* **SCR 16**
Everlasting grace *Carpenter* **VIN6 58**
For by grace *Nicholas* **W&P 38**
For me *Hanson* **SCR 176**
Jesus, I believe *Batstone* **MAR 130**
Only by grace *Gustafson* **HCW 140, W&P 112**

LUKE 7: 36-8:3
The woman anointing the feet of Jesus is forgiven
Before you now *Butler/Osbrink* **VIN7 44**
Love you so much *Fragar* **HMS13 1088**
O Lord to you *Sadler* **HMS11 937**
The summons *Bell* **W&P 137, GC 700**
Two fishermen *Toolan* **RS 812, GC 688**
You, Lord *Hanson* **SCR 42, W&P 162**

ADDITIONAL SONGS FOR THE DAY/SEASON
O love of God/Amor de Dios *Hurd* **G&P 541**

Proper 7

Sunday between June 19 and 25 Inclusive

(If after Trinity Sunday)

Year A

In today's gospel reading, Jesus gives a brief teaching on the nature of discipleship: do not be afraid, for I am with you; tell others what you hear me say; give your life to the good news and you will discover the riches of life. This teaching appears simple, yet it is spoken in an anxious and troubled world where it is easier to be fearful than courageous and more common to look out for oneself than to care for the neighbor in need.

JEREMIAH 20:7-13
The prophet must speak despite opposition
Lord, my strength *Krippaehne* **W&P 93**

PSALM 69:8-11 [12-17] 18-20
Answer me, O Lord, for your love is kind.
Be my home *Hanson/Murakami* **SCR 45, W&P 16**
Lord, in your great love *Guimont* **GC 68**
Lord, in your great love *Peloquin* **RS 98**
Turn to the Lord in your need *Guimont* **RS 97, GC 69**

GENESIS 21:8-21
The rescue of Hagar and Ishmael
Lead me, guide me *Akers* **TFF 70**
You've delivered me again *Ylvisaker* **BC**

PSALM 86:1-10, 16-17
Have mercy upon me; give strength to your servant.
Lord, listen to your children praying *Medema* **W&P 92, WOV 775**
Lord, listen to your children *Hanson* **SCR 23, W&P 91**
Lord, you are good and forgiving *Dean* **PS3**

ROMANS 6:1B-11
Buried and raised with Christ by baptism
Christ is alive *Traditional* **RS 601**
I don't belong to me *Hanson* **SCR 152**
I saw water *Young* **BL**
I'm going on a journey *Bonnemere* **TFF 115**
In the water *McLean* **WIS 14**
Waterlife *Hanson* **SCR 129, W&P 145**

MATTHEW 10: 24-39
The cost of discipleship
Come and follow me *O'Brien* **G-3028**
Embrace my way and cross *Glover* **G-4594**
First love *Baloche/Sadler* **HMS13 1062**
I belong to a mighty God *DeShazo* **HMS8 654**
O Lord to you *Sadler* **HMS11 937**

ADDITIONAL SONGS FOR THE DAY/SEASON
The summons *Bell* **W&P 137, GC 700**

Year B

Life is sometimes like a storm that causes our hearts to fear. In today's gospel the disciples encounter a storm on the waters while Jesus is asleep. Upon waking, Jesus bids the wind to cease, and he speaks words of peace to his troubled disciples. We gather amid life's obstacles and hardships to hear words of comfort and promise, to greet one another with peace, and to celebrate Jesus' enduring presence among us at the Lord's table and in the community of faith.

JOB 38:1-11
The creator of earth and sea
God the sculptor of the mountains *Thornburg/Husberg* **TFF 222**
Mighty is our God *Walker* **HCW 118**

PSALM 107:1-3, 23-32
God stilled the storm and quieted the waves of the sea.
Ancient of days *Sadler/Harvill* **HCW 11**
Awesome God *Mullins* **W&P 13**
Give thanks to the Lord *Carroll* **RS 147**
Give thanks to the Lord *Stewart* **GC 102**
Lord most high *Harris/Sadler* **HMS11 930**

1 SAMUEL 17:[1A, 4-11, 19-23] 32-49

David and Jonathan; Saul fears David's success

Freely, given freely *Hanson/Murakami* **SCR 74**

Lord, my strength *Krippaehne* **W&P 93**

1 SAMUEL 17:57-18:5, 10-16

David and Jonathan; Saul fears David's success

Freely, given freely *Hanson/Murakami* **SCR 74**

Lord, my strength *Krippaehne* **W&P 93**

PSALM 9:9-20

The LORD will be a refuge in time of trouble.

God my refuge *Montemayer* **HCW 50**

God of love, have mercy *Makeever* **DH 10**

PSALM 133

How good and pleasant it is to live together in unity.

God of glory *Hanson* **SCR 89**

The family of the Lord *Hanson* **SCR 39**

2 CORINTHIANS 6:1-13

Paul's defense of his ministry

Let the river flow *Evans* **HMS12 1015**

MARK 4:35-41

Christ calming the sea

Be my home *Hanson/Murakami* **SCR 45, W&P 16**

Flowing river *Baloche* **HMS13 1064**

How can I keep from singing *Lowry* **RS 733, G&P 616, GC 603**

Let the peace of God reign *Zschech* **HMS11 926**

Night storm: Song of Mark *Haugen* **G-4416**

Precious Lord, take my hand *Dorsey* **G&P 478**

Who can this be? *Haas* **G-3499**

You have rescued me *Dufford* **G&P 475**

ADDITIONAL SONGS FOR THE DAY/SEASON

You have come down to the lakeshore *Gabaraín* **WOV 784**

Year C

Before God saves us in baptism, we are held prisoner to hostile spiritual forces. Some of them are known to us and some are of our own making. Often we do not see or recognize the spirits that trouble us. As we come into God's presence today, a word of liberation is announced to us.

ISAIAH 65:1-9

The prophet sent to a rebellious people

You have called us *DeShazo/Nystrom* **HCW 199**

PSALM 22:18-27

In the midst of the congregation I will praise you.

As the deer longs *Hurd* **G&P 207**

Just like a deer *Joncas* **G&P 205**

Like a deer that longs *Bauman* **RS 77**

Like a deer that longs *Haugen* **G-3261**

O God, for you I long *Farrell* **G&P 206**

Praises resound *Ylvisaker/Casabolt* **BC**

Song of longing *Cooney* **GC 51**

Stand in the congregation *Batstone* **W&P 131**

Stand up and give him the praise *DeShazo* **HMS10 867**

We will glorify *Paris* **HCW 187, W&P 154**

You are the Lord of me *Sims* **SCR 76**

1 KINGS 19:1-4 [5-7] 8-15A

Elijah hears the word of the Lord in the midst of silence

I want to know you *Evans* **HMS12 1008**

You are my hiding place *Ledner* **MAR 167, W&P 160**

PSALM 42 AND 43

Send out your light and truth that they may lead me.

As the deer longs *Hurd/Kingsbury* **PS2**

As the deer *Nystrom* **HMS11 892, W&P 9**

My heart yearns for thee *Baroni* **HMS12 1022**

Why so downcast? *Berrios/Brooks* **HCW 191**

GALATIANS 3:23-29

In baptism, clothed with Christ; no longer Jew or Greek

Faithful Father *Doerksen* **VIN7 72**

I belong to a mighty God *DeShazo* **HMS8 654**

In Christ there is no east or west *Spiritual* **TFF 214**

One bread, one body *Foley* **WOV 710, G&P 499**

Put on love *Makeever* **DH 78**

LUKE 8:26-39

Jesus casts out demons possessing a man of the Gerasenes

All the power you need *Fragar* **HMS11 888**

Arise, oh Lord *Carpenter* **VIN6 16**

In Christ, a new creation *Ylvisaker* **BC**

New life again and again *Hanson/Murakami* **SCR 102**

We declare your name *Baloche/Baloche* **HMS10 874**

You are mine *Haas* **GC 649, RS 762**

ADDITIONAL SONGS FOR THE DAY/SEASON

Be light for our eyes *Haas* **GC 509**

God beyond all names *Farrell* **GC 491, RS 634, G&P 667**

Pan de vida *Hurd* **G&P**

Satan, we're going to tear your kingdom down *Spiritual* **TFF 207**

Tell what God has done for us *Makeever* **DH 97**

Proper 8

Sunday between June 26 and July 2 Inclusive

Year A

Without God's loving presence, we are like a parched and waterless land. In the waters of baptism, Christ becomes our life-giving spring, quenching our thirst and pouring God's love into our hearts. In today's gospel, Christ promises that the disciple who gives a cup of cold water to one in need serves Christ himself. Our baptism leads us to hear Jesus' words as words concerning our baptismal mission to serve those in need in this world—with a gesture as simple as offering a cup of cold water.

JEREMIAH 28:5-9
The test of a true prophet
Let the peace of God reign *Zschech* **HMS11 926**

PSALM 89:1-4, 15-18
Your love, O LORD, forever will I sing.
For ever I will sing *Guimont* **RS 117**
For ever I will sing *Haugen* **GC 82, RS 118**
For ever I will sing *Kogut* **G-4718**
I could sing of your love forever *Smith* **VIN8 89, HMS13 1075**
I will sing *Odgen* **PS1**
Throughout all time *Haas* **G-4579**
You have been good *Paris* **HCW 198**

GENESIS 22:1-14
The testing of Abraham
We bring the sacrifice of praise *Dearman* **W&P 150**

PSALM 13
I put my trust in your mercy, O LORD.
Jesus, help me see *Ylvisaker* **BC**

ROMANS 6:12-23
No longer under law but under grace
Alive in Christ Jesus *Haas* **GC 799**
Life in his hands *Hanson* **SCR 10**
Nothing at all but love *Ylvisaker* **BC**
Sanctuary *Thompson/Scruggs* **HCW 154**
Song about grace *Ylvisaker* **BC**
Thank you for the gift *Hanson* **SCR 144**
Thank you, Lord *Park* **VIN8 202**

MATTHEW 10:40-42
Welcome Christ in those he sends
All are welcome *Haugen* **GC 753, RS 846**
God without and within *Hanson/Murakami* **SCR 70**
Meet us *Rethmeier* **VIN8 136**
Where two or three *Kendrick* **HMS12 1050**

ADDITIONAL SONGS FOR THE DAY/SEASON
God beyond all names *Farrell* **GC 491, RS 634, G&P 667**

Year B

The Christian assembly gathers each Lord's day to praise God's faithfulness and steadfast love. With faith we come to hear the word and share the meal, and to know the healing that sets us free from sin and the ailments of body, mind, and soul. We go in peace to tell others of God's power to bring life from death.

LAMENTATIONS 3:22-33
Great is the LORD's faithfulness
God is so good *Anonymous* **COK 75, TFF 275**
Great is the Lord *Smith* **W&P 53, MAR, CEL**
Great is thy faithfulness *Runyan* **WOV 771, REN 249**
You have been good *Paris* **HCW 198**

WISDOM OF SOLOMON 1:13-15; 2:23-24
God created humankind for immortality

PSALM 30
I will exalt you, O LORD, because you have lifted me up.
I will praise you *Smith* **PS2**
I will praise you, Lord *Inwood* **GC 41, G&P 192**
I will praise you, Lord *Ridge* **G&P 193**
Mourning into dancing *Walker* **HCW 125, W&P 99**
We can be lifted up *Hanson* **SCR 105**

2 SAMUEL 1:1, 17-27
Lamentation over Saul and Jonathan
Broken hearts *Hanson/Murakami* **SCR 170**

PSALM 130
Out of the depths have I called to you, O LORD.
Bright and morning star *Makeever* **DH 50**
De profundis blues *Wellicome* **PS3**
My heart yearns for thee *Baroni* **HMS12 1022**
Only by grace *Gustafson* **HCW 140, W&P 112**

2 CORINTHIANS 8:7-15
Excel in generosity, following the Lord Jesus
Give thanks *Smith* **HCW 46, W&P 41, TFF 292**
God is so good *Anonymous* **COK 75, TFF 275**
I am loved *Gaither/Gaither* **COK 80**
Someone in need of your love *Makeever* **DH 94**

MARK 5:21-43
Christ healing a woman and Jairus' daughter
Holy love *Park* **VIN7 107**
I was on the outside/Song of Mark *Haugen* **G-4416**
Jesus, amazing *Hanson/Murakami* **SCR 79**
Wake up *Hanson* **SCR 13**
We can be lifted up *Hanson* **SCR 105**

ADDITIONAL SONGS FOR THE DAY/SEASON
Lay hands upon us *Glover* **G-4591**
You are mine *Haas* **GC 649, RS 762**

Year C

As we are called by Jesus, we leave one life behind and take up another. The readings for this day invite us to take the bold step that brings us into a new world.

1 KINGS 19:15-16, 19-21
Elijah says to Elisha, Follow me and do not continue plowing
Jesus lead on *Helming* **VIN8 114**
You have called us *DeShazo/Nystrom* **HCW 199**

PSALM 16
I have set the LORD always before me.
Harbor of my heart *Warner* **VO 31**
I love to be in your presence *Baloche/Kerr* **HCW 75**
Keep me safe, O God *Foley* **GC 23, RS 35**
Show me the path *Haas* **G-4579**
The Lord is my portion *Ylvisaker* **BC**
You will show me the path of life *Haugen* **GC 24, RS 36**

2 KINGS 2:1-2, 6-14
Elijah ascends into heaven in a whirlwind
Draw me into your presence *Muller* **MAR**
I will be with you always *Hanson/Murakami* **SCR 118**
Shine, Jesus, shine *Kendrick* **HCW 155, WOV 651, W&P 123**
Swing low, sweet chariot *Spiritual* **TFF 171**

PSALM 77:1-2, 11-20
By your strength you have redeemed your people.
Rock of ages *Baloche* **HMS13 1099**

GALATIANS 5:1, 13-25
Love is the whole law, gift of the Spirit
Arise, oh Lord *Carpenter* **VIN6 16**
Lead me, guide me *Akers* **TFF 70**
Spirit calls, rejoice! *Hanson/Murakami* **SCR 1**
Spirit of the living God *Iverson* **W&P 129**
Spirit of the living God *Sanchez* **HCW 158**

LUKE 9:51-62
Jesus says, Follow me and do not look back
Come and follow me *O'Brien* **G-3028**
Lead me, oh lead me *Smith* **HMS13 1085**
The summons *Bell* **W&P 137, GC 700**
With all my heart *Avery* **CC 11**

ADDITIONAL SONGS FOR THE DAY/SEASON
Eye has not seen *Haugen* **G-3726**
Let us talents and tongues employ *Jamaican* **WOV 754**

Proper 9

Sunday between July 3 and 9 Inclusive

Year A

Jesus chose to be with people who believed that they were excluded from God's mercy and love: the poor, the sick, the dying, and the deranged. Where many religious people saw only the dark and sinful shadows in these people, Jesus recognized their need for the transforming power of mercy, forgiveness, and healing. To them he said: Come to me and find rest. Today he comes to us in the waters of healing, in the word of mercy, in the meal of forgiveness. And he asks the church to bring these good gifts—signs of the Spirit's presence—into daily life.

ZECHARIAH 9:9-12
The king will come in humility and peace
- He has made me glad *Brethorst* **COK 3**
- I will enter his gates *Brethorst* **TFF 291**
- Lift up your heads *Fry* **HCW 111**
- Shout to the Lord *Zschech* **HMS10 862, W&P 124**

PSALM 145:8-14
The Lord is gracious and full of compassion.
- Glorious God *Baroni/Fitts/Smith* **HMS10 823**
- God is always near *Kemp* **CGA 31**
- He answers all our needs *Bolduc* **VO 33**
- I will praise your name forever *Roberts* **RS 192**
- I will praise your name *Haas* **GC 137, RS 193**
- Our God is compassion *Cotter* **GC 138**
- Psalm 145 *Folkemer* **G-2337**

GENESIS 24:34-38, 42-29, 58-67
The marriage of Isaac and Rebekah
- Holy love *Park* **VIN7 107**

PSALM 45:10-17
God has anointed you with the oil of gladness.
- The queen stands at your right hand *Rees* **PS3**

SONG OF SOLOMON 2:8-13
Arise, my love, my fair one, and come away

ROMANS 7:15-25A
The struggle within the self
- Purify my heart *Greco* **HCW 148**
- You, Lord *Hanson* **SCR 42, W&P 162**

MATTHEW 11:16-19, 25-30
The yoke of discipleship
- Age to age *Vogt* **OCP 10900**
- Come to me *Joncas* **GC 647, G-3373**
- God is here *Moen/Overstreet* **HMS12 995**
- I heard the voice of Jesus say *Bonar/Traditional* **TFF 62**
- Rest in my love *Hanson/Swanson* **SCR 93**
- Rest in your love *Sadler* **HMS11 945**

ADDITIONAL SONGS FOR THE DAY/SEASON
- Just a closer walk with thee *Spiritual* **TFF 253**
- Come unto me *Makeever* **DH 26**

Year B

The prophets of God speak with both conviction and compassion. Because prophetic words can threaten the security of even the most devout people, prophets are seldom popular in the church or in society as a whole. Yet in baptism, each Christian has been made a prophet, one who speaks on behalf of God in this time and place. Finding strength in God's grace, we are able to offer our merciful words and actions on behalf of all those who suffer in our world.

EZEKIEL 2:1-5
The call of Ezekiel
- Stand up and give him the praise *DeShazo* **HMS10 867**

PSALM 123
Our eyes look to you, O God, until you show us your mercy.
- God of love, have mercy *Makeever* **DH 10**
- Jesus, help me see *Ylvisaker* **BC**
- Mercy *DeShazo/Sadler* **HMS14**

Our eyes are fixed on the Lord *Guimont* **RS 168, GC 122**
Our eyes are on the Lord *Duffy* **PS3**

2 SAMUEL 5:1-5, 9-10
The reign of David
Arise, oh Lord *Carpenter* **VIN6 16**
Lord, my strength *Krippaehne* **W&P 93**

PSALM 48
God shall be our guide forevermore.
Step by step *Beaker* **HMS13 1103, W&P 132**

2 CORINTHIANS 12:2-10
God's power made perfect in weakness
Give thanks *Smith* **HCW 46, W&P 41, TFF 292**
I can do all things *Baloche/Harris* **HMS11 913**
I can do all things *Smith* **HMS13 1074**
Let the river flow *Evans* **HMS12 1015**
You are my all in all *Jernigan* **MAR**

MARK 6:1-13
Sending of the Twelve to preach and heal
Go in peace and serve the Lord *Hanson* **SCR 120, W&P 46**
Go, make disciples *Hanson* **SCR 114, W&P 47**
God will make a way *Moen* **HCW 52**

ADDITIONAL SONGS FOR THE DAY/SEASON
Let us talents and tongues employ *Jamaican* **WOV 754**

Year C

We are nurtured; we are nurturing. Today's readings remind us how God cares for us. We are called to adopt God's sustaining style. We are fed at the table and we are sent into the world to care for others.

ISAIAH 66:10-14
Jerusalem, a nursing mother giving life to her children
A song of unity *Jahn* **W&P 1**
The river is here *Park* **CMH 58, VIN6 232**

PSALM 66:1-9
God holds our souls in life.
Let all the earth *Haugen* **GC 65, RS 93**
Let all the world sing praises *Falson* **MAR 216**
Shout with joy *Smith* **PS2**
Sing unto the Lord *Makeever* **DH 47**

2 KINGS 5:1-14
Elisha heals a warrior with leprosy
Healing word *McCoy* **VIN6 82**

PSALM 30
My God, I cried out to you, and you restored me to health.
I will praise you *Smith* **PS2**
Mourning into dancing *Walker* **HCW 125, W&P 99**
Trading my sorrows *Evans* **HMS14**

GALATIANS 6:[1-6] 7-16
Do what is right now and reap at the harvest time
At the foot of the cross *Bond* **W&P 11**
I come to the cross *Summa/Batstone* **MAR 122**
May you run and not be weary *Hanson* **SCR 116, W&P 97**

LUKE 10:1-11, 16-20
Jesus sends out seventy disciples into the harvest
Glory and praise to our God *Schutte* **W&P 43, G&P 671, GC 522**
Go forth *Rathmann* **CPH 98-3332**
Go in peace and serve the Lord *Hanson* **W&P 46, SCR 120**
Go now in peace *Sleeth* **COK 96**
Here I am *Batstone* **MAR 115**
I heard the voice of Jesus say *Bonar/Traditional* **TFF 62**
Spirit song *Wimber* **CMH 6, W&P 130**

ADDITIONAL SONGS FOR THE DAY/SEASON
Be my home *Hanson/Murakami* **W&P 16**
My chosen one *Young* **BL, AFP 11-10753**

Proper 10

Sunday between July 10 and 16 Inclusive

Year A

For the next three Sundays, the gospel readings present the image of the seed. Though it is very small and seemingly insignificant, the seed contains its entire future; with light and nourishment it will grow and prosper. The seed is a vital image of faith in God, baptism, a congregation's life, the word, and the great paradox at the center of Christian faith: God brings flourishing life out of what appears to be little, dormant, even dead. It is a primary image of faith's central mystery: the dying and rising of Christ. There is ground for hope here.

ISAIAH 55:10-13
The growth of the word to accomplish God's purpose
- Come to the river of life *Moen/Cloninger* **HMS10 818**
- Let it rain *Park* **VIN8 126**
- Most holy one *Willard/Baloche* **MAR 223**
- Open our lives to the word *Makeever* **DH 8**

PSALM 65:[1-8] 9-13
Your paths overflow with plenty.
- The river is here *Park* **VIN6 232, HMS11 958**
- The seed that falls on good ground *Guimont* **GC 64, RS 92**

GENESIS 25:19-34
Esau sells his birthright to Jacob

PSALM 119:105-112
Your word is a lantern to my feet and a light upon my path.
- Show me your ways *Fragar* **HMS11 949**
- Teach me, O God *Walker* **PS3**
- Thy word *Smith/Grant* **W&P 144, TFF 132**
- Thy word *Webb* **W&P 143**

ROMANS 8:1-11
Live according to the Spirit
- Arise, oh Lord *Carpenter* **VIN6 16**
- Show me your ways *Fragar* **HMS11 949**
- Spirit calls, rejoice! *Hanson/Murakami* **SCR 1**
- Spirit of the living God *Iverson* **W&P 129**
- Spirit of the living God *Sanchez* **HCW 158**
- The Spirit is singing *Hanson/Murakami* **SCR 72**

MATTHEW 13:1-9, 18-23
The parable of the sower and the seed
- As the grains of wheat *Haugen/Haas* **W&P 10**
- Come and grow *McLean* **WIS 1, CCJ**
- Glory and praise to our God *Schutte* **G&P 671, GC**
- Good soil *Hanson* **SCR 30, WOV 713, W&P 52**
- Parable *Ridge* **G&P 481**

ADDITIONAL SONGS FOR THE DAY/SEASON
- Lord, I lift your name on high *Founds* **W&P 90, MAR**
- Seed, scattered and sown *Feiten* **W&P 121, RS 918**

Year B

In today's gospel reading, we recognize the danger of being a prophetic voice in the world. John the Baptist denounced the intrigues of the Herodian court and eventually lost his head. Jesus criticized religious leaders who twisted life-giving practices into heavy burdens. He pointed to a justice suffused with love for all people of the earth. Jesus was put to death, as if the grave would silence him. Our worship leads us to believe just the opposite: he is alive among us, still challenging us with the vision of God's justice for this world and inspiring us to be ministers of peace.

AMOS 7:7-15
The sign of the plumb line: God's judgment on Israel
- El Shaddai *Card/Thompson* **UM 123**

PSALM 85:8-13
I will listen to what the LORD God is saying.
- Come, O Lord, and set us free *Balhoff/Daigle/Ducote* **GC 80, RS 114**
- Dancing at the harvest *Makeever* **DH 40**
- Let us see, O Lord, your mercy *Smith* **PS1**
- Lord, let us see your kindness *Haugen* **GC 79, RS 112**
- Lord, make us turn to you *Haugen* **GC 75**
- O Lord, let us see your kindness *Harbor* **TFF 8**
- Open our eyes, Lord *Cull* **MAR 59, W&P 113**
- Over and over *Baloche* **HMS13 1096**
- Your mercy like rain *Cooney* **GC 330, G-3971**

2 SAMUEL 6:1-5, 12B-19
David and the house of Israel dance before the Lord
- My God reigns *Evans* **HMS12 1021**
- Reason to celebrate *Chumchal* **VIN8 165**
- Through our God we shall do valiantly *Garratt* **REN 262**

PSALM 24
Lift up your heads, O gates, and the King of glory shall come in.
- Let the Lord enter! *Ollis* **PS3**
- Lift up your heads *Kendrick* **W&P 88**
- Stretch towards heaven *Smith* **PS1**
- The King of glory *Ylvisaker* **BC**
- Welcome the King *Kendrick* **HMS12 1048**

EPHESIANS 1:3-14
Chosen in Christ to live to the praise of God's glory
- Freely, given freely *Hanson/Murakami* **SCR 74**
- Holy love, holy light *Batstone* **MAR 118**
- Thank you for the gift *Hanson* **SCR 144**

MARK 6:14-29
The death of John the Baptist
- Arise, shine *Urspringer/Robinson* **HCW 14**
- God will make a way *Moen* **HCW 52**
- My heart will trust *Morgan* **HMS14**
- There is a redeemer *Green* **REN 232**

ADDITIONAL SONGS FOR THE DAY/SEASON
- Moved by the gospel, let us move *English* **RS 801**
- We are marching in the light of God *South African* **WOV 650, W&P 148, REN 306**

Year C

God can be as near as a neighbor, and our opportunities to share God's love are as close as the words that leave our lips. The peace of Christ we exchange in this community we also take with us into the world to share with others.

DEUTERONOMY 30:9-14

The LORD will take delight in your fruitfulness

Be near us, Lord Jesus *Hanson/Murakami* **SCR 4**

We will draw near *Nystrom/Harris* **HMS11 966**

PSALM 25:1-9

Show me your ways, O LORD, and teach me your paths.

Remember *Cooney* **G-3972**

Remember your love *Ducote/Daigle* **G&P 474**

Remember your mercies *Haas* **GC 35, RS 54**

Remember your mercy, Lord *Inwood* **G&P 476**

Show me your ways *Fragar* **HMS11 949**

To you, O God, I lift up my soul *Hurd* **G&P 302**

To you, O Lord I lift my soul *Roberts* **G-4601**

To you, O Lord *Haugen* **GC 36, RS 53**

To you, O Lord *Thompson* **RS 50**

AMOS 7:7-17

A plumb line will judge the people

El Shaddai *Card/Thompson* **UM 123**

PSALM 82

Arise, O God, and rule the earth.

Arise *Barnett* **VIN7 33**

Arise, oh Lord *Carpenter* **VIN6 16**

Faithful One *Doerksen* **CMH2 60**

COLOSSIANS 1:1-14

The gospel is growing, bearing fruit in the whole world

Glorious God *Baroni/Fitts/Smith* **HMS10 823**

I will never be *Bullock* **HMS11 920**

LUKE 10:25-37

The parable of the merciful Samaritan

Mercy *DeShazo/Sadler* **HMS14**

My life is in you, Lord *Gardner* **HCW 128**

Send me, Jesus *South African* **WOV 773, REN 308**

Someone in need of your love *Makeever* **DH 94**

The people on your heart *DeShazo/Sadler* **HMS10 869**

With all my heart *Avery* **CC 11**

ADDITIONAL SONGS FOR THE DAY/SEASON

Help me, Jesus *Bonnemere* **TFF 224**

I will call upon the Lord *O'Shields* **W&P 70, REN 15**

Proper 11

Sunday between July 17 and 23 Inclusive

Year A

The parable in today's gospel reading sets forth what we may experience every day: evil coexists with the good. The conclusion to the parable—the weeds will be burned—seems simple, except for this: the one who speaks gives his life over to death, that God's mercy for all people may be revealed and that God's power to bring good out of evil may be known. Is it possible that even weeds and thorns will be transformed into beautiful flowers and lush vines? Here is each Christian's mission: to speak and to act with mercy and justice in a world that knows too well the presence of evil.

ISAIAH 44:6-8

There is no other God than the LORD

- Age to age, everlasting *Ylvisaker* **BC**
- Ancient of days *Sadler/Harvill* **HCW 11**
- It has always been you *Butler/Butler* **VIN6 120**
- Rock of ages *Baloche* **HMS13 1099**

WISDOM OF SOLOMON 12:13, 16-19

God's sovereignty: both righteous and forbearing

PSALM 86:11-17

Teach me your way, O LORD, and I will walk in your truth.

- Glorify thy name *Adkins* **W&P 42**
- Lord, you are good and forgiving *Guimont* **GC 81**
- Lord, you are good and forgiving *Smith* **PS3**
- Purify my heart *Greco* **HCW 148**
- We will glorify *Paris* **HCW 187, W&P 154**

GENESIS 28:10-19A

Jacob's dream of the ladder to heaven

- I will be with you always *Hanson/Murakami* **SCR 118**
- Surely it is God who saves me *White* **REN 122**
- Surely the presence of the Lord *Wolfe* **COK 1**

PSALM 139:1-12, 23-24

You have searched me out and known me.

- I was there to hear your borning cry *Ylvisaker* **BC, W&P 69, WOV 752**
- O God, you search me *Farrell* **PS3**

ROMANS 8:12-25

The revealing of the children of God

- Alive in Christ Jesus *Haas* **GC 799**
- Faithful Father *Doerksen* **VIN7 72**
- Lord, listen to your children praying *Medema* **W&P 92**
- Lord, listen to your children *Hanson* **W&P 91**
- My chosen one *Young* **BL, AFP 11-10753**
- You are my child *Ylvisaker* **BC**

MATTHEW 13:24-30, 36-43

The parable of the weeds

- Beauty for brokenness *Kendrick* **W&P 17**
- Good soil *Hanson* **SCR 30, WOV 713, W&P 52**
- He who began a good work *Mohr* **HCW 60**

ADDITIONAL SONGS FOR THE DAY/SEASON

- Bring forth the kingdom *Haugen* **W&P 22**
- Seed, scattered and sown *Feiten* **W&P 121, RS 918**

Year B

Built on the living foundation of the apostles and prophets, the local congregation is called to be an agent of reconciliation in a world filled with division and violence. For Christians, the ministry of peace begins and ends with Christ the shepherd, who gathers the scattered children of the world. He is the source of our life together and the center of the church's mission. To those who seek nourishment for daily life, we point to Christ who guides and feeds us in our journey.

JEREMIAH 23:1-6

From David's line, a righteous shepherd for Israel

- All we like sheep *Moen* **HCW 7**
- Like a shepherd *Moen/Simpson* **HCW 112**

PSALM 23

The LORD is my shepherd; I shall not be in want.

See Easter 4.

2 SAMUEL 7:1-14A

The promise of the LORD to David

Be my home *Hanson/Murakami* **SCR 45, W&P 16**
Life in his hands *Hanson* **SCR 10**

PSALM 89:20-37

Your love, O LORD, forever will I sing.

I could sing of your love forever *Smith* **HMS13 1075**
I will sing *Ogden* **PS1**
The festival psalm *Ylvisaker* **BC**

EPHESIANS 2:11-22

Reconciled to God through Christ, our peace

Building block *Stookey* **BC**
No longer strangers *Ylvisaker* **BC, W&P 102**
We are his hands *Gersmehl* **COK 85**
We are members of each other *McLean* **WIS 37**

MARK 6:30-34, 53-56

Christ healing the multitudes

I am the Good Shepherd *Ylvisaker* **BC**
Jesus, Jesus *Bullock* **HMS11 923**
Lamb of God *Paris* **HCW 100**
Lead me, oh lead me *Smith* **HMS13 1085**
Like a shepherd *Moen/Simpson* **HCW 112**

ADDITIONAL SONGS FOR THE DAY/SEASON

Amazing grace *Traditional* **REN 189**
Let the walls fall down *Batstone/Barbour* **MAR**
Make me a servant *Willard* **W&P 96**

Year C

Stay alert! You might be entertaining God! Today we are introduced to people who hosted God in their homes, although they were not always aware of God's presence. God comes close to us—even within us, as Paul exclaims.

GENESIS 18:1-10A

The hospitality of Abraham and Sarah to three visitors of the LORD

Welcome the King *Kendrick* **HMS12 1048**

PSALM 15

Who may abide upon your holy hill? Whoever leads a blameless life and does what is right.

Sanctuary *Thompson/Scruggs* **HCW 154**
The just will live *Batastini* **RS 33**
They who do justice *Haas* **GC 22**

AMOS 8:1-12

A famine of hearing the words of the LORD

Open our lives to the word *Makeever* **DH 8**
We cry out for grace again *Kerr* **HMS12 1045**

PSALM 52

I am like a green olive tree in the house of God.

God my refuge *Montemayer* **HCW 50**
Thank you, Lord *Park* **VIN8 202**
Your steadfast love *Sandquist* **HCW 200**

COLOSSIANS 1:15-28

Hymn to Christ, the firstborn of all creation

Because we believe *Gordon/Harvill* **HMS12 985**
It has always been you *Butler/Butler* **VIN6 120**
King of life *Sadler* **HMS12 1014**

LUKE 10:38-42

Jesus says: Martha, your sister Mary has chosen the better part

Closer *Butler* **VIN6 36**
Come closer *Hanson* **SCR 47**
Meet us *Rethmeier* **VIN8 136**
We have come into his house *Ballinger* **TFF 136**
We will draw near *Nystrom/Harris* **HMS11 966**

ADDITIONAL SONGS FOR THE DAY/SEASON

I love you, Lord *Klein* **W&P 67**
Jesus, we are gathered *Matsikenyiri* **TFF 140**

Proper 12

Sunday between July 24 and 30 Inclusive

Year A

The mission of the church and each baptized Christian is to serve the reign of God. But what is the reign of God? In today's gospel reading, Jesus offers images drawn from ordinary life that reveal something of the reign of God. It is like a tree that becomes a safe and sheltering home, like yeast that penetrates and expands, like a treasured pearl, like a net that gains a great catch. The reign of God is God's steadfast desire to unite the human family, with all its great diversity, in a justice and mercy so great and thoroughly life-giving that people will rejoice at its advent. How are baptism and the eucharist signs of its presence among us?

1 KINGS 3:5-12
Solomon's prayer for wisdom
- Teach me how to pray *Hanson/Murakami* **SCR 25**

PSALM 119:129-136
When your word goes forth, it gives light and understanding.
- Happy are those who follow *Cooney* **GC 116**
- Happy are those who follow *Cooney* **GC 116**
- Hear me, O God *Tate* **VO 35**
- Open our lives to the word *Makeever* **DH 8**
- Thy word *Smith/Grant* **W&P 144, CEL 184**
- Thy word *Webb* **W&P 143**

GENESIS 29:15-28
Leah and Rachel become Jacob's wives

PSALM 105:1-11, 45B
Make known the deeds of the LORD among the peoples. Hallelujah!
- Tell what God has done for us *Makeever* **DH 97**

PSALM 128
Happy are they who follow in the ways of the LORD.
- Bless us, O God *Makeever* **DH 44**
- O blessed are those who fear the Lord *Ollis* **PS1**

ROMANS 8:26-39
Nothing can separate us from God's love
- Alive in Christ Jesus *Haas* **GC 799**
- For all you've done *Moen* **HMS12 992**
- Holy love *Park* **VIN7 107**
- I'll belong to you *Hanson* **SCR 126**
- Leave your heart with me *Hanson* **SCR 150**
- Nothing can come between us *Young* **BL, AFP 11-10848**
- Oh how he loves you and me *Kaiser* **TFF 82**
- Spirit of the living God *Iverson* **W&P 129 TFF 101**
- Spirit of the living God *Sanchez* **HCW 158**
- The love of God *Tate* **VO 89**
- The people on your heart *DeShazo/Sadler* **HMS10 869**
- Your everlasting love *Batstone* **MAR 85**

MATTHEW 13:31-33, 44-52
Parables of the reign of heaven
- First love *Baloche/Sadler* **HMS13 1062**
- Give us your vision *Hanson/Murakami* **SCR 85**
- More precious than silver *DeShazo* **HCW 122**
- Seek ye first *Lafferty* **W&P 122, TFF 149, WOV 783**
- You, Lord *Hanson* **W&P 162, SCR 142**

ADDITIONAL SONGS FOR THE DAY/SEASON
- Eat this bread, drink this cup *Young* **WOV 706**

Year B

The psalms speak of God as the One who feeds humanity: You open wide your hand O God and give us food in every season. This implies that humans have bodily as well as spiritual hungers hungers that will be satisfied only by God. In Christ God satisfies our thirst with living waters and offers us living bread. These are images of our desire for communion with the One who is greater than our frailty and fears. They are biblical images of Christ's presence among us in the waters of baptism and the bread and cup of the eucharist.

2 KINGS 4:42-44
Elisha feeding a hundred people
- Thank you for the gift *Hanson* **SCR 144**
- Thank you Lord *Park* **VIN8 202**
- We are an offering *Liles* **W&P 146, HCW 182**

PSALM 145:10-18
You open wide your hand and satisfy the needs of every living creature.
- Glorious God *Baroni/Fitts/Smith* **HMS10 823**
- God be gracious *Kendrick* **HMS12 994**
- God is compassionate *Makeever* **DH 46**
- He answers all our needs *Bolduc* **VO 33**
- I will praise your name for ever *Roberts* **RS 192**
- I will praise your name *Haas* **GC 137, RS 193, PS2**
- Our God is compassion *Cotter* **GC 138**
- The hand of the Lord *Stewart* **PCY5**

2 SAMUEL 11:1-15
Bathsheba and Uriah wronged by David
- Closer *Butler* **VIN6 36**

PSALM 14
God is in the company of the righteous.

EPHESIANS 3:14-21
Prayer for wisdom, strength, and Christ's indwelling
- Come to me *Ylvisaker* **BC**
- Dwelling place *Foley* **G&P 591**
- I bend my knees again *Butler/Butler* **VIN8 85**
- Paul's doxology *Ylvisaker* **BC**
- Shine, Jesus, shine *Kendrick* **W&P 123, TFF 64, WOV 651, HCW 155**
- Spirit song *Wimber* **W&P 130, CMH 6, TFF 105**
- We bow down *Paris* **W&P 149, HCW 183**

JOHN 6:1-21
Christ feeding the five thousand
- As bread that is broken *Baloche/Cloninger* **HMS10 811**
- Be magnified *DeShazo* **HCW 20**
- Bread to share: Song of Mark *Haugen* **RS 927**
- Come to the feast *Haugen* **RS 642, GC 503**
- Eat this bread *Taizé* **TFF 125, WOV 709**
- Freely given freely *Hanson/Murakami* **SCR 74**
- Hallelujah! We sing your praises *South African* **TFF 158**
- Here is bread *Kendrick* **W&P 58**
- Rain down on us *Butler/Butler/Butler* **VIN8 160**
- Table of plenty *Schutte* **G&P 530**
- You only *McCoy* **VIN8 242**

ADDITIONAL SONGS FOR THE DAY/SEASON
- Just as Jesus told us *Makeever* **DH 29**
- Let us talents and tongues employ *Jamaican* **WOV 754, BC**
- You who are thirsty *Ross* **SPW**

Year C

The source of all Christian prayer is the Lord's Prayer. Since the earliest days of the Christian community these simple words have been prayed daily in the morning at noon and at bedtime. These are words through which the community is prepared for communion at the holy supper. These words are filled with the promise that God desires to give us all good things. God does this in the Son who is our open door, our bread and cup, our food and drink.

GENESIS 18:20-32

Abraham bargains with God for the righteous of Sodom and Gomorrah

God of love have mercy *Makeever* **DH 10**

PSALM 138

Your love endures forever; do not abandon the works of your hands.

I praise your name *Ylvisaker* **BC**
In the presence of the angels *Haas* **PCY3**
In the presence of the angels *Inwood* **PS3**
In the sight of the angels *Guimont* **RS 185**
Lord, your love is eternal *Stewart* **GC 133**

HOSEA 1:2-10

Hosea's marriage; a message to Israel

Father I adore you *Coelho* **W&P 37**
Hosea: Come back to me *Norbet* **REN 126**

PSALM 85

Righteousness and peace shall go before the LORD.

Dancing at the harvest *Makeever* **DH 40**
For the Lord is good *DeShazo/Sadler* **HMS13 1065**
God is good (All the time) *Chapman* **MAR 186**
God is so good *Anonymous* **TFF 275, COK 75**
O Lord let us see your kindness *Harbor* **TFF 8**
Turn my heart *DeShazo* **HCW 179**

COLOSSIANS 2:6-15 [16-19]

Buried with Christ in baptism, raised with him through faith

Forever my friend *Carpenter* **CMH2 51**
I don't belong to me *Hanson* **SCR 152**
My life is in you, Lord *Gardner* **HCW 128**
The Spirit is singing *Hanson/Murakami* **SCR 72**
Waterlife *Hanson* **W&P 145, SCR 129**

LUKE 11:1-13

Jesus teaches the disciples to pray

First love *Baloche/Sadler* **HMS13 1062**
Heavenly Father *Park* **VIN7 92**
I thank you Lord for love unknown *Ylvisaker* **BC**
Lord we pray *Gustafson* **HMS8 668**
Seek ye first *Lafferty* **W&P 122, TFF 149, WOV 783**
Teach me how to pray *Hanson/Murakami* **SCR 25**
The Lord's prayer *West Indian* **REN 180**

ADDITIONAL SONGS FOR THE DAY/SEASON

Let my prayer be a fragrant offering *Sappington* **W&P 86**
Lord, listen to your children *Hanson* **W&P 91**
Lord, listen to your children praying *Medema* **W&P 92, WOV 775**
Stretch out your hand *Smith/duPlessis* **MAR**

Proper 13

Sunday between July 31 and August 6 Inclusive

Year A

In the gospel reading for this day, we hear familiar words about Jesus' meal practice: he took the loaves, blessed them, broke them, and gave them for all to eat. Here the church sees the pattern for its meal. To this supper the church welcomes all the baptized. The gifts of God are given freely, equally, and without discrimination. "You that have no money," shouts Isaiah, "come and eat." And yet we recognize that this gracious communion takes place in a world where many eat and many go hungry each day. How is this sacred meal a sign of what God intends for life in this world?

ISAIAH 55:1-5
Eat and drink that which truly satisfies
- All around your throne *DeShazo/Kerr* **HMS10 808**
- Eat this bread, drink this cup **BL**
- Reason to celebrate *Chumchal* **VIN8 165**
- You satisfy the hungry heart *Kreutz* **WOV 711**

PSALM 145:8-9, 14-21
You open wide your hand and satisfy the needs of every living creature.
- Glorious God *Baroni/Fitts/Smith* **HMS10 823**
- He answers all our needs *Bolduc* **VO 33**
- I will praise your name for ever *Roberts* **RS 192**
- I will praise your name *Haas* **GC 137, RS 193**
- Our God is compassion *Cotter* **GC 138**

GENESIS 32:22-31
Jacob receives a blessing from God
- I'll bless the Lord for evermore *Ylvisaker* **BC**
- Make your presence known *Barbour* **MAR 221**

PSALM 17:1-7, 15
I shall see your face; when I awake, I shall be satisfied.
- That we may be filled *Hanson/Murakami* **SCR 182, W&P 134**

ROMANS 9:1-5
The glory of God's people Israel
- Before you now *Butler/Osbrink* **VIN7 44**

MATTHEW 14:13-21
Christ feeding five thousand
- As bread that is broken *Baloche/Cloninger* **HMS10 811**
- Be magnified *DeShazo* **HCW 20**
- Come to the water *Foley* **GC 502, OCP**
- Freely, given freely *Hanson/Murakami* **SCR 74**
- Rain down on us *Butler/Butler/Butler* **VIN8 160**
- You only *McCoy* **VIN8 242**

ADDITIONAL SONGS FOR THE DAY/SEASON
- Arise, shine, for your light is come *Class* **REN 123**
- Come to the feast *Haugen* **G-3543**
- We come to the hungry feast *Makeever* **DH 84, WOV 766**

Year B

Even when they grumbled and complained, God provided food for the Israelites. In today's gospel, when the disciples ask Jesus for an impressive sign, he offers them himself, the bread of life to all who truly hunger. This gift enables all believers to grow in Christ and to become one with his mission in the world. Though our hunger will always return, Christ is present to nourish us with his very life.

EXODUS 16:2-4, 9-15
The LORD gives manna in the wilderness
- Come and taste *Hanson/Murakami* **W&P 30, SCR 186**

PSALM 78:23-29
The LORD rained down manna upon them to eat.
- Rain down on us *Butler/Butler/Butler* **VIN8 160**
- Raining down manna *Haas* **G-4579**
- The Lord gave them bread *Guimont* **GC**

2 SAMUEL 11:26-12:13A

David rebuked by the prophet Nathan

Closer *Butler* **VIN6 36**

Come closer *Hanson* **SCR 47**

Here is my heart *Nystrom* **HMS13 1070**

PSALM 51:1-12

Have mercy on me, O God, according to your lovingkindness.

Create in me a clean heart *Anonymous* **HCW 36**

Create in me a clean heart *Hopkins* **W&P 35**

EPHESIANS 4:1-16

Maintain the unity of the faith

Here I am *Batstone* **MAR 115**

In unity and peace *Chepponis* **G-4452**

One *Hanson/Murakami* **SCR 160**

Only for your glory *Hanson* **SCR 34**

They'll know we are Christians *Traditional* **COK 78**

JOHN 6:24-35

Christ the bread of life

As bread that is broken *Baloche/Cloninger* **HMS10 811**

Because we believe *Gordon/Harvill* **HMS12 985**

Broken in love *Hanson* **SCR 177, W&P 24**

Eat this bread *Taizé* **WOV 709**

Here is bread *Kendrick* **W&P 58**

I am the Bread of life *Toolan* **WOV 702**

Let it rain *Park* **VIN8 126**

Year C

The church prays, "We offer with joy and thanksgiving what you have first given us—our selves, our time, and our possessions." We do much more than support the work of our congregation as we make our contribution. We actually reorient ourselves to what we possess and what we value the most. God's word speaks to us about this fundamental realignment of our lives.

ECCLESIASTES 1:2, 12-14, 2:18-23

Search out wisdom, for all is vanity

First love *Baloche/Sadler* **HMS13 1062**

More precious than silver *DeShazo* **HCW 122**

PSALM 49:1-12

We can never ransom ourselves or deliver to God the price of our life.

I belong to a mighty God *DeShazo* **HMS8 654**

My life is in you, Lord *Gardner* **HCW 128**

HOSEA 11:1-11

Like a mother, God will love Israel forever

Be my home *Hanson/Murakami* **SCR 45, W&P 16**

Come to me today *Hanson* **SCR 174**

PSALM 107:1-9, 43

Give thanks to the LORD, all those whom the LORD has redeemed.

His love endures forever *Clark* **VIN6 94**

COLOSSIANS 3:1-11

Clothed in Christ, your life is hidden with him in God

Over and over *Baloche* **HMS13 1096**

Sanctuary *Thompson/Scruggs* **HCW 154**

You are my all in all *Jernigan* **HMS11 976**

You are my hiding place *Ledner* **MAR 167, W&P 160**

LUKE 12:13-21

Jesus says: Be on guard against greed; be rich toward God, your treasure

All that is hidden *Farrell* **G&P 585**

Give thanks *Smith* **HCW 46, W&P 41, TFF 292**

Let the river flow *Evans* **HMS12 1015**

Turn your eyes upon Jesus *Lemmel* **COK 55**

ADDITIONAL SONGS FOR THE DAY/SEASON

Eat this bread, drink this cup *Young* **WOV 706, BL**

Hide me in your holiness *Ragsdale* **MAR**

I will choose Christ *Booth* **OCP 10592**

I'm not afraid *Ylvisaker* **BC**

Proper 14

Sunday between August 7 and 13 Inclusive

Year A

Lord, save me." One of the most ancient prayers of the liturgy is this cry of Peter in today's gospel reading. Lord, save me. How many times in frightening moments have we not shouted or murmured this simple prayer? Faced with a threatening situation or devastating news, we recognize that left to our own devices we will not survive. Such a moment of recognition signals our deep need for God's merciful presence in our lives. Today we hear these words again. Lord, have mercy. In our singing and speaking of these words, we ask Christ to strengthen our faith so that we might hear the cry for help in daily life and respond with Christ's own words: Take heart; do not be afraid.

1 KINGS 19:9-18
The LORD speaks to Elijah on Mount Horeb
- I want to know you *Evans* **HMS12 1008**
- You are my hiding place *Ledner* **MAR 167, W&P 160**

PSALM 85:8-13
I will listen to what the LORD God is saying.
- Come, O Lord, and set us free *Balhoff/Daigle/Ducote* **GC 80, RS 114**
- Dancing at the harvest *Makeever* **DH 40**
- Let us see, O Lord, your mercy *Smith* **PS1**
- Lord, let us see your kindness *Haugen* **GC 79, RS 112**
- Lord, make us turn to you *Haugen* **GC 75**
- Open our eyes, Lord *Cull* **MAR 59, W&P 113**
- Over and over *Baloche* **HMS13 1096**
- Your mercy like rain *Cooney* **GC 330**

GENESIS 37:1-4,12-28
Joseph sold by his brothers
- Mercy *DeShazo/Sadler* **HMS14**

PSALM 105:1-6, 16-22, 45B
Make known the deeds of the LORD among the peoples. Hallelujah!
- Tell what God has done for us *Makeever* **DH 97**

ROMANS 10:5-15
Hearing and confessing the word of faith
- Because we believe *Gordon/Harvill* **HMS12 985**
- I believe in Jesus *Nelson* **HCW 71**
- I do believe *Ylvisaker* **BC**

MATTHEW 14:22-33
Jesus walking on the sea
- Closer *Butler* **VIN6 36**
- I want Jesus to walk with me *Traditional* **TFF 66, WOV 660**
- Jesus, help me see *Ylvisaker* **BC**
- Lord we pray *Gustafson* **HMS8 668**
- May we have peace *Ylvisaker* **BC**
- Peace *Hanson* **SCS 20**
- Precious Lord, take my hand *Dorsey* **WOV 731, RS 754**
- Who can this be? *Haas* **G-3499**

ADDITIONAL SONGS FOR THE DAY/SEASON
- Lord, we pray *Gustafson* **MAR**
- Remember *Keesecker* **AFP 11-10743**

Year B

Christ has given his flesh for the life of the world. He sustains the pilgrim people of God with the word of life and the bread of heaven. Through the holy supper, Christ comes to us so that we might find the source of our unity and follow him in the way of sacrificial love. Though we will experience frustration or despair, we know that God is ever eager to nourish us back to life. We need only come to the table and receive the gift of life.

1 KINGS 19:4-8
Elijah receives bread for his journey
- For the Lord is good *DeShazo/Sadler* **HMS13 1065**
- God is so good *Anonymous* **COK 75, TFF 275**

PSALM 34:1-8
Taste and see that the LORD is good.
- Come and taste *Hanson/Murakami* **SCR 186, W&P 30**
- Eat this bread, drink this cup *Young* **WOV 706, BL**
- I will always thank the Lord *Soper* **G&P 202**
- I will bless the Lord *Gouin* **GC 46**
- Taste and see *Hurd* **G&P 199**
- Taste and see *Dean* **RS 72, G&P 200**
- Taste and see *Haugen* **RS 70, GC 47**
- Taste and see *Young* **BL, AFP 11-10895**
- The cry of the poor *Foley* **RS 69, GC 48, G&P 203**
- The Lord is close to the brokenhearted *Brown* **PS1**

2 SAMUEL 18:5-9, 15, 31-33
David laments his son Absalom's death
- Broken hearts *Hanson/Murakami* **SCR 170**

PSALM 130
Out of the depths have I cried to you, O LORD.
- Bright and morning star *Makeever* **DH 50**
- Only by grace *Gustafson* **HCW 140, W&P 112**

EPHESIANS 4:25-5:2
Put away evil, live in love
- I am loved *Gaither/Gaither* **COK 80**
- Live in my love *Young* **BL**
- Turn our hearts *Kendrick* **HMS12 1043**
- We are an offering *Liles* **W&P 146**
- We are members of each other *McLean* **WIS 37**

JOHN 6:35, 41-51
Christ the bread of life
- As bread that is broken *Baloche/Cloninger* **HMS10 811**
- Cup we bless *Young* **BL**
- I am the Bread of life *Toolan* **WOV 702**
- I am the living bread *Keesecker* **AFP 11-10684**
- Jesus, we want to meet *Oiude* **TFF 145**
- Rain down on us *Butler/Butler/Butler* **VIN8 160**
- That we may be filled *Hanson/Murakami* **SCR 182, W&P 134**

ADDITIONAL SONGS FOR THE DAY/SEASON
- God has spoken, bread is broken *Young* **BL, AFP 11-10733**
- What feast of love *English* **WOV 701**

Year C

Faith is the conviction of things not seen," the second reading announces. "We've come this far by faith, leaning on the Lord," the hymn by Albert Goodson proclaims. This day we gather as a community of faith and seek renewed vision so that we might make our way more boldly into the world as bearers of God's saving love.

GENESIS 15:1-6

God's promise of a child for Abram and Sarai

- Faithful Father *Doerksen* **VIN7 72**
- Faithful One *Doerksen* **CMH2 60**
- My chosen one *Young* **BL, AFP 11-10753**

PSALM 33:12-22

Let your lovingkindness be upon us, as we have put our trust in you.

- He is exalted *Paris* **HCW 57, W&P 55**
- Rain down *Cortez* **G&P 713**
- Rest in your love *Ogden* **PS2**

ISAIAH 1:1, 10-20

Learn to do good, seek justice, and rescue the oppressed

- Closer *Butler* **VIN6 36**
- Here is my heart *Nystrom* **HMS13 1070**
- The first song of Isaiah *White* **REN 122**

PSALM 50:1-8, 22-23

To those who keep in my way will I show the salvation of God.

- I will show God's salvation *Dean* **PS3**
- Jesus lead on *Helming* **VIN8 114**
- Lead me, oh lead me *Smith* **HMS13 1085**
- Show me your ways *Fragar* **HMS11 949**

HEBREWS 11:1-3, 8-16

A model for us: Abraham's faith in a new home given by God

- Be my home *Hanson/Murakami* **SCR 45, W&P 16**
- Open our lives to the Word *Makeever* **DH 8**
- We walk by faith *Ylvisaker* **BC**

LUKE 12:32-40

God will give you the treasure of the kingdom; sell all that you have

- Give it away *Makeever* **DH 96**
- My life is in you, Lord *Gardner* **HCW 128**
- Now in this banquet *Haugen* **W&P 104**
- Our hope is alive *Ylvisaker* **BC**
- Stir up the love *Ylvisaker* **BC**
- When the Lord comes *Flowers* **VIN6 262**

ADDITIONAL SONGS FOR THE DAY/SEASON

- That Christ be known *Schaefer* **W&P 133**

Proper 15

Sunday between August 14 and 20 Inclusive

Year A

What parents would not cry out for help to someone who could save their sick or tormented children? Here, in the gospel reading, we see a mother who will not abandon her mission to find relief for her suffering daughter. She is persistent and unflinching in her request for Christ's healing. In this Canaanite woman, the church finds an image of its mission. The world is filled with people who are tormented, sick, and oppressed. In the prayers, the church asks for God's healing in a world that is troubled and wounded. In the eucharistic meal, the church receives the strength to enter this world and bring comfort, healing, and justice to those in need.

ISAIAH 56:1, 6-8
A house of prayer for all peoples
- Let all the world sing praises *Falson* **MAR 216**
- We've come to praise you *Grant/Darnall* **MAR 80**

PSALM 67
Let all the peoples praise you, O God.
- God, be gracious *Kendrick* **HMS12 994**
- Let all the people praise *Makeever* **DH 38**
- May God bless us in his mercy *Batastini* **RS 95**
- May God bless us in his mercy *Guimont* **RS 94, GC 66**
- May we have peace *Ylvisaker* **BC**
- O God, be gracious *Brown* **PS1**

GENESIS 45:1-15
Joseph reconciles with his brothers
- Mercy *DeShazo/Sadler* **HMS14**

PSALM 133
How good and pleasant it is to live together in unity.
- Only for your glory *Hanson* **SCR 34**
- The family of the Lord *Hanson* **SCR 39**

ROMANS 11:1-2A, 29-32
God's mercy to all, Jew and Gentile
- Change my heart, O God *Espinoza* **HCW 28, W&P 28**
- God of love, have mercy *Makeever* **DH 10**
- Mercy *DeShazo/Sadler* **HMS14**
- Turn our hearts *Kendrick* **HMS12 1043**

MATTHEW 15:[10-20] 21-28
The healing of the Canaanite woman's daughter
- Faithful One *Doerksen* **CMH2 60**
- Forever grateful *Altrogge* **HCW 44**
- Thank you for the gift *Hanson* **SCR 144**
- Thank you, Lord *Park* **VIN8 202**

ADDITIONAL SONGS FOR THE DAY/SEASON
- Healer of our every ill *Haugen* **WOV 738, RS 958**
- Thank you for the gift *Hanson* **SCR**

Year B

Wisdom sets a table and invites all to taste the wine and bread. Jesus Christ, our Wisdom, gives his life for all, inviting everyone to drink and eat. Wisdom nourishes us with the word of life and the bread from heaven. In all this, we experience the abundant grace of God. How can this congregation be gracious and hospitable to any and all who seek the Lord?

PROVERBS 9:1-6
Invited to dine at wisdom's feast
- Now in this banquet *Haugen* **W&P 104**

PSALM 34:9-14
Those who seek the L*ORD* *lack nothing that is good.*
- God is so good *Anonymous* **COK 75, TFF 275**
- I will always thank the Lord *Soper* **G&P 202**
- I will bless the Lord *Gouin* **GC 46**
- I will bless you, O God *Makeever* **DH 34**
- Taste and see *Dean* **RS 72, G&P 200**
- Taste and see *Haugen* **RS 70, GC 47**
- Taste and see *Hurd* **G&P 199**
- Taste and see *Young* **BL**
- The cry of the poor *Foley* **RS 69, GC 48, G&P 203**
- You have been good *Paris* **HCW 198**

1 KINGS 2:10-12, 3:3-14
Solomon's prayer for wisdom
Jesus lead on *Helming* **VIN8 114**
Show me your ways *Fragar* **HMS11 949**
Where you lead me *DeShetler/Craig* **HMS13 1113**

PSALM 111
The fear of the LORD *is the beginning of wisdom.*
Rise up and praise him *Baloche/Sadler* **HMS13 1098**
Stand up and give him the praise *DeShazo* **HMS10 867**

EPHESIANS 5:15-20
Filled with the Spirit, sing thanks to God
Give thanks *Smith* **HCW 46, W&P 41, TFF 292**
Spirit of the living God *Iverson* **W&P 129**
Spirit of the living God *Sanchez* **HCW 158**
Thank you, Lord *Park* **VIN8 202**
Wake up sleeper *Ylvisaker* **BC**
Wake up *Hanson* **SCR 13**

JOHN 6:51-58
Christ the true food and drink
Come to me today *Hanson* **SCR 174**
Cup we bless *Young* **BL**
Eat this bread *Taizé* **TFF 125, WOV 709**
Everlasting grace *Carpenter* **VIN6 58**
Hallelujah! We sing your praises *South African* **TFF 158, WOV 722**
Life in his hands *Hanson* **SCR 10**
Poured out and broken *Hanson/Murakami* **SCR 184**
That we may be filled *Hanson/Murakami* **SCR 182, W&P 134**

ADDITIONAL SONGS FOR THE DAY/SEASON
Come, let us eat *Kwillia* **TFF 119, REN 197**

Year C

The candles that grace our worship seem like gentle lights, but fire is a powerful and purging force. Ancient peoples used fire to purify molten ore and burn away the dross. In this day's worship, God's word comes among us like raging fire, consuming what is false and leaving behind pure gold.

JEREMIAH 23:23-29
God's word is like fire, like a hammer that breaks rocks
Let your fire fall *DeShazo/Sadler* **HMS12 1016**
Revival fire, fall *Baloche* **HMS11 946**
The fire of your love *Baloche/Kerr* **HMS12 1037**

PSALM 82
Arise, O God, and rule the earth.
Arise, oh Lord *Carpenter* **VIN6 16**

ISAIAH 5:1-7
The vineyard of the Lord is destroyed
Come closer *Hanson* **SCR 47**
Hear our cry *Kendrick* **HMS12 1001**
We've come to praise you *Grant/Darnall* **MAR 80**

PSALM 80:1-2, 8-19
Look down from heaven, O God; behold and tend this vine.
God of hosts, bring us back *Furlong* **PS1**
We cry out for grace again *Kerr* **HMS12 1045**

HEBREWS 11:29-12:2
The faith of the Hebrew people, a great cloud of witnesses
May you run and not be weary *Hanson* **SCR 116, W&P 97**
O, mighty cross *Baroni/Chisum* **HCW 136**

LUKE 12:49-56
Jesus brings fire on earth and has a baptism with which to be baptized
I don't belong to me *Hanson* **SCR 152**
Let it rain *Park* **VIN8 126**
Let your fire fall *DeShazo/Sadler* **HMS12 1016**
Revival fire, fall *Baloche* **HMS11 946**
Water from heaven *Hanson/Murakami* **SCR 136**

ADDITIONAL SONGS FOR THE DAY/SEASON
Be bold, be strong *Chapman* **W&P 15**
Guide my feet *Spiritual* **TFF 153**
One Lord *Soper* **G&P**

Proper 16

Sunday between August 21 and 27 Inclusive

Year A

At any time and in any place, the Christian may ask God to forgive sin that separates one from God and others. At the same time, it is good to remember that to be a Christian is to be united to a community that bears the wounds of sin and human folly. The worshiping assembly—as a community—confesses the truth of its own unloving words, thoughts, and deeds. It hears and feels and tastes the merciful and forgiving love of God: in the absolution, in the waters of baptism, in receiving the body and blood of Christ, in the words of forgiveness spoken by a friend or family member, in the sharing of the Peace. These acts of confession and forgiveness are gifts of grace. How, then, might our words and actions extend this grace in daily life?

ISAIAH 51:1-6
The enduring foundation of God's salvation

- I see you *Mullins* **CC 90**
- Turn to me *Foley* **G&P 342**
- Your everlasting love *Batstone* **MAR 85**

PSALM 138
O LORD, your love endures forever.

- A joyous psalm *Butler* **CGA 74**
- For he alone is worthy *Traditional/Wade* **TFF 284**
- I praise your name *Ylvisaker* **BC**
- In the presence of the angels *Inwood* **PS3**
- In the sight of the angels *Guimont* **RS 185**
- Lord, your love is eternal *Stewart* **GC 133**

EXODUS 1:8-2:10
Pharaoh's daughter takes Moses as her son

- The wise may bring their learning *Ylvisaker* **BC**

PSALM 124
We have escaped like a bird from the snare of the fowler.

- Mighty is our God *Walker* **HCW 118**
- Our help is in the name *Baroni* **HMS11 938**

ROMANS 12:1-8
One body in Christ, with gifts that differ

- Before you now *Butler/Osbrink* **VIN7 44**
- Holy One, in you alone *Makeever* **DH 83**
- O Lord to you *Sadler* **HMS11 937**
- Somos uno en Cristo *Spanish* **TFF 221**
- We are an offering *Liles* **HCW 182, W&P 146**
- You, Lord *Hanson* **SCR 42, W&P 162**

MATTHEW 16:13-20
The profession of Peter's faith

- I believe in Jesus *Nelson* **HCW 71**
- Jesus, I believe *Batstone* **MAR 130**
- Only God for me *Harris* **HMS14**
- You alone *Hanson/Murakami* **SCR 36**
- You only *McCoy* **VIN8 242**

ADDITIONAL SONGS FOR THE DAY/SEASON

- Deep within *Haas* **RS 546**
- Faith that's sure *Lord* **CGA 695**
- I give you thanks *Lindh* **CGA 561**
- One bread, one body *Foley* **W&P 111, G&P 499, WOV 710**

Year B

In the midst of life's challenges and uncertainties we seek to understand God's words of truth and life for us. Like Joshua we make a commitment not to worship the passing gods of the day, but to serve the Lord alone. Today's reading from John includes words some Christians sing before the gospel is proclaimed: "Lord, to whom shall we go? You have the words of eternal life." Our hearts yearn for the good news that sets us free and strengthens us for service.

JOSHUA 24:1-2A, 14-18
Joshua calls all Israel to serve the LORD
- Let your fire fall *DeShazo/Sadler* **HMS12 1016**
- Only God for me *Harris* **HMS14**
- You are my God *Delavan* **HCW 196**

PSALM 34:15-22
The eyes of the LORD are upon the righteous.
- I will always thank the Lord *Soper* **G&P 202**
- I will bless the Lord *Gouin* **GC 46**
- I'll bless the Lord for evermore *Ylvisaker* **BC**
- Taste and see *Dean* **RS 72, G&P 200**
- Taste and see *Haugen* **RS 70, GC 47**
- Taste and see *Hurd* **G&P 199**
- Taste and see *Young* **BL, AFP 11-10895**
- The cry of the poor *Foley* **RS 69, GC 48, G&P 203**

1 KING 8:[1, 6, 10-11] 22-30, 41-43
Solomon's prayer at the temple dedication
- All around your throne *DeShazo/Kerr* **HMS10 808**
- Lord most high *Harris/Sadler* **HMS11 930**
- Our heart *Chisum/Searcy* **HCW 143**

PSALM 84
How dear to me is your dwelling, O LORD.
- Don't be anxious *Hanson* **SCR 141**
- I could sing of your love forever *Smith* **HMS13 1075**
- Lord, you've been our dwelling place *Ylvisaker* **BC**
- My heart yearns for thee *Baroni* **HMS12 1022**

EPHESIANS 6:10-20
Put on the armor of God
- I have kept the faith *Baloche* **HMS13 1076**
- Let it be said of us *Fry* **MAR 217**
- Lord, my strength *Krippaehne* **W&P 93**

JOHN 6:56-69
The bread of eternal life
- Alleluia. Lord, to whom shall we go *Cain/Kadidlo* **W&P 7**
- Because we believe *Gordon/Harvill* **HMS12 985**
- I am the living bread *Keesecker* **AFP 11-10684**
- I believe in Jesus *Nelson* **HCW 71**
- Life in his hands *Hanson* **SCR 10**
- You alone *Hanson/Murakami* **SCR 36**

ADDITIONAL SONGS FOR THE DAY/SEASON
- Eat this bread, drink this cup *Young* **WOV 706, BL, AFP 11-10651**

Year C

Early Christians referred to Sunday as the Lord's Day, the eighth day of the week, the day beyond time in which a new creation is born. We gather this day for new beginnings, eager to be recreated by the Word that raises us to new life.

ISAIAH 58:9B-14
Do not trample the sabbath, but feed the hungry
- Before the sun burned bright *Schutte* **G&P 577**
- Morning has broken *Farjeon/Traditional* **W&P 98**
- Rest in my love *Hanson/Swanson* **SCR 93**

PSALM 103:1-8
The LORD crowns you with mercy and lovingkindness.
- Bless his holy name *Crouch* **W&P 19**
- Bless the Lord *Makeever* **DH 42**
- Bless the Lord, O my soul *Taizé* **REN 114**
- Here is my heart *Nystrom* **HMS13 1070**
- The Lord is kind and merciful *Bolduc* **VO 90**
- The Lord is kind and merciful *Cotter* **GC 99**
- The Lord is kind and merciful *Haugen* **GC 100**
- With all my heart *Avery* **CC 11**

JEREMIAH 1:4-10
Jeremiah is called to be a prophet
- Open our eyes, Lord *Cull* **MAR 59, W&P 113**
- Open our lives to the Word *Makeever* **DH 8**

PSALM 71:1-6
From my mother's womb you have been my strength.
- You are my rock *Carpenter* **VIN6 278**

HEBREWS 12:18-29
You have come to the city of the living God and to Jesus
- Before you now *Butler/Osbrink* **VIN7 44**
- Let your fire fall *DeShazo/Sadler* **HMS12 1016**
- Thank you, Lord *Park* **VIN8 202**

LUKE 13:10-17
Jesus heals a crippled woman on the sabbath and is condemned
- Before you now *Butler/Osbrink* **VIN7 44**
- Celebrate love *Hanson* **SCR 16**
- Life in his hands *Hanson* **SCR 10**
- Share your bread with the hungry *Haas* **G-4734**

ADDITIONAL SONGS FOR THE DAY/SEASON
- Canticle of the turning *Cooney* **RS 678, W&P 26**
- I will bless thee, O Lord *Watanabe* **MAR**
- Let justice roll like a river *Haugen* **W&P 85**
- Our confidence is in the Lord *Richards* **W&P 114**

Proper 17

Sunday between August 28 and September 3 Inclusive

Year A

Today's gospel reading reminds us that life in Christ, rather than simply comforting us or excusing us from the pain of this world, strengthens us to face what we fear most: suffering and death. Jesus does not turn from pain and loss; indeed, he offers strength and hope to his people. God's adoption of us in the waters of baptism and our communion in Christ's body and blood—signs of healing and community—strengthen us to offer ourselves as servants to a weary and frightened world.

JEREMIAH 15:15-21
God fortifies the prophet against opposition
- God my refuge *Montemayer* **HCW 50**
- Lord, my strength *Krippaehne* **W&P 93**

PSALM 26:1-8
Your love is before my eyes; I have walked faithfully with you.
- O Lord, I love the habitation of your house *Bender* **CPH 98-2859**
- Psalm 26 *Gerike* **G-2632**

EXODUS 3:1-15
From the blazing bush God calls Moses
- I Am *Hanson* **SFL**
- We will glorify *Paris* **HCW 187, W&P 154**
- You are I Am *Evans* **HMS12 1051**

PSALM 105:1-6, 23-26, 45C
Make known the deeds of the LORD among the peoples. Hallelujah!
- We declare your name *Baloche/Baloche* **HMS10 874**

ROMANS 12:9-21
Live in harmony
- Only for your glory *Hanson* **SCR 34**
- The people on your heart *DeShazo/Sadler* **HMS10 869**
- Turn our hearts *Kendrick* **HMS12 1043**

MATTHEW 16:21-28
The passion prediction and rebuke to Peter
- I want Jesus to walk with me *Traditional* **TFF 66, WOV 660**
- Jesus lead on *Helming* **VIN8 114**
- Step by step *Beaker* **HMS13 1103, W&P 132**
- Turn our hearts *Kendrick* **HCW, MAR**
- You have called us *DeShazo/Nystrom* **HCW 199**

ADDITIONAL SONGS FOR THE DAY/SEASON
- Broken hearts *Hanson/Murakami* **SCR**
- Stir up the love *Ylvisaker/Dragseth* **BC**

Year B

In our worship, we pray to God who is the giver of every good and perfect gift. We ask God to bring to fruition the word of truth sown in our hearts by Christ, so that we will live the law of love. It is this liberating law that judges all other laws of human origin. It is this gracious command that is sealed with Christ's blood. In this supper Christ forgives us and strengthens us to be communal witnesses to his love.

DEUTERONOMY 4:1-2. 6-9
God's law: a sign of a great nation
- Lead me, oh lead me *Smith* **HMS13 1085**

PSALM 15
LORD, who may dwell in your tabernacle?
- Sanctuary *Thompson/Scruggs* **HCW 154**
- The just will live *Batastini* **RS 33**
- They who do justice *Haas* **GC 22**

SONG OF SOLOMON 2:8-13
Song of two lovers
- You are the Lord of me *Sims* **SCR 76**

PSALM 45:1-2, 6-9
God has anointed you with the oil of gladness.
- The queen stands at your right hand *Rees* **PS3**

JAMES 1:17-27

Be doers of the word, not hearers only

Go and do *Hanson* **SCR 123**
Purify my heart *Greco* **HCW 148**
The gift of giving *Ylvisaker* **BC**
We are his hands *Gersmehl* **COK 85**

MARK 7:1-8, 14-15, 21-23

Authentic religion

Cry of my heart *Butler* **MAR**
Good soil *Hanson* **SCR 30, W&P 52, WOV 713**
Holy love *Park* **VIN7 107**
Purify my heart *Greco* **HCW 148**
Turn my heart *DeShazo* **HCW 179**

ADDITIONAL SONGS FOR THE DAY/SEASON

All things bright and beautiful *Mitchell* **CGA-492**
We choose the fear of the Lord *Dearman* **MAR**
Who shall live on that holy mountain *Ylvisaker* **BC**

Year C

Who is welcome in your community of faith? And how would they know that they are? Today's readings ask us to think about hospitality, especially as it is practiced at the table. The feast of God's radical grace calls us into this place and connects friends and strangers with each other.

PROVERBS 25:6-7

Do not put yourself forward

I bend my knees again *Butler/Butler* **VIN8 85**

SIRACH 10:12-18

Judgment upon the proud

PSALM 112

The righteous are merciful and full of compassion.

A light rises in the darkness *Guimont* **RS 149**
Sing with joy to God *Currie* **RS 109**
Sing with joy to God *Guimont* **GC 76**
You're a child of God *Ylvisaker* **BC**

JEREMIAH 2:4-13

The people of Israel forsake the Lord

Come to the fount of creation *Ylvisaker* **BC**
Come to the river of life *Moen/Cloninger* **HMS10 818**

PSALM 81:1, 10-16

I feed you with the finest wheat and satisfy you with honey from the rock.

God is so good *Anonymous* **COK 75, TFF 275**

HEBREWS 13:1-8, 15-16

God is with us: let acts of mutual love continue

Come to the table *Nystrom* **W&P 33**
From A to O *Hanson* **SCR 56**
It has always been you *Butler/Butler* **VIN6 120**
Someone in need of your love *Makeever* **DH 94**
The people on your heart *DeShazo/Sadler* **HMS10 869**
Turn our hearts *Kendrick* **HMS12 1043**
We are an offering *Liles* **HCW 182, W&P 146**
We bring the sacrifice of praise *Dearman* **W&P 150**

LUKE 14:1, 7-14

An image of God's reign: invite the poor, crippled to your banquet

Let the river flow *Evans* **HMS12 1015**
Now in this banquet *Haugen* **W&P 104**
That we may be filled *Hanson/Murakami* **SCR 182, W&P 134**

ADDITIONAL SONGS FOR THE DAY/SEASON

Anybody ask you *Ylvisaker* **BC**
Come to the feast *Haugen* **G-3543**

Proper 18

Sunday between September 4 and 10 Inclusive

Year A

Life in community is a precious thing, but it easily breaks down if rumors and idle talk are given free reign. In today's gospel, Jesus prescribes a manner for dealing with conflict in community life. The intent of such a form of church discipline is to restore people to community life. May all who come to hear and to taste the presence of Christ in word and meal today also find communities which seek to understand one another in truth and in love.

EZEKIEL 33:7-11
The prophet's responsibility to warn the people
- Awake, O sleeper *Haugen* **GC 803**
- Here is my heart *Nystrom* **HMS13 1070**
- I bend my knees again *Butler/Butler* **VIN8 85**

PSALM 119:33-40
I desire the path of your commandments.
- Happy are they *Guimont* **RS**
- Happy are those who follow *Cooney* **GC 116**
- Lord, I love your commands *Guimont* **GC 117**
- Show me your ways *Fragar* **HMS11 949**
- Step by step *Beaker* **W&P 132**
- Teach me, O Lord *Hurd* **G-2715**

EXODUS 12:1-14
The passover of the L*ORD*
- The Lamb *Coleman* **TFF 89**

PSALM 149
Sing the praise of the L*ORD in the congregation of the faithful.*
- Stand up and give him the praise *DeShazo* **HMS10 867**

ROMANS 13:8-14
Live honorably as in the day
- Awake, O sleeper *Haugen* **GC 803**
- Put on love *Makeever* **DH 78**
- Someone in need of your love *Makeever* **DH 94**
- Wake up *Hanson* **SCR 13**

MATTHEW 18:15-20
Reconciliation in the community of faith
- Be near us, Lord Jesus *Hanson/Murakami* **SCR 4**
- God is here *Moen/Overstreet* **HMS12 995**
- Seek first the kingdom *Haas* **G-3955**
- Where two or three *Kendrick* **HMS12 1050**

ADDITIONAL SONGS FOR THE DAY/SEASON
- There's a song *Hanson* **SFL**

Year B

In today's gospel Jesus heals a deaf and mute man using the word *ephphatha*, which means "be opened." The author of James exhorts the community of faith to guard against favoritism among its members. In baptism we have died to any distinctions that would separate us from each other. Likewise, at the Lord's table each one receives the free gift of Christ equally and without discrimination. Through word, bath, and meal, God opens our minds and hearts to the healing and liberating gospel of Christ.

ISAIAH 35: 4-7A
Like streams in the desert, God comes with healing
- Flow, river, flow *Hurd* **G&P 455**
- Let the river flow *Evans* **HMS12 1015**

PSALM 146
I will praise the L*ORD as long as I live.*
- As long as I live *Haas* **G-4681**
- He shall reign *Chopinsky* **HMS12 999**
- Lord, I lift your name on high *Founds* **W&P 90**
- Maranatha, alleluia! *Wellicome* **PS2**
- Sing unto the Lord *Makeever* **DH 47**

PROVERBS 22:1-2, 8-9, 22-23
Sayings concerning a good name and generosity
- Faithful One *Doerksen* **CMH2 60**
- We can be lifted up *Hanson* **SCR 105**

PSALM 125
Those who trust in the L*ORD stand fast forever.*
- My heart will trust *Morgan* **HMS14**

JAMES 2:1-1- [11-13] 14-17

Faith without works is dead

- Go and do *Hanson* **SCR 123**
- They'll know we are Christians *Traditional* **COK 78**
- We've come to praise you *Grant/Darnall* **MAR 80**

MARK 7:24-37

Christ healing a little girl and a deaf man

- Come and taste *Hanson/Murakami* **SCR 186, W&P 30**
- Come touch *Hanson* **SCR 180**
- Healer of our every ill *Haugen* **WOV 738, GC 882**
- Open our eyes, Lord *Cull* **MAR 59, W&P 113**

ADDITIONAL SONGS FOR THE DAY/SEASON

- Bring forth the kingdom *Haugen* **W&P 22, GC 658**
- He who began a good work in you *Mohr* **W&P 56**
- In my life be glorified *Kilpatrick* **SPW**

Year C

In remembrance of our baptism, many Christians make the sign of the cross. We are the people marked with Jesus' cross. But that cross is costly, and those who bear it must be prepared to let go of everything in order to take up the new life that comes from Jesus' cross and open tomb.

DEUTERONOMY 30:15-20

Walk in the way of life and hold fast to God

- Freely, given freely *Hanson/Murakami* **SCR 74**
- Lord, my strength *Krippaehne* **W&P 93**
- Show me your ways *Fragar* **HMS11 949**
- Take up your cross *Traditional* **GC 698**
- Turn my heart *DeShazo* **HCW 179**

PSALM 1

Their delight is in the law of the LORD.

- Happy are they *Harbor* **TFF 1**
- I will delight *Harrah/Schreiner* **W&P 72**
- I will never be *Bullock* **HMS11 920**
- In Christ, a new creation *Ylvisaker* **BC**
- Planted by the waters *Kline* **REN**
- Roots in the earth *Cooney* **G-3969**

JEREMIAH 18:1-11

Like a potter, the Lord will reshape Israel

- Change my heart, O God *Espinoza* **W&P 28**
- Now God our Father *Dearman/Mills* **W&P 103**

PSALM 139:1-6, 13-18

You have searched me out and known me.

- Here is my heart *Nystrom* **HMS13 1070**
- I was there to hear your borning cry *Ylvisaker* **BC, W&P 69, WOV 770**
- Write it on my heart *McLean* **WIS 41**

PHILEMON 1-21

Paul says: Receive Onesimus as a coworker

- Mercy *DeShazo/Sadler* **HMS14**
- Nothing at all but love *Ylvisaker* **BC**
- Song about grace *Ylvisaker* **BC**

LUKE 14:25-33

Jesus says: Disciples, give up your possessions and carry the cross

- I come to the cross *Somma/Batstone* **MAR 122**
- I want Jesus to walk with me *Traditional* **TFF 66, WOV 660**
- More precious than silver *DeShazo* **HCW 122**
- Nothing is as wonderful *Underwood* **VIN8 150**
- Two fishermen *Toolan* **GC 688**

ADDITIONAL SONGS FOR THE DAY/SEASON

- Embrace my way and cross *Glover* **G-4594**
- Take up your cross *Traditional* **GC 698**
- We shall not be moved *Ylvisaker* **BC**

Proper 19

Sunday between September 11 and 17 Inclusive

Year A

In today's Gospel reading, Jesus invites us to forgive one another. His invitation, however, is not an optional activity for Christians. It is the heart of the gospel and the distinctive character of Christian life. Out of love for us in our weakness and sin, God forgives us, heals us, and strengthens us to be a forgiving people. The sign of the cross invites us to the daily ministry of reconciliation.

GENESIS 50:15-21
Joseph reconciles with his brothers
- God of love, have mercy *Makeever* **DH 10**
- Mercy *DeShazo/Sadler* **HMS14**

PSALM 103:[1-7] 8-13
The Lord is full of compassion and mercy.
- Bless the Lord *Makeever* **DH 42**
- God of love, have mercy *Makeever* **DH 10**
- How blessed *Hampton* **VIN6 106**
- I'll bless the Lord for evermore *Ylvisaker* **BC**
- The Lord is kind and merciful *Bolduc* **VO 90**
- The Lord is kind and merciful *Cotter* **GC 99**
- The Lord is kind and merciful *Haugen* **GC 100, RS**

EXODUS 14:19-31
Israel's deliverance at the Red Sea
- Standing on the Lord's side *Ylvisaker* **BC**
- Where you lead me *DeShetler/Craig* **HMS13 1113**

PSALM 114
Tremble, O earth, at the presence of the LORD.
- Alleluia *Sinclair* **HMS11 889, W&P 6**

EXODUS 15:1B-11, 20-21
I will sing to the LORD who has triumphed gloriously
- Glory be! *Ylvisaker* **BC**
- Sing unto the Lord *Makeever* **DH 47**

ROMANS 14:1-12
Accepting diversity in the community of faith
- For to this end *Makeever* **DH 104**
- I belong to a mighty God *DeShazo* **HMS8 654**
- In unity and peace *Chepponis* **G-4452**
- Jesus, name above all names *Cain* **W&P 77**
- Life in his hands *Hanson* **SCR 10**
- My life is in you, Lord *Gardner* **HCW 128**
- We declare your name *Baloche/Baloche* **HMS10 874**

MATTHEW 18:21-35
A parable of forgiveness in the community of faith
- God of love, have mercy *Makeever* **DH 10**
- Mercy *DeShazo/Sadler* **HMS14**
- Turn our hearts *Kendrick* **HMS12 1043**
- When we eat this bread *Joncas* **G&P 510**

ADDITIONAL SONGS FOR THE DAY/SEASON
- Change our hearts *Cooney* **G&P 349, GC 394**
- I'll belong to you *Hanson* **SCR**
- Return to me *Hurd* **G&P 347**

Year B

Those who confess Jesus as Messiah are called to deny themselves, take up their cross, and follow Christ. As we face the suffering of the world and the brokenness of our own lives, we learn the meaning of losing our lives for the sake of the gospel. Each time we make the sign of the cross, and share the broken bread and the cup of salvation, we remember the good news that our baptism into Christ's death is also the promise of the resurrection.

ISAIAH 50:4-9A
The servant is vindicated by God
- Awaken the song *Rethmeier* **VIN6 22**

PSALM 116:1-9
I will walk in the presence of the LORD.
- An offering of thanksgiving *Ylvisaker* **BC**
- I love to be in your presence *Baloche/Kerr* **HCW 75**
- I will call upon the name of the Lord *Roberts* **TFF 14**
- I will walk in the presence of God *Cooney* **GC 109**
- Lord, how can I repay *Glynn* **PS2**
- Our blessing cup *Joncas* **G&P 257**
- Our blessing-cup *Haugen* **RS 155, GC 107**
- The blessing cup *Brown* **PS2**
- The name of God *Haas* **RS 152, GC 110**
- Walk in the land *Mattingly* **VO 94**

PROVERBS 1:20-33
Wisdom's rebuke to the foolish
Be magnified *DeShazo* **HCW 20**

PSALM 19
The statutes of the LORD are just and rejoice the heart.
Praised be the rock *Haya* **TFF 290**
Psalm 19 *Butler* **VIN7 190**

WISDOM OF SOLOMON 7:26—8:1
God loves nothing so much as the person who lives with wisdom.

JAMES 3:1-12
Dangers of the unbridled tongue
Here is my heart *Nystrom* **HMS13 1070**
Sanctuary *Thompson/Scruggs* **HCW 154**
We are an offering *Liles* **HCW 182, W&P 146**
We are his hands *Gersmehl* **COK 85**

MARK 8:27-38
Peter's confession of faith
I believe in Jesus *Nelson* **HCW 71**
Jesus, I believe *Batstone* **MAR 130**
Only God for me *Harris* **HMS14**
Take up your cross *Traditional* **GC 698**
The summons *Bell* **W&P 137**
You alone *Hanson/Murakami* **SCR 36**
You only *McCoy* **VIN8 242**

ADDITIONAL SONGS FOR THE DAY/SEASON
Be thou my vision *Irish* **WOV 776, REN 151**
For the life of the world *Haas* **GC 801**
Meet us here *Marks* **MAR**

Year C

Only the lost can be found. The confession of sins is our admission that we do not know the way to God. But God has been looking for us. This day we are surrounded by images of people who "once were lost." Those who are found enter the joy of the Lord.

EXODUS 32:7-14
Moses begs the LORD to turn from anger against the Hebrews
Go down, Moses *Spiritual* **GC 715, TFF 87**
Standing on the Lord's side *Ylvisaker* **BC**

PSALM 51:1-10
Have mercy on me, O God, according to your lovingkindness.
Please have mercy on me *Ylvisaker* **BC**
See also Ash Wednesday.

JEREMIAH 4:11-12, 22-28
Judgment is spoken against Jerusalem
Awesome God *Mullins* **W&P 13**
God the sculptor of the mountains *Thornburg/Husberg* **TFF 222**
The trumpets sound, the angels sing *Kendrick* **W&P 139**

PSALM 14
The LORD looks down from heaven upon us all.
As we gather *Coomes/Fay* **MAR 6**

1 TIMOTHY 1:12-17
Christ Jesus came for sinners
Bless the body broken for my sin *Ylvisaker* **BC**
Come to me today *Hanson* **SCR 174**
Come, you sinners, poor and needy *American* **RS 954**

LUKE 15:1-10
Looking for the lost sheep, silver coin: Jesus eating with sinners
All we like sheep *Moen* **HCW 7**
Come home *Mattingly* **VO 16**
I am the Good Shepherd *Ylvisaker* **BC**
Like a shepherd *Moen/Simpson* **HCW 112**
Softly and tenderly Jesus is calling *Thompson* **WOV 734, REN 147**

ADDITIONAL SONGS FOR THE DAY/SEASON
Come home *Landry* **G&P 468**

Proper 20

Sunday between September 18 and 24 Inclusive

Year A

People like to keep score. If our team wins by a point, we rejoice and claim victory. But our relationships begin to dissolve when we count up little mistakes, losing trust and patience. We learn today that God is not interested in playing counting games. In the reign of God, mercy is freely given to those who come late, as well as to those who have labored for many hours or years. Any claim to partiality, any impulse to keep score, is undercut by the grace of God received in word and meal. In the presence of God's mercy, we are all beggars.

JONAH 3:10-4:11
God's concern for the city of Nineveh
- Jonah's song *Williams* **REN 125**
- You've delivered me again *Ylvisaker* **BC**

PSALM 145:1-8
The LORD is slow to anger and of great kindness.
- Glorious God *Baroni/Fitts/Smith* **HMS10 823**
- He answers all our needs *Bolduc* **VO 33**
- I will praise your name for ever *Roberts* **RS 192**
- I will praise your name *Haas* **GC 137, RS 193, PS2**
- Our God is compassion *Cotter* **GC 138**

EXODUS 16:2-15
Manna and quails feed the Israelites in the wilderness
- Come and taste *Hanson/Murakami* **SCR 186, W&P 30**
- God is so good *Anonymous* **COK 75, TFF 275**
- God of glory *Hanson* **SCR 89**
- Thanksgiving to the living God *Makeever* **DH 3**

PSALM 105:1-6, 37-45
Make known the deeds of the LORD among the peoples. Hallelujah!
- Great is the Lord *Smith/Smith* **W&P 53**
- Step by step *Beaker* **HMS13 1103, W&P 132**
- We declare your name *Baloche/Baloche* **HMS10 874**

PHILIPPIANS 1:21-30
Standing firm in the gospel
- Be magnified *DeShazo* **HCW 20**
- Rise up and praise him *Baloche/Sadler* **HMS13 1098**
- Stand firm *Glover* **G-4593**
- They'll know we are Christians *Traditional* **COK 78**

MATTHEW 20:1-16
The parable of the vineyard workers
- A taste of the joys of heaven *Ylvisaker* **BC**
- Lead me, oh lead me *Smith* **HMS13 1085**
- Precious Lord, take my hand *Dorsey* **TFF 193, WOV 731**
- The wondrous day of our God *Haugen* **G-4416**

ADDITIONAL SONGS FOR THE DAY/SEASON
- Somos uno *Traditional* **TFF 221**
- We gather as one *Dinise/Howard* **VO 100**

Year B

In worship we learn the reversals in the kingdom of God: greatness is not defined by wealth, power, or prestige. Rather, all people are welcomed in the name of Christ. The children in our midst are a sign of the hospitality that God offers to all persons regardless of their status in the world. We go forth from our Sunday assemblies to be servants who find greatness in humble service on behalf of those who are often forgotten or rejected in society.

JEREMIAH 11:18-20
The prophet led like a lamb to slaughter
- Here is my heart *Nystrom* **HMS13 1070**

WISDOM OF SOLOMON 1:16—2:1, 12-22
The righteous shall live

PSALM 54
God is my helper; it is the LORD who sustains my life.
- My life is in you, Lord *Gardner* **HCW 128**
- The Lord upholds my life *Guimont* **GC 58**
- The Lord upholds my life *Haas* **G-3563**
- You've delivered me again *Ylvisaker* **BC**

PROVERBS 31:10-31
Poem celebrating the capable wife
Women of faith *Harvill/Arterburn* **HMS13 117**

PSALM 1
Their delight is in the law of the LORD.
I will never be *Bullock* **HMS11 920**
In Christ, a new creation *Ylvisaker* **BC**

JAMES 3:13—4:3, 7-8A
The wisdom from above
First love *Baloche/Sadler* **HMS13 1062**
Give us your vision *Hanson/Murakami* **SCR 85**
Take up your cross *Traditional* **GC 698**
We will draw near *Nystrom/Harris* **HMS11 966**

MARK 9:30-37
Prediction of the passion
Beauty for brokenness *Kendrick* **W&P 17**
Broken hearts *Hanson/Murakami* **SCR 170**
Broken in love *Hanson* **SCR 177, W&P 24**
For God so loved the world *Dauermann* **W&P 39**
Unless you learn *Haugen* **G-4416**

ADDITIONAL SONGS FOR THE DAY/SEASON
Bring the children *Makeever* **DH 74**
I will offer you my life *Ylvisaker* **BC**
We gather as one *Dinise/Howard* **VO 100**

Year C

Early in the academic year may seem a strange time to think about the final exam, but on this day Jesus reminds us that each of us needs to give an accounting of all that is entrusted to us. In the new logic of God's reign, knowing the riches of grace we possess demands resolute action from us; we risk it all for possessing the lavish love of God offered to us.

AMOS 8:4-7
Warnings to those who trample on the needy and poor
Let justice roll like a river *Haugen* **GC 716**
Open our lives to the word *Makeever* **DH 8**
We cry out for grace again *Kerr* **HMS12 1045**

PSALM 113
The LORD lifts up the poor from the ashes.
Praise God's name *Joncas* **RS**
Praise the Lord *Guimont* **GC 106**
We can be lifted up *Hanson* **SCR 105**

JEREMIAH 8:18-9:1
The LORD laments over Judah
Broken hearts *Hanson/Murakami* **SCR 170**

PSALM 79:1-9
Deliver us and forgive us our sins, for your name's sake.
Let your fire fall *DeShazo/Sadler* **HMS12 1016**

1 TIMOTHY 2:1-7
One God, one mediator—Christ Jesus—who gave himself for all people
I love to be in your presence *Baloche/Kerr* **HCW 75**
One *Hanson/Murakami* **SCR 160**

LUKE 16:1-13
A shrewd manager: faithful in little, faithful in much; serving God/wealth
More precious than silver *DeShazo* **HCW 122**
Nothing is as wonderful *Underwood* **VIN8 150**
Only God for me *Harris* **HMS14**
Unless you learn *Haugen* **G-4416**

ADDITIONAL SONGS FOR THE DAY/SEASON
From where the sun rises *Kendrick* **W&P 40**
Here is love *Lowry* **MAR**
Praise the name of Jesus *Hayford* **MAR**
The love of the Lord *Joncas* **GC 702, RS 814**

Proper 21

Sunday between September 25 and October 1 Inclusive

Year A

As we gather today we become more than a collection of individuals. We have been united to each other in the waters of baptism and welcomed by Christ to his holy supper. While some may be strangers to us, we are invited to recognize the deep communion we share in Christ Jesus. Our worship does not protect us from others; it teaches us to be a people of hospitality, generous in faith, hope, and love.

EZEKIEL 18:1-4, 25-32
The fairness of God's way
- God provides a brand new heart *Ylvisaker* **BC**
- New life again and again *Hanson/Murakami* **SCR 102**

PSALM 25:1-9
Remember, O LORD, your compassion and love.
- Remember *Cooney* **G-3972**
- Remember your love *Ducote/Daigle* **G&P 474**
- Remember your mercies *Haas* **GC 35, RS 54**
- Remember your mercy, Lord *Inwood* **G&P 476**
- Remember your mercy, Lord *Wellicome* **PS1**
- Show me your ways *Fragar* **HMS11 949**
- Thy word *Smith/Grant* **W&P 144, TFF 132**
- Thy word *Webb* **W&P 143**
- To you, O God, I lift up my soul *Hurd* **G&P 302**
- To you, O Lord *Thompson* **RS 50**
- To you, O Lord I lift my soul *Roberts* **G-4601**
- To you, O Lord *Haugen* **G-2653, GC, RS**

EXODUS 17:1-7
Water from the rock in the wilderness
- Faithful Father *Doerksen* **VIN7 72**
- Let it rain *Park* **VIN8 126**

PSALM 78:1-4, 12-16
We will recount to generations to come the power of the LORD.
- All the power you need *Fragar* **HMS11 888**
- Arise, oh Lord *Carpenter* **VIN6 16**
- Glorious God *Baroni/Fitts/Smith* **HMS10 823**

PHILIPPIANS 2:1-13
Christ humbled to the point of death on a cross
- At the name of Jesus *Bolduc* **VO 5**
- At the name of Jesus *Webb* **W&P 12**
- Come share the spirit *Hanson/Murakami* **SCR 116**
- For the life of the world *Haas* **GC 801**
- He is exalted *Paris* **HCW 57, W&P 55**
- He is Lord *Smith* **HMS12 998**
- I come to the cross *Somma/Batstone* **MAR 122**
- In unity and peace *Chepponis* **G-4452**
- Jesus, name above all names *Cain* **W&P 77**
- We bow before his holy name *Ylvisaker* **BC**
- You have been given *Kauflin* **HCW 197**

MATTHEW 21:23-32
A parable of doing God's will
- Go and do *Hanson* **SCR 123**
- Here I am *Batstone* **MAR 115**

ADDITIONAL SONGS FOR THE DAY/SEASON
- For the life of the world *Haas* **GC 801**
- Gather us in *Haugen* **WOV 718, RS 850**

Year B

The disciples ask Jesus how to deal with those who are doing good in his name, but are not a part of their company. The Lord's response assures them that the reign of God can be served in many and diverse ways. Such words invite the contemporary church to be attentive to those who serve Christ in new or unexpected ministries. Even as Jesus encourages us to be seasoned with salt and to be at peace with one another, James urges us to confess our sins and to pray for the healing of all who are sick.

NUMBERS 11:4-6, 10-16, 24-29
The LORD's spirit comes upon seventy elders
- Spirit song *Wimber* **CMH 6, W&P 130**

PSALM 19:7-14
The commandment of the LORD gives light to the eyes.
- Lord, you have the words *Bolduc* **VO 61**
- Lord, you have the words *Haas* **GC 27**
- Lord, you have the words *Haugen* **VO 62**
- More precious than silver *DeShazo* **HCW 122**
- Psalm 19 *Butler* **VIN7 190**
- You, Lord, have the message *Ogden* **PS2**

ESTHER 7:1-6, 9-10; 9:20-22
Esther's intercession spares the lives of her people
- Women of faith *Harvill/Arterburn* **HMS13 117**

PSALM 124
We have escaped like a bird from the snare of the fowler.
- Mighty is our God *Walker* **HCW 118**
- Our help is in the name *Baroni* **HMS11 938**

JAMES 5:13-20
Prayer and anointing in the community
- Heavenly Father *Park* **VIN7 92**
- Lord, we pray *Gustafson* **HMS8 668**
- The people on your heart *DeShazo/Sadler* **HMS10 869**
- Turn our hearts *Kendrick* **HMS12 1043**

MARK 9:38-50
Warnings to those who obstruct faith
- Bring forth the kingdom *Haugen* **GC 658**
- Make me a servant *Willard* **W&P 96**
- Make my life a candle *Hanson* **SCR 163**
- Someone in need of your love *Makeever* **DH 94**

ADDITIONAL SONGS FOR THE DAY/SEASON
- Lay down that Spirit *Mattingly* **VO 52**

Year C

The readings for this day continue the theme of the past several weeks asking God's people to consider their relationship to wealth. Our money can be a powerful tool for alleviating suffering in the world, but it can just as easily become a strong force that alienates us from the riches of God's love. We need to know where we place our deepest values.

AMOS 6:1A, 4-7
Warnings to those who are comfortable or wealthy
- Let justice roll like a river *Haugen* **GC 716**
- More precious than silver *DeShazo* **HCW 122**
- Nothing is as wonderful *Underwood* **VIN8 150**

PSALM 146
The LORD gives justice to those who are oppressed.
- As long as I live *Haas* **G-4681**
- He shall reign *Chopinsky* **HMS12 999**
- Lord I lift your name on high *Founds* **W&P 90**
- Lord, come and save us *Haugen* **GC 140**
- Maranatha, alleluia! *Wellicome* **PS1**
- Sing unto the Lord *Makeever* **DH 47**

JEREMIAH 32:1-3A, 6-15
Jeremiah buys a field

PSALM 91:1-6, 14-16
You are my refuge and my stronghold, my God in whom I put my trust.
- On eagle's wings *Joncas* **W&P 110, WOV 779**
- We can be lifted up *Hanson* **SCR 105**

1 TIMOTHY 6:6-19
Eager to be rich or eager to pursue richness of God's justice?
- I have kept the faith *Baloche* **HMS13 1076**
- King of life *Sadler* **HMS12 1014**
- Shine, Jesus, shine *Kendrick* **HCW 155, W&P 123, WOV 651**

LUKE 16:19-31
Story of poor Lazarus and the wealthy man
- Come, you sinners, poor and needy *American* **RS 954**
- Give thanks *Smith* **HCW 46, W&P 41, TFF 292**
- Let the river flow *Evans* **HMS12 1015**
- Nothing is as wonderful *Underwood* **VIN8 150**

ADDITIONAL SONGS FOR THE DAY/SEASON
- As the deer *Nystrom* **MAR**
- Gather us in *Haugen* **WOV 718, G-2651**
- Make me a servant *Willard* **MAR**

Proper 22

Sunday between October 2 and 8 Inclusive

Year A

In today's gospel reading, Jesus tells a parable of the vineyard, an image of Israel, the prophets' mission, and Christ's death. For Christians, the vineyard also speaks of God's love poured out in the blood of Christ, given to us for the forgiveness of sin. Grafted into Christ the vine at baptism, we are nourished with his blood and drawn to each other by his love.

ISAIAH 5:1-7
The song of the vineyard
- Be magnified *DeShazo* **HCW 20**
- Taste and see *Young* **BL**

PSALM 80:7-14
Look down from heaven, O God; behold and tend this vine.
- Behold and tend this vine *Makeever* **DH 39**
- The vineyard of the Lord *Guimont* **GC 74**

EXODUS 20:1-4, 7-9, 12-20
The commandments given at Sinai
- Open our lives to the Word *Makeever* **DH 8**
- Thy word *Smith/Grant* **W&P 144**
- Thy word *Webb* **W&P 143**

PSALM 19
The statutes of the LORD *are just and rejoice the heart.*
- Psalm 19 *Butler* **VIN7 190**
- You, Lord, have the message *Ogden* **PS2**

PHILIPPIANS 3:4B-14
Nothing surpasses the value of knowing Christ
- Amen *Fitts* **HMS12 982**
- Broken hearts *Hanson/Murakami* **SCR 170**
- Change my heart, O God *Espinoza* **HCW 28, W&P 28**
- Hop on the bus *Underwood* **VIN7 120**
- I want to know you *Evans* **HMS12 1008**
- The love of the Lord *Joncas* **RS 814, GC 702**

MATTHEW 21:33-46
The parable of the vineyard owner's son
- Building block *Stookey* **BC**
- Holy love *Park* **VIN7 107**
- May you run and not be weary *Hanson* **SCR 116, W&P 97**
- Save us, O Lord (st. 3) *Dufford* **G&P 301**
- Send me, Jesus *South African* **TFF 244, WOV 773**

ADDITIONAL SONGS FOR THE DAY/SEASON
- Amazing love *Kendrick* **REN**
- Only this I want *Schutte* **GC 695**

Year B

The psalmist sings that human beings are the crown of God's creation. Our loving human relationships, though marred by sin, are a sign of the kingdom of God among us. In their mutual respect and love, they symbolize the wholeness intended for all life. Yet neither husband nor wife nor the creation itself is the property of humans to do with as they will. The world, and all that lives within it, belongs to God, who transforms all things through Christ.

GENESIS 2:18-24
Created for relationship
- Blessing the marriage *Bell* **GC 871**
- God, in the planning *Bell* **GC 868**
- Put on love *Makeever* **DH 78**

PSALM 8
You adorn us with glory and honor.
- All my days *Schutte* **G&P 701**
- Come and see *LeBlanc* **W&P 29**
- He is Lord *Traditional* **SPW**
- How glorious is your name *Cooney* **GC 20**
- How majestic is your name *Smith* **W&P 66**
- Psalm 8 *Hanson* **SCR**
- Who are we *Makeever* **DH 33**
- Your name is praised *Geary* **PS3**
- Your wonderful name *Haas* **G-5041**

JOB 1:1; 2:1-10

Job's integrity in the face of suffering

Don't be anxious *Hanson* **SCR 141**

PSALM 26

Your love is before my eyes; I have walked faithfully with you.

Love you so much *Fragar* **HMS13 1088**

Thanksgiving to the living God *Makeever* **DH 3**

HEBREWS 1:1-4; 2:5-12

God has spoken by a Son

God of glory *Hanson* **SCR 89**

Jesus, child of God *Ylvisaker* **BC**

Who are we *Makeever* **DH 33**

You are my all in all *Jernigan* **HMS11 976**

MARK 10:2-16

Teaching on marriage

God without and within *Hanson/Murakami* **SCR 70**

I Am *Hanson* **SFL**

Lord, listen to your children *Hanson* **SCR 23, WOV 775, W&P 91**

Lord, listen to your children praying *Medema* **W&P 92**

ADDITIONAL SONGS FOR THE DAY/SEASON

Bind us together *Gilman* **W&P 18, WOV 748**

How majestic is your name *Smith* **W&P 66, MAR**

When love is found *Traditional* **WOV 749, GC 865**

Year C

Faith is the substance of our worship. It is the "stuff" we need to be people of God. It is transmitted from one generation to the next. We confess it in the creed but we live it in daily life.

HABAKKUK 1:1-4; 2:1-4

Wicked surround the righteous; wait for the LORD

Be bold, be strong *Chapman* **W&P 15**

My heart yearns for thee *Baroni* **HMS12 1022**

Stand firm *Glover* **G-4593**

PSALM 37:1-10

Commit your way to the LORD; put your trust in the LORD.

I will never be *Bullock* **HMS11 920**

Purify my heart *Greco* **HCW 148**

LAMENTATIONS 1:1-6

Jerusalem is empty and destroyed

LAMENTATIONS 3:19-26

Great is your faithfulness, O LORD.

God of love, have mercy *Makeever* **DH 10**

Great is thy faithfulness *Runyon* **WOV 771, REN 149**

Your everlasting love *Batstone* **MAR 85**

PSALM 137

Remember the day of Jerusalem, O LORD.

By the Babylonian rivers *Latvian* **WOV 656**

2 TIMOTHY 1:1-14

Guard the treasure entrusted to you: faith and love in Christ

All the power you need *Fragar* **HMS11 888**

Life in his hands *Hanson* **SCR 10**

My life is in you, Lord *Gardner* **HCW 128**

We walk by faith *Ylvisaker* **BC**

LUKE 17:5-10

Faith the size of a mustard seed

Come and grow *McLean* **CCJ, WIS 1**

Faith that's sure *Lord* **CGA 695**

Good soil *Hanson* **SCR 30, W&P 52, WOV 713**

Increase our faith *Haas* **G-4736**

Let the peace of God reign *Zschech* **HMS11 926**

Song of the mustard seed *Hopson* **G-2239**

ADDITIONAL SONGS FOR THE DAY/SEASON

Keep the faith *Makeever* **DH 98**

Your wonderful name *Haas* **G-5041**

Proper 23

Sunday between October 9 and 15 Inclusive

Year A

Three sets of meals cluster around the readings today: the meals of Jesus; the church's celebration of the holy supper; and the wedding feast of heaven. In each meal, the invitation is given to all who hunger for God's love: Come to the banquet. Come and feast on the bread of heaven; come and drink God's mercy; come and be strengthened for service to the needy. As Augustine once said to his congregation, Become the bread that you hold in your hand. Come to the holy supper and learn what it means to be a Christian.

ISAIAH 25:1-9
The feast of victory
- Now the feast and celebration *Haugen* **WOV 789**
- On the mountain top *Ylvisaker* **BC**
- This is the feast of victory *Hillert* **RSH 199**
- This is the feast of victory *Makeever* **DH 12**
- This is the feast of victory *Young* **W&P 142**

PSALM 23
You spread a table before me and my cup is running over.
See Lent 4.

EXODUS 32:1-14
The Israelites forge a golden calf
- Standing on the Lord's side *Ylvisaker* **BC**

PSALM 106:1-6, 19-23
Remember, O LORD, the favor you have for your people.
- Be magnified *DeShazo* **HCW 20**

PHILIPPIANS 4:1-9
Rejoice in the Lord always
- Forever grateful *Altrogge* **HCW 44**
- Give thanks *Smith* **HCW 46, W&P 41, TFF 292**
- God is here *Moen/Overstreet* **HMS12 995**
- Let the peace of God reign *Zschech* **HMS11 926**
- Teach me how to pray *Hanson/Murakami* **SCR 25**

MATTHEW 22:1-14
The parable of the unwelcome guest at the wedding feast
- All around your throne *DeShazo/Kerr* **HMS10 808**
- Celebrate love *Hanson* **SCR 16**
- I will celebrate *Baloche* **MAR 43**
- Meet us *Rethmeier* **VIN8 136**
- Reason to celebrate *Chumchal* **VIN8 165**
- We come to your feast *Joncas* **GC 850**

ADDITIONAL SONGS FOR THE DAY/SEASON
- Come to the feast *Haugen* **GC 503**
- Praise, rejoice and sing *Pote* **CGA 392**
- The trumpets sound, the angels sing *Kendrick* **W&P 139**
- We come to the hungry feast *Makeever* **WOV 766, DH 84**

Year B

Jesus knows our weaknesses, especially the weakness of clinging to those things that could be given away or shared for the good of others. In the gospel reading, Jesus states that it will be difficult for those who pursue wealth to enter the reign of God. Living in a culture that seems driven by the pursuit of money and comfort, we may find these words difficult to hear. Yet Jesus announces that nothing is impossible with God who is our life, our treasure, and our salvation.

AMOS 5:6-7, 10-15
Turn from injustice to the poor, that you may live
- God of love, have mercy *Makeever* **DH 10**
- Let justice roll like a river *Haugen* **GC 716**

PSALM 90:12-17
So teach us to number our days that we may apply our hearts to wisdom.
- Jesus, help me see *Ylvisaker* **BC**
- Restless is the heart *Farrell* **G&P 483**
- Shelter *Lisicky* **G-4426**
- Turn my heart *DeShazo* **HCW 179**

JOB 23:1-9, 16-17

The Almighty hidden from Job's searching

Amen *Fitts* **HMS12 982**

King of life *Sadler* **HMS12 1014**

PSALM 22:1-15

My God, my God, why have you forsaken me?

Praises resound *Ylvisaker/Casabolt* **BC**

We will glorify *Paris* **HCW 187, W&P 154**

You are the Lord of me *Sims* **SCR 76**

HEBREWS 4:12-16

Approach the throne of grace with boldness

A taste of the joys of heaven *Ylvisaker* **BC**

First love *Baloche/Sadler* **HMS13 1062**

God with us *Kendrick* **HMS5 392**

Only by grace *Gustafson* **HCW 140, W&P 112**

MARK 10:17-31

Teaching on wealth and reward

Give it away *Makeever* **DH 96**

More precious than silver *DeShazo* **HCW 122**

No greater love *Walker* **MAR 54**

Nothing is as wonderful *Underwood* **VIN8 150**

Offering *McLean* **WIS 31**

Seek first the kingdom *Haas* **G-3955**

We are an offering *Liles* **HCW 182, W&P 146**

We bring the sacrifice of praise *Dearman* **W&P 150**

ADDITIONAL SONGS FOR THE DAY/SEASON

Blessed be Yahweh *Young* **AFP 11-10669**

The church song *Beech* **W&P 135**

Year C

Kyrie, eleison," the church cries: "Lord, have mercy." In Jesus, God does have mercy—mercy upon lepers who are outcasts, mercy on apostles who are in chains. God has mercy upon foreigners, breaking through boundaries of nationality and political alienation. God has mercy on *us*.

2 KINGS 5:1-3, 7-15C

Naaman washes in the Jordan and is cleansed

Come to the river of life *Moen/Cloninger* **HMS10 818**

I've just come from the fountain *Spiritual* **WOV 696, GC 802**

The river is here *Park* **VIN6 232**

Wade in the water *Spiritual* **TFF 114**

PSALM 111

I will give thanks to the L*ORD* *with my whole heart.*

Blessed be the name *Park* **VIN7 48**

Majesty *Hayford* **W&P 94**

The name of the Lord *Utterback* **MAR 245**

JEREMIAH 29:1, 4-7

Israel builds houses and plants gardens in Babylon

May we have peace *Ylvisaker* **BC**

PSALM 66:1-12

God holds our souls in life.

Ancient of days *Sadler/Harvill* **HCW 11**

Awesome God *Mullins* **W&P 13**

Come, all you people *South African* **WOV 717, TFF 138**

Let all the world sing praises *Falson* **MAR 216**

Sing unto the Lord *Makeever* **DH 47**

2 TIMOTHY 2:8-15

If we die with Christ, we will live with Christ

Broken in love *Hanson* **SCR 177, W&P 24**

I don't belong to me *Hanson* **SCR 152**

Song of fire and water *Haugen* **GC 154**

LUKE 17:11-19

One leper made clean by Jesus gives thanks to God

Come touch *Hanson* **SCR 180**

Give thanks to God on high *Chepponis* **GC 792**

Glory and praise to our God *Schutte* **W&P 43, G&P 671, GC 522**

Heal me, O Lord *Moen* **HMS10 828**

Healing word *McCoy* **VIN6 82**

Jesus, Jesus *Bullock* **HMS11 923**

Let your healing love *Butler* **VIN6 144**

Mercy *DeShazo/Sadler* **HMS14**

Now we remain *Haas* **W&P 106**

When I think of the goodness of Jesus *Traditional* **TFF 269**

ADDITIONAL SONGS FOR THE DAY/SEASON

Awake, O sleeper *Haugen* **GC 803**

Kyrie eleison *Olson* **W&P 81**

Proper 24

Sunday between October 16 and 22 Inclusive

Year A

In today's gospel reading, Jesus' words are more than a clever response to a trap set by his opponents. Give the tax that is due to the ruler, he says, but offer to God what is God's: the very life given you by the Creator. These words of Jesus remind us that no earthly authority can claim the church's ultimate allegiance to God; its life comes from God so that it might serve the world in the labor of love.

ISAIAH 45:1-7
An earthly ruler as the instrument of God's will
- Turn to me *Foley* **G&P 342**
- We bow down *Paris* **HCW 183, W&P 149**

PSALM 96:1-9 [10-13]
Ascribe to the LORD honor and power.
- Come let us sing *Lindh* **CGA 478**
- Give the Lord glory and honor *Haas* **GC 93**
- Great is the Lord *Smith/Smith* **W&P 53**
- He is Lord *Smith* **HMS12 998**
- Rise up and praise him *Baloche/Sadler* **HMS13 1098**
- Sing unto the Lord *Makeever* **DH 47**
- We declare your name *Baloche/Baloche* **HMS10 874**

EXODUS 33:12-23
The glory of God revealed to Moses
- Arise, oh Lord *Carpenter* **VIN6 16**
- Make your presence known *Barbour* **MAR 221**

PSALM 99
Proclaim the greatness of the LORD our God.
- He is exalted *Paris* **HCW 57, W&P 55**
- He is Lord *Smith* **HMS12 998**
- King of life *Sadler* **HMS12 1014**
- Mighty is our God *Walker* **HCW 118**
- You are holy *Brown* **HMS10 884**

THESSALONIANS 1:1-10
Thanksgiving for the church at Thessalonica
- For all people Christ was born *Makeever* **DH 52**
- God sent his Son *Gaither/Gaither* **TFF 93**
- Thanksgiving to the living God *Makeever* **DH 3**
- This is the gospel of Christ *Brown* **HMS10 870**

MATTHEW 22:15-22
A teaching on giving to the emperor and to God
- For he alone is worthy *Traditional* **TFF 284**
- Glory and praise to our God *Schutte* **W&P 43, G&P 671, GC 522**
- Only you *Baloche/Kerr* **HMS13 1092**
- You alone *Hanson/Murakami* **SCR 36**
- You only *McCoy* **VIN8 242**
- You, Lord *Hanson* **SCR 42, W&P 162**

ADDITIONAL SONGS FOR THE DAY/SEASON
- Come let us sing out our praise *Tate* **VO 17**
- Give thanks to God on high *Chepponis* **GC 792**
- I'll give thanks to God above *Ylvisaker* **BC**

Year B

Baptism into Christ is our entrance into the Lord's mission. This calling is made abundantly clear at the end of the liturgy when the assembly is charged to go in peace and serve the Lord. Such service cannot avoid the cup of suffering. Indeed, the good news is that, in Christ, God has embraced us in love where we are most weak and frail. How shall we do this for each other and for those who are in need?

ISAIAH 53:4-12
The suffering servant
- All we like sheep *Moen* **HCW 7**
- Amazing love *Kendrick* **CW10, W&P 8**
- Behold the lamb of God *Willet* **GC 823**
- Make me a servant *Willard* **REN, W&P 96**

PSALM 91:9-16
You have made the LORD your refuge, and the Most High your habitation.
- God my refuge *Montemayer* **HCW 50**
- On eagle's wings *Joncas* **WOV 779, W&P 110, RS 740, G&P 598, GC 611**
- Shelter *Lisicky* **G-4426**

JOB 38:1-7 [34-41]
Challenge to Job from God, the creator
Ancient of days *Sadler/Harvill* **HCW 11**
God the sculptor of the mountains *Thornburg/Husberg* **TFF 222**
I was there to hear your borning cry *Ylvisaker* **BC, W&P 69, WOV 770**

PSALM 104:1-9, 24, 35C
O LORD, how manifold are your works! In wisdom you have made them all.
Come to the fount of creation *Ylvisaker* **BC**
Mighty is our God *Walker* **HCW 118**

HEBREWS 5:1-10
Through suffering Christ becomes the source of salvation
Broken hearts *Hanson/Murakami* **SCR 170**
For me *Hanson* **SCR 176**
I don't belong to me *Hanson* **SCR 152**
Leave your heart with me *Hanson* **SCR 150**

MARK 10:35-45
Warnings to ambitious disciples
Jesus lead on *Helming* **VIN8 114**
Turn my heart *DeShazo* **HCW 179**
We will drink the cup *Haas* **GC 709**

ADDITIONAL SONGS FOR THE DAY/SEASON
We are the hope *Tate* **VO 97**

Year C

The life of faith means that we might wrestle with God. Jesus commends to us the story of a widow who would not take "No" for an answer. And Paul commends to Timothy a life of persistence in proclaiming good news, even when a world may not be eager to hear it. We contend with God, but find our peace when our true identity is named by God in the heart of our being, telling us who we are.

GENESIS 32:22-31
Jacob's struggle with the angel: I'll not let go until you bless me
Blessed be the Lord *Daigle/Ducote* **G&P 442**
I'll bless the Lord for evermore **BC**
Make your presence known *Barbour* **MAR 221**

PSALM 121
My help comes from the LORD, the maker of heaven and earth.
God is ever wakeful *Haas* **G-4579**
Hebrew traveling psalm *Ylvisaker* **BC**
Our help comes from the Lord *Joncas* **GC 119**
The Lord will keep me safe & holy *Ylvisaker* **BC**

JEREMIAH 31:27-34
The LORD promises a new covenant
I want to know you *Evans* **HMS12 1008**
Write it on my heart *McLean* **WIS 41**
You are mine *Haas* **W&P 158**

PSALM 119:97-104
Your words are sweeter than honey to my mouth.
Lead me, guide me *Akers* **TFF 70**
Lead me, oh lead me *Smith* **HMS13 1085**
Where you lead me *DeShetler/Craig* **HMS13 1113**

2 TIMOTHY 3:14-4:5
In the presence of Christ the judge, proclaim the message
Amen *Fitts* **HMS12 982**
Open our lives to the Word *Makeever* **DH 8**
Thy word *Smith/Grant* **TFF 132, W&P 144**
Thy word *Webb* **W&P 143**
We are the hope *Tate* **VO 97**

LUKE 18:1-8
The widow begs for justice; God grants justice to those who cry to him
God of love, have mercy *Makeever* **DH 10**
Increase our faith *Haas* **G-4736**
Lord, listen to your children praying *Medema* **W&P 92**
Lord, listen to your children *Hanson* **SCR 23, W&P 91**
Teach me how to pray *Hanson/Murakami* **SCR 25**
We cry out for grace again *Kerr* **HMS12 1045**

ADDITIONAL SONGS FOR THE DAY/SEASON
The trumpet in the morning *Cooney* **G-4970**

Proper 25

Sunday between October 23 and 29 Inclusive

Year A

In the era of "sound bites" and headline news, Jesus' summary of the entire law and the prophets to just two commandments is no doubt quite appealing. But what commandments they are! Love God with all your heart, soul, and mind. And love your neighbor as yourself. These are easy commandments to speak, but they will take more than a lifetime for any of us to be able to put into practice. So we have gathered here this day to deepen our desire and our commitment to love God and to love our fellow human beings. May the words we hear and our communion in the body of Christ strengthen us to do those very things.

LEVITICUS 19:1-2, 15-18
Holiness revealed in acts of justice
- I am loved *Gaither/Gaither* **COK 80**
- Someone in need of your love *Makeever* **DH 94**
- We are the hope *Tate* **VO 97**

PSALM 1
Their delight is in the law of the LORD.
- Happy are they *Haas* **GC 18, PCY3**
- Happy are they *Schoenbachler* **STP2**
- I will never be *Bullock* **HMS11 920**
- In Christ, a new creation *Ylvisaker* **BC**
- Planted by the waters *Kline* **REN**

DEUTERONOMY 34:1-12
The death of Moses

PSALM 90:1-6, 13-17
Show your servants your works, and your splendor to their children.
- Ancient of days *Sadler/Harvill* **HCW 11**
- Jesus, help me see *Ylvisaker* **BC**
- Lord, you've been our dwelling place *Ylvisaker* **BC**
- Turn my heart *DeShazo* **HCW 179**

1 THESSALONIANS 2:1-8
The apostle's tender care for the Thessalonians
- Our heart *Chisum/Searcy* **HCW 143**

MATTHEW 22:34-46
Two great commandments: love for God and neighbor
- I am loved *Gaither/Gaither* **COK 80**
- I love you, Lord *Klein* **TFF 288, W&P 67**
- Jesu, Jesu *Ghana* **GC 409, WOV 765**
- Love you so much *Fragar* **HMS13 1088**
- With all my heart *Avery* **CC 11**
- With all your heart *Makeever* **DH 95**

ADDITIONAL SONGS FOR THE DAY/SEASON
- Change my heart, O God *Espinosa* **MAR, CMH**
- Restless is the heart *Farrell* **G&P 483**

Year B

Bartimaeus, a blind beggar, beseeches Jesus with these words, "Son of David, have mercy on me." We too seek God's mercy on behalf of the world, the church, and all those in need. In the words of the ancient Kyrie, we pray, "Lord, have mercy." Gathered as God's people, we pray for a faith that will enable us to see the signs of God's merciful presence among us even as we become signs of healing in the world.

JEREMIAH 31:7-9
The LORD *gathers the remnant of Israel*
- Mourning into dancing *Walker* **HCW 125, W&P 99**
- We declare your name *Baloche/Baloche* **HMS10 874**

PSALM 126
Those who sowed with tears will reap with songs of joy.
- God has done great things *Haugen* **GC 124**
- Mourning into dancing *Walker* **HCW 125, W&P 99**
- The Lord has done great things *Smith* **PS1**
- Trading my sorrows *Evans* **HMS14**

JOB 42:1-6, 10-17
Job's restoration
- Faithful One *Doerksen* **CMH2 60**
- I'm so glad Jesus lifted me *Spiritual* **TFF 191, WOV 673**
- We can be lifted up *Hanson* **SCR 105**

PSALM 34:1-8 [19-22]
Taste and see that the LORD is good.
- Come and taste *Hanson/Murakami* **SCR 186, W&P 30**
- I will bless you, O god *Makeever* **DH 34**
- I'll bless the Lord for evermore *Ylvisaker* **BC**
- Taste and see *Young* **BL**
- The trumpets sound, the angels sing *Kendrick* **W&P 139**

HEBREWS 7:23-28
Christ the merciful high priest
- Everlasting grace *Carpenter* **VIN6 58**
- For he alone is worthy *Traditional/Wade* **TFF 284**
- Lamb of God *Paris* **HCW 100**
- The fire of your love *Baloche/Kerr* **HMS12 1037**

MARK 10:46-52
Christ healing the blind man Bartimaeus
- First love *Baloche/Sadler* **HMS13 1062**
- I see you *Mullins* **CC 90**
- In the light *Poirier* **VO 48**
- Jesus, heal us *Haas* **GC 875**
- O Lord, open my eyes *Ghana* **TFF 134**
- Open our eyes, Lord *Cull* **MAR 59, W&P 113, REN**
- Open the eyes of my heart *Baloche* **HMS12 1027**
- Seek ye first *Lafferty* **W&P 122, WOV 783**

ADDITIONAL SONGS FOR THE DAY/SEASON
- Kyrie eleison *Olson* **W&P 81**
- Take, O, take me as I am *Bell* **G**
- There is a redeemer *Green* **REN 232**

Year C

Those who seem the farthest from God may be the closest to mercy. That is the theme of today's gospel, and it is echoed in the other readings. It is the dynamic that supports the dialogue in the first reading. We get close to God as we confess that we are in need of grace.

JEREMIAH 14:7-10, 19-22
Jerusalem will be defeated
- Age to age *Vogt* **OCP 10900**
- Here is my heart *Nystrom* **HMS13 1070**
- May we have peace *Ylvisaker* **BC**
- Out of the depths *Hay* **VO 74**
- The cry of the poor *Foley* **GC 48**

SIRACH 35:12-17
God is impartial in justice and hears the powerless

PSALM 84:1-7
Happy are the people whose strength is in you.
- As the deer *Nystrom* **MAR, W&P 9**
- Happy are they *Porter* **GC 77, G-3026**
- How lovely is your dwelling place *Goebel-Komala* **G-4406**
- How lovely is your dwelling place *Joncas* **STP1**
- My heart yearns for thee *Baroni* **HMS12 1022**

JOEL 2:23-32
The LORD promises to restore Israel
- In the last days *Makeever* **DH 70**
- Let it rain *Park* **VIN8 126**
- Rain down on us *Butler/Butler/Butler* **VIN8 160**
- Singing through the water *Hanson/Murakami* **SCR 132**

PSALM 65
Your paths overflow with plenty.
- The river is here *Park* **CMH 58, VIN6 232**

2 TIMOTHY 4:6-8, 16-18
The good fight of faith
- I have kept the faith *Baloche* **HMS13 1076**
- Keep the faith *Makeever* **DH 98**
- Let it be said of us *Fry* **MAR 217**
- The trumpet in the morning *Cooney* **G-4970**

LUKE 18:9-14
A Pharisee and tax collector pray together
- God of love, have mercy *Makeever* **DH 10**
- Increase our faith *Haas* **G-4736**
- Lord we pray *Gustafson* **HMS8 668**
- Lord, listen to your children *Hanson* **SCR 23, W&P 91**
- Mercy *DeShazo/Sadler* **HMS14**
- O Lord to you *Sadler* **HMS11 937**
- Teach me how to pray *Hanson/Murakami* **SCR 25**
- We will draw near *Nystrom/Harris* **HMS11 966**

ADDITIONAL SONGS FOR THE DAY/SEASON
- Guide my feet *Spiritual* **TFF 153**
- Increase our faith *Haas* **G-4736**
- Lord, I lift your name on high *Founds* **MAR**
- Praise to you, O God of mercy *Haugen* **W&P 119, WOV 790**

Proper 26

Sunday between October 30 and November 5 Inclusive

Year A

As we come to the final month of a church year, the scripture readings become more urgent, encouraging us to think about things of ultimate importance. Today's readings strongly urge us to obey God's teachings and to act fairly and charitably in our dealings with others.

MICAH 3:5-12
Judgment upon corrupt rulers

Give us your vision	*Hanson/Murakami*	**SCR 85**
Jesus, help me see	*Ylvisaker*	**BC**

PSALM 43
Send out your light and truth that they may lead me.

As a doe	*Fitzgerald*	**G-2032**
As the deer longs	*Hurd*	**G&P 207**
Be my home	*Hanson/Murakami*	**SCR 45, W&P 16**
Just like a deer	*Joncas*	**G&P 205**
Like a deer that longs	*Bauman*	**RS 77**
Like a deer that longs	*Haugen*	**G-3261**
O God, for you I long	*Farrell*	**G&P 206**
Song of longing	*Cooney*	**GC 51**
Why so downcast?	*Berrios/Brooks*	**HCW 191**

JOSHUA 3:7-17
Israel crosses the Jordan into the land of promise

Go down, Moses	*Spiritual*	**TFF 87, WOV 670**
Jesus lead on	*Helming*	**VIN8 114**
Lead me, guide me	*Akers*	**TFF 70**
Where you lead me	*DeShetler/Craig*	**HMS13 1113**

PSALM 107:1-7, 33-37
Give thanks to the LORD, all those whom the LORD has redeemed.

For the Lord is good	*DeShazo/Sadler*	**HMS13 1065**
Forever grateful	*Altrogge*	**HCW 44**
Thank you, Lord	*Park*	**VIN8 202**

1 THESSALONIANS 2:9-13
The apostle's teaching accepted as God's word

Open our lives to the word	*Makeever*	**DH 8**
This kingdom	*Bullock*	**HMS11 962**

MATTHEW 23:1-12
All who humble themselves will be exalted

Faithful Father	*Doerksen*	**VIN7 72**
Father, I adore you	*Coelho*	**W&P 37**
Heavenly Father	*Park*	**VIN7 92**
I will bow down and worship	*Chambers/Brewster*	**HMS13 1081**
We shall behold him	*Rambo*	**MAR**

ADDITIONAL SONGS FOR THE DAY/SEASON

Come let us sing out our praise	*Tate*	**VO 17**
Gather us in	*Haugen*	**WOV 718, G-2651**
Glory and praise to our God	*Schutte*	**W&P 43, G&P 671, GC 522**
We are an offering	*Liles*	**W&P 146, MAR**

Year B

In today's gospel Jesus speaks of the two great commandments—love of God, and love of neighbor—yet how difficult it is to observe them diligently. A well-known prayer of confession includes these words: "We have not loved you with our whole heart; we have not loved our neighbors as ourselves." As we hear the word and share the meal we receive the forgiveness, strength, and courage to offer our lives in God's service, loving God through our gracious acts of mercy and kindness.

DEUTERONOMY 6:1-9
The blessing of keeping the words of God

Open our lives to the Word	*Makeever*	**DH 8**
With all my heart	*Avery*	**CC 11**

PSALM 119:1-8
Happy are they who seek the LORD with all their hearts.

First love	*Baloche/Sadler*	**HMS13 1062**
Happy are those who follow	*Cooney*	**GC 116**
Hear me, O God	*Tate*	**VO 35**

Seek ye first *Lafferty* **W&P 122, WOV 783**
Step by step *Beaker* **HMS13 1103, W&P 132**

RUTH 1:1-8
Ruth's dedication to her mother-in-law
For all the faithful women *Potter* **TFF 219, WOV 692**
Women of faith *Harvill/Arterburn* **HMS13 117**

PSALM 146
The LORD *lifts up those who are bowed down.*
He shall reign *Chopinsky* **HMS12 999**
Lord I lift your name on high *Founds* **W&P 90**
Sing unto the Lord *Makeever* **DH 47**

HEBREWS 9:11-14
Redeemed through the blood of Christ
O, mighty cross *Baroni/Chisum* **HCW 136**
Poured out and broken *Hanson/Murakami* **SCR 184**
Purify my heart *Greco* **HCW 148**
Refiner's fire *Doerksen* **CMH 10**

MARK 12:28-34
Two great commandments: loving God and neighbor
Faith, hope and love *Haas* **GC 624**
I am loved *Gaither/Gaither* **COK 80**
I love you, Lord *Klein* **W&P 67**
Love you so much *Fragar* **HMS13 1088**
My life is in you, Lord *Gardner* **HCW 128**
With all my heart *Avery* **CC 11**

ADDITIONAL SONGS FOR THE DAY/SEASON
Broken for me *Lunt* **W&P 23**
Jesu, Jesu *Ghana* **WOV 765, GC 409**
Nothing can come between us *Young* **BL, AFP 11-10848**

Year C

In today's gospel, Jesus invites himself to the home of a known sinner. This day God invites us into grace, even though we do not deserve it. "Today salvation has come to this house." Therefore, we always "enter God's courts with praise."

ISAIAH 1:10-18
Learn to do good, seek justice, and rescue the oppressed
Let justice roll like a river *Haugen* **W&P 85**

PSALM 32:1-7
All the faithful will make their prayers to you in time of trouble.
I turn to you *Cooney* **GC 44**
Shout to God, O faithful people *Ylvisaker* **BC**
You are my hiding place *Ledner* **MAR 167, W&P 160**

HABAKKUK 1:1-4, 2:1-4
The righteous live by their faith
My heart yearns for thee *Baroni* **HMS12 1022**

PSALM 119:137-144
Grant me understanding, that I may live.
Step by step *Beaker* **HMS13 1103, W&P 132**

2 THESSALONIANS 1:1-4, 11-12
Faith and love amid persecution and adversity
Firm foundation *Gordon/Harvill* **HCW 42**

LUKE 19:1-10
Zacchaeus climbs into a tree to see Jesus
Mercy *DeShazo/Sadler* **HMS14**
Someone in need of your love *Makeever* **DH 94**
The people on your heart *DeShazo/Sadler* **HMS10 869**

ADDITIONAL SONGS FOR THE DAY/SEASON
Come let us reason *Medema* **REN**
Come let us sing out our praise *Tate* **VO 17**
For by grace *Nicholas* **W&P 38**

Proper 27

Sunday between November 6 and 12 Inclusive

Year A

Why does the bridegroom come so late to the wedding celebration? Why, asked the early Christians, does Christ seemingly delay his promised return? And we, who live in an unjust and violent world may ask, Where is the Lord when we need him? We do not know the hour of his final coming. But we do know that Christ has claimed us in holy baptism as his servants in this world. We have the witness of the word of God to enlighten our path in life. We are strengthened in holy communion as heralds of the coming reign of God's justice and peace. Between his first advent and his final coming, the church is called to serve the Lord Jesus in faith, hope, and love.

AMOS 5:18-24
Let justice roll down like waters
- I will never be *Bullock* **HMS11 920**
- It won't be long *Makeever* **DH 89**
- Let justice roll like a river *Haugen* **W&P 85, GC 716**

WISDOM OF SOLOMON 6:12-16
Wisdom makes herself known

PSALM 70
You are my helper and deliverer; O Lord, do not tarry.

WISDOM OF SOLOMON 6:17-20
The beginning of wisdom is the most sincere desire for instruction.
- Be magnified *DeShazo* **HCW 20**

JOSHUA 24:1-3A, 14-25
Joshua calls Israel to serve the Lord
- Come, let us worship God *Makeever* **DH 2**
- Jehovah *Springer* **VIN6 124**
- Shout to God, O faithful people *Ylvisaker* **BC**

PSALM 78:1-7
We will recount to generations to come the power of the LORD.
- Almighty *Watson* **HMS10 810, HCW 8**

1 THESSALONIANS 4:13-18
The promise of the resurrection
- Because we believe *Gordon/Harvill* **HMS12 985**
- The trumpets sound, the angels sing *Kendrick* **W&P 139**

MATTHEW 25:1-13
The story of the wise and foolish bridesmaids
- All through the night *Heber/Traditional* **BC**
- I'll be waitin' *Ylvisaker* **BC**
- My heart yearns for thee *Baroni* **HMS12 1022**
- The trumpet in the morning *Cooney* **G-4970**
- When the Lord in glory comes *Moore* **GC 765**

ADDITIONAL SONGS FOR THE DAY/SEASON
- Lift up your heads *Kendrick* **W&P 88**
- We are called *Haas* **W&P 147**

Year B

All that we have—our lives, families, possessions, labor, and talents—comes from God and belongs to God. From the Christian perspective, we are not owners but stewards of all that the Creator has given us. And all that we have is given to us for the good of others. The divine economy works with equity for all, a hand always open to the poor, the outcast, and the forgotten ones. God's bounty gives us the grace to hold nothing back in serving God.

1 KINGS 17:8-16
God feeds Elijah and the widow at Zarephath
- God is so good *Anonymous* **COK 75, TFF 275**
- Thank you for the gift *Hanson* **SCR 144**

PSALM 146
The LORD lifts up those who are bowed down.
- As long as I live *Haas* **G-4681**
- Awesome God *Mullins* **W&P 13, MAR**
- He shall reign *Chopinsky* **HMS12 999**
- I will praise the Lord *Joncas* **G-3434**
- Lord, I lift your name on high *Founds* **W&P 90**
- Sing unto the Lord *Makeever* **DH 47**

RUTH 3:1-5, 4:13-17
Ruth wins the favor of Boaz
Women of faith *Harvill/Arterburn* **HMS13 117**

PSALM 127
Children are a heritage from the LORD.
You're a child of God *Ylvisaker* **BC**

HEBREWS 9:24-28
The once for all sacrifice of Christ
At the name of Jesus *Bolduc* **VO 5**
For the life of the world *Haas* **GC 801**
I'll belong to you *Hanson* **SCR 126**
Once and for all time *Hanson/Murakami* **SCR 200**
One *Hanson/Murakami* **SCR 160**
When the Lord comes *Flowers* **VIN6 262**

MARK 12:38-44
A widow's generosity reveals the hypocrisy of the scribes
More precious than silver *DeShazo* **HCW 122**
Offering *McLean* **WIS 31**
Sanctuary *Thompson/Scruggs* **HCW 154**
Take, O, take me as I am *Bell* **G**
We are an offering *Liles* **HCW 182, W&P 146**
We bring the sacrifice of praise *Dearman* **MAR**

ADDITIONAL SONGS FOR THE DAY/SEASON
All that we have *Ault* **GC 601, W&P 5**
Make me a servant *Willard* **W&P 96**
My Lord will come again *Haas* **G-3654**

Year C

In these final weeks of the church year, the church cries out, "Come, Lord Jesus!" We are always awaiting God's coming, and God does not disappoint us, making the divine presence known in water, bread, wine, and in this very human community of faith.

JOB 19:23-27A
I know that my Redeemer lives and I shall see God
I know that my redeemer lives *Haas* **GC 854**
King of life *Sadler* **HMS12 1014**
New life again and again *Hanson/Murakami* **SCR 102**
Open the eyes of my heart *Baloche* **HMS12 1027**
There is a Redeemer *Green* **W&P 140, REN 232**
We can be lifted up *Hanson* **SCR 105**

PSALM 17:1-9
Keep me as the apple of your eye; hide me under the shadow of your wings.
Blessed be the name *Park* **VIN7 48**
Lord, when your glory appears *Stewart* **GC 25**
Psalm 17 *Marshall* **CGA 18**

HAGGAI 1:15B-2:9
The LORD promises to restore Judah to prosperity
Our heart *Chisum/Searcy* **HMS13 1094, HCW 143**

PSALM 145:1-5, 17-21
Great is the LORD and greatly to be praised.
Glorious God *Baroni/Fitts/Smith* **HMS10 823**
Glorious *Daniels* **VIN7 82**
Great is the Lord *Smith/Smith* **W&P 53**

PSALM 98
In righteousness shall the LORD judge the world.
God has done marvelous things *Brokering/Haas* **W&P 51**
I will sing, I will sing *Dyer* **W&P 73, GC**
Shout to the Lord *Zschech* **HMS10 862, W&P 124**

2 THESSALONIANS 2:1-5, 13-17
The coming of the Lord Jesus
Soon and very soon *Crouch* **W&P 128, WOV 744**
Stand in the congregation *Batstone* **W&P 131**
The trumpet in the morning *Cooney* **G-4970**
When the Lord comes *Flowers* **VIN6 262**

LUKE 20:27-38
Jesus speaks of the resurrection; the God of the living
I know that my redeemer lives *Haas* **GC 854**
My life is in you, Lord *Gardner* **HCW 128**
New life again and again *Hanson/Murakami* **SCR 102**
Thanksgiving to the living God *Makeever* **DH 3**
We can be lifted up *Hanson* **SCR 105**

ADDITIONAL SONGS FOR THE DAY/SEASON
Hide me in your holiness *Ragsdale* **MAR**
Song of the angels *Dufford* **G&P**
The trumpet in the morning *Cooney* **G-4970**

Proper 28

Sunday between November 13 and 19 Inclusive

Year A

In a world marked by much suspicion and back-biting, those who offer encouragement, trust, and hope are like an oasis of green-growing life. In a world wounded by rugged individualism, cutthroat competition, and much greed, the Holy Spirit blesses each Christian with the ability to use one's gifts for the greater and common good, to build up the body of Christ, and to serve those who suffer injustice. The gospel reading for this day encourages us to use our God-given talents wisely while we still have time to do so. We do not know the hour of the Lord's final coming among us. But we do know that we have been formed into a body of servants who live according to the light of faith, nourished by word and meal, eager to share the riches of God's love with all in need.

ZEPHANIAH 1:7, 12-18
The day of the LORD
The day is near *Conry* **GC 768**

PSALM 90:1-8 [9-11] 12
So teach us to number our days, that we may apply our hearts to wisdom.
Jesus, help me see *Ylvisaker* **BC**
Lord, you've been our dwelling place *Ylvisaker* **BC**
Restless is the heart *Farrell* **G&P 483, STP2**
Turn my heart *DeShazo* **HCW 179**

JUDGES 4:1-7
The judgeship of Deborah
Women of faith *Harvill/Arterburn* **HMS13 117**

PSALM 123
Our eyes look to you, O God, until you show us your mercy.
God of love, have mercy *Makeever* **DH 10**
In the morning *Houge* **W&P 75**
Mercy *DeShazo/Sadler* **HMS14**

1 THESSALONIANS 5:1-11
Be alert for the day of the Lord
As the deer *Nystrom* **W&P 9, HMS11 892**
I'll be waitin' *Ylvisaker* **BC**
My heart yearns for thee *Baroni* **HMS12 1022**
Stand firm *Cameroon/Glover* **G-4593**

MATTHEW 25:14-30
The story of the slaves entrusted with talents
Come and grow *McLean* **CCJ**
Go and do *Hanson* **SCR 123**
Good soil *Hanson* **W&P 52, WOV 713**
The gift of giving *Ylvisaker* **BC**

ADDITIONAL SONGS FOR THE DAY/SEASON
All that is hidden *Farrell* **OCP 7161**
Go forth in his name *Kendrick* **REN 290**
Praise, praise, praise the Lord *Cameroon* **W&P 116**

Year B

During November the scripture readings lead the worshiping assembly to visions of the last day, to a reflection on the resurrection of the body and life everlasting. Some religious people see only panic and doom in the future. They dwell in the land of fear. The conclusion to the Lord's Prayer offers another view: the kingdom, the power, and the glory are yours, now and forever. It is a bold confession of faith in God, who is our refuge and our strength. Such a hope, according to Hebrews, leads us to encourage one another in love and good deeds.

DANIEL 12:1-3
The deliverance of God's people at the end
- Eternity *Doerksen* **CMH 28**
- I'll belong to you *Hanson* **SCR 126**
- The day is near *Conry* **GC 768**

PSALM 16
My heart is glad and my spirit rejoices; my body shall rest in hope.
- Centre of my life *Inwood* **PS2**
- Forever my friend *Carpenter* **CMH2 51**
- Harbor of my heart *Warner* **VO 31**
- I love to be in your presence *Baloche/Kerr* **HCW 75**
- Keep me safe, O God *Foley* **GC 23, RS 35**
- Show me the path *Haas* **G-4579**
- The Lord is my portion *Ylvisaker* **BC**
- You will show me the path of life *Haugen* **GC 24, RS 36**

1 SAMUEL 1:4-20
Hannah's prayers for a child answered
- For all the faithful women *Potter* **TFF 219, WOV 692**
- Forever grateful *Altrogge* **HCW 44**
- Thank you, Lord *Park* **VIN8 202**

1 SAMUEL 2:1-10
My heart exults in the LORD; my strength is exalted in my God.
- Lord most high *Harris/Sadler* **HMS11 930**
- Rock of ages *Baloche* **HMS13 1099**
- You are holy *Brown* **HMS10 884**

HEBREWS 10:11-14 [15-18] 19-25
The way to God opened through Christ's death
- Amazing love *Kendrick* **W&P 8, HCW 10**
- Our hope is alive *Ylvisaker* **BC**
- Stir up the love *Ylvisaker* **BC**
- The cloud's veil *Lawton* **G-4664**
- We will draw near *Nystrom/Harris* **HMS11 966**
- We've come to worship you *Kerr* **HMS10 878**
- You are holy *Brown* **HMS10 884**

MARK 13:1-8
The end and the coming of the Son
- For he alone is worthy *Traditional/Wade* **TFF 284**
- Only you *Baloche/Kerr* **HMS13 1092**
- When the Lord comes *Flowers* **VIN6 262**
- When the Lord in glory comes *Moore* **GC 765**
- You only *McCoy* **VIN8 242**

ADDITIONAL SONGS FOR THE DAY/SEASON
- All that is hidden *Farrell* **OCP 7161**
- Come let us sing out our praise *Tate* **VO 17**
- We bow down *Paris* **REN 38**

Year C

Signs of the end time fill today's gospel. Christ will come again "to judge the living and the dead," we confess in the creed. How, then, shall we live our lives, knowing that everything around us will one day pass away? We can live with hope if we know that history is heading toward the God who loves us. But it also means that we live in the present moment ready for action, making the most of the time given to us as a gift.

MALACHI 4:1-2A

A day of blistering heat for the arrogant; a day of healing sun for the righteous

- Say the name *McLean* **WIS 33**
- Shine, Jesus, shine *Kendrick* **HCW 155, WOV 651, W&P 123**
- The day is near *Conry* **GC 768**

PSALM 98

In righteousness shall the LORD *judge the world.*

- All the ends of the earth *Haugen/Haas* **PCY**
- Shout to the Lord *Zschech* **HMS10 862, W&P 124**
- The Lord comes to the earth *Haas/Kodner* **GC 95**

ISAIAH 65:17-25

God promises a new heaven and a new earth

- Heaven and earth *DeShazo/Harvill* **HMS10 829**

ISAIAH 12

In your midst is the Holy One of Israel.

- Lord, my strength *Krippaehne* **W&P 93**
- The first song of Isaiah *White* **REN 122**

2 THESSALONIANS 3:6-13

Do not be idle, but do what is right for the sake of Christ

- As you go on your way *Ylvisaker* **BC**
- Go and do *Hanson* **SCR 123**
- Into the life *McLean* **WIS 11**

LUKE 21:5-19

Jesus speaks of wars, endurance, betrayal, and suffering for his sake

- Firm foundation *Gordon/Harvill* **HCW 42**
- I have kept the faith *Baloche* **HMS13 1076**
- My heart will trust *Morgan* **HMS14**
- The trumpet in the morning *Cooney* **G-4970**
- When the Lord in glory comes *Moore* **GC 765**

ADDITIONAL SONGS FOR THE DAY/SEASON

- Beauty for brokenness *Kendrick* **W&P 17**
- Between the times *Makeever* **DH 103**
- Go *Patillo* **CG 454**
- Let justice roll like a river *Haugen* **W&P 85, GC 716**

Christ the King

Proper 29

Last Sunday after Pentecost

Sunday between November 20 and 26 Inclusive

Year A

The Lord Jesus was not wealthy or famous. He did not promise his followers that they would possess riches, power, or prestige. He was named a king only in his death. He reigned from the cross, leaving his disciples the treasure of his body and blood. We gather at the table of Christ, our merciful and loving ruler. We wear the crown of baptism and his royal sign, the holy cross. We leave here strengthened to serve those who are hungry, thirsty, strangers, naked, sick, and imprisoned. We look for the day when all earth's people will see him coming with the scepter of peace and the crown of justice.

EZEKIEL 34:11-16, 20-24
God will shepherd Israel

- All we like sheep *Moen* **HCW 7**
- In the arms of the shepherd *Weckler* **VO 47**
- Lead me, oh lead me *Smith* **HMS13 1085**
- Like a shepherd *Moen/Simpson* **HCW 112**
- Shepherd me, O God *Haugen* **G-3107**
- You are my shepherd *Haas* **G-4994**

PSALM 95:1-7A
We are the people of God's pasture and the sheep of God's hand.

- I will come and bow down *Nystrom* **HCW 87**
- Sing a song to the Lord *Lawton* **G-4661**
- We are God's people *Haas* **GC 97, RS 138**
- We bow down *Paris* **HCW 183, W&P 149**

EZEKIEL 34:11-16, 20-24
God will shepherd Israel

- All we like sheep *Moen* **HCW 7**
- Lead me, oh lead me *Smith* **HMS13 1085**
- Like a shepherd *Moen/Simpson* **HCW 112**

PSALM 100
We are God's people and the sheep of God's pasture.

- For the Lord is good *DeShazo/Sadler* **HMS13 1065**
- God is good (All the time) *Chapman* **MAR 186**
- He has made me glad *Brethorst* **TFF 291, COK 3**
- Thanksgiving to the living God *Makeever* **DH 3**
- You have been good *Paris* **HCW 198**

EPHESIANS 1:15-23
The reign of Christ

- He is exalted *Paris* **REN 238**
- I do believe *Ylvisaker* **BC**
- Open our eyes, Lord *Cull* **MAR 59, W&P 113**
- Open the eyes of my heart *Baloche* **HMS12 1027**
- The fullness of the Lord *Ylvisaker* **BC**

MATTHEW 25:31-46
The coming of the Son of Man; the separation of sheep and goats

- Eternity *Doerksen* **CMH 28**
- For he alone is worthy *Traditional/Wade* **TFF 284**
- God of the hungry *Soper* **G&P 560**
- I will be with you always *Hanson/Murakami* **SCR 118**
- I'll belong to you *Hanson* **SCR 126**
- My God reigns *Evans* **HMS12 1021**
- One is the body *Cooney* **GC 846**

ADDITIONAL SONGS FOR THE DAY/SEASON

- Come, worship the Lord *Talbot* **G&P 536, OCP 10331**
- Gathered as one *Tate/ Light* **VO 25**
- Majesty *Hayford* **W&P 94, REN 63**

Year B

We proclaim Christ our king as he goes to the throne of the cross. We acclaim him our ruler as he sheds his blood. We acknowledge him as our Lord as he gives himself to us in bread and cup. Christ is our king as he reigns from the tree, sharing our fears and experiencing our frailties. In the reign of God, the powerful one does not intimidate the weak, but cares for them. In the reign of God, the person of authority does not use others, but seeks them out and crowns them with mercy.

DANIEL 7:9-10, 13-14

The one coming with the clouds rules over all

- Ancient of days *Sadler/Harvill* **HCW 11**
- Heaven and earth *DeShazo/Harvill* **HMS10 829**
- King of kings *Batya/Conty* **W&P 80**
- King of life *Sadler* **HMS12 1014**
- The day is near *Conry* **GC 768**

PSALM 93

Ever since the world began, your throne has been established.

- Majesty *Hayford* **W&P 94**
- Mighty is our God *Walker* **HCW 118**
- The Lord is king *Guimont* **GC 87**

2 SAMUEL 23:1-7

The just ruler is like the light of morning

- Bright and morning star *Makeever* **DH 50**
- We see the Lord *Anonymous* **REN 274**

PSALM 132:1-12 [13-18]

Let your faithful people sing with joy.

- I will come and bow down *Nystrom* **HCW 87**
- Sanctuary *Thompson/Scruggs* **HCW 154**
- Shout to God, O faithful people *Ylvisaker* **BC**

REVELATION 1:4B-8

Glory to the one who made us a kingdom

- Be glorified *Funk* **HCW 19**
- Blessed be the Lord *Daigle/Ducote* **G&P 442**
- Glorious *Daniels* **VIN7 82**
- Glory be! *Ylvisaker* **BC**
- God of glory *Hanson* **SCR 89**
- To God be the glory *Crouch* **TFF 272**

JOHN 18:33-37

The kingdom of Christ

- Bring forth the kingdom *Haugen* **W&P 22, GC 658**
- He is exalted *Paris* **HCW 57, W&P 55**
- He is Lord *Smith* **HMS12 998**
- He shall reign *Chopinsky* **HMS12 999**
- The kingdom song *Evans* **HMS12 1040**
- This kingdom *Bullock* **HMS11 962**
- We are the hope *Tate* **VO 97**

ADDITIONAL SONGS FOR THE DAY/SEASON

- At the name of Jesus *Bolduc* **VO 5**
- At the name of Jesus *Webb* **W&P 12**
- For the life of the world *Haas* **GC 801**
- King of kings *Dauermann* **REN 268**
- Soon and very soon *Crouch* **WOV 74, GC 770, G&P 723**

Year C

Jesus shall reign where'er the sun does its successive journeys run," wrote the English hymnist Isaac Watts. On this last Sunday of the church year, we honor Christ who reigns as king from the cross. All space and all time belong to the one who offers paradise to those who live and die with him.

JEREMIAH 23:1-6

Coming of the shepherd and righteous Branch who will execute justice

- He is exalted *Paris* **HCW 57, W&P 55**
- Jesus is our king *Prebble* **REN 273**
- King of kings *Batya/Conty* **W&P 80**
- King of life *Sadler* **HMS12 1014**
- Like a shepherd *Moen/Simpson* **HCW 112**

PSALM 46

I will be exalted among the nations.

- Awesome God *Mullins* **W&P 13**
- Come to the river of life *Moen/Cloninger* **HMS10 818**
- God my refuge *Montemayer* **HCW 50**
- He is exalted *Paris* **VO 32**
- I will praise your name *Bolduc* **VO 44**
- The river is here *Park* **HMS11 958, VIN6 232**
- You are mine *Haas* **W&P 158**

LUKE 1:68-79

God has raised up for us a mighty savior.

- Arise, shine *Urspringer/Robinson* **HCW 14**
- Holy love, holy light *Batstone* **MAR 118**
- Light the darkness *McLean* **WIS 22**
- Shine, Jesus, shine *Kendrick* **WOV 651, HCW 155, W&P 123**

COLOSSIANS 1:11-20

Hymn to Christ, firstborn of all creation; peace through his blood

- At the name of Jesus *Bolduc* **VO 5**
- Come share the Spirit *Hanson/Murakami* **SCR 116**
- For the life of the world *Haas* **GC 801**
- Glorious God *Baroni/Fitts/Smith* **HMS10 823**
- I will never be *Bullock* **HMS11 920**
- It has always been you *Butler/Butler* **VIN6 120**

LUKE 23:33-43

Jesus is crucified between two thieves: you will be with me in Paradise

- Amazing love *Kendrick* **REN 272**
- Crux fidelis *Warner* **VO 19**
- I come to the cross *Somma/Batstone* **MAR 122**
- Jesus, remember me *Berthier* **WOV 740, W&P 78**
- O, mighty cross *Baroni/Chisum* **HCW 136**
- Strange King *Makeever* **DH 61**

ADDITIONAL SONGS FOR THE DAY/SEASON

- Blessed be the Lord *Daigle/Ducote* **G&P 442**
- Church of God *Denton* **GC 664, G&P 571, RS 783**
- Gathered as one *Tate/ Light* **VO 25**
- The King of glory *Israeli* **REN 267**
- We shall not be silent *Conry* **G&P 559**

Songs for the Church Year

Special Days

New Year's Day

January 1

Years A, B, C

God is continually making all things new—a truth we long to grasp again as the calendar's cycle moves from one year into another. A new year of grace stretches before us, providing opportunities for new beginnings. We need not wait for the calendar, however, to experience the new thing God has done for us in Christ. In the word, in the bath, in the holy meal, we meet the one in whom is our beginning, our ending, and our beginning again every day of our lives.

ECCLESIASTES 3:1-13
For everything there is a season
I see you *Mullins* **CC 90**
The steadfast love of the Lord *McNeill* **REN 23**

PSALM 8
How exalted is your name in all the world.
Come and see *LeBlanc* **W&P 29**
How majestic is your name *Smith* **W&P 66**
Who are we *Makeever* **DH 33**
Your name is praised *Geary* **PS3**

REVELATION 21:1-6A
A new heaven and a new earth
Come to the fount of creation *Ylvisaker* **BC**
Heaven and earth *DeShazo/Harvill* **HMS10 829**
Jehovah *Springer* **VIN6 124**
Mourning into dancing *Walker* **W&P 99, HCW 125**
Soon and very soon *Crouch* **WOV 744, W&P 128, TFF 38**

MATTHEW 25:31-46
The Son of Man will separate the sheep and the goats
Eternity *Doerksen* **CMH 28**
For he alone is worthy *Traditional/Wade* **TFF 284**
I will be with you always *Hanson/Murakami* **SCR 118**
I'll belong to you *Hanson* **SCR 126**
Make me a servant *Willard* **W&P 96**
My God reigns *Evans* **HMS12 1021**
Parable *Ridge* **G&P 481**
We are his hands *Gersmehl* **COK 85**

ADDITIONAL SONGS FOR THE DAY/SEASON
Great is the Lord *Smith* **W&P 53, REN 22**
It has always been you *Butler/Butler* **VIN6 120**
Once and for all time *Hanson/Murakami* **SCR 200**
You are God: Te deum *Haugen* **G-5100**

Presentation of the Lord

February 2

Years A, B, C

Forty days after the birth of Christ the church celebrates his presentation in the temple by his parents. Two aged saints, Anna and Simeon, recognize him as the promised messiah. Simeon speaks the words of the beloved Nunc dimittis in which he calls Jesus a "light for the nations." On this festival in the midst of the Epiphany season, we are reminded again of our hope in Christ, the Light of the world.

MALACHI 3:1-4

My messenger is a refiner and purifier

- Purify my heart *Greco* **CW 148**
- Refiner's fire *Doerksen* **CMH 10**
- Streams of living water *Consiglio* **OCP 10898**
- The fire of your love *Baloche/Kerr* **HMS12 1037**

PSALM 84

How dear to me is your dwelling, O LORD.

- I will always thank the Lord *Soper* **GP 202**
- I will bless the Lord *Gouin* **GC 46**
- Lord, you've been our dwelling place *Ylvisaker* **BC**
- My heart yearns for thee *Baroni* **HMS12 1022**
- The cry of the poor *Foley* **RS 69, GC 48, G&P 203**

PSALM 24:7-10

Lift up your heads, O gates, and the King of glory shall come in.

- King of kings *Batya/Conty* **W&P 80**
- King of life *Sadler* **HMS12 1014**
- Lift up your heads *Fry* **CEL 111**
- The King of glory *Ylvisaker/Traditional* **BC**
- Welcome the King *Kendrick* **HMS12 1048**

HEBREWS 2:14-18

Jesus shares human flesh and sufferings

- God with us *Kendrick* **HMS5 392**

LUKE 2:22-40

The child is brought to the temple

- Give thanks to God on high *Chepponis* **GC 792**
- Sanctuary *Thompson/Scruggs* **CEL 154**
- Shalom, my good friends *Traditional* **BC**

ADDITIONAL SONGS FOR THE DAY/SEASON

- Gathered as one *Tate/Light* **VO 25**
- Song of the chosen *Cooney* **GC 813**
- That boy-child of Mary *Malawi* **TFF 54**
- We long to see your face *Keil* **RS 47**

Annunciation of the Lord

March 25

Years A, B, C

With Mary, the church hears these words: Do not be afraid, you have found favor with God. You, the people of God. You, the baptized Christian. In an anxious and uncertain world, you need not be fearful, the Lord is with you. With these words of consolation, we also hear Mary's openness to the mysterious will of God: I am the servant of the Lord. Baptized into the Lord's death and resurrection, and strengthened by his body and blood, we are sent into the world to witness to God's favor for all creation in the incarnation of Jesus.

ISAIAH 7:10-14
A young woman will bear a son

- Emmanuel *McGee* **TFF 45, W&P 36**
- He came down *Cameroon* **GC 370**

PSALM 45
I will make your name to be remembered from one generation to another.

- The queen stands at your right hand *Kodner* **GC 52**

PSALM 40:5-10
I love to do your will, O my God.

- Here am I *Batastini* **RS 75**
- Here I am *Batstone* **MAR 115**
- Here I am *Cooney* **GC 49**
- Jesus, Jesus *Bullock* **HMS11 923**

HEBREWS 10:4-10
The offering of Jesus' body sanctifies us

- Now God our Father *Dearman/Mills* **W&P 103**
- Our hope is alive *Ylvisaker* **BC**
- Shine down on me *O'Brien* **MAR**
- Stir up the love *Ylvisaker* **BC**

LUKE 26:38
The angel greets Mary

- Be glorified *Funk* **CEL 19**
- Magnificat *Ylvisaker* **BC**
- Magnify the Lord *Berthier* **REN 131**
- Mary's song *Rethmeier* **VIN6 160**

ADDITIONAL SONGS FOR THE DAY/SEASON

- Ave Maria *Kantor* **RS 896**
- Canticle of the turning *Irish* **W&P 26**
- My soul in stillness waits *Haugen* **GC 328**
- No wind at the window *Bell* **RS 876**
- Sing, my soul *Traditional* **REN 129**

Visitation of Mary to Elizabeth

May 31

Years A, B, C

Elizabeth welcomes Mary's visit with great joy, and declares that Mary is indeed blessed for believing that God's word would be fulfilled in her. Mary's song announces the great things God is doing. A new day is being birthed into existence and we are meant to be a part of it. Like the baby who leaps for joy in Elizabeth's womb, we rejoice in the news that God is near.

1 SAMUEL 2:1-10

Hannah prays and exults in the LORD

- Forever grateful *Altrogge* **HCW 44**
- Rock of ages *Baloche* **HMS13 1099**
- Thank you, Lord *Park* **VIN8 202**
- You are holy *Brown* **HMS10 884**

PSALM 113

Let the name of the LORD be blessed from this time forth forevermore.

- Praise God's name *Joncas* **RS 150**
- Praise the Lord *Guimont* **RS 151**
- We can be lifted up *Hanson* **SCR 105**

ROMANS 12:9-16B

Rejoice with those who rejoice, weep with those who weep

- Only for your glory *Hanson* **SCR 34**
- The people on your heart *DeShazo/Sadler* **HMS10 869**
- Turn our hearts *Kendrick* **HMS12 1043**

LUKE 1:39-57

Mary greets Elizabeth and exults in the Lord

- Canticle of the turning *Irish* **W&P 26**
- Faithful One *Doerksen* **CMH2 60**
- Magnificat *Joncas* **RS 656**
- Magnificat *Ylvisaker* **BC**
- Mary's song *Rethmeier* **VIN6 160**
- No wind at the window *Bell* **RS 876**
- Thanks be to you *Haugen* **RS 708**

ADDITIONAL SONGS FOR THE DAY/SEASON

- A story for all people *Collins* **W&P 2**
- Bless his holy name *Crouch* **W&P 19**
- Send me, Jesus *South African* **WOV 773, REN 308**
- Surely it is God who saves me *White* **REN 122**

Mary, Mother of the Lord

August 15

Years A, B, C

Mary has been important to Christian devotion throughout history because in her, the God-bearer, is seen a representation of the church itself. Mary's song (the Magnificat) is a powerful statement of justice, still apt for us today as we come with our own neediness to experience God's justice and mercy in word and sacrament. Can Mary also serve as a model for us, leading us not only to pray for those in need, but also to just action on their behalf?

ISAIAH 61:7-11

God will cause righteousness and praise to spring up before all nations

- He is Lord *Smith* **HMS12 998**
- I Am *Hanson* **SFL**
- The kingdom song *Evans* **HMS12 1040**

PSALM 45:11-16

I will make your name to be remembered from one generation to another.

GALATIANS 4:4-7

We are no longer slaves, but children

- Faithful Father *Doerksen* **VIN7 72**
- I belong to a mighty God *DeShazo* **HMS8 654**
- Let the peace of God reign *Zschech* **HMS11 926**
- Saved by the grace of a miracle *Ylvisaker* **BC**

LUKE 1:46-55

Mary exults in the Lord

- Canticle of the turning *Irish* **W&P 26**
- Faithful One *Doerksen* **CMH2 60**
- Magnificat *Ylvisaker* **BC**
- Mary's song *Rethmeier* **VIN6 160**
- My soul does magnify the Lord *Brown* **TFF 168**
- Sanctuary *Thompson/Scruggs* **CW 154**

ADDITIONAL SONGS FOR THE DAY/SEASON

- Ave Maria *Kantor* **RS 896**
- For all the faithful women *Wesley* **WOV 692, TFF 219**
- Make me a servant *Willard* **W&P 96**
- Thanks be to you *Haugen* **WOV 790, RS 708**
- The virgin Mary had a baby boy *West Indian* **TFF 53, RS 501**

Holy Cross

September 14

Years A, B, C

We proclaim Christ crucified: the power and wisdom of God. Jesus is lifted up on the cross so that all who hold to him will be healed. Does the cross have central place in the life of your congregation—in its worship, education, evangelism, and social ministry? Do you teach children (and adults) to make the sign of the cross in remembrance of their baptism into Jesus' death and resurrection?

NUMBERS 21:4B-9
Moses lifts up a bronze serpent in the wilderness
- God my refuge *Montemayer* **HCW 50**

PSALM 98:1-4
The LORD has done marvelous things.
- God has done marvelous things *Brokering/Haas* **W&P 51**
- I will sing, I will sing *Dyer* **W&P 73, GC**
- Oh, sing to the Lord *Brazilian* **TFF 274, WOV 795**
- Shout to the Lord *Zschech* **HMS10 862, W&P 124**

PSALM 78:1-2, 34-38
God was their rock and the Most High God their redeemer.

1 CORINTHIANS 1:18-24
The cross is the power of God to those who are being saved
- Hop on the bus *Underwood* **VIN7 120**
- I come to the cross *Somma/Batstone* **MAR 122**
- Lift high the cross *Nicholson* **REN**
- O, mighty cross *Baroni/Chisum* **HCW 136**
- Only God for me *Harris* **HMS14**

JOHN 3:13-17
The Son of Man will be lifted up
- Eternity *Doerksen* **CMH 28**
- For God so loved *Dauermann* **W&P 39**
- Jesus, I believe *Batstone* **MAR 130**
- Singing through the water *Hanson/Murakami* **SCR 132**
- Spirit calls, rejoice! *Hanson/Murakami* **SCR 1**
- This is the gospel of Christ *Brown* **HMS10 870**
- Waterlife *Hanson* **SCR 129, W&P 145**
- Wind of the spirit *Hanson/Murakami* **SCR 18, W&P 157**

ADDITIONAL SONGS FOR THE DAY/SEASON
- At the foot of the cross *Bond* **W&P 11**
- By grace we have been saved *Traditional* **W&P 25**
- Now we remain *Haas* **W&P 106, RS 813**

St. Michael and All Angels

September 29

Years A, B, C

In the book of Revelation, Michael the archangel fights in a cosmic battle against Satan. In the book of Daniel, Michael is portrayed as the heavenly being who leads the faithful dead to God's throne on the day of resurrection. On this day we remember the important roles angels play in the biblical story—defender, message-bearer, protector, herald of glad tidings—and marvel at the many ways in which we continue to be assured of God's presence, help, and love.

DANIEL 10:10-14, 12:1-3
All who are dead shall arise on the day of the Lord

- My Lord, what a morning *Spiritual* **WOV 627, BC**
- We can be lifted up *Hanson* **SCR 105**

PSALM 103:1-5, 20-22
Bless the Lord, *you angels of the* Lord.

- God of love, have mercy *Makeever* **DH 10**
- How blessed *Hampton* **VIN6 106**
- I'll bless the Lord for evermore *Ylvisaker* **BC**

REVELATION 12:7-12
Michael defeats Satan in a cosmic battle

- I belong to a mighty God *DeShazo* **HMS8 654**
- Let the peace of God reign *Zschech* **HMS11 926**
- Mighty is our God *Walker* **HCW 118**

LUKE 10:17-20
Jesus gives his followers authority over the enemy

- All the power you need *Fragar* **HMS11 888**
- Arise, oh Lord *Carpenter* **VIN6 16**
- Lord, my strength *Krippaehne* **W&P 93**

ADDITIONAL SONGS FOR THE DAY/SEASON

- On eagle's wings *Joncas* **W&P 110, WOV 779**
- The trumpets sound, the angels sing *Kendrick* **W&P 139**

Reformation

October 31

Years A, B, C

This day invites the daughters and sons of the Reformation to celebrate the perennial source of reform in the church: the word of God and the gifts of forgiveness and new life. Indeed, when the church welcomes a new member in holy baptism or gathers around the table of holy communion, the Holy Spirit's reforming labor continues among us. This is a day to acknowledge that our souls are captive to the word of God, that we share the life of Christ with other Christians through holy baptism, and that we are urged by the Holy Spirit to pray for the ongoing renewal of the church in our day.

JEREMIAH 31:31-34
I will write my law in their hearts, says the LORD
- I want to know you *Evans* **HMS12 1008**
- Write it on my heart *McLean* **WIS 41**
- Write your law upon our hearts *Makeever* **DH 91**
- You are mine *Haas* **W&P 158**

PSALM 46
The LORD of hosts is with us; the God of Jacob is our stronghold.
- Awesome God *Mullins* **W&P 13**
- Come to the river of life *Moen/Cloninger* **HMS10 818**
- God my refuge *Montemayer* **HCW 50**
- The river is here *Park* **CMH 58, VIN6 232**
- You are mine *Haas* **W&P 158**

ROMANS 3:19-28
Justified by God's grace as a gift
- Because we believe *Gordon/Harvill* **HMS12 985**
- By grace have we been saved *Edwards* **W&P 25**
- Everlasting grace *Carpenter* **VIN6 58**
- For by grace *Nicholas* **W&P 38**
- Only by grace *Gustafson* **HCW 140, W&P 112**

JOHN 8:31-36
Jesus says, Continue in my word and you will know the truth
- Come share the Spirit *Hanson/Murakami* **SCR 116**
- I will sing, I will sing *Dyer* **W&P 73**
- These things are true of you *Walker* **MAR 248**

ADDITIONAL SONGS FOR THE DAY/SEASON
- Our confidence is in the Lord *Richards* **W&P 114**
- The church song *Beech* **W&P 135**
- We rejoice in the grace of God *Cook/Cook/Christopher* **MAR**
- What a mighty God we serve! *Traditional* **TFF 295**
- What a mighty word God gives! *Traditional* **W&P 155**
- You are the rock of my salvation *Muller* **W&P 161**

All Saints

November 1

Year A

As November heralds the dying of the landscape in many northern regions, the readings call us to remember those who have died in Christ. As the church year draws to a close, we hear warnings about the end of time, stories of crisis and judgment, and parables of loss and death. The Christian community speaks honestly about human frailty and mortality. At the same time, we confess our faith in the risen Lord, in the communion of saints, the resurrection of the body, and life everlasting. While we may face dying or death with fear, we are called to hear the Lord's promise that he is with us in life and in death. Christ has claimed us in baptism. He nourishes us with his body and blood. He leads us to the new Jerusalem. There we shall join all the saints in praise of God, who has turned our graves into the doorway to eternal life.

REVELATION 7:9-17
The multitudes of heaven worship the Lamb
- All around your throne *DeShazo/Kerr* **HMS10 808**
- Comes a new song *Makeever* **DH 101**
- Eternity *Doerksen* **CMH 28**
- He is exalted *Paris* **HCW 57, W&P 55**
- Praise we render *Ylvisaker* **BC**
- Sing with all the saints in glory *Traditional* **WOV 691, GC 442**
- Water from heaven *Hanson/Murakami* **SCR 136**
- Worthy the Lamb that was slain *Moen* **HCW 192**

PSALM 34:1-10, 22
Fear the L*ORD*, *you saints of the* L*ORD*.
- Beauty for brokenness *Kendrick* **W&P 17**
- Come and taste *Hanson/Murakami* **SCR 186, W&P 30**
- I'll bless the Lord for evermore *Ylvisaker* **BC**
- Taste and see *Young* **BL, AFP 11-10895**
- The trumpets sound, the angels sing *Kendrick* **W&P 139**

1 JOHN 3:1-3
We are God's children
- Behold what manner of love *vanTine* **TFF 218**
- Change my heart, O God *Espinoza* **HCW 28, W&P 28**
- Make me a servant *Willard* **W&P 96**
- Open our eyes, Lord *Cull* **MAR 59, W&P 113**

MATTHEW 5:1-12
Blessed are the poor in spirit
- Blest are they *Haas* **WOV 764, REN 127**
- Give thanks *Evans* **VIN6 128**
- Give thanks *Smith* **HCW 46, W&P 41, TFF 292**
- Let the river flow *Evans* **HMS12 1015**
- We are the light of the world *Greif* **REN 288**

ADDITIONAL SONGS FOR THE DAY/SEASON
- Eat this bread, drink this cup *Young* **BL, AFP 11-10651**
- I am the bread of life *Toolan* **WOV 702, REN**
- The trees of the field *Dauermann* **REN 302**
- We are marching in the light of God *South African* **W&P 148, WOV 650**

Year B

All Saints Sunday celebrates the baptized people of God, living and dead, who make up the body of Christ. With thanksgiving we remember all the faithful departed, especially those most dear to us who have died. Today's readings are filled with rich images of the eternal life promised to all the saints. The holy meal is a foretaste of that great and promised feast where death or pain will be no more. Even in the midst of loss and grief God wipes away the tears from our eyes and makes all things new.

ISAIAH 25:6-9
The banquet of the L*ORD*
- On the mountain top *Ylvisaker* **BC**
- The trumpets sound, the angels sing *Kendrick* **W&P 139**
- This is the feast of victory *Young* **W&P 142, BL**

WISDOM OF SOLOMON 3:1-9
The righteous are with God

PSALM 24

They shall receive a blessing from the God of their salvation.

Eat this bread, drink this cup *Young* BL, AFP 11-10651
The King of glory *Ylvisaker* BC
Welcome the King *Kendrick* HMS12 1048

REVELATION 21:1-6A

A new heaven and a new earth

Come to the fount of creation *Ylvisaker* BC
Heaven and earth *DeShazo/Harvill* HMS10 829
Jehovah *Springer* VIN6 124
Mourning into dancing *Walker* HCW 125, W&P 99
Soon and very soon *Crouch* REN 278, WOV 744, W&P 128

JOHN 11:32-44

The raising of Lazarus

Because we believe *Gordon/Harvill* HMS12 985
I am the resurrection *Ylvisaker* BC
I do believe *Ylvisaker* BC
Only God for me *Harris* HMS14
You only *McCoy* VIN8 242

ADDITIONAL SONGS FOR THE DAY/SEASON

I am the Bread of life *Toolan* WOV 702, REN 246
I will sing, I will sing *Dyer* W&P 73
Oh, when the saints go marching in *Spiritual* TFF 180
We are called *Haas* W&P 137

Year C

With the Church on earth and the hosts of heaven, we praise your name and join their unending hymn," proclaims the presiding minister in the eucharistic prayer. On the festival of All Saints we remember with thanksgiving those who have lived and died in the faith. They are the sign of our hope and an image of the glory we shall inherit. But even more, they are worshipers with us this day as we sing the praises of the God who brings life out of death.

DANIEL 7:1-3, 15-18

The holy ones of the Most High shall receive the kingdom

Ancient of days *Sadler/Harvill* HCW 11

PSALM 149

Sing the praise of the LORD in the congregation of the faithful.

Sing unto the Lord *Makeever* DH 47
Stand up and give him the praise *DeShazo* HMS10 867

EPHESIANS 1:11-23

God raised Christ from the dead and made him head over all the church

Freely, given freely *Hanson/Murakami* SCR 74
Open our eyes, Lord *Cull* MAR 59, W&P 113
Open the eyes of my heart *Baloche* HMS12 1027
Thank you for the gift *Hanson* SCR 144

LUKE 6:20-31

Jesus speaks blessings and woes

Give thanks *Evans* VIN6 128
Give thanks *Smith* HCW 46, W&P 41, TFF 292
Let the river flow *Evans* HMS12 1015
The gift of giving *Ylvisaker* BC
We are the light of the world *Greif* REN 288

ADDITIONAL SONGS FOR THE DAY/SEASON

As the deer *Nystrom* REN 9, W&P 9
Bring forth the kingdom *Haugen* W&P 22
Death be never last *Makeever* DH 102
Deep river *Spiritual* TFF 174
Oh, when the saints go marching in *Spiritual* TFF 180

Thanksgiving Day

Fourth Thursday of November (United States)

Second Monday of October (Canada)

Year A

While North Americans celebrate one day of thanksgiving each year, Christians gather frequently to celebrate a thanksgiving meal at the table of Christ. In communion, the church receives the body and blood of Christ, the food and drink of the promised land. His abundant grace is the reason for our thanksgiving. Indeed, when we gather at the holy supper, there is always enough for everyone. No one is turned away. At the same time, many people in our rich country go without food, shelter, and clothing. Here, in the meal where there is enough for everyone, we find the source of our service in the world to those who have little or nothing. As Christ has blessed us with the riches of his life, so we are called to give ourselves freely to all in need.

DEUTERONOMY 8:7-18

God will lead you into a land of flowing streams

- Glory and praise to our God *Schutte* — **W&P 43, G&P 671, GC 522**
- God is so good *Anonymous* — **COK 75, TFF 275**

PSALM 65

You crown the year with your goodness, and your paths overflow with plenty.

- Glory and praise to our God *Schutte* — **W&P 43, G&P 671, GC 522**
- The river is here *Park* — **VIN6 232, HMS11 958**

2 CORINTHIANS 9:6-15

God provides every blessing in abundance

- An offering of thanksgiving *Ylvisaker* — **BC**
- Give thanks *Smith* — **W&P 41, TFF 292**
- Now we raise our thanks to you *Ylvisaker* — **BC**
- Thanksgiving to the living God *Makeever* — **DH 3**

LUKE 17:11-19

The healed leper returns to give thanks to Jesus

- Come touch *Hanson* — **SCR 180**
- Heal me, O Lord *Moen* — **HMS10 828**
- Healing word *McCoy* — **VIN6 82**
- Jesus, Jesus *Bullock* — **HMS11 923**
- Let your healing love *Butler* — **VIN6 144**
- Mercy *DeShazo/Sadler* — **HMS14**
- Your steadfast love *Sandquist* — **HCW 200**

ADDITIONAL SONGS FOR THE DAY/SEASON

- Age to age *Vogt* — **OCP 10900**
- All that we have *Ault* — **G&P 18**
- As the grains of wheat *Haas* — **W&P 10**
- As the grains of wheat *Haugen* — **WOV 705**
- Gathered as one *Tate/Light* — **VO 25**
- Rain down *Cortez* — **LBG**

Year B

As winter darkness crosses the land, the nation takes time to offer thanks for the harvest and the abundant resources of this land. While this holiday witnesses many households gathering for a festive meal, Christians recognize that the source of all good things is the God who feeds the birds and clothes the grass of the field. Gathered at Christ's supper, we offer thanksgiving for the bread of life and the cup of blessing. And here, as we share these gifts, we are knit together into a community whose mission is among those who are poor and in need. We offer thanks to God for the bounty of the land and seek to share these riches with all in need.

JOEL 2:21-27

The LORD promises to restore Jerusalem

- Let it rain *Park* **VIN8 126**
- Rain down on us *Butler/Butler/Butler* **VIN8 160**
- Rain down *Cortez* **LBG**
- Singing through the water *Hanson/Murakami* **SCR 132**

PSALM 126

The LORD has done great things for us, and we are glad indeed.

- Give thanks *Smith* **HCW 46, W&P 41, TFF 292**
- Mourning into dancing *Walker* **W&P 99**
- The Lord has done great things *Smith* **PS1**
- Trading my sorrows *Evans* **HMS14**

1 TIMOTHY 2:1-7

Make supplications, prayers, intercessions, and thanksgivings

- I love to be in your presence *Baloche/Kerr* **HCW 75**
- One *Hanson/Murakami* **SCR 160**

MATTHEW 6:25-33

God will care for all our needs

- Don't be anxious *Hanson* **SCR 141**
- Leave your heart with me *Hanson* **SCR 150**
- Lord, I'm in your hands *Weeks* **MAR 133**
- My heart will trust *Morgan* **HMS14**
- Nothing is as wonderful *Underwood* **VIN8 150**
- Seek ye first *Lafferty* **W&P 122, TFF 149, WOV 783**

ADDITIONAL SONGS FOR THE DAY/SEASON

- Glory and praise to our God *Schutte* **W&P 43**
- I will sing, I will sing *Dyer* **GC, W&P 73**
- Living thanksgiving *Makeever* **DH 99**

Year C

One of the names for holy communion is eucharist. It comes from a Greek word meaning "to give thanks." Food and thanksgiving always go together, for life is a precious gift from God. Every meal, every harvest, is an occasion for giving thanks and for acknowledging that all God's gifts are on loan for us to use in acts of praise.

DEUTERONOMY 26:1-11
The offering of the first fruits
- King of life *Sadler* **HMS12 1014**

PSALM 100
Enter the gates of the LORD with thanksgiving.
- For the Lord is good *DeShazo/Sadler* **HMS13 1065**
- God is good (All the time) *Chapman* **MAR 186**
- He has made me glad *Brethorst* **COK 3, TFF 291**
- Indeed, how good is the Lord *Roberts* **TFF 12**
- Shout joy to the Lord *d'Inverno* **PS 2**
- Thanksgiving to the living God *Makeever* **DH 3**
- You have been good *Paris* **HCW 198**

PHILIPPIANS 4:4-9
Do not worry about anything
- Deep is the prayer *Young* **BL**
- Forever grateful *Altrogge* **HCW 44**
- Give thanks *Smith* **HCW 46, TFF 292, W&P 41**
- God is here *Moen/Overstreet* **HMS12 995**
- Let the peace of God reign *Zschech* **HMS11 926**
- Teach me how to pray *Hanson/Murakami* **SCR 25**

JOHN 6:25-35
Jesus is the bread of life
- As bread that is broken *Baloche/Cloninger* **HMS10 811**
- Because we believe *Gordon/Harvill* **HMS12 985**
- Broken in love *Hanson* **SCR 177, W&P 24**
- Here is bread *Kendrick* **W&P 58**
- Let it rain *Park* **VIN8 126**
- One in the bread *Young* **BL**

ADDITIONAL SONGS FOR THE DAY/SEASON
- Hallelujah! We sing your praises *South African* **WOV 722, RS 692**
- I'm forever grateful *Altrogge* **MAR 44**
- Thankgiving to the living God *Makeever* **DH 3**
- We bring the sacrifice of praise *Dearman* **MAR 251**

Additional Resources

Barrett, Bob. *Contemporary Music Styles: The Worship Band's Guide to Excellence*. Mission Viejo, CA: Tailor Made Music, 1996.

Benedict, Daniel and Craig Kennet Miller. *Contemporary Worship for the 21st Century*. Nashville, Discipleship Resources, 1994.

Collins, Dori Erwin and Scott Weidler. *Sound Decisions: Evaluating Contemporary Music for Lutheran Worship*. Chicago: Evangelical Lutheran Church in America, 1997.

Farlee, Robert Buckley, General Editor. *Leading the Church's Song*. Minneapolis: Augsburg Fortress, 1998.

Haugen, Marty. *Instrumentation and the Liturgical Ensemble*. Chicago: GIA Publications, Inc., 1991.

Liesch, Barry. *The New Worship*. New York: Baker Bros., 1996.

McLean, Terri. *New Harmonies: Choosing Contemporary Music for Worship*. Bethesda, MD: The Alban Institute, 1999.

Morgenthaler, Sally. *Worship Evangelism*. Grand Rapids, MI: Zondervan, 1995.

Siewert, Crouch, Frazier & Frazier. *The Worship Team Handbook*. Downers Grove, IL: InterVarsity Press, 1998.

The Ultimate Fake Book. Milwaukee, WI: Hal Leonard, 1994.

Wright, Timothy. *A Community of Joy: How to Create Contemporary Worship*. Nashville: Abingdon Press, 1996.

Index to the Revised Common Lectionary

During the season after Pentecost, Old Testament selections without an asterisk are thematically related to the gospel; the alternate selections, marked with an an asterisk (*), form a semi-continuous pattern of readings. Either series is designed to be read in its entirety.

GENESIS

1:1—2:4a	Holy Trinity		A
1:1—2:4a	Vigil of Easter		A, B, C
1:1-5	Baptism of the Lord		B
2:15-17; 3:1-7	1 Lent		A
2:18-24	S. btwn. Oct. 2 and 8	Pr. 22	B
3:8-15	S. btwn. June 5 and 11	Pr. 5	B
6:9-22; 7:24; 8:14-19	S. btwn. May 29 and June 4*	Pr. 4	A
7:1-5, 11-18; 8:6-18; 9:8-13	Vigil of Easter		A, B, C
9:8-17	1 Lent		B
11:1-9	Day of Pentecost		C
12:1-4a	2 Lent		A
12:1-9	S. btwn. June 5 and 11*	Pr. 5	A
15:1-6	S. btwn. Aug. 7 and 13	Pr. 14	C
15:1-12, 17-18	2 Lent		C
17:1-7, 15-16	2 Lent		B
18:1-10a	S. btwn. July 17 and 23	Pr. 11	C
18:1-15 [21:1-7]	S. btwn. June 12 and 18*	Pr. 6	A
18:20-32	S. btwn. July 24 and 30	Pr. 12	C
21:8-21	S. btwn. June 19 and 25*	Pr. 7	A
22:1-14	S. btwn. June 26 and July 2*	Pr. 8	A
22:1-18	Vigil of Easter		A, B, C
24:34-38, 42-49, 58-67	S. btwn. July 3 and 9*	Pr. 9	A
25:19-34	S. btwn. July 10 and 16*	Pr. 10	A
28:10-19a	S. btwn. July 17 and 23*	Pr. 11	A
29:15-28	S. btwn. July 24 and 30*	Pr. 12	A
32:22-31	S. btwn. July 31 and Aug. 6*	Pr. 13	A
32:22-31	S. btwn. Oct. 16 and 22	Pr. 24	C
37:1-4, 12-28	S. btwn. Aug. 7 and 13*	Pr. 14	A

JOSHUA

3:7-17	S. btwn. Oct. 30 and Nov. 5*	Pr. 26	A
5:9-12	4 Lent		C
24:1-2a, 14-18	S. btwn. Aug. 21 and 27	Pr. 16	B
24:1-3a, 14-25	S. btwn. Nov. 6 and 12*	Pr. 27	A

JUDGES

4:1-7	S. btwn. Nov. 13 and 19*	Pr. 28	A

RUTH

1:1-18	S. btwn. Oct. 30 and Nov. 5*	Pr. 26	B
3:1-5; 4:13-17	S. btwn. Nov. 6 and 12*	Pr. 27	B

1 SAMUEL

1:4-20	S. btwn. Nov. 13 and 19*	Pr. 28	B
2:1-10	S. btwn. Nov. 13 and 19*	Pr. 28	B
2:1-10	Visitation of Mary to Elizabeth		A, B, C
2:18-20, 26	1 Christmas		C
3:1-10 [11-20]	2 Epiphany		B
3:1-10 [11-20]	S. btwn. May 29 and June 4*	Pr. 4	B
8:4-11 [12-15] 16-20 [11:14-15]	S. btwn. June 5 and 11*	Pr. 5	B
15:34—16:13	S. btwn. June 12 and 18*	Pr. 6	B
16:1-13	4 Lent		A
17:[1a, 4-11, 19-23] 32-49	S. btwn. June 19 and 25*	Pr. 7	B
17:57—18:5, 10-16	S. btwn. June 19 and 25*	Pr. 7	B

2 SAMUEL

1:1, 17-27	S. btwn. June 26 and July 2*	Pr. 8	B
5:1-5, 9-10	S. btwn. July 3 and 9*	Pr. 9	B
6:1-5, 12b-19	S. btwn. July 10 and 16*	Pr. 10	B
7:1-11, 16	4 Advent		B
7:1-14a	S. btwn. July 17 and 23*	Pr. 11	B
11:1-15	S. btwn. July 24 and 30*	Pr. 12	B
11:26—12:10, 13-15	S. btwn. June 12 and 18	Pr. 6	C
11:26—12:13a	S. btwn. July 31 and Aug. 6*	Pr. 13	B
18:5-9, 15, 31-33	S. btwn. Aug. 7 and 13*	Pr. 14	B
23:1-7	Christ the King*		B

1 KINGS

2:10-12; 3:3-14	S. btwn. Aug. 14 and 20*	Pr. 15	B
3:5-12	S. btwn. July 24 and 30	Pr. 12	A
8:[1, 6, 10-11] 22-30, 41-43	S. btwn. Aug. 21 and 27*	Pr. 16	B
8:22-23, 41-43	S. btwn. May 29 and June 4	Pr. 4	C
17:8-16	S. btwn. Nov. 6 and 12	Pr. 27	B
17:8-16 [17-24]	S. btwn. June 5 and 11*	Pr. 5	C
17:17-24	S. btwn. June 5 and 11	Pr. 5	C
18:20-21 [22-29] 30-39	S. btwn. May 29 and June 4*	Pr. 4	C
19:1-4 [5-7] 8-15a	S. btwn. June 19 and 25*	Pr. 7	C
19:4-8	S. btwn. Aug. 7 and 13	Pr. 14	B
19:9-18	S. btwn. Aug. 7 and 13	Pr. 14	A
19:15-16, 19-21	S. btwn. June 26 and July 2	Pr. 8	C
21:1-10 [11-14] 15-21a	S. btwn. June 12 and 18*	Pr. 6	C

2 KINGS

2:1-12	Transfiguration of the Lord		B
2:1-2, 6-14	S. btwn. June 26 and July 2*	Pr. 8	C
4:42-44	S. btwn. July 24 and 30	Pr. 12	B
5:1-3, 7-15c	S. btwn. Oct. 9 and 15	Pr. 23	C
5:1-14	6 Epiphany		B
5:1-14	S. btwn. July 3 and 9*	Pr. 9	C

NEHEMIAH

8:1-3, 5-6, 8-10	3 Epiphany		C

ESTHER

7:1-6, 9-10; 9:20-22	S. btwn. Sept. 25 and Oct. 1*	Pr. 21	B

JOB

1:1; 2:1-10	S. btwn. Oct. 2 and 8*	Pr. 22	B
14:1-14	Saturday in Holy Week		A, B, C
19:23-27a	S. btwn. Nov. 6 and 12	Pr. 27	C
23:1-9, 16-17	S. btwn. Oct. 9 and 15*	Pr. 23	B
38:1-7 [34-41]	S. btwn. Oct. 16 and 22*	Pr. 24	B
38:1-11	S. btwn. June 19 and 25	Pr. 7	B
42:1-6, 10-17	S. btwn. Oct. 23 and 29*	Pr. 25	B

PSALMS

1	6 Epiphany		C
1	7 Easter		B
1	S. btwn. Sept. 4 and 10	Pr. 18	C
1	S. btwn. Sept. 18 and 24*	Pr. 20	B
1	S. btwn. Oct. 23 and 29	Pr. 25	A
2	Transfiguration of the Lord		A
4	3 Easter		B
5:1-8	S. btwn. June 12 and 18*	Pr. 6	C
8	Holy Trinity		A, C
8	New Year's Day		A, B, C
8	S. btwn. Oct. 2 and 8	Pr. 22	B
9:9-20	S. btwn. June 19 and 25*	Pr. 7	B
13	S. btwn. June 26 and July 2*	Pr. 8	A
14	S. btwn. July 24 and 30*	Pr. 12	B
14	S. btwn. Sept. 11 and 17*	Pr. 19	C
15	4 Epiphany		A
15	S. btwn. Aug. 28 and Sept. 3	Pr. 17	B
15	S. btwn. July 17 and 23	Pr. 11	C
16	2 Easter		A
16	S. btwn. June 26 and July 2	Pr. 8	C
16	S. btwn. Nov. 13 and 19	Pr. 28	B
16	Vigil of Easter		A, B, C
17:1-7, 15	S. btwn. July 31 and Aug. 6*	Pr. 13	A
17:1-9	S. btwn. Nov. 6 and 12	Pr. 27	C
19	3 Epiphany		C
19	3 Lent		B
19	S. btwn. Oct. 2 and 8*	Pr. 22	A
19	S. btwn. Sept. 11 and 17*	Pr. 19	B
19	Vigil of Easter		A, B, C
19:7-14	S. btwn. Sept. 25 and Oct. 1	Pr. 21	B
20	S. btwn. June 12 and 18*	Pr. 6	B

22	Good Friday		A, B, C
22:1-15	S. btwn. Oct. 9 and 15*	Pr. 23	B
22:19-28	S. btwn. June 19 and 25	Pr. 7	C
22:23-31	2 Lent		B
22:25-31	5 Easter		B
23	4 Easter		A, B, C
23	4 Lent		A
23	S. btwn. July 17 and 23	Pr. 11	B
23	S. btwn. Oct. 9 and 15	Pr. 23	A
24	All Saints		B
24	S. btwn. July 10 and 16*	Pr. 10	B
24:7-10	Presentation of the Lord		A, B, C
25:1-9	S. btwn. Sept. 25 and Oct. 1	Pr. 21	A
25:1-10	1 Advent		C
25:1-10	1 Lent		B
25:1-10	S. btwn. July 10 and 16	Pr. 10	C
26	S. btwn. Oct. 2 and 8*	Pr. 22	B
26:1-8	S. btwn. Aug. 28 and Sept. 3	Pr. 17	A
27	2 Lent		C
27:1, 4-9	3 Epiphany		A
29	Baptism of the Lord		A, B, C
29	Holy Trinity		B
30	3 Easter		C
30	6 Epiphany		B
30	S. btwn. July 3 and 9*	Pr. 9	C
30	S. btwn. June 26 and July 2	Pr. 8	B
30	S. btwn. June 5 and 11	Pr. 5	C
31:1-4, 15-16	Saturday in Holy Week		A, B, C
31:1-5, 15-16	5 Easter		A
31:1-5, 19-24	S. btwn. May 29 and June 4	Pr. 4	A
31:9-16	Sunday of the Passion		A, B, C
32	1 Lent		A
32	4 Lent		C
32	S. btwn. June 12 and 18	Pr. 6	C
32:1-7	S. btwn. Oct. 30 and Nov. 5	Pr. 26	C
33:1-12	S. btwn. June 5 and 11*	Pr. 5	A
33:12-22	S. btwn. Aug. 7 and 13	Pr. 14	C
33:12-22	Vigil of Pentecost		A, B, C
34:1-8	S. btwn. Aug. 7 and 13	Pr. 14	B
34:1-8 [19-22]	S. btwn. Oct. 23 and 29*	Pr. 25	B
34:1-10, 22	All Saints		A
34:9-14	S. btwn. Aug. 14 and 20	Pr. 15	B
34:15-22	S. btwn. Aug. 21 and 27	Pr. 16	B
36:5-10	2 Epiphany		C
36:5-11	Monday in Holy Week		A, B, C
37:1-9	S. btwn. Oct. 2 and 8	Pr. 22	C
37:1-11, 39-40	7 Epiphany		C
40:1-11	2 Epiphany		A
40:5-10	Annunciation of the Lord		A, B, C
41	7 Epiphany		B
42 and 43	S. btwn. June 19 and 25*	Pr. 7	C
42 and 43	Vigil of Easter		A, B, C
43	S. btwn. Oct. 30 and Nov. 5	Pr. 26	A
43	Vigil of Easter		C
45	Annunciation of the Lord		A, B, C

PSALMS *(continued)*

84	S. btwn. Aug. 21 and 27*	Pr. 16	B
84:1-7	S. btwn. Oct. 23 and 29	Pr. 25	C
85	S. btwn. July 24 and 30*	Pr. 12	C
85:1-2, 8-13	2 Advent		B
85:8-13	S. btwn. Aug. 7 and 13	Pr. 14	A
85:8-13	S. btwn. July 10 and 16	Pr. 10	B
86:1-10, 16-17	S. btwn. June 19 and 25*	Pr. 7	A
86:11-17	S. btwn. July 17 and 23	Pr. 11	A
89:1-4, 15-18	S. btwn. June 26 and July 2	Pr. 8	A
89:1-4, 19-26	4 Advent		B
89:20-37	S. btwn. July 17 and 23*	Pr. 11	B
90:1-6, 13-17	S. btwn. Oct. 23 and 29*	Pr. 25	A
90:1-8 [9-11] 12	S. btwn. Nov. 13 and 19	Pr. 28	A
90:12-17	S. btwn. Oct. 9 and 15	Pr. 23	B
91:1-2, 9-16	1 Lent		C
91:1-6, 14-16	S. btwn. Sept. 25 and Oct. 1*	Pr. 21	C
91:9-16	S. btwn. Oct. 16 and 22	Pr. 24	B
92:1-4, 12-15	8 Epiphany		C
92:1-4, 12-15	S. btwn. June 12 and 18	Pr. 6	B
92:1-4, 12-15	S. btwn. May 24 and 28	Pr. 3	C
93	Ascension of the Lord		A, B, C
93	Christ the King	Pr. 29	B
95	3 Lent		A
95:1-7a	Christ the King	Pr. 29	A
96	Christmas Eve (I)		A, B, C
96	S. btwn. May 29 and June 4*	Pr. 4	C
96:1-9	S. btwn. May 29 and June 4	Pr. 4	C
96:1-9 [10-13]	S. btwn. Oct. 16 and 22	Pr. 24	A
97	7 Easter		C
97	Christmas Dawn (II)		A, B, C
98	6 Easter		B
98	Christmas Day (III)		A, B, C
98	S. btwn. Nov. 13 and 19	Pr. 28	C
98	S. btwn. Nov. 6 and 12*	Pr. 27	C
98	Vigil of Easter		A, B, C
98:1-5	Holy Cross		A, B, C
99	S. btwn. Oct. 16 and 22*	Pr. 24	A
99	Transfiguration of the Lord		A, C
100	Christ the King*	Pr. 29	A
100	S. btwn. June 12 and 18	Pr. 6	A
100	Thanksgiving		C
103:1-5, 20-22	St. Michael and All Angels		A, B, C
103:[1-7] 8-13	S. btwn. Sept. 11 and 17	Pr. 19	A
103:1-8	S. btwn. Aug. 21 and 27	Pr. 16	C
103:1-13, 22	8 Epiphany		B
103:1-13, 22	S. btwn. May 24 and 28	Pr. 3	B
104:1-9, 24, 35c	S. btwn. Oct. 16 and 22*	Pr. 24	B
104:24-34, 35b	Day of Pentecost		A, B, C
105:1-11, 45b	S. btwn. July 24 and 30*	Pr. 12	A
105:1-6, 16-22, 45b	S. btwn. Aug. 7 and 13*	Pr. 14	A
105:1-6, 23-26, 45c	S. btwn. Aug. 28 and Sept. 3*	Pr. 17	A
105:1-6, 37-45	S. btwn. Sept. 18 and 24*	Pr. 20	A
106:1-6, 19-23	S. btwn. Oct. 9 and 15*	Pr. 23	A
107:1-3, 17-22	4 Lent		B
107:1-3, 23-32	S. btwn. June 19 and 25	Pr. 7	B

PSALMS *(continued)*

137	S. btwn. Oct. 2 and 8*	Pr. 22	C
138	5 Epiphany		C
138	S. btwn. Aug. 21 and 27	Pr. 16	A
138	S. btwn. July 24 and 30	Pr. 12	C
138	S. btwn. June 5 and 11*	Pr. 5	B
139:1-6, 13-18	S. btwn. Sept. 4 and 10*	Pr. 18	C
139:1-6, 13-18	2 Epiphany		B
139:1-6, 13-18	S. btwn. May 29 and June 4*	Pr. 4	B
139:1-12, 23-24	S. btwn. July 17 and 23*	Pr. 11	A
143	Vigil of Easter		A, B, C
145:1-5, 17-21	S. btwn. Nov. 6 and 12*	Pr. 27	C
145:1-8	S. btwn. Sept. 18 and 24	Pr. 20	A
145:8-14	S. btwn. July 3 and 9	Pr. 9	A
145:8-9, 14-21	S. btwn. July 31 and Aug. 6	Pr. 13	A
145:10-18	S. btwn. July 24 and 30	Pr. 12	B
146	S. btwn. June 5 and 11*	Pr. 5	C
146	S. btwn. Nov. 6 and 12	Pr. 27	B
146	S. btwn. Oct. 30 and Nov. 5*	Pr. 26	B
146	S. btwn. Sept. 25 and Oct. 1	Pr. 21	C
146	S. btwn. Sept. 4 and 10	Pr. 18	B
146:5-10	3 Advent		A
147:1-11, 20c	5 Epiphany		B
147:12-20	2 Christmas		A, B, C
148	1 Christmas		A, B, C
148	5 Easter		C
149	All Saints Day		C
149	S. btwn. Sept. 4 and 10*	Pr. 18	A
150	2 Easter		C
PROVERBS			
1:20-33	S. btwn. Sept. 11 and 17*	Pr. 19	B
8:1-4, 22-31	Holy Trinity		C
8:1-8, 19-21; 9:4b-6	Vigil of Easter		A, B, C
9:1-6	S. btwn. Aug. 14 and 20	Pr. 15	B
22:1-2, 8-9, 22-23	S. btwn. Sept. 4 and 10*	Pr. 18	B
25:6-7	S. btwn. Aug. 28 and Sept. 3	Pr. 17	C
31:10-31	S. btwn. Sept. 18 and 24*	Pr. 20	B
ECCLESIASTES			
1:2, 12-14; 2:18-23	S. btwn. July 31 and Aug. 6	Pr. 13	C
3:1-13	New Year's Day		A, B, C
SONG OF SOLOMON			
2:8-13	S. btwn. Aug. 28 and Sept. 3*	Pr. 17	B
2:8-13	S. btwn. July 3 and 9*	Pr. 9	A
ISAIAH			
1:1, 10-20	S. btwn. Aug. 7 and 13*	Pr. 14	C
1:10-18	S. btwn. Oct. 30 and Nov. 5	Pr. 26	C
2:1-5	1 Advent		A
5:1-7	S. btwn. Aug. 14 and 20*	Pr. 15	C
5:1-7	S. btwn. Oct. 2 and 8	Pr. 22	A
6:1-8	Holy Trinity		B
6:1-8 [9-13]	5 Epiphany		C
7:10-14	Annunciation of the Lord		A, B, C

ISAIAH *(continued)*

JEREMIAH			
1:4-10	4 Epiphany		C
1:4-10	S. btwn. Aug. 21 and 27*	Pr. 16	C
2:4-13	S. btwn. Aug. 28 and Sept. 3*	Pr. 17	C
4:11-12, 22-28	S. btwn. Sept. 11 and 17*	Pr. 19	C
8:18—9:1	S. btwn. Sept. 18 and 24*	Pr. 20	C
11:18-20	S. btwn. Sept. 18 and 24	Pr. 20	B
14:7-10, 19-22	S. btwn. Oct. 23 and 29	Pr. 25	C
15:15-21	S. btwn. Aug. 28 and Sept. 3	Pr. 17	A
17:5-10	6 Epiphany		C
18:1-11	S. btwn. Sept. 4 and 10*	Pr. 18	C
20:7-13	S. btwn. June 19 and 25	Pr. 7	A
23:1-6	Christ the King	Pr. 29	C
23:1-6	Christ the King*	Pr. 29	C
23:1-6	S. btwn. July 17 and 23	Pr. 11	B
23:23-29	S. btwn. Aug. 14 and 20	Pr. 15	C
28:5-9	S. btwn. June 26 and July 2	Pr. 8	A
29:1, 4-7	S. btwn. Oct. 9 and 15*	Pr. 23	C
31:1-6	Easter Day		A
31:7-9	S. btwn. Oct. 23 and 29	Pr. 25	B
31:7-14	2 Christmas		A, B, C
31:27-34	S. btwn. Oct. 16 and 22*	Pr. 24	C
31:31-34	5 Lent		B
31:31-34	Reformation		A, B, C
32:1-3a, 6-15	S. btwn. Sept. 25 and Oct. 1*	Pr. 21	C
33:14-16	1 Advent		C
LAMENTATIONS			
1:1-6	S. btwn. Oct. 2 and 8*	Pr. 22	C
3:1-9, 19-24	Saturday in Holy Week		A, B, C
3:19-26	S. btwn. Oct. 2 and 8*	Pr. 22	C
3:22-33	S. btwn. June 26 and July 2	Pr. 8	B
EZEKIEL			
2:1-5	S. btwn. July 3 and 9	Pr. 9	B
17:22-24	S. btwn. June 12 and 18	Pr. 6	B
18:1-4, 25-32	S. btwn. Sept. 25 and Oct. 1	Pr. 21	A
33:7-11	S. btwn. Sept. 4 and 10	Pr. 18	A
34:11-16, 20-24	Christ the King	Pr. 29	A
36:24-28	Vigil of Easter		A, B, C
37:1-14	5 Lent		A
37:1-14	Day of Pentecost		B
37:1-14	Vigil of Easter		A, B, C
DANIEL			
3:1-29	Vigil of Easter		A, B, C
7:1-3, 15-18	All Saints Day		C
7:9-10, 13-14	Christ the King	Pr. 29	B
10:10-14; 12:1-3	St. Michael and All Angels		A, B, C
12:1-3	S. btwn. Nov. 13 and 19	Pr. 28	B
HOSEA			
1:2-10	S. btwn. July 24 and 30*	Pr. 12	C
2:14-20	8 Epiphany		B
2:14-20	S. btwn. May 24 and 28	Pr. 3	B
5:15—6:6	S. btwn. June 5 and 11	Pr. 5	A
11:1-11	S. btwn. July 31 and Aug. 6*	Pr. 13	C

JOEL			
2:1-2, 12-17	Ash Wednesday		A, B, C
2:21-27	Thanksgiving		B
2:23-32	S. btwn. Oct. 23 and 29*	Pr. 25	C
AMOS			
5:6-7, 10-15	S. btwn. Oct. 9 and 15	Pr. 23	B
5:18-24	S. btwn. Nov. 6 and 12	Pr. 27	A
6:1a, 4-7	S. btwn. Sept. 25 and Oct. 1	Pr. 21	C
7:7-15	S. btwn. July 10 and 16	Pr. 10	B
7:7-17	S. btwn. July 10 and 16*	Pr. 10	C
8:1-12	S. btwn. July 17 and 23*	Pr. 11	C
8:4-7	S. btwn. Sept. 18 and 24	Pr. 20	C
JONAH			
2:1-3 [4-6] 7-9	Vigil of Easter		A, B, C
3:1-5, 10	3 Epiphany		B
3:1-10	Vigil of Easter		A, B, C
3:10—4:11	S. btwn. Sept. 18 and 24	Pr. 20	A
MICAH			
3:5-12	S. btwn. Oct. 30 and Nov. 5	Pr. 26	A
5:2-5a	4 Advent		C
6:1-8	4 Epiphany		A
HABAKKUK			
1:1-4; 2:1-4	S. btwn. Oct. 2 and 8	Pr. 22	C
1:1-4; 2:1-4	S. btwn. Oct. 30 and Nov. 5*	Pr. 26	C
ZEPHANIAH			
1:7, 12-18	S. btwn. Nov. 13 and 19	Pr. 28	A
3:14-20	3 Advent		C
3:14-20	Vigil of Easter		A, B, C
HAGGAI			
1:15b—2:9	S. btwn. Nov. 6 and 12*	Pr. 27	C
ZECHARIAH			
9:9-12	S. btwn. July 3 and 9	Pr. 9	A
MALACHI			
3:1-4	Presentation of the Lord		A, B, C
3:1-4	2 Advent		C
4:1-2a	S. btwn. Nov. 13 and 19	Pr. 28	C
WISDOM OF SOLOMON			
1:13-15; 2:23-24	S. btwn. June 26 and July 2	Pr. 8	B
1:16—2:1, 12-22	S. btwn. Sept. 18 and 24	Pr. 20	B
3:1-9	All Saints		B
6:12-16	S. btwn. Nov. 6 and 12	Pr. 27	A
6:17-20	S. btwn. Nov. 6 and 12	Pr. 27	A
7:26—8:1	S. btwn. Sept. 11 and 17*	Pr. 19	B
10:15-21	2 Christmas		A, B, C
12:13, 16-19	S. btwn. July 17 and 23	Pr. 11	A

SIRACH

10:12-18	S. btwn. Aug. 28 and Sept. 3	Pr. 17	C
15:15-20	6 Epiphany		A
24:1-12	2 Christmas		A, B, C
27:4-7	S. btwn. May 24 and 28	Pr. 3	C
27:4-7	8 Epiphany		C
35:12-17	S. btwn. Oct. 23 and 29	Pr. 25	C

BARUCH

3:9-15, 32—4:4	Vigil of Easter		A, B, C
5:1-9	2 Advent		C

SONG OF THREE YOUNG MEN

35–65	Vigil of Easter		A, B, C

MATTHEW

1:18-25	4 Advent		A
2:1-12	Epiphany		A, B, C
2:13-23	1 Christmas		A
3:1-12	2 Advent		A
3:13-17	Baptism of the Lord		A
4:1-11	1 Lent		A
4:12-23	3 Epiphany		A
5:1-12	4 Epiphany		A
5:1-12	All Saints		A
5:13-20	5 Epiphany		A
5:21-37	6 Epiphany		A
5:38-48	7 Epiphany		A
6:1-6, 16-21	Ash Wednesday		A, B, C
6:24-34	8 Epiphany		A
6:24-34	S. btwn. May 24 and 28	Pr. 3	A
6:25-33	Thanksgiving		B
7:21-29	S. btwn. May 29 and June 4	Pr. 4	A
9:9-13, 18-26	S. btwn. June 5 and 11	Pr. 5	A
9:35—10:8 [9-23]	S. btwn. June 12 and 18	Pr. 6	A
10:24-39	S. btwn. June 19 and 25	Pr. 7	A
10:40-42	S. btwn. June 26 and July 2	Pr. 8	A
11:2-11	3 Advent		A
11:16-19, 25-30	S. btwn. July 3 and 9	Pr. 9	A
13:1-9, 18-23	S. btwn. July 10 and 16	Pr. 10	A
13:24-30, 36-43	S. btwn. July 17 and 23	Pr. 11	A
13:31-33, 44-52	S. btwn. July 24 and 30	Pr. 12	A
14:13-21	S. btwn. July 31 and Aug. 6	Pr. 13	A
14:22-33	S. btwn. Aug. 7 and 13	Pr. 14	A
15:[10-20] 21-28	S. btwn. Aug. 14 and 20	Pr. 15	A
16:13-20	S. btwn. Aug. 21 and 27	Pr. 16	A
16:21-28	S. btwn. Aug. 28 and Sept. 3	Pr. 17	A
17:1-9	Transfiguration of the Lord		A
18:15-20	S. btwn. Sept. 4 and 10	Pr. 18	A
18:21-35	S. btwn. Sept. 11 and 17	Pr. 19	A
20:1-16	S. btwn. Sept. 18 and 24	Pr. 20	A
21:1-11	Sunday of the Passion (palms)		A
21:23-32	S. btwn. Sept. 25 and Oct. 1	Pr. 21	A
21:33-46	S. btwn. Oct. 2 and 8	Pr. 22	A
22:1-14	S. btwn. Oct. 9 and 15	Pr. 23	A

LUKE

1:26-38	4 Advent		B
1:26-38	Annunciation of the Lord		A, B, C
1:39-45 [46-55]	4 Advent		C
1:39-57	Visitation of Mary to Elizabeth		A, B, C
1:46-55	Mary, Mother of the Lord		A, B, C
1:47-55	3 Advent		A, B
1:47-55	4 Advent		B, C
1:68-79	2 Advent		C
1:68-79	Christ the King*	Pr. 29	C
2:[1-7] 8-20	Christmas Dawn (II)		A, B, C
2:1-14 [15-20]	Christmas Eve (I)		A, B, C
2:22-40	1 Christmas		B
2:22-40	Presentation of the Lord		A, B, C
2:41-52	1 Christmas		C
3:1-6	2 Advent		C
3:7-18	3 Advent		C
3:15-17, 21-22	Baptism of the Lord		C
4:1-13	1 Lent		C
4:14-21	3 Epiphany		C
4:21-30	4 Epiphany		C
5:1-11	5 Epiphany		C
6:17-26	6 Epiphany		C
6:20-31	All Saints Day		C
6:27-38	7 Epiphany		C
6:39-49	8 Epiphany		C
6:39-49	S. btwn. May 24 and 28	Pr. 3	C
7:1-10	S. btwn. May 29 and June 4	Pr. 4	C
7:11-17	S. btwn. June 5 and 11	Pr. 5	C
7:36—8:3	S. btwn. June 12 and 18	Pr. 6	C
8:26-39	S. btwn. June 19 and 25	Pr. 7	C
9:28-36 [37-43]	Transfiguration of the Lord		C
9:51-62	S. btwn. June 26 and July 2	Pr. 8	C
10:1-11, 16-20	S. btwn. July 3 and 9	Pr. 9	C
10:17-20	St. Michael and All Angels		A, B, C
10:25-37	S. btwn. July 10 and 16	Pr. 10	C
10:38-42	S. btwn. July 17 and 23	Pr. 11	C
11:1-13	S. btwn. July 24 and 30	Pr. 12	C
12:13-21	S. btwn. July 31 and Aug. 6	Pr. 13	C
12:32-40	S. btwn. Aug. 7 and 13	Pr. 14	C
12:49-56	S. btwn. Aug. 14 and 20	Pr. 15	C
13:1-9	3 Lent		C
13:10-17	S. btwn. Aug. 21 and 27	Pr. 16	C
13:31-35	2 Lent		C
14:1, 7-14	S. btwn. Aug. 28 and Sept. 3	Pr. 17	C
14:25-33	S. btwn. Sept. 4 and 10	Pr. 18	C
15:1-3, 11b-32	4 Lent		C
15:1-10	S. btwn. Sept. 11 and 17	Pr. 19	C
16:1-13	S. btwn. Sept. 18 and 24	Pr. 20	C
16:19-31	S. btwn. Sept. 25 and Oct. 1	Pr. 21	C
17:5-10	S. btwn. Oct. 2 and 8	Pr. 22	C
17:11-19	S. btwn. Oct. 9 and 15	Pr. 23	C
17:11-19	Thanksgiving		A
18:1-8	S. btwn. Oct. 16 and 22	Pr. 24	C
18:9-14	S. btwn. Oct. 23 and 29	Pr. 25	C

LUKE *(continued)*

19:1-10	S. btwn. Oct. 30 and Nov. 5	Pr. 26	C
19:28-40	Sunday of the Passion		C
20:27-38	S. btwn. Nov. 6 and 12	Pr. 27	C
21:5-19	S. btwn. Nov. 13 and 19	Pr. 28	C
21:25-36	1 Advent		C
22:14—23:56	Sunday of the Passion		C
23:1-49	Sunday of the Passion		C
23:33-43	Christ the King	Pr. 29	C
24:1-12	Vigil of Easter		C
24:1-12	Easter Day		C
24:13-35	3 Easter		A
24:13-49	Easter Evening		A, B, C
24:36b-48	3 Easter		B
24:44-53	Ascension of the Lord		A, B, C

JOHN

1:[1-9] 10-18	2 Christmas		A, B, C
1:1-14	Christmas Day (III)		A, B, C
1:6-8, 19-28	3 Advent		B
1:29-42	2 Epiphany		A
1:43-51	2 Epiphany		B
2:1-11	2 Epiphany		C
2:13-22	3 Lent		B
3:1-17	2 Lent		A
3:1-17	Holy Trinity		B
3:13-17	Holy Cross		A, B, C
3:14-21	4 Lent		B
4:5-42	3 Lent		A
5:1-9	6 Easter		C
6:1-21	S. btwn. July 24 and 30	Pr. 12	B
6:24-35	S. btwn. July 31 and Aug. 6	Pr. 13	B
6:25-35	Thanksgiving		C
6:35, 41-51	S. btwn. Aug. 7 and 13	Pr. 14	B
6:51-58	S. btwn. Aug. 14 and 20	Pr. 15	B
6:56-69	S. btwn. Aug. 21 and 27	Pr. 16	B
7:37-39	Day of Pentecost		A
7:37-39	Vigil of Pentecost		A, B, C
8:31-36	Reformation		A, B, C
9:1-41	4 Lent		A
10:1-10	4 Easter		A
10:11-18	4 Easter		B
10:22-30	4 Easter		C
11:1-45	5 Lent		A
11:32-44	All Saints		B
12:1-8	5 Lent		C
12:1-11	Monday in Holy Week		A, B, C
12:12-16	Sunday of the Passion (palms)		B
12:20-33	5 Lent		B
12:20-36	Tuesday in Holy Week		A, B, C
13:1-17, 31b-35	Maundy Thursday		A, B, C
13:21-32	Wednesday in Holy Week		A, B, C
13:31-35	5 Easter		C
14:1-14	5 Easter		A
14:8-17 [25-27]	Day of Pentecost		C
14:15-21	6 Easter		A

14:23-29	6 Easter		C
15:1-8	5 Easter		B
15:9-17	6 Easter		B
15:26-27; 16:4b-15	Day of Pentecost		B
16:12-15	Holy Trinity		C
17:1-11	7 Easter		A
17:6-19	7 Easter		B
17:20-26	7 Easter		C
18:1—19:42	Good Friday		A, B, C
18:33-37	Christ the King	Pr. 29	B
19:38-42	Saturday in Holy Week		A, B, C
20:1-18	Easter Day		A, B, C
20:19-23	Day of Pentecost		A
20:19-31	2 Easter		A, B, C
21:1-19	3 Easter		C

ACTS

1:1-11	Ascension of the Lord		A, B, C
1:6-14	7 Easter		A
1:15-17, 21-26	7 Easter		B
2:1-11	Vigil of Pentecost		A, B, C
2:1-21	Day of Pentecost		A, B, C
2:14a, 22-32	2 Easter		A
2:14a, 36-41	3 Easter		A
2:42-47	4 Easter		A
3:12-19	3 Easter		B
4:5-12	4 Easter		B
4:32-35	2 Easter		B
5:27-32	2 Easter		C
7:55-60	5 Easter		A
8:14-17	Baptism of the Lord		C
8:26-40	5 Easter		B
9:1-6 [7-20]	3 Easter		C
9:36-43	4 Easter		C
10:34-43	Baptism of the Lord		A
10:34-43	Easter Day		A, B, C
10:44-48	6 Easter		B
11:1-18	5 Easter		C
16:9-15	6 Easter		C
16:16-34	7 Easter		C
17:22-31	6 Easter		A
19:1-7	Baptism of the Lord		B

ROMANS

1:1-7	4 Advent		A
1:16-17; 3:22b-28 [29-31]	S. btwn. May 29 and June 4	Pr. 4	A
3:19-28	Reformation		A, B, C
4:1-5, 13-17	2 Lent		A
4:13-25	2 Lent		B
4:13-25	S. btwn. June 5 and 11	Pr. 5	A
5:1-5	Holy Trinity		C
5:1-8	S. btwn. June 12 and 18	Pr. 6	A
5:1-11	3 Lent		A
5:12-19	1 Lent		A
6:1b-11	S. btwn. June 19 and 25	Pr. 7	A
6:12-23	S. btwn. June 26 and July 2	Pr. 8	A

ROMANS *(continued)*

6:3-11	Vigil of Easter		A, B, C
7:15-25a	S. btwn. July 3 and 9	Pr. 9	A
8:1-11	S. btwn. July 10 and 16	Pr. 10	A
8:6-11	5 Lent		A
8:12-17	Holy Trinity		B
8:12-25	S. btwn. July 17 and 23	Pr. 11	A
8:14-17	Day of Pentecost		C
8:14-17, 22-27	Vigil of Pentecost		A, B, C
8:22-27	Day of Pentecost		B
8:26-39	S. btwn. July 24 and 30	Pr. 12	A
9:1-5	S. btwn. July 31 and Aug. 6	Pr. 13	A
10:5-15	S. btwn. Aug. 7 and 13	Pr. 14	A
10:8b-13	1 Lent		C
11:1-2a, 29-32	S. btwn. Aug. 14 and 20	Pr. 15	A
12:1-8	S. btwn. Aug. 21 and 27	Pr. 16	A
12:9-16b	Visitation of Mary to Elizabeth		A, B, C
12:9-21	S. btwn. Aug. 28 and Sept. 3	Pr. 17	A
13:8-14	S. btwn. Sept. 4 and 10	Pr. 18	A
13:11-14	1 Advent		A
14:1-12	S. btwn. Sept. 11 and 17	Pr. 19	A
15:4-13	2 Advent		A
16:25-27	4 Advent		B

1 CORINTHIANS

1:1-9	2 Epiphany		A
1:3-9	1 Advent		B
1:10-18	3 Epiphany		A
1:18-24	Holy Cross		A, B, C
1:18-25	3 Lent		B
1:18-31	4 Epiphany		A
1:18-31	Tuesday in Holy Week		A, B, C
2:1-12 [13-16]	5 Epiphany		A
3:1-9	6 Epiphany		A
3:10-11, 16-23	7 Epiphany		A
4:1-5	8 Epiphany		A
4:1-5	S. btwn. May 24 and 28	Pr. 3	A
5:6b-8	Easter Evening		A, B, C
6:12-20	2 Epiphany		B
7:29-31	3 Epiphany		B
8:1-13	4 Epiphany		B
9:16-23	5 Epiphany		B
9:24-27	6 Epiphany		B
10:1-13	3 Lent		C
11:23-26	Maundy Thursday		A, B, C
12:1-11	2 Epiphany		C
12:3b-13	Day of Pentecost		A
12:12-31a	3 Epiphany		C
13:1-13	4 Epiphany		C
15:1-11	5 Epiphany		C
15:1-11	Easter Day		B
15:12-20	6 Epiphany		C
15:19-26	Easter Day		C
15:35-38, 42-50	7 Epiphany		C
15:51-58	8 Epiphany		C
15:51-58	S. btwn. May 24 and 28	Pr. 3	C

2 CORINTHIANS

1:18-22	7 Epiphany		B
3:1-6	8 Epiphany		B
3:1-6	S. btwn. May 24 and 28	Pr. 3	B
3:12—4:2	Transfiguration of the Lord		C
4:3-6	Transfiguration of the Lord		B
4:5-12	S. btwn. May 29 and June 4	Pr. 4	B
4:13—5:1	S. btwn. June 5 and 11	Pr. 5	B
5:6-10 [11-13] 14-17	S. btwn. June 12 and 18	Pr. 6	B
5:16-21	4 Lent		C
5:20b—6:10	Ash Wednesday		A, B, C
6:1-13	S. btwn. June 19 and 25	Pr. 7	B
8:7-15	S. btwn. June 26 and July 2	Pr. 8	B
9:6-15	Thanksgiving		A
12:2-10	S. btwn. July 3 and 9	Pr. 9	B
13:11-13	Holy Trinity		A

GALATIANS

1:1-12	S. btwn. May 29 and June 4	Pr. 4	C
1:11-24	S. btwn. June 5 and 11	Pr. 5	C
2:15-21	S. btwn. June 12 and 18	Pr. 6	C
3:23-29	S. btwn. June 19 and 25	Pr. 7	C
4:4-7	1 Christmas		B
4:4-7	Mary, Mother of the Lord		A, B, C
5:1, 13-25	S. btwn. June 26 and July 2	Pr. 8	C
6:[1-6] 7-16	S. btwn. July 3 and 9	Pr. 9	C

EPHESIANS

1:3-14	2 Christmas		A, B, C
1:3-14	S. btwn. July 10 and 16	Pr. 10	B
1:11-23	All Saints Day		C
1:15-23	Ascension of the Lord		A, B, C
1:15-23	Christ the King	Pr. 29	A
2:1-10	4 Lent		B
2:11-22	S. btwn. July 17 and 23	Pr. 11	B
3:1-12	Epiphany of the Lord		A, B, C
3:14-21	S. btwn. July 24 and 30	Pr. 12	B
4:1-16	S. btwn. July 31 and Aug. 6	Pr. 13	B
4:25—5:2	S. btwn. Aug. 7 and 13	Pr. 14	B
5:8-14	4 Lent		A
5:15-20	S. btwn. Aug. 14 and 20	Pr. 15	B
6:10-20	S. btwn. Aug. 21 and 27	Pr. 16	B

PHILIPPIANS

1:3-11	2 Advent		C
1:21-30	S. btwn. Sept. 18 and 24	Pr. 20	A
2:1-13	S. btwn. Sept. 25 and Oct. 1	Pr. 21	A
2:5-11	Sunday of the Passion		A, B, C
3:4b-14	5 Lent		C
3:4b-14	S. btwn. Oct. 2 and 8	Pr. 22	A
3:17—4:1	2 Lent		C
4:1-9	S. btwn. Oct. 9 and 15	Pr. 23	A
4:4-7	3 Advent		C
4:4-9	Thanksgiving		C

10:4-10	Annunciation of the Lord		A, B, C
10:5-10	4 Advent		C
10:11-14 [15-18] 19-25	S. btwn. Nov. 13 and 19	Pr. 28	B
10:16-25	Good Friday		A, B, C
11:1-3, 8-16	S. btwn. Aug. 7 and 13	Pr. 14	C
11:29—12:2	S. btwn. Aug. 14 and 20	Pr. 15	C
12:1-3	Wednesday in Holy Week		A, B, C
12:18-29	S. btwn. Aug. 21 and 27	Pr. 16	C
13:1-8, 15-16	S. btwn. Aug. 28 and Sept. 3	Pr. 17	C
JAMES			
1:17-27	S. btwn. Aug. 28 and Sept. 3	Pr. 17	B
2:1-10 [11-13] 14-17	S. btwn. Sept. 4 and 10	Pr. 18	B
3:1-12	S. btwn. Sept. 11 and 17	Pr. 19	B
3:13—4:3, 7-8a	S. btwn. Sept. 18 and 24	Pr. 20	B
5:7-10	3 Advent		A
5:13-20	S. btwn. Sept. 25 and Oct. 1	Pr. 21	B
1 PETER			
1:3-9	2 Easter		A
1:17-23	3 Easter		A
2:2-10	5 Easter		A
2:19-25	4 Easter		A
3:13-22	6 Easter		A
3:18-22	1 Lent		B
4:1-8	Saturday in Holy Week		A, B, C
4:12-14; 5:6-11	7 Easter		A
2 PETER			
1:16-21	Transfiguration of the Lord		A
3:8-15a	2 Advent		B
1 JOHN			
1:1—2:2	2 Easter		B
3:1-3	All Saints		A
3:1-7	3 Easter		B
3:16-24	4 Easter		B
4:7-21	5 Easter		B
5:1-6	6 Easter		B
5:9-13	7 Easter		B
REVELATION			
1:4-8	2 Easter		C
1:4b-8	Christ the King	Pr. 29	B
5:11-14	3 Easter		C
7:9-17	4 Easter		C
7:9-17	All Saints		A
12:7-12	St. Michael and All Angels		A, B, C
21:1-6	5 Easter		C
21:1-6a	All Saints		B
21:1-6a	New Year's Day		A, B, C
21:10, 22—22:5	6 Easter		C
22:12-14, 16-17, 20-21	7 Easter		C

Index of Scripture References

49:1-7 I come to the cross
Make my life a candle
We bow before his holy name
You are my hiding place
49:8-16a All around your throne
Though the mountains may fall
You've delivered me again
50:4-9a Awaken the song
Lord, my strength
No greater love
51:1-6 I see you
Your everlasting love
52:7-10 How beautiful upon the mountains
Lord, most high
The King of glory
52:13—53:12 All we like sheep
Amazing love
How beautiful upon the mountains
53:4-12 All we like sheep
Amazing love
55 Come to the water
Seek the Lord
55:1-5 All around your throne
Come to us
Reason to celebrate
Seek the Lord
55:1-9 Come to the river of life
Let it rain
Most holy one
55:10-13 Come to the river of life
He shall reign
Let it rain
Most holy one
Open our lives to the word
Sow the word
56:1, 6-8 Let all the world sing praises
We've come to praise you
58:1-12 Arise
Arise, oh Lord
Arise, shine
Faithful one
Morning has broken
Return to God
Rise up and praise him
58:9b-14 Morning has broken
Rest in my love
Return to God
60:1-6 Arise, shine
Here I am, Lord
I, the Lord of sea and sky
Shine, Jesus, shine
61:1-4, 8-11 He is Lord
God has chosen me
Good news
Great is the Lord
I Am
The Spirit of God
The Kingdom song
61:10—62:3 Beauty for brokenness
Before you now
Jesus, Jesus
62:1-5 My God reigns
62:6-12 Faithful one
You are mine
You have called us
63:7-9 I could sing of your love forever
The King of glory
64:1-9 Change my heart, O God
I bend my knees again
Now God our Father
65:1-9 You have called us
65:17-25 Heaven and earth
66:1-2 Mighty is our God
66:10-14 The river is here

JEREMIAH
1:4-10 Awaken the song
Before the sun burned bright
Open our eyes, Lord
Open our lives to the word
Teach me how to pray
2:4-13 Come to the fount of creation
Come to the river of life
4:11-12, 22-28 Awesome God
God the sculptor of the mountains
5:23 Here I am, Lord
8:18—9:1 Broken hearts
11:18-20 Here is my heart
14:7-10, 19-22 Here is my heart
May we have peace
15:15-21 God my refuge
Lord, my strength
17:5-10 Holy love
Water from heaven
18:1-11 Change my heart, O God
Now God our Father
20:7-13 Lord my strength
23:1-6 All we like sheep
He is exalted
King of kings
King of life
Like a shepherd
23:23-29 Let your fire fall
Revival fire, fall
The fire of your love
26:[1-6] 7-16 Open our lives to the word

MATTHEW *(continued)*

LUKE *(continued)*
10:17-20 All the power you need
Arise, oh Lord
Lord my strength
10:25-37 Mercy
My life is in you, Lord
Someone in need of your love
The people on your heart
With all my heart
10:38-42 Closer
Come closer
Meet us
We will draw near
When Jesus came preaching
11:1-13 First love
Heavenly Father
Lord we pray
Seek ye first
Song of the body of Christ
Teach me how to pray
12:2-3 All that is hidden
12:13-21 Give thanks
Let the river flow
Turn your eyes upon Jesus
12:32-40 My life is in you, Lord
Now in this banquet
Stir up the love
When the Lord comes
12:49-56 I don't belong to me
Let it rain
Let your fire fall
Revival fire, fall
Water from heaven
13:1-9 Change my heart, O God
Life in his hands
Turn my heart
13:10-17 Before you now
Celebrate love
Life in his hands
13:29 As the grains of wheat
13:31-35 All around your throne
Closer
Come and see
Come closer
Shelter me, O God
14:1, 7-14 Let the river flow
Now in this banquet
That we may be filled
14:25-33 I come to the cross
I want Jesus to walk with me
More precious than silver
Nothing is as wonderful
15:1-3, 11b-32 Come closer
Come to me today
God of love, have mercy
Mercy
We cry out for grace again
We love you
15:1-10 All we like sheep
I am the good shepherd
Like a shepherd
15:11-24 Come home
16:1-13 More precious than silver
Nothing is as wonderful
Only God for me
16:19-31 Give thanks
Let the river flow
Nothing is as wonderful
17:5-10 Come and grow
Good soil
Let the peace of God reign
17:11-19 Come touch
Healing word
Heal me, O Lord
Jesus, Jesus
Let your healing love
Mercy
Your steadfast love
18:1-8 God of love, have mercy
Lord, listen to your children praying
Teach me how to pray
We cry out for grace again
18:9-14 Gather us in
God of love, have mercy
Lord, listen to your children
Lord, we pray
Mercy
O Lord to you
Teach me how to pray
We will draw near
18:22 Two fishermen
19:1-10 Mercy
Someone in need of your love
The people on your heart
We shall not be silent
20:27-38 My life is in you, Lord
New life again and again
Thanksgiving to the living God
We can be lifted up
21:5-19 Firm foundation
I have kept the faith
My heart will trust
21:25-36 Eternity
Heaven and earth
My heart yearns for thee
The Kingdom song
This Kingdom
22:14—23:56 Bless the body broken for my sin
Broken in love

JOHN *(continued)*

ACTS *(continued)*

9:36-43	New life again and again
	We can be lifted up
10:34-43	He is Lord
	One
	Only God for me
	Singing through the water
10:44-48	Let it rain
	Rain down on us
	The river is here
11:1-18	Building block
11:19-30; 13:1-3	All the power you need
	Go, make disciples
11:27—12:3a	I have kept the faith
	Let it be said of us
12:15	The servant song
13:13-26	For all people Christ was born
13:26-33a	Because we believe
	This is the gospel of Christ
16:9-15	Give us your vision
16:16-34	I believe in Jesus
	I bend my knees again
	Saved by the grace of a miracle
17:22-31	Awesome God
	Heaven and earth
	Wind of God
19:1-7	I don't belong to me
	Spirit song

ROMANS

1:1-7	God sent his son
	Jesus, child of God
1:16-17; 3:22b-28	Because we believe
	For all you've done
	Only by grace
	Thanksgiving to the living God
	We've come to praise you
3:19-28	Because we believe
	Everlasting grace
	For by grace
	Only by grace
4:1-5, 13-17	Everlasting grace
	We walk by faith
	Your everlasting love
4:13-25	Firm foundation
	I have kept the faith
	We walk by faith
5:1-11	Amazing love
	Firm foundation
	For all you've done
	Lamb of God
	Leave your heart with me
	Rain down on us
	Saved by the grace of a miracle
	Spirit calls, rejoice!
5:12-19	King of life
	Life in his hands
	One
6:1b-11	I don't belong to me
	In the water
	Waterlife
6:3-11	Arise, shine
	For me
	Put on love
6:12-23	Life in his hands
	Sanctuary
	Song about grace
	Thank you for the gift
	Thank you, Lord
7:15-25a	Breathe on me
	Purify my heart
	You, Lord
8	Everyone moved by the Spirit
8:1-11	Arise, oh Lord
	Show me your ways
	Spirit calls, rejoice!
	Spirit of the living God
	The Spirit is singing
8:6-11	Come share the Spirit
	Life in his hands
	My life is in you, Lord
	Spirit of the living God
8:12-17	Lord, listen to your children praying
	Whom shall I fear?
8:12-25	Faithful Father
	Lord, listen to your children praying
	You're a child of God
8:14-17, 22-27	Spirit of the living God
	Teach me how to pray
	That we may be filled
	The people on your heart
8:26-39	For all you've done
	Holy love
	I'll belong to you
	Leave your heart with me
	Oh, how he loves you and me
	Spirit of the living God
	The people on your heart
	Your everlasting love
9:1-5	Before you now
10:5-15	Because we believe
	I believe in Jesus
	I do believe
10:8b-13	Because we believe
	Jesus, I believe
10:10-18	Because we believe
	I heard the voice of Jesus say
	Open our lives to the word

1 CORINTHIANS

PHILIPPIANS

COLOSSIANS

COLOSSIANS *(continued)*
My life is in you, Lord
The Spirit is singing
Waterlife
3:1-4 Jesus, amazing
My life is in you, Lord
3:1-11 Jesus, Lamb of God (All in all)
Over and over
Sanctuary
You are my hiding place
3:12-17 Forever grateful
Give thanks
Let the peace of God reign
Put on love
Someone in need of your love
Turn our hearts

1 THESSALONIANS
1:1-10 For all people Christ was born
God sent his son
Thanksgiving to the living God
This is the gospel of Christ
2:1-8 Our heart
2:9-13 Open our lives to the word
This Kingdom
3:9-13 All through the night
I'll belong to you
Only you
Turn our hearts
4:13-18 Because we believe
The trumpets sound, the angels sing
5:1-11 As the deer
I'll be waitin'
My heart yearns for thee
5:5 For the life of the world
5:16-24 Purify my heart
Sanctuary

2 THESSALONIANS
1:1-4, 11-12 Firm foundation
1:1-4; 2:5-12 God of glory
Jesus, child of God
Jesus, Lamb of God (All in all)
Who are we
2:1-5, 13-17 Soon and very soon
When the Lord comes
3:6-13 As you go on your way
Go and do
Into the life

1 TIMOTHY
1:12-17 Bless the body broken for my sin
Come to me today
2:1-7 I love to be in your presence
One
2:11 Alleluia, alleluia! Give thanks
6:6-19 I have kept the faith
King of life
Shine, Jesus, shine

2 TIMOTHY
1:1-14 All the power you need
Life in his hands
My life is in you, Lord
We walk by faith
2 Now we remain
We shall rise again
2:8-15 Broken in love
I don't belong to me
3:14—4:5 Amen
Open our lives to the word
Thy word
4:6-11, 16-18 I have kept the faith
Let it be said of us

TITUS
2:11-14 Everlasting grace
3:4-7 Saved by the grace of a miracle
The Spirit is singing

PHILEMON
1–21 Mercy
Song about grace

HEBREWS
1:1-4 [5-12] Like a rose in winter
Majesty
2:10-18 Come to me today
Everlasting grace
For all people Christ was born
God with us
4:12-16; 5:7-9 A taste of the joys of heaven
First love
God with us
How blessed
Only by grace
5:1-10 Broken hearts
For me
I don't belong to me
Leave your heart with me
5:5-10 Broken hearts
Lamb of God
You, Lord
7:23-28 Everlasting grace
For he alone is worthy
Lamb of God
The fire of your love
9 The King of glory
9:11-15 O, mighty cross

1 JOHN *(continued)*

	More like Jesus Christ
	Open our eyes, Lord
3:16-24	As bread that is broken
	Someone in need of your love
	Turn our hearts
	We love you
4:1-6	I belong to a mighty God
	I'll belong to you
4:12	Love one another
4:7-21	Come closer
	Forever grateful
	I love you, Lord
	Jesus, I believe
	O, mighty cross
	This Kingdom
	Turn our hearts
	We love you
	We will draw near
4:16	Many are the lightbeams
	Ubi caritas
5:1-6	I have kept the faith
	Rock of ages
	You are my rock
5:9-13	Life in his hands
	My life is in you, Lord
	New life again and again

REVELATION

1:4-8	Be glorified
	From A to O
	Glorious
	Glory be!
	God of glory
	It has always been you
	Soon and very soon
	To God be the glory
5:11-14	Glorify thy name
	We will glorify
	Worthy the Lamb that was slain
	You are holy
	You are the Lord of me
7:9-17	All around your throne
	Eternity
	He is exalted
	Praise we render
	Water from heaven
	Worthy the Lamb that was slain
12:7-12	I belong to a mighty God
	Let the peace of God reign
	Mighty is our God
21:1-6	Christ is risen! Shout hosanna!
	Come to the fount of creation
	Heaven and earth
	Jehovah
	Mourning into dancing
	Soon and very soon
	When we eat this bread
21:10; 22—22:5	All around your throne
	Come to the river of life
22:12-14, 16-17, 20-21	Bright and morning star
	Each winter
	From A to O
	Soon and very soon
22:16	Come to set us free
22:20	Each winter as the year grows older
	Soon and very soon

Index of Seasons and Topics

ADORATION
All hail King Jesus
All in all
All is ready now
All the ends of the earth
Alleluia, alleluia! Give thanks
Amen
Arise, shine
At the name of Jesus
Bless his holy name
Blessing, honor and glory
Break into songs of joy
Center of my life
Come and see
Come, worship the Lord
Emmanuel
Glorify thy name
Glory and praise to our God
Glory to God
He has made me glad
Holy, holy
How majestic is your name
I love you, Lord
I was glad
I will celebrate
I will delight
I will sing of the mercies of the Lord
I will sing, I will sing
Jesus, name above all names
King of kings
Let there be praise
Let us go rejoicing
Lord, I lift your name on high
Majesty
Morning has broken
Mourning into dancing
Now God our Father
Praise, praise, praise the Lord
Shout to the Lord
Sing a joyful song
Sing a new song
Sing of the Lord's goodness
Sing out, earth and skies
Sing to the mountains
Step by step
The trumpets sound, the angels sing
This is the day
This is the feast of victory
We are called
We bow down
We bring the sacrifice of praise
We see the Lord
We will glorify

ADVENT
A message came to maiden young
A story for all people
A voice cries out
Advent song
All earth is hopeful
Arise
Arise, shine
As the deer
Awake! Awake, and greet the new morn
Beauty for brokenness
Bright and morning star

ADVENT *(continued)*
Canticle of the turning
Carol of the child
Change my heart, O God
Come to set us free
Come, let us worship God
Cry out with joy and gladness
Each winter as the year grows older
Emmanuel
Eternity
Every valley
Faithful one
First love
For all people Christ was born
Give us your vision
Glorious
God sent his son
God with us
Good news
He came down
He came to be baptized
He is Jesus
He shall reign
He who began a good work in you
Hear our cry
Here begins the good news
Holy love, holy light
I see the Lord
I see you
I want to be ready
I want to know you
I'll be waitin'
I'll bless the Lord for evermore
Jesus, child of God
King of kings
Let the king of glory come
Let the valleys be raised
Lift up your heads
Lift up your hearts
Light the darkness
Like a shepherd
Look to the one
Lord, you've been our dwelling place
Magnificat
Maranatha
Maranatha, come
Mary's song
Meet us
My heart yearns for thee
My Lord will come again
My soul in stillness waits
No wind at the window
Now in this banquet
O come, O come, Emmanuel
On Jordan's bank
On the mountain top
Open our eyes
Patience until the coming of the Lord
Peace
Peace child
Refiner's fire
Rejoice in the mission
Save us, O Lord
Send out your grace abundantly
Shine on us
Soon and very soon
Stand firm
Star of David
Stir up
Take of the wonder
The angel Gabriel from heaven came
The king of glory
The Lord of glory
The wondrous day of our God
This kingdom
Turn my heart
Unto thee, O Lord
Wake up, sleeper
Walk in the reign
We cry out for grace again
We will draw near
When the Lord in glory comes
While we are waiting
Who has known
Who will stand up
Whom shall I fear?
Within our hearts be born
Wonderful counselor

AFFIRMATION OF BAPTISM
Be bold, be strong
For by grace
God, here is my life and my will
He who began a good work in you
I believe in Jesus
I belong to a mighty God
I do believe
I don't belong to me
I was there to hear your borning cry
Jesus, I believe
My chosen one
Nothing can come between us
Now God our Father
Our confidence is in the Lord
Singing through the water
The river is here
The summons
This is the gospel of Christ
Waterlife
You are mine

You are my God
You, Lord
You're a child of God

ALL SAINTS DAY/SAINTS DAYS

All around your throne
Alleluia
As the deer
Because we believe
Blest are they
Bring forth the kingdom
Come and taste
Come to the fount of creation
Deep river
Eat this bread, drink this cup
Eternity
Firm foundation
Give thanks
Glory, glory! Hallelujah!
Go and do
Go in peace and serve the Lord
Go, make disciples
Heaven and earth
Here I am, Lord
I am the bread of life
I am the good shepherd
I am the resurrection
I believe in Jesus
I do believe
I was there to hear your borning cry
I will sing, I will sing
Jehovah
Let it be said of us
Let the river flow
Mourning into dancing
No longer strangers
Oh, when the saints go marching in
On the mountain top
Only God for me
Praise we render
Saved by the grace of a miracle
Sing with all the saints in glory
Soon and very soon
Stand up and give him the praise
Taste and see
The gift of giving
The king of glory
The trees of the field
The trumpets sound, the angels sing
This is the feast of victory
We are called
We are marching in the light of God
We are the light of the world
Worthy the lamb that was slain
You only

ANNUNCIATION OF THE LORD

A message came to a maiden young
Ave Maria
Be glorified
Canticle of the turning
Emmanuel
Faithful one
He came down
Here am I
Here I am, Lord
Jesus, Jesus
Magnificat
Magnify the Lord
Mary's song
My soul in stillness waits
No wind at the window
Now God our Father
Our hope is alive
Shine down on me
Sing, my soul
Stir up the love
The queen stands at your right hand

ARTS AND MUSIC

All the ends of the earth
Come let us sing out our praise
I will enter his gates
I will sing, I will sing
Morning has broken
Praise, praise, praise the Lord
Shout to the Lord
Sing a new song
Sing a song to the Lord
Sing my soul
Sing out, earth and skies
Song of the angels
The spirit is singing
The trumpet in the morning
The trumpets sound, the angels sing
We are an offering

ASCENSION OF THE LORD

Age to age everlasting
Arise
Arise, oh Lord
Awesome God
Clap your hands
Come touch
El Shaddai
Emmanuel
Glorious God
Go
Go and do
Go in peace and serve the Lord
Go to the world!

ASCENSION OF THE LORD *(continued)*
Go, make disciples
God mounts his throne
God mounts his throne to shouts
God without and within
I see the Lord
I will be with you
I will be with you always
It has always been you
Lord, I lift your name on high
Love you so much
Majesty
My God reigns
Our God is lifted up
Shout to the Lord
Soon and very soon
Who will stand up

ASH WEDNESDAY
Ashes
Be my home
Beauty for ashes
Change our hearts
Create in me
Create in me a clean heart
Deep within
Dust and ashes
Give me a new heart
Give thanks
God of love, have mercy
Here is my heart
I bend my knees again
I want Jesus to walk with me
Lord, listen to your children
Mourning into dancing
Please have mercy on me
Return to God
Seek the Lord
Share your bread with the hungry
We can be lifted up
We cry out for grace

ASSURANCE
A taste of the joys of heaven
As you go on your way
Come to me today
Don't be anxious
Firm foundation
Forever my friend
From A to O
God is here
God my refuge
God provides a brand new heart
God sent his son
God will make a way
God without and within
He who began a good work
Here is bread
I am
I am the resurrection
I was there to hear your borning cry
I will be with you always
Leave your heart with me
Make your presence known
On eagle's wings
Our help is in the name
Rest in my love
Seek ye first
Surely the presence of the Lord
The Lord will keep me safe and holy
There's a sweet, sweet spirit
We will draw near
Whom shall I fear?
You are mine

ATONEMENT
Amazing love
At the foot of the cross
How blessed
I come to the cross
I don't belong to me
Lamb of God
Saved by the grace of a miracle
Taste of the joys of heaven
We bring the sacrifice of praise

BAPTISM OF THE LORD
Come to the fount of creation
Come to the river of life
Come to the water
Create in me a clean heart
Flowing river
Glory be!
He came to be baptized
Holy love
I don't belong to me
I saw water
In the water
King of kings
Lay down that spirit
Let the fire fall
O star of beauty
O'er the river Jordan
Shine on us, Lord
Singing through the water
Song over the waters
The holy Lamb of God
The Lord will bless all people
The river is here
Wade in the water

Waterlife
You are mine
You have anointed me

CELEBRATION

All around your throne
Alleluia
Almighty
Awesome God
Celebrate Jesus
Celebrate love
Happy are they
He has made me glad
He is exalted
His love endures forever
I could sing of your love forever
I love to be in your presence
I was glad
I will call upon the Lord
I will celebrate
In Christ, a new creation
Join in the dance
Let there be praise
Mourning into dancing
My God reigns
Now God our Father
Praise to you, O Christ
Reason to celebrate
Ring, ring all the living bells
Sing out, earth and skies
The festival psalm
The river is here
The spirit is singing
The trees of the field
The trumpets sound, the angels sing
This is the day
This is the feast of victory
We rejoice in the grace of God

CHRIST THE KING

All we like sheep
Alleluia
Amazing love
Ancient of days
Arise, shine
At the name of Jesus
Awesome God
Be glorified
Blessed be the Lord
Bright and morning star
Bring forth the kingdom
Church of God
Come and see
Come share the spirit
Come, worship the Lord
Crux fidelis
Eternity
For he is worthy
For the life of the world
Gathered as one
Glorious
Glory be!
God is good
God of glory
He has made me glad
He is exalted
He is Lord
He shall reign
Heaven and earth
I belong to a mighty God
I come to the cross
I love you, Lord
I praise your name
I see the Lord
I will be with you always
I will bow down and worship
I will come and bow down
I will enter his gates
I will never be
In the arms of the shepherd
It has always been you
Jehovah
Jesus is our king
King of kings
King of life
Let all the world sing praises
Light the darkness
Like a shepherd
Lord most high
Majesty
Mighty is our God
My God reigns
O mighty cross
Reason to celebrate
Shine, Jesus, shine
Shout to the Lord
Soon and very soon
Strange king
Thanksgiving to the living God
The King of glory
The kingdom song
The Lord is king
The Lord reigns
This kingdom
To God be the glory
We bow down
We see the Lord
We shall not be silent
You are my rock

CHRISTMAS
A stable lamp is lighted
All is Christmas
Arise and sing
Arise, shine
Awake! Awake, and greet the new morn
Carol at the manger
Child of mercy
Child of the poor
Christ is born in bethlehem
City of God
Emmanuel
Faithful one
For all people Christ was born
Gentle night
Give thanks
Glory be!
He brings peace
He came down
He is Jesus
Hear the angels
Holy child
Holy child within the manger
Holy love, holy light
How beautiful upon the mountains
I wonder as I wander
I wonder if he knew
Jehovah
Jesus, child of God
Jesus, Jesus
Joy came down at Christmastide
Let the heavens rejoice
Like a rose in winter
Make my life a candle
Nativity carol
Night of silence
O star of beauty
On a holy night
On Christmas night
Once and for all time
Peace child
People of the night
Proclaim to the nations
Ring the chimes, ring the Christmas bells
Rise up, shepherd, and follow
Song of the stable
Star of David
That boy-child of Mary
The aye carol
The Lord of glory
The tiny child to Bethlehem came
The virgin Mary had a baby boy
Today a Savior is born
Wake from your sleep
We declare your name
Welcome the child
Within our hearts be born

CHURCH
Because we believe
Blessed be Yahweh
Blessing, honor and glory
Building block
Built on a rock
Church of God
Come worship the Lord
For by grace
Gathered as one
Hop on the bus
I was glad
Lord, be glorified
Make your presence known
No longer strangers
One bread, one body
Sanctuary
Seed, scattered and sown
Send out your grace abundantly
Stand in the congregation
The church song
There is a redeemer

COMFORT AND REST
All through the night
Be my home
Beauty for brokenness
Blessed be the name
Broken hearts
Cares chorus
Come closer
Come to me
Come to me today
Come, let us worship God
Don't be anxious
God is here
God without and within
How beautiful upon the mountains
I am
I am the good shepherd
I heard the voice of Jesus say
I will be with you always
I'll bless the Lord for evermore
Leave your heart with me
Make your presence known
On the mountain top
Rest in my love
Rest in your love
Where you lead me
You are mine
You are my all in all
You are my hiding place

COMMISSIONING, LAY MINISTRY
As bread that is broken
Bring forth the kingdom
Here am I
Here I am, Lord
In Christ, a new creation
My chosen one
Rejoice in the mission
Someone in need of your love
Step by step
The summons

COMMITMENT
Alleluia
An offering of thanksgiving
As bread that is broken
Here I am
Here I am, Lord
Hop on the bus
I have decided to follow Jesus
I have kept the faith
I will never be
Jesus, I believe
O Lord to you
Standing on the Lord's side
Step by step
We are an offering

CONFESSION OF SIN
All we like sheep
Be magnified
Be merciful, O Lord
Change our hearts
Create in me
Create in me a clean heart
Faithful Father
Give me a new heart
God of love, have mercy
Here is my heart
I bend my knees again
I'll belong to you
Please have mercy on me
Return to God
Shout to God, O faithful people
We cry for grace
We've come to praise you

CREATION
Age to age, everlasting
Awesome God
Beauty for brokenness
Because we believe
Before the sun burned bright
Blessed be yahweh
Creation/Tales of wonder
For all you've done
From A to O
Give thanks
Glory and praise to our God
God has done marvelous things
God the sculptor of the mountains
Great is the Lord
Heaven and earth
His love endures forever
I am
I do believe
I see you
I will sing, I will sing
Jehovah
Majesty
Mighty is our God
Morning has broken
Now we raise our thanks to you
Oh sing to the Lord
Rain down
Rain down on us
Shout to the Lord
Singing through the water
Song over the waters
This is the day
To God be the glory
We bow down
You are the I Am
You are the Lord of me

CROSS, THE
Amazing love
Carol of the thorn tree
Embrace my way and cross
Forever grateful
How blessed
I come to the cross
I do believe
Leave your heart with me
Let it be said of us
Lord, I lift your name on high
New life again and again
O, mighty cross
Only by grace
Only God for me
Praise we render
Strange king
The cross of Jesus
Tree of life

DEATH AND RESURRECTION
A taste of the joys of heaven
Alleluia! Jesus is risen!
As the grains of wheat
Broken hearts

DEATH AND RESURRECTION *(continued)*
Come to the fount of creation
Eat this bread, drink this cup
Eternity
Faithful Father
For God is love
God sent his son
He is exalted
Here is bread
Holy ground
I am the resurrection
I see the Lord
I was there to hear your borning cry
I will sing, I will sing
Jesus, help me see
Jesus, remember me
Join the dance
Live in my love
Majesty
Mourning into dancing
My life is in you, Lord
No more strangers
Now we remain
On eagle's wings
On the mountain top
Our confidence is in the Lord
Precious Lord, take my hand
Soon and very soon
Step by step
Taste and see
The love of the Lord
The trees of the field
The trumpets sound, the angels sing
Trading my sorrows
Up from the earth
We see the Lord
You are my all in all

DEVOTION
As the deer
First love
Flow like a river
Flowing river
Here I am
Holy, holy
I bend my knees again
I could sing of your love forever
I want to know you
I will bow down and worship
I'll belong to you
Lamb of God
Lead me, oh lead me
Let your fire fall
Love you so much
Make my life a candle
Nothing is as wonderful
Now God our Father
O Lord to you
Offering
Only God for me
Rest in your love
Sanctuary
Spirit of the living God
The gift of giving
We are an offering
Wonderful counselor
You are I Am
You've delivered me again

EASTER
All things new
Alleluia
Alleluia! Jesus is risen!
Alleluia, alleluia! Give Thanks
Amazing love
Arise, shine
Be exalted
Be glorified
Celebrate Jesus
Christ is risen
Christ is risen! Shout hosanna
Christ the Lord is risen
Come away to the skies
Come to me today
Come to the river of life
Eastertide carol
Glory, glory, hallelujah!
God sent his son
Hallelujah! Praise the Lord
He is Lord
Heaven and earth
I am the living bread
I am the resurrection
I believe in Jesus
I cannot tell it all
I come with joy
I will be with you always
I will celebrate
I will enter his gates
I will give you peace
In Christ, a new creation
Jesus, amazing
Join in the dance
King of life
Let all the world sing praises
Let the heavens rejoice
Lord, I lift your name on high
Mourning into dancing
New life again and again
Now in this banquet

Now the green blade rises
On the mountain top
On the road to Emmaus.
One
Only God for me
Our God reigns
Praise God with the trumpet
Praise we render
Praises resound
Reason to celebrate
Ring, ring all the living bells
Rise up and praise him
Shine on us
Shout to the Lord
Sing out, earth and skies
The honduras alleluia
The trumpets sound, the angels sing
This day was made by the Lord
This is the day
Trading my sorrows
We walk by faith
Welcome the King

EASTER VIGIL

A canticle of creation
A taste of the joys of heaven
Amazing love
Ancient of days
Be exalted
Behold the glory of God
Celebrate Jesus
Come to the feast
Come to the river of life
Come to the water
Deep within
Eternity
Everlasting grace
From A to O
Glorious
God provides a brand new heart
Heaven and earth
Join in the dance
Ring, ring all the living bells
Roll away the stone
Song over the waters
Strange king
Streams of living water
Table of plenty
Tales of wonder
Up from the earth
Water from heaven
Wind of the spirit
You are my all in all

EPIPHANY

All the earth, proclaim God's glory
Alleluia
Arise, shine out
Arise, shine!
Every nation on earth
Follow me
Glory be
God has spoken, bread is broken
God, be gracious
Good news
He came down
He came to be baptized
He is exalted
Heal me, O Lord
Healing word
Hear the angels
Here I am, Lord
Holy child
Holy love
I am
I am the light of the world
I do believe
I heard the voice of Jesus say
I saw water
It has always been you
Jesus lead on
Jesus, help me see
Jesus, I believe
King of kings
Lay down that spirit
Let the fire fall
Let the river flow
Lord, my strength
Lord, every nation
Lord, today
Make me a servant
Make my life a candle
Morning has broken
Mourning into dancing
O Lord, be my help
O star of beauty
O'er the river Jordan
Open our lives to the word
Our heart
'Round the table
Send out your grace abundantly
Shine on us
Shine on us, Lord
Shine, Jesus, shine
Singing through the water
Song over the waters
Speak now, O Lord
The God of all grace
The Lord will bless all people

EPIPHANY *(continued)*
The spirit of God
The summons
This little light of mine
Thy word
Two fishermen
Waterlife
We bow before his holy name
We receive power
When Jesus came preaching
Where you lead me
Whom shall I fear?
You are mine
You are my hiding place
You have anointed me
You have called us

EVANGELISM. *SEE* PROCLAMATION

EXALTATION
All hail, King Jesus
Alleluia
Awesome God
Be exalted
Be glorified
Be magnified
Glorify thy name
Glorious
Glory and praise to our God
He is exalted
Holy ground
Holy, holy, holy
How majestic is your name
I see the Lord
I will call upon the Lord
I will celebrate
I will sing, I will sing
King of kings
King of life
Lift up your heads
Lord, I lift your name on high
Lord most high
Lord of heaven
Lord, be glorified
Majesty
Now God our Father
Shine down
Shine, Jesus, shine
Shout to the Lord
The King of glory
The trumpets sound, the angels sing
This is the feast of victory
We bow down
We bring the sacrifice of praise
We will glorify

FAITH
All the power you need
Alleluia
As the deer
At the name of Jesus
Be bold, be strong
Beauty for brokenness
Because we believe
Building block
By grace have we been saved
For all you've done
He who began a good work in you
I believe in Jesus
I do believe
I have kept the faith
I see you
I was there to hear your borning cry
I will call upon the Lord
I will celebrate
I will delight
I will sing of the mercies of the Lord
Into the life
Jesus, I believe
Lead me, guide me
Lord, be glorified
Lord, listen to your children
Lord, my strength
Make me a servant
Name above all names
Now in this banquet
Now we remain
Out in the wilderness
Rest in your love
Say to the mountain
Shout to the Lord
Stand in the congregation
Step by step
That Christ be known
The summons
We walk by faith
We've come to worship you
What a mighty word God gives
Women of faith
You are mine
You are the rock of my salvation

FAMILY
All the ends of the earth
An offering of thanksgiving
Bind us together
Come to the water
Come to us
Faith, hope and love
Gather your people
I was there to hear your borning cry
I will not die

Justice shall fourish
Let all the earth cry out
Let us go rejoicing
My chosen one
No longer strangers
Now God our Father
One bread, one body
Pan de vida
Sing of the Lord's goodness
The family of the Lord

FORGIVENESS, HEALING
A taste of the joys of heaven
All the power you need
All we like sheep
Amazing love
An offering of thanksgiving
Bless the body broken for my sin
Breathe on me
Broken hearts
Change my heart, O God
Come closer
Come to me
Come to me today
Come touch
Come touch
Everlasting grace
God is here
Heal me, O Lord
Healing word
Here is my heart
Holy love, holy light
How blessed
I believe in Jesus
I bend my knees again
I come to the cross
Jesus, Jesus
Lamb of God
Leave your heart with me
Let it rain
Let your healing love
Lord my strength
Mercy
Mourning into dancing
O, mighty cross
Refiner's fire
Say the name
Shout to God, O faithful people
The Lamb
Turn my heart
Turn our hearts
White as snow

FREEDOM
Almighty
Arise, oh Lord
Breathe on me
Flow like a river
Glory be!
Healing word
How beautiful upon the mountains
I could sing of your love forever
In Christ, a new creation
Let your healing love
Most holy one
Only God for me
Only you
Sing unto the Lord
We declare your name

GATHERING
A story for all people
All around your throne
All hail King Jesus
All is ready now
Alleluia, alleluia! Give thanks
As the deer
As the grains of wheat
Awake! Awake and greet the new morn
Awesome God
Come and see
Come and taste
Come away to the skies
Come share the spirit
Come to the mountain
Emmanuel
Father, I adore you
Gather us in
Glory and praise to our God
God has done marvelous things
God is here
Great is the Lord
He has made me glad
He is exalted
Holy ground
How majestic is your name
I love you, Lord
I was glad
I will celebrate
I will enter his gates
I will sing, I will sing
Jesus, name above all names
King of kings
Let justice roll like a river
Let us rejoice
Lord, I lift your name on high
Majesty
Make your presence known
Morning has broken
Mourning into dancing
Now God our Father
Oh sing to the Lord

As the grains of wheat
For the Lord is good
Gathered as one
Give thanks
Glory and praise to our God
God is so good
God the sculptor of the mountains
I will sing, I will sing
Indeed, how good is the Lord
Now we raise our thanks to you
Rain down
Taste and see
Thanksgiving to the living God
You have been good

HOLY BAPTISM
Be not afraid
Come to the fount of creation
Come to the water
He came to be baptized
I don't belong to me
I saw water
I was there to hear your borning cry
In the water
Lord, bless your people
Make me a servant
O'er the river Jordan
On eagle's wings
Only for your glory
Shine on us, Lord
Singing through the water
Song over the waters
Spirit song
The river is here
Wade in the water
Water from heaven
Waterlife
Wind of the spirit
You have anointed me
You have been given

HOLY COMMUNION
Amazing love
As bread that is broken
As the grains of wheat
Bless the body broken for my sin
Broken in love
Come to me today
Cup we bless
Eat this bread, drink this cup
For me
God has spoken, bread is broken
Here is bread
How blessed
I am the resurrection
I come with joy
Live in my love
Now in this banquet
One
One bread, one body
One in the bread
Poured out and broken
That we may be filled
The night of his betrayal

HOLY CROSS DAY
Amazing love
At the foot of the cross
By grace we have been saved
Crux fidelis
Embrace my way and cross
For God so loved
Forever grateful
Hop on the bus
How blessed
I come to the cross
I have decided to follow Jesus
Jesus, remember me
Lift high the cross
Now we remain
O, mighty cross
Only God for me
Strange king
The cross of Jesus
There is a redeemer
Tree of life
We love you

HOLY SPIRIT
Breathe on me
Envia tu espiritu
Every time I feel the spirit
Everyone moved by the spirit
Flow like a river
Go to the world
God without and within
I do believe
I want to be ready
Let it rain
Let the peace of God reign
Let the river flow
Let your fire fall
Lord, send out your spirit
One bread, one body
Over and over
Precious Lord, take my hand
Rain down
Rain down on us
Revival fire, fall
Send down the fire

HOLY SPIRIT *(continued)*
Send forth your spirit, O Lord
Spirit blowing through creation
Spirit calls, rejoice!
Spirit of the living God
Spirit song
Spirit-Friend
Teach me how to pray
That we may be filled
The river is here
The spirit is singing
The spirit of God
They'll know we are Christians
We are many parts
We know and believe
When you send forth your spirit
Wind of God
Wind of the spirit

HOLY TRINITY
All the earth, proclaim God's glory
Alleluia, sing!
Because we believe
Eternity
Father, I adore you
Glorify thy name
God beyond all names
Great one in three
Holy, holy
How wonderful the three in one
I do believe
Jesus, I believe
Let there be praise
My Lord, what a morning
Praise to the trinity
Praises resound
Spirit song
Stand up friends

HOPE
Alleluia! Jesus is risen!
As the deer
Be my home
Beauty for brokenness
Come, let us worship God
Don't be anxious
Everything I am
Firm foundation
Forever my friend
Freely, given freely
Go in peace and serve the Lord
He who began a good work in you
May you run and not be weary
My heart will trust
My life is in you, Lord
Name above all names
No longer strangers
Now in this banquet
Now we remain
Our confidence is in the Lord
Soon and very soon
The king of glory
Why so downcast?
You are mine
You are the rock of my salvation

HUMILITY
An offering of thanksgiving
At the name of Jesus
Be merciful, O Lord
Beauty for ashes
Beauty for brokenness
Change my heart, O God
Closer
I come to the cross
I place my life
I will come and bow down
Jesu, Jesu, fill us with your love
Jesus, keep me near the cross
Make me a servant
Mourning into dancing
No greater love
Nothing at all but love
O God of love, have mercy
Please have mercy on me
Reach out and take a hand
So you must do
The servant song
We bow before his holy name
We bow down
We cry out for grace
We cry out for grace again
Who are we
You are my God

HUNGER
A taste of the joys of heaven
As bread that is broken
As the deer
Be thou my vision
Beauty for brokenness
Come, let us worship God
Commune with me
I need you
Praises resound
So you must do

INCARNATION
A message came to a maiden young
Ave Maria

Canticle of the turning
Carol at the manger
Child of Mary
Child of mercy
Emmanuel
Faithful one
For all the faithful women
Forever grateful
God the sculptor of the mountains
God with us
God, beyond all names
He brings peace
He came down
Hold us in your mercy
Jesus Christ, yesterday, today and forever
Lord, today
Many and great
Nativity carol
Now the feast and celebration
Praise to you, O Christ, our Savior
Rise up, shepherd, and follow
Song of the chosen
Song of the stable
Sow the word
Thanks be to you
The tiny child to Bethlehem came

INNER LIFE

All that is hidden
As you go on your way
Be my home
Be thou my vision
Breathe on me
Change my heart oh God
Closer
Come and grow
Create in me a clean heart
Flow like a river
Flowing river
Give us your vision
God without and within
Good soil
Guide my feet
I will be with you always
Jesus, help me see
Jesus, I believe
Jesus, Jesus
My heart yearns for thee
Restless is the heart
Turn my heart
Turn your eyes upon Jesus
You are I Am
You are my all in all

INVITATION

Come adore
Come and follow me
Come and see
Come and taste
Come away to the skies
Come closer
Come share the spirit
Come to me
Come to me today
Come to the feast
Come to the fount of creation
Come to the mountain
Come to the river of life
Come to the table
Come to the water
Come to us
Come, let us worship God
Gather us in
Gather your people
Hop on the bus
I come to the cross
I'll bless the Lord for evermore
Taste and see
The trumpets sound, the angels sing
We've come to praise you

INVOCATION

Arise
As the deer
Awaken the song
Come to me
Come to me today
Come, let us worship God
I thank you Lord for love unknown
Into the life
Let the river flow
Let your fire fall
Meet us
Teach me how to pray
We cry out for grace again
Wind of God

JESUS THE SON

Alive in Christ Jesus
All hail King Jesus
All we like sheep
Amazing love
At the foot of the cross
At the name of Jesus
Be near us, Lord Jesus
Blessings on the king
Broken in love
Calvary
Carol of the thorn tree

JESUS THE SON *(continued)*

Christ is risen! Shout hosanna
Come to me
Come to me today
Come touch
Crucifixion/Song of Mark
Cup we bless
Do not let your hearts be troubled
Each winter as the year grows older
Emmanuel
Father, I put my life in your hands
For God so loved
For the life of the world
Glorious in majesty
Glory be!
Go
Good news
He came down
He came to be baptized
He is exalted
He is Lord
Here I am, Lord
Holy child
Hosanna to the son of David
How blessed
I come to the cross
I danced in the morning
I do believe
I have decided to follow Jesus
I see the Lord
I want Jesus to walk with me
I'm so glad Jesus lifted me
In Christ, a new creation
In the breaking of the bread
Into your hands, O Lord, I commend my spirit
Jesu, Jesu
Jesus in the morning
Jesus is here right now
Jesus lead on
Jesus reigns
Jesus walked this lonesome valley
Jesus, amazing
Jesus, child of God
Jesus, heal us
Jesus, help me see
Jesus, I believe
Jesus, Jesus
Jesus, mighty God
Jesus, name above all names
Jesus, remember me
Jesus, shepherd of our souls
Jesus, the Lord
King of life
Kyrie eleison
Lamb of God
Life in his hands
Like a shepherd
Live in me
Lord of heaven
Meet us
More like Jesus Christ
Morning has broken
Name above all names
No greater love
O mighty cross
Out in the wilderness
Over and over
People of the night
Poured out and broken
Praise to you, O Christ, our Savior
Precious Lord, take my hand
Rest in my love
Ride on, Jesus, ride
Ride on, King Jesus
Rise up, shepherd, and follow
Rock of ages
Send me, Jesus
Shake up the morning
Shine, Jesus, shine
Step by step
Strange king
Take of the wonder
Thank you, Lord
That Christ be known
The night of his betrayal
The summons
The tiny child to Bethlehem came
There is a balm in Gilead
There is a redeemer
They'll know we are Christians
This kingdom
To know you more
Tree of life
Two fishermen
We bow before his holy name
Welcome the king
You are my all in all
You are my rock
You are the branches
You only

JOY

Blest are they
Go out with joy
God has done marvelous things
God is good
He has made me glad
He is exalted
Holy ground
I come with joy

I will celebrate
I will enter his gates
I will sing, I will sing
I'm so glad Jesus lifted me
King of kings
Let there be praise
Lift up your heads
May you run and not be weary
Mourning into dancing
Oh sing to the Lord
Open our lives to the word
Praise, praise, praise the Lord
Praises resound
Rise up and praise him
Shout joy to the Lord
Shout to the Lord
Spirit calls, rejoice!
Stand in the congregation
The trees of the field
The trumpets sound, the angels sing
This is the day
Trading my sorrows
Write it on my heart

JUDGMENT
All the ends of the earth
Ancient of days
Awesome God
Beauty for brokenness
Bright and morning star
Bring forth the kingdom
Eternity
Firm foundation
Forever my friend
He is exalted
He shall reign
Heaven and earth
King of kings
King of life
Kyrie eleison
Let justice roll like a river
Majesty
Make me a channel of your peace
Make me a servant
Mighty is our God
My chosen one
My heart will trust
Now in this banquet
Say the name
Send out your grace abundantly
Shine, Jesus, shine
Shout to the Lord
Sing out, earth and skies
Song over the waters
Soon and very soon
Stand in the congregation
Stir up the love
The day is near
The kingdom song
The Lord comes to the earth
The Lord is King
The trumpet in the morning
We are called
What have we to offer
You are mine

JUSTICE
All the ends of the earth
Anthem
Canticle of the turning
Come to the feast
Dust and ashes
Each winter as the year grows older
For the life of the world
Great is the Lord
Happy are they
Hosea
How good it is
I say "Yes," Lord
I will lift up my eyes
I will not die
Lead me, guide me
Lord, let us see your kindness
Now in this banquet
Ride on, Jesus, ride
Sing a new song to the Lord
Song of the chosen
Taste and see
The cloud's veil
The harvest of justice
The Lord is King
We are called
We bow down
We see the Lord
We will draw near
When the Lord comes
When the Lord in glory comes
You only
Your mercy like rain

KINGDOM OF GOD
All around your throne
Ancient of days
Awesome God
Beauty for brokenness
Bring forth the kingdom
God has chosen me
God, be gracious
Great is the Lord
He is Lord

KINGDOM OF GOD *(continued)*
He shall reign
Hear our cry
I see the Lord
It has always been you
Jesus reigns
Jesus, name above all names
Jesus, remember me
King of kings
King of life
Lord, I lift your name on high
Majesty
Mighty is our God
My chosen one
My God reigns
My Lord will come again
Praise we render
Rejoice, the Lord is king
Seek ye first
Send down the fire
Soon and very soon
The kingdom song
The Lord is king
This kingdom
Thy kingdom come
We bow down
We will drink the cup
We will glorify

LAST THINGS
All that is hidden
All the ends of the earth
Bright and morning star
Come to the fount of creation
For he alone is worthy
Go
Heaven and earth
I have kept the faith
I see the Lord
I'll be waitin'
Let justice roll like a river
Shine, Jesus, shine
Shout to the Lord
The cloud's veil
The day is near
The Lord comes to earth
The trumpet in the morning
The trumpets sound, the angels sing
We bow down
We will draw near
When the Lord comes
When the Lord in glory comes
You only

LENT
A story for all people
All that is hidden
All we like sheep
Amazing love
Ashes
Be magnified
Be my home
Be near us, Lord Jesus
Beauty for ashes
Before the sun burned bright
Broken hearts
Broken in love
By grace have we been saved
By the waters of Babylon
Cares chorus
Carol of the thorn tree
Change my heart, O God
Change our hearts
Closer
Come and taste
Come closer
Come to me
Create in me
Create in me a clean heart
Cup we bless
Deep within
Dust and ashes
Embrace my way and cross
First love
For God so loved the world
Forever grateful
Forever my friend
Give me a new heart
God is here
God my refuge
God of love, have mercy
God provides a brand new heart
God so loved the world
God the sculptor of the mountains
God will make a way
God with us
He who began a good work
Here I am, Lord
Here is my heart
Holy love
Hop on the bus
I am the resurrection
I believe this is Jesus
I can do all things
I come to the cross
I have kept the faith
I want Jesus to walk with me
I want to know you
I'll belong to you

In the wilderness
Into the life
Jesus walked this lonesome valley
Jesus, amazing
Jesus, I believe
Jesus keep me near the cross
Jesus, tempted in the desert
John 3:16
Lead me, guide me
Lead me, oh lead me
Lord my strength
May you run and not be weary
Mercy
Morning has broken
Mourning into dancing
My heart will trust
My life is in you, Lord
Nothing is as wonderful
Now in this banquet
Only by grace
Out in the wilderness
Please have mercy on me
Return to God
Seek the Lord
Shout to the Lord
Show me your ways
Step by step
That priceless grace
The cross of Jesus
The Lord will keep me safe and holy
The river is here
This is the time of fulfillment
To know you more
Tree of life
Turn my heart
Turn to me
Up from the earth
We are an offering
We can be lifted up
We cry out for grace again
We shall rise again
What you are
Where you lead me
Whom shall I fear?
You are mine
You are my all in all
You are my hiding place
You are the rock of my salvation
You only

LIFE, CHRISTIAN
All through the night
Amen
As you go on your way
Be my home
Beauty for brokenness
Come and grow
Come to me today
Everlasting grace
Forever my friend
Freely, given freely
Give us your vision
Go and do
God, the sculptor of the mountains
I am loved
I am the resurrection
I belong to a mighty God
I can do all things
I don't belong to me
I have decided to follow Jesus
I have kept the faith
I see you
I want to know you
I was there to hear your borning cry
I will be with you always
In Christ, a new creation
Into the life
Jesus, help me see
King of life
Life in his hands
Lord, you've been our dwelling place
Make my life a candle
May you run and not be weary
My life is in you, Lord
Nothing is as wonderful
Now God our Father
Open our lives to the word
Put on love
Someone in need of your love
Thanksgiving to the living God
The Lord will keep me safe and holy
We are an offering

LIGHT
A light rises in the darkness
All hail, King Jesus
Anthem
Arise, shine
Awake, O sleeper
Beauty for brokenness
Bring forth the kingdom
City of God
Come to the mountain
Come to the water
For all people Christ was born
From the sunrise
Gather us in
Glory and praise to our God
God is love
Holy love, holy light

LIGHT *(continued)*
I am the light of the world
I see you
Jesus Christ, yesterday, today and forever
Jesus lead on
Jesus, help me see
Lead me, guide me
Light of Christ
Light the darkness
Lord my strength
Make me a channel of your peace
Make my life a candle
Mourning into dancing
Nativity carol
No longer strangers
Now in this banquet
On the mountain top
Praise to you, O Christ, our savior
Send out your grace abundantly
Shine on us
Shine, Jesus, shine
Song over the waters
Stand up
Take and eat
Thanksgiving to the living God
The Lord is near
This is the day
This little light of mine
Thy word
'Tis good, Lord, to be here
Transfiguration
Tree of life
We are called
We are marching in the light of God
We are the light of the world
What star is this
When the Lord in glory comes
Whom shall I fear?
You are mine
You have called us

LOVE
A song of unity
A story for all people
All are welcome
Amazing love
Awesome God
Bind us together
Bring forth the kingdom
Broken for me
Broken in love
By grace we have been saved
Celebrate love
Change my heart, O God
Come and taste
Faith, hope and love
First love
For God so loved
Glorify thy name
Go and do
Go now in peace
Good soil
Great is the Lord
Here I am, Lord
Holy love
Holy love, holy light
I am loved
I could sing of your love forever
I love you, Lord
I say "Yes," Lord
Jesu, Jesu
Jesus, amazing
Jesus, I believe
Let there be praise
Love one another
Make me a channel of your peace
Mercy
Most holy one
No greater love
Now in this banquet
One bread, one body
Open our eyes, Lord
Put on love
Seek ye first
Shout to the Lord
Sing a new song
Sing out, earth and skies
Someone in need of your love
Song about grace
Spirit song
Stir up the love
Thank you, Lord
That we may be filled
The fire of your love
The summons
The trumpets sound, the angels sing
There is a redeemer
They'll know we are Christians
Thy word
We are called
We love you
We remember you
We will draw near
What have we to offer
What you are
Who are we
Wind of the spirit
You are mine
You, Lord
Your constant love

Your everlasting love
Your steadfast love

MARRIAGE
Bind us together
For God is love
God be with you
I was there to hear your borning cry
I will praise your name
Let there be praise
Let us go rejoicing
Live in my love
Love one another
My chosen one
No greater love
Nothing can come between us
Sing out, earth and skies
Taste and see
That we may be filled
The Lord is near
We have been told
We praise you

MARY, MOTHER OF THE LORD
A story for all people
Ave Maria
Canticle of the turning
Emmanuel
Faithful one
For all the faithful women
He came down
He is Lord
Here am I
Magnificat
Magnify the Lord
Mary's song
My soul does magnify the Lord
My soul in stillness waits
No wind at the window
Sing, my soul
Song of the chosen
Thanks be to you
The queen stands at your right hand
The virgin Mary had a baby boy

MAUNDY THURSDAY
A song of unity
An offering of thanksgiving
As bread that is broken
As the grains of wheat
Broken in love
Come and taste
Come to me today
Create in me a clean heart
Cup we bless
Eat this bread, drink this cup
For God is love
Here is bread
I love you, Lord
Jesu, Jesu
Lamb of God
Live in my love
Make me a servant
No greater love
One bread we bless and share
One bread, one body
Our blessing cup
Poured out and broken
Remember
So you must do
Song of the Lord's command
Take off your shoes
That we may be filled
The name of God
The night of his betrayal
The servant song
When we eat this bread
You are my all in all

MERCY
All we like sheep
Amazing love
An offering of thanksgiving
Arise, oh Lord
As we remember
Awesome God
Be exalted, O God
Be merciful, O Lord
Bless the Lord
Bring forth the kingdom
Calvary
Canticle of the turning
Eternal is his mercy
Father, I adore you
Father, I put my life in your hands
For God so loved
Give thanks
God is good (All the time)
God of love, have mercy
Great is the Lord
Great is thy faithfulness
Have mercy, Lord
Here I am
Hold us in your mercy
How blessed
I come to the cross
I danced in the morning
I will bless the Lord
Jesus, remember me
Justice shall flourish

MERCY *(continued)*
Lamb of God
Lead me, Lord
Let justice roll like a river
Let us see your kindness
Let us see, O Lord, your mercy
Like a shepherd
Lord, let us see your kindness
Lord, let your mercy
Magnificat
Mercy
Most holy one
O Lord, let us see your kindness
Peace prayer
Praise to you, O Christ, our savior
Remember your mercy, Lord
Seek the Lord
Sing of the Lord's goodness
Taste and see
The cry of the poor
The Lord has revealed
The Lord is kind and merciful
The Lord is near
There is a redeemer
They who do justice
Thy kingdom come
With our God there is mercy
With the Lord there is mercy
Your everlasting love
Your mercy flows
Your mercy like rain

MINISTRY
All that is hidden
Alleluia, alleluia! Give thanks
Anthem
As bread that is broken
Beauty for brokenness
Blessed be the Lord
Bring forth the kingdom
Centre of my life
City of God
Earthen vessels
For ever I will sing
Go
Go in peace and serve the Lord
Go, make disciples
Good news
Here am I
Here I am
Here I am, Lord
I am the vine
I will be with you
In Christ, a new creation
Jesu, Jesu
Jesus took a towel
Lift high the cross
Lord, you have come
Make me a channel of your peace
Make me a servant
My chosen one
My God, my God
Now in this banquet
O love of God
Peace prayer
Praise God's name
Rejoice in the mission
Send us your spirit
Servant song
Sing a new song
Song over the waters
The summons
They'll know we are Christians
This is the day
Tree of life
We are an offering
We are called
We are God's people
We are one bdy
We shall draw water
Without you
You have anointed me

MORNING
Arise, shine
Awake! Awake, and greet the new morn
Create in me
God mounts his throne
Great is thy faithfulness
I danced in the morning
I will praise the Lord
Jesus in the morning
Let all the earth
Lord, let us see your kindness
Morning has broken
My Lord, what a morning
My soul is thirsting
Oh, sing to our God
Shine, Jesus, shine
Sing a new song
Sing to the mountains
Song of the three children
This is the day
We are marching in the light of God
You will draw water

NAME OF JESUS
Age to age, everlasting
All hail, King Jesus
Blessing, honor, and glory

Emmanuel
For he alone is worthy
How majestic is your name
Jehovah
Jesus, I believe
Jesus, Jesus
Jesus, name above all names
King of kings
Majesty
Name above all names
Only you
Our help is in the name
Praise the name of Jesus
Say the name
The fullness of the Lord
The name of the Lord
We bow before his holy name
We declare your name
We've come to worship you
You are my all in all

NEW YEAR
Awaken the song
Come and see
Eternity
Firm foundation
Give us your vision
Heaven and earth
How majestic is your name
I have kept the faith
I was there to hear your borning cry
I will be with you always
I will never be
It has always been you
Life in his hands
Once and for all time
Soon and very soon
This is the day
You are God—Te deum
Your name is praised

OFFERTORY
A song of unity
Age to age
All is ready now
All that we have
An offering of thanksgiving
As the grains of wheat
Broken in love
Create in me a clean heart
Deep is the prayer
For the Lord is good
Forever grateful
Give thanks
Glory and praise to our God
God is good
He has made me glad
I'm forever grateful
Indeed, how good is the Lord
Let there be praise
Let your fire fall
Make me a servant
Now in this banquet
Now we remain
O Lord to you
Offering
One bread, one body
Seed, scattered and sown
Shout to the Lord
Thanksgiving to the living God
The wise may bring their learning
We are an offering
We bow down
We bring the sacrifice of praise
What have we to offer?
You have been good
You, Lord

PEACE
All who hunger
As you go on your way
Awake! Awake, and greet the new morn
Blest are they
Bring forth the kingdom
Each winter as the year grows older
Go in peace and serve the Lord
Go now in peace
Go out with joy
Good soil
He came down
Healer of our every ill
How can I keep from singing
I say "Yes," Lord
I was glad
I will give you peace
Kyrie eleison
Lamb of God
Let justice roll like a river
Let the peace of God reign
Let there be peace on earth
Let us go rejoicing
Lord, let us see your kindness
Lord, listen to your children
Make me a channel of your peace
May we have peace
Nativity carol
No longer strangers
O God of love
Peace
Praise the Lord

PEACE *(continued)*
Put on love
Renew your people
Song of the body of Christ
Song over the waters
Take and eat
Taste and see
You are mine

PENTECOST
Amen
Arise
As the deer
As you go on your way
Awaken the song
Because we believe
Breathe on me
Bring forth the kingdom
Building block
Celebrate love
Change my heart oh God
Come and grow
Come share the spirit
Come, let us worship God
Every time I feel the spirit
Flow like a river
Freely, given freely
Glorify thy name
Go and do
Go ye therefore
Go, make disciples
God without and within
Good soil
Here is bread
Holy ground
Holy, holy
Hop on the bus
I could sing of your love forever
I love to be in your presence
I was glad
I will delight
I will never be
Let it rain
Let the peace of God reign
Let the river flow
Let your fire fall
Let your healing love
Like a shepherd
Lord, listen to your children
Lord, listen to your children praying
Make me a channel of your peace
My Lord, what a morning
No longer strangers
Now God our Father
Now in this banquet
Over and over
Rain down
Rain down on us
Revival fire, fall
Seek ye first
Shine, Jesus, shine
Spirit calls, rejoice!
Spirit of the living God
Spirit song
The fire of your love
The river is here
The summons
There is a redeemer
Turn my heart
Waterlife
Wind of God
Wind of the spirit

PRAISE, ADORATION
A joyous psalm
Age to age, everlasting
All around your throne
All hail, King Jesus
Alleluia
Alleluia! Jesus is risen!
Alleluia, alleluia! Give thanks
Almighty
Ancient of days
Arise
At the foot of the cross
At the name of Jesus
Awake! Awake, and greet the new morn
Awesome God
Before you now
Bless his holy name
Blessed be the name
Blessing, honor and glory
Canticle of the sun
Canticle of the turning
Celebrate Jesus
Child of mercy
Come and see
Dancing at the harvest
El Shaddai
Emmanuel
Everlasting grace
Faithful Father
Father, I adore you
For all the faithful women
For all you've done
For he alone is worthy
For the Lord is good
Forever my friend

From where the sun rises
Give thanks
Glorify thy name
Glorious
Glorious God
Glorious in majesty
Glory and praise to our God
Glory be!
Go, make disciples
God has done marvelous things
God of glory
God without and within
Great is the Lord
Hallelujah! We sing your praises
He has made me glad
He is exalted
He is Lord
Heaven and earth
Holy ground
Holy love, holy light
Holy! Holy! Holy Lord
How beautiful upon the mountains
How blessed
How majestic is your name
I danced in the morning
I love to be in your presence
I love you, Lord
I praise your name
I was glad
I will celebrate
I will come and bow down
I will delight
I will praise you
I will praise you, Lord
I will praise your name
I will sing of the mercies of the Lord
I will sing, I will sing
It is good
Jesus, Jesus
Jesus, name above all names
Join in the dance
King of kings
King of life
Let all the world sing praises
Let there be praise
Lift up your heads
Lord, I lift your name on high
Lord, most high
Lord, be glorified
Love you so much
Majesty
Maranatha, alleluia!
Mark's Sanctus
Meet us
More precious than silver
Morning has broken
Mourning into dancing
My life is in you, Lord
No greater love
Nothing is as wonderful
Now God our Father
Oh, come, let us sing
Only for your glory
Only you
Praise to you, O Christ, our savior
Praise to you, O God of mercy
Praise we render
Praise, praise, praise the Lord
Praises resound
Reason to celebrate
Ring, ring all the living bells
Rise up and praise him
Rise up and sing
Santo, santo, santo
Shine, Jesus, shine
Shout to the Lord
Sing a new song
Sing out, earth and skies
Sing unto the Lord
Spirit calls, rejoice
Stand up and give him the praise
Stand up, friends
Step by step
Taste and see
The King of glory
The Lord is my portion
The trees of the field
The trumpets sound, the angels sing
These things are true of you
This is the day
This is the feast of victory
To God be the glory
We are called
We are marching in the light of God
We bow down
We bring the sacrifice of praise
We love you
We rejoice in the grace of God
We see the Lord
We will glorify
We've come to praise you
What you are
With all my heart
You alone
You are holy
You are my God
You are my rock
You are the Lord of me

PRAISE, ADORATION *(continued)*
You have been given
You have been good
You, Lord
Your constant love
Your steadfast love

PRAYER
All I ask of you
All that we have
Answer me
Answer when I call
As the deer
At the foot of the cross
Be merciful, O Lord
Be my home
Beauty for brokenness
Bless the Lord
By your cross
Cares chorus
Change my heart, O God
Create in me
Dust and ashes
Father, I put my life in your hands
Gather us in
Give me a new heart
God of love, have mercy
Healer of our every ill
Healing word
Hear my prayer
Hear our cry
Hear us, almighty Lord
Heavenly Father
Here I am
I bend my knees again
I need you
I want to know you
I will call upon the Lord
Jesus, Lord
Jesus, remember me
Just like a deer
Let justice roll like a river
Let your healing love
Like a deer that longs
Like a little child
Lord, we pray
Lord, forgive the wrong
Lord, heal my soul
Lord, I lift your name on high
Lord, let us see your kindness
Lord, listen to your children
Lord, listen to your children praying
Lord, my strength
Loving and forgiving
Make me a channel of your peace
Make me a servant
My God, come to my aid
My God, my God
Nothing is as wonderful
Now in this banquet
O God, for you I long
O Lord, my heart is not proud
Open our eyes, Lord
Precious Lord, take my hand
Psalm of hope
Rain down
Remember your mercy, Lord
Seek ye first
Send me, Jesus
Send us your spirit
Shelter me, O God
Shepherd me, O God
Shine on us, Lord
Song of longing
Spirit of the living God
Spirit, come
Teach me how to pray
The people on your heart
The summons
These things are true of you
Thy kingdom come
To you, O Lord
Wind of the spirit

POWER, GOD'S MIGHTY
All the power you need
Almighty
Ancient of days
Arise
Arise, oh Lord
Awesome God
Be bold, be strong
Glorious God
Great is the Lord
How majestic is your name
I will call upon the Lord
Lead me, guide me
Let the river flow
Let your fire fall
Lord, my strength
Majesty
Mighty is our God
My God reigns
Our confidence is in the Lord
Paul's doxology
Say to the mountain
Stand up and give him the praise
The fullness of the Lord
The trumpets sound, the angels sing
This kingdom

What a mighty word God gives
You are my hiding place
You are the rock of my salvation

PRESENTATION OF THE LORD
God with us
How beautiful upon the mountains
I love to be in your presence
King of kings
Lift up your heads
Sanctuary
Song of the chosen
That boy-child of Mary
The King of glory
We long to see your face
Welcome the King

PROCLAMATION
A story for all people
All you who are thirsty
Anthem
As bread that is broken
Beauty for ashes
Bring forth the kingdom
Come to the mountain
Come unto me
Deep within
Glorious
Go
Go and do
Go in peace and serve the Lord
Go out with joy
Go ye therefore
Go, make disciples
Good news
Good soil
Halleluya! We sing your praises
I believe in Jesus
I danced in the morning
I want to know you
In Christ, a new creation
Jesu, Jesu
Jesus, help me see
Jesus, the Lord
Let it be said of us
Lord, when you came
Make my life a candle
Many are the lightbeams
Nothing is as wonderful
Now we remain
Open our lives to the word
Our heart
Rejoice in the mission
Seed, scattered and sown
Send me, Jesus
Spirit, come
That Christ be known
The church song
They'll know we are Christians
Thy word
We are called
We are marching in the light of God
We declare your name
We have been told
What a mighty word God gives
Without you
You have called us
You, Lord, have the message

PROCESSIONS
All around your throne
Gather us in
Lead me, guide me
Lift high the cross
Lift up your heads
Praise, praise, praise the Lord
Soon and very soon
Step by step
We are marching in the light of God

RECONCILIATION
All around your throne
All we like sheep
Amazing love
As the grains of wheat
As we gather at your table
Building block
Change my heart, O God
Come to me today
Come to the feast
Create in me
Give back to me
God, be gracious
He is Lord
He is our peace
I am loved
I danced in the morning
I was glad
In Christ, a new creation
Lead me, guide me
Let the walls fall down
Magnificat
Make us one
Many are the lightbeams
May God bless us in his mercy
No longer strangers
Praise to you, O Christ, our Savior
Reach out and take a hand
Sing a new song to the Lord
Somos uno

RECONCILIATION *(continued)*
There is a balm in Gilead
They'll know we are Christians
Turn my heart
Turn our hearts
You have been given

REFORMATION DAY
Awesome God
Because we believe
By grace we have been saved
Everlasting grace
For by grace
God my refuge
I belong to a mighty God
Only by grace
Our confidence is in the Lord
Saved by the grace of a miracle
Song about grace
The church song
We cry out for grace again
We rejoice in the grace of God
You are the rock of my salvation

REVIVAL, RENEWAL, RESTORATION
Arise
Arise, oh Lord
Arise, shine
Awake! Awake, and greet the new morn
Awaken the song
Celebrate love
Change my heart, O God
Come and taste
Come to me today
Come to the river of life
Come touch
Create in me a clean heart
Everlasting grace
God provides a brand new heart
Here is my heart
Hop on the bus
I bend my knees again
I will never be
In Christ, a new creation
In the wilderness
Leave your heart with me
Let it rain
Let your healing love
Lord of heaven
Mercy
New life again and again
Purify my heart
Rain down
Refiner's fire
Revival fire, fall
Send out your grace abundantly
Shout to God, O faithful people
Song over the waters
Spirit song
The fire of your love
Turn my heart
Turn our hearts
We can be lifted up

SENDING
As you go on your way
At the name of Jesus
Be bold, be strong
Blessing, honor, and glory
Bring forth the kingdom
Every time I feel the spirit
Give thanks
Glory and praise to our God
Go
Go and do
Go in peace and serve the Lord
Go now in peace
Go, make disciples
I will be with you always
I will celebrate
I will delight
I will sing, I will sing
Into the life
Lead me, guide me
May you run and not grow weary
Oh, when the saints go marching in
Paul's doxology
Praise to you, O God of mercy
Send me, Jesus
Shalom, my good friends
Shine, Jesus, shine
Sing a new song
Soon and very soon
Stand in the congregation
The summons
The trees of the field
The trumpets sound, the angels sing
We are called
We are marching in the light of God
We rejoice in the grace of God
What have we to offer
You are the seed

SERVICE
A song of unity
Amen
An offering of thanksgiving
As bread that is broken
As bread that is broken
Bread of life

Broken in love
Change my heart, oh God
Come to the mountain
Glorious in majesty
Go in peace and serve the Lord
Go, make disciples
Here I am
Here I am, Lord
Jesu, Jesu
Jesus, help me see
Lord, when you came
Make me a servant
Many are the lightbeams
No greater love
Pan de vida
Psalm 19
Rain down on us
Reach out and take a hand
Remember
So you must do
Song of the Lord's command
Stir up the love
Take off your shoes
The servant song
We are an offering
We are called
We are his hands
We bring the sacrifice of praise
We have been told
What have we to offer?
You are my all in all
You are my God
You are my hiding place

SOCIETY
A song of unity
Age to age, everlasting
All around your throne
All who hunger
All you who are thirsty
Anthem
Beauty for brokenness
Bind us together
Bring forth the kingdom
Canticle of the turning
Church of God
City of God
Come to the water
Earthen vessels
Everyone moved by the spirit
For the life of the world
Gather us in
Glorious in majesty
God beyond all names
Good news
Great is the Lord
Here I am, Lord
I don't belong to me
I say "Yes," Lord
I will not die
Jesu, Jesu
Kyrie eleison
Let the river flow
On holy ground
'Round the table
Sanctuary
Send down the fire
Sing out earth and skies
Song of the chosen
Song over the waters
The God of all grace
The summons
They who do justice
We are called

SORROW, SUFFERING
Amazing love
As bread that is broken
Ashes
At the foot of the cross
Be my home
Beauty for brokenness
Blest are they
Broken for me
Broken hearts
Cares chorus
Come closer
Come to me
Come touch
Glory and praise to our God
He who began a good work
Holy love
How can I be free from sin?
I am
I danced in the morning
I heard the voice of Jesus say
I need you to listen
I want Jesus to walk with me
Jesus walked this lonesome valley
Leave your heart with me
Lord, heal my soul
Lord, let your mercy
My heart will trust
My Lord will come again
On the mountain top
Only in God
Open our lives to the word
Pan de vida
Precious Lord, take my hand
Psalm of hope

SORROW, SUFFERING *(continued)*
Taste and see
The Lord will keep me safe and holy
The love of the Lord
Trading my sorrows
You are mine
You are my hiding place

SUNDAY OF THE PASSION/PALM SUNDAY
At the name of Jesus
Bless the body broken for my sin
Blessed be the name
Blessings on the King
Broken in love
Calvary
Carol of the thorn tree
Come to me today
He is exalted
He is Lord
I come to the cross
I will enter his gates
Jesus, name above all names
King of life
Lift up your heads
Lord of heaven
Lord, my strength
Poured out and broken
Ride on Jesus ride
Ride on, King Jesus
Stand up and give him the praise
Strange king
The cross of Jesus
The servant of the Lord submits to suffering
Tree of life
We bow before his holy name
Welcome the King

TESTIMONY
God is so good
I belong to a mighty God
I could sing of your love forever
I have kept the faith
To God be the glory

THANKSGIVING DAY
A song of unity
Age to age
All that we have
An offering of thanksgiving
As the grains of wheat
Come and see
Come and taste
For all you've done
For the Lord is good
Forever grateful
Gathered as one
Give thanks
Glory and praise to our God
God is good
God is so good
God of glory
Halleluya! We sing your praises
He has made me glad
His love endures forever
I will delight
I will enter his gates
I will sing, I will sing
I'm forever grateful
Indeed, how good is the Lord
It is good
King of life
Let there be praise
Love you so much
Mercy
Now we raise our thanks to you
One
One in the bread
Praise to you, O God of mercy
Rain down
Rain down on us
Shout joy to the Lord
Singing through the water
Thank you for the gift
Thank you, Lord
Thanksgiving to the living God
The gift of giving
The Lord has done great things
The trees of the field
Trading my sorrows
We are an offering
We bring the sacrifice of praise
What have we to offer
You have been good
You've delivered me again

TRANSFIGURATION OF THE LORD
Arise, oh Lord
Arise, shine
Awesome God
Before you
Before you now
Come to the mountain
Glory
God of glory
God sent his son
He is Lord
Holy ground
I believe in Jesus
I see you
I will be with you always

I will show God's salvation
Jesus, you reign over all
Let it be said of us
Let your glory fill this place
Majesty
My chosen one
On the mountain top
Open our eyes, Lord
Open the eyes of my heart
Praise God with the trumpet
Praise to you, O Christ
Shake up the morning
Shine on us
Shine, Jesus, shine
Stand up
Thy word
'Tis good, Lord, to be here
Transfiguration
Transform us
We see the Lord
You are holy

TRAVELERS/PILGRIMAGE
All that we have
Anthem
As you go on your way
Be my home
Be not afraid
City of God
Gather us in
Glory and praise to our God
Go in peace and serve the Lord
Go now in peace
I see you
I want Jesus to walk with me
I was there to hear your borning cry
I will be with you always
In the breaking of the bread
Jesus lead on
Jesus walked this lonesome valley
Journeysong
Lead me, guide me
Lead me, Lord
Praise to you, O Christ, our Savior
Soon and very soon
Spirit song
Step by step
The Lord will keep me safe and holy
We are marching in the light of God
Where you lead me

TRUST, GUIDANCE
All that we have
All the power you need
Amen
As the deer
Awake! Awake and greet the new morn
Be my home
Be not afraid
Change my heart oh God
Closer
Come to me
Don't be anxious
Each winter as the year grows older
Eat this bread
Eye has not seen
Fill us with your love
For by grace
Gather us in
Glory and praise to our God
God provides a brand new heart
God will make a way
Great is the Lord
Happy are they
He who began a good work in you
Here I am
Here is bread
His love endures forever
I am the good shepherd
I long for you
I put my life in your hands
I see you
I want Jesus to walk with me
I was there to hear your borning cry
I will call upon the Lord
I will sing
I will sing of the mercies of the Lord
I'll belong to you
In God alone
Jesu, Jesu
Jesus lead on
Jesus, remember me
Keep me safe, O God
Lead me, guide me
Lead me, oh lead me
Let your mercy be on us
Like a shepherd
Lord, be glorified
Lord, listen to your children
Lord, my strength
Lord, you've been our dwelling place
Lord, your love is eternal
Make me a servant
May you run and not be weary
Mourning into dancing
My God, my God
My heart will trust
My soul is thirsting
Now in this banquet
On eagle's wings

TRUST, GUIDANCE *(continued)*
Our confidence is in the Lord
Our help comes from the Lord
Out in the wilderness
Precious Lord, take my hand
Purify my heart
Remember your love
Seek ye first
Shepherd me, O God
Shepherd of my heart
Shout to the Lord
Show me your ways
Stand in the congregation
Step by step
Taste and see
The Lord upholds my life
The Lord will keep me safe and holy
There is a balm in Gilead
Thy word
Turn my heart
Wait for the Lord
Waterlife
We shall rise again
Where you lead me
With the Lord there is mercy
Write it on my heart
You are mine
You are my hiding place
You will draw water

UNITY/COMMUNITY IN CHRIST
A song of unity
A story for all people
All are welcome
All around your throne
As the grains of wheat
Awake! Awake, and greet the new morn
Baptized and set free
Bind us together
Broken for me
Come share the spirit
Come to the table
Cup we bless
Eat this bread, drink this cup
From where the sun rises
Gather us in
God has spoken, bread is broken
God is love
God the sculptor of the mountains
He shall reign
Here is bread
I am for you
I am loved
I come with joy
I was glad
Let it be said of us
Life in his hands
Make your presence known
Many are the lightbeams
No longer strangers
Nothing can come between us
One bread, one body
One in the bread
Only for your glory
Pan de vida
Praise to you, O God of mercy
Put on love
Reach out and take a hand
Seed, scattered and sown
Sing a new song
Sing out, earth and skies
Someone in need of your love
Somos uno
Song of the body of Christ
Song over the waters
Spirit song
Stir up the love
Take of the wonder
That Christ be known
That we may be filled
The church song
The summons
There is a redeemer
They'll know we are Christians
Waterlife
We are called
We are members of each other
We are your people
We remember you
What have we to offer?
Wind of the spirit
You are mine

VISION
As the deer
Be my home
Bright and morning star
Bring forth the kingdom
Come to me
Lift up your heads
My heart yearns for thee
On the mountain top
Rejoice in the mission
The trees of the field
There is a redeemer
We are marching in the light of God
We rejoice in the grace of God

VISITATION
A story for all people
Bless his holy name
Canticle of the turning
Faithful one
Forever grateful
I want to know you
Magnificat
Mary's song
My chosen one
No wind at the window
Send me, Jesus
Thanks be to you
You are holy

WITNESS
Bring forth the kingdom
Glory and praise to our God
Go in peace and serve the Lord
Go out with joy
Go ye therefore
Go, make disciples
Good news
Good soil
Halleluyah! We sing your praises
He is Lord
Here I am
I will be with you
Lord, you have come
Out in the wilderness
Praise to you, O Christ, our Savior
Send down the fire
Shine, Jesus, shine
Spirit of the living God
Take and eat this bread
That Christ be known
The church song
The trumpets sound, the angels sing
We are an offering
We are called
We will drink the cup
What have we to offer
You, Lord

WORD, THE
Amen
Bring forth the kingdom
Change our hearts
Come to set us free
Come to the mountain
Firm foundation
First love
Go out with joy
God will make a way
Good soil
Healing word
Here I am
I see you
I will delight
Jesus, name above all names
Like a shepherd
Morning has broken
Open our lives to the word
Praise to you, O Christ, our Savior
Praise to you, O God of mercy
Seed, scattered and sown
Seek ye first
Shine, Jesus, shine
Spirit of the living God
The fullness of the Lord
This is the gospel of Christ
Thy word
What a mighty word God gives
Write it on my heart

WORK, DAILY
All through the night
Bind us together
Jesu, Jesu
No greater love
One bread, one body
Reach out and take a hand
The people of God
The servant song
The summons
They'll know we are Christians
We are his hands
We are many parts

WORSHIP
Alleluia! Jesus is risen!
Ancient of days
As the deer
Be glorified
Before you now
Come, let us worship God
I love to be in your presence
I was glad
I will bow down and worship
I will come and bow down
My God reigns
Open our lives to the word
Shout to the Lord
We bow down
We've come to worship you
You are holy
You have been given

Alphabetical Index of Titles

As bread that is broken *Baloche/Cloninger* **HMS10 811**
As long as I live *Haas* **G-4681**
As the deer longs *Hurd* **G&P 207**
As the deer longs *Hurd/Kingsbury* **PS2**
As the deer *Nystrom* **HMS11 892, W&P 9, CEL 548, MAR, REN 9,**
As the grains of wheat *Haas* **W&P 10**
As the grains of wheat *Haugen* **WOV 705**
As we gather *Coomes/Fay* **MAR 6**
As you go on your way *Ylvisaker* **BC**
Ashes *Conry* **G&P 340, RS 957, LBG 25**
At the foot of the cross *Bond* **W&P 11**
At the name of Jesus *Bolduc* **VO 5**
At the name of Jesus *Cain* **TFF 268**
At the name of Jesus *Webb* **W&P 12**
Ave Maria *Kantor* **GC 785, RS 896**
Awake! Awake, and greet the new morn *Haugen* **WOV 633, GC 346, RS 494**
Awake, O sleeper *Haugen* **GC 803, RS 650**
Awaken the song *Rethmeier* **VIN6 22**
Awesome God *Mullins* **MAR 92, W&P 13**
Awesome power *Elliott* **CEL 150**

B

Baptized in water *Bisbee* **WOV 693**
Be bold, be strong *Chapman* **W&P 15**
Be exalted *Butler/Butler/Park* **VIN8 10**
Be glad in the Lord *Manalo* **G-4363**
Be glorified *Funk* **CW 19, HCW 19**
Be light for our eyes *Haas* **GC 509**
Be magnified *DeShazo* **HCW 20**
Be merciful, O Lord *Haugen* **GC 56, RS 83**
Be my home *Hanson/Murakami* **SCR 45, W&P 16**
Be near us, Lord Jesus *Hanson/Murakami* **SCR 4**
Be not afraid *Dufford* **G&P 602, GC 608**
Be thou my vision *Irish* **WOV776, REN 151**
Be with me *Haugen* **RS 123, GC 85**
Be with me, Lord *Mattingly* **VO 10**
Beauty for ashes *Manzano* **MAR**
Beauty for brokenness *Kendrick* **W&P 17**
Because we believe *Gordon/Harvill* **HMS12 985**
Before the sun burned bright *Schutte* **G&P 577**
Before you now *Butler/Osbrink* **VIN7 44**
Behold and tend this vine *Makeever* **DH 39**
Behold I make all things new *Bell* **G-4391, SSW**
Behold the glory of God *O'Connor* **G&P 385**
Behold the Lamb of God *Bell* **SSW, G-4391**
Behold the Lamb of God *Dufford* **G&P 360**
Behold the Lamb of God *Willet* **GC 823**
Behold the wood *Schutte* **G&P 369, GC 420**
Behold what manner of love *vanTine* **TFF 218**
Bend my knees again *Butler/Butler* **VIN8 85**
Benedictus *Jones* **PS1**
Between the times *Makeever* **DH 103**
Bind us together *Gillman* **W&P 18, WOV 748**
Bless his holy name *Crouch* **W&P 19**
Bless the body broken for my sin *Ylvisaker* **BC**
Bless the Lord *Crouch* **W&P 19, TFF 273**
Bless the Lord *Makeever* **DH 42**
Bless the Lord, my soul *Haugen* **GC 141**
Bless the Lord, O my soul *Taizé* **REN 114**
Bless us, O God *Makeever* **DH 44**
Blessed are you *Makeever* **DH 86**
Blessed be the Lord God of Israel *Sappington* **W&P 20**
Blessed be the Lord *Daigle/Ducote* **G&P 442**
Blessed be the name *Park* **VIN7 48**
Blessed be Yahweh *Young* **AFP 11-10669**
Blessing the marriage *Bell* **GC 871**
Blessing, honor and glory *Bullock/Reidy* **W&P 21**
Blessings on the King *Lynch* **G&P 357**
Blest are they *Haas* **WOV 764, GC 659, RS 774, REN 127**
Born from the gospel *Glover* **G-4587**
Bread for the world *Farrell* **G&P 528, GC 827**
Bread of life *Fisher* **G&P 522**
Bread to share: Song of Mark *Haugen* **RS 927**
Bridegroom and bride *Irish* **RS 944, GC 868**
Bright and morning star *Makeever* **DH 50**
Brighter than the sun *Makeever* **DH 64**
Bring forth the kingdom *Haugen* **GC 658, RS 772, W&P 22**
Bring the children *Makeever* **DH74**
Broken for me *Lunt* **W&P 23**
Broken hearts *Hanson/Murakami* **SCR 170**
Broken in love *Hanson* **SCR 177, W&P 24**
Building block *Stookey* **BC**
Built on a rock *James* **G-3525**
By grace have we been saved *Edwards* **W&P 25**
By the Babylonian rivers *Latvian* **WOV 656**
By the waters of Babylon *Jamaican* **TFF 67**

C

Calvary *Spiritual* **TFF 85**
Canticle of Moses *Inwood* **G&P 286**
Canticle of the turning *Irish/Cooney* **RS 678, W&P 26**
Cares chorus *Willard* **W&P 27, MAR**
Carol at the manger *Haugen* **GC 369, RS 516, WOV 638**
Carol of the child *Haas* **G-4344**
Carol of the thorn tree *Haugen* **G-4416**
Celebrate Jesus *Oliver* **HCW 27**
Celebrate love *Hanson* **SCR 16**
Centre of my life *Inwood* **PS2**
Change my heart oh God *Espinoza* **HCW 28, W&P 28, MAR, CMH, SPW**
Change my heart, O God *Espinoza* **HCW 28, W&P 28**
Change our hearts *Cooney* **G&P 349, GC 394**
Child of mercy *Haas* **GC 357, RS 506**
Child of the poor/What child is this *Soper* **G&P 336/337**
Children, go where I send thee *Haugen* **G-3814**
Christ has arisen, alleluia *Tanzanian* **WOV 678**
Christ is alive! *Williams* **RS 601**

Christ is risen *Hanson* **SCR 156**
Christ is risen! Shout hosanna *Haas* **GC 431**
Christ the Lord is risen *Ghanaian* **GC 439, RS 600**
Christ, be our light *Farrell* **G&P 656**
Church of God *Denton* **GC 664, G&P 571, RS 783**
City of God *Schutte* **G&P 548, GC 678**
Clap your hands *Hanson/Murakami* **SCR 32**
Clap your hands *Owens* **MAR**
Closer *Butler* **VIN6 36**
Come and follow me *O'Brien* **G-3028**
Come and grow *McLean* **CCJ, WIS 1**
Come and see *LeBlanc* **W&P 29**
Come and see *Makeever* **DH 56**
Come and taste *Hanson/Murakami* **SCR 186, W&P 30, W&P 30**
Come as you are *Helming* **MAR 178**
Come away to the skies *American* **WOV 669, GC 440**
Come closer *Hanson* **SCR 47**
Come home *Landry* **G&P 468**
Come home *Mattingly* **VO 16**
Come just as you are *Sabolick* **MAR 179**
Come let us reason *Medema* **REN 190**
Come let us sing out our praise *Tate* **VO 17**
Come let us sing *Lindh* **CGA 478**
Come share the spirit *Hanson/Murakami* **SCR 116**
Come to me today *Hanson* **SCR 174**
Come to me *Joncas* **GC 647, G-3373**
Come to me *Ylvisaker* **BC**
Come to set us free *Farrell* **GC 338, G&P 298**
Come to the feast *Haugen* **G-3543, GC 503, RS 642**
Come to the fount of creation *Ylvisaker* **BC**
Come to the mountain *Tunseth* **W&P 32**
Come to the river of life *Moen/Cloninger* **HMS10 818**
Come to the table *Nystrom* **W&P 33**
Come to the water *Foley* **G&P 706, GC 502, OCP**
Come touch *Hanson* **SCR 180**
Come unto me *Makeever* **DH26**
Come with joy *Makeever* **DH 41**
Come with me into the fields *Schutte* **G&P 553**
Come, all you people *South African* **WOV 717, TFF 138**
Come, let us eat *Kwillia* **TFF 119, REN 197**
Come, let us worship God *Makeever* **DH 2**
Come, O Lord, and set us free *Balhoff/Daigle/Ducote* **GC 80, RS 114**
Come, worship the Lord *Talbot* **G&P 536, OCP 10331**
Come, you sinners, poor and needy *American* **RS 954**
Comes a new song *Makeever* **DH 101**
Commune with me *Dearman* **MAR 20**
Create in me a clean heart *Hopkins* **W&P 35**
Create in me a clean heart, O God *Anonymous* **W&P 34, HCW 36**
Create in me *Haas* **GC 57, RS 85**
Create in me *Hurd* **G&P 209**
Creating God *Haas* **GC 580**
Crucifixion: Song of Mark *Haugen* **G-4416**
Crux fidelis *Warner* **VO 19**
Cry of my heart *Butler* **MAR**
Cry out to the Lord *Warner* **G&P 217**
Cry out with joy and gladness *Haugen* **GC 148**
Cup we bless *Young* **BL**

D

Dancing at the harvest *Makeever* **DH 40**
De profundis blues *Wellicome* **PS3**
Death be never last *Makeever* **DH102**
Deep is the prayer *Young* **BL**
Deep river *Spiritual* **TFF 174**
Deep within *Haas* **GC 399, RS 546**
Do not let your hearts be troubled *Haas* **G-349**
Don't be anxious *Hanson* **SCR 141**
Don't be worried *Brown* **TFF 212**
Don't you know where you are *Ylvisaker* **BC**
Draw me into your presence *Muller* **MAR**
Dust and ashes *Haas* **GC 381, RS 539**
Dwelling place *Foley* **G&P 591**

E

Each winter as the year grows older *Gay/Haugen* **GC 339, RS 481**
Earthen vessels *Foley* **G&P 584**
Eastertide carol *Ridge* **G&P 380**
Eat this bread *Taizé* **TFF 125, WOV 709**
Eat this bread, drink this cup *Young* **BL, AFP 11-10651, WOV 706**
El Shaddai *Card/Thompson* **UM 123**
Embrace my way and cross *Glover* **G-4594**
Emmanuel *Manion* **G&P 329**
Emmanuel *McGee* **SPW, TFF 45, W&P 36**
Envia tu Espiritu *Hurd* **GC 459, G&P 407**
Eternal Lord of love *Joncas* **RS 554, GC 385**
Eternity *Doerksen* **CMH 28**
Everlasting grace is yours *Haas* **G-4579**
Everlasting grace *Carpenter* **VIN6 58**
Every nation on earth *Joncas* **GC 72**
Every time I feel the spirit *Spiritual* **TFF 241, BC**
Every valley *Dufford* **G&P 297**
Everyone moved by the Spirit *Landry* **G&P 412**
Everyone who calls upon the name *Makeever* **DH 17**
Everything I am *Dyer/Horness* **MAR**
Eye has not seen *Haugen* **G-3726, GC 638, RS 758**

F

Faith that's sure *Lord* **CGA 695**
Faith, hope and love *Haas* **GC 624**
Faithful Father *Doerksen* **VIN7 72**
Faithful One *Doerksen* **CMH2 60, VIN7 72**
Father, I adore you *Coelho* **W&P 37**
Father, I put my life in your hands *Hughes* **RS 62**
Father, I put my life in your hands *Talbot* **G&P 195**
Father, into your hands *Smith* **PS2**

Fill us with your Spirit *Makeever* **DH 71**
Filling me with joy *Lisicky* **GC 135**
Firm foundation *Gordon/Harvill* **HCW 42**
First love *Baloche/Sadler* **HMS13 1062**
Flow like a river *Funk* **HMS13 1063**
Flow, river, flow *Hurd* **G&P 455**
Flowing river *Baloche* **HMS13 1064**
Follow me *Haugen* **G-4416**
For all people Christ was born *Makeever* **DH 52**
For all the faithful women *Potter* **TFF 219, WOV 692**
For all you've done *Moen* **HMS12 992**
For by grace *Nicholas* **W&P 38**
For ever I will sing *Guimont* **RS 117**
For ever I will sing *Haugen* **GC 82, RS 118**
For ever I will sing *Kogut* **G-4718**
For God so loved the world *Dauermann* **W&P 39**
For he alone is worthy *Traditional/Wade* **TFF 284**
For me *Hanson* **SCR 176**
For the life of the world *Haas* **GC 801**
For the Lord is good *DeShazo/Sadler* **HMS13 1065**
For to this end *Makeever* **DH 104**
Forever grateful *Altrogge* **HCW 44**
Forever my friend *Carpenter* **CMH2 51**
Freely given freely *Hanson/Murakami* **SCR 74**
From A to O *Hanson* **SCR 56**
From the depths *Smith* **PS2**
From the sunrise *Walker* **MAR 184**
From where the sun rises *Kendrick* **W&P 40**

G

Gather us in *Haugen* **RS 850, GC 744, WOV 718, G-2651**
Gathered as one *Tate/ Light* **VO 25**
Gathered in the love of Christ *Haugen* **G-5066**
Gentle night *Manion* **G&P 323**
Give it away *Makeever* **DH 96**
Give me a new heart *Walker* **G&P 210**
Give strength to your people, Lord *Smith* **PS1**
Give thanks to God on high *Chepponis* **GC 792**
Give thanks to the Lord *Carroll* **RS 147**
Give thanks to the Lord *Stewart* **GC 102**
Give thanks *Evans* **VIN6 128**
Give thanks *Smith* **W&P 41, TFF 292, HCW 46**
Give the Lord glory and honor *Haas* **GC 93**
Give us your vision *Hanson/Murakami* **SCR 85**
Gloria, gloria, gloria *Sosa* **WOV 637**
Glorify thy name *Adkins* **W&P 42**
Glorious God *Baroni/Fitts/Smith/Cloninger* **HMS10 823**
Glorious *Daniels* **VIN7 82**
Glory and praise for ever *Ash* **G&P 289**
Glory and praise to our God *Schutte* **G&P 671, RS 696, GC 522, W&P 43**
Glory be! *Ylvisaker* **BC**
Glory to the Lamb *Batstone* **MAR 28**
Glory *Bullock* **MAR 185**
Glory, glory, hallelujah! *Spiritual* **TFF 148**
Go and do *Hanson* **SCR 123**
Go down, Moses *Spiritual* **GC 715, TFF 87, WOV 670**
Go forth in his name *Kendrick* **REN 290**
Go forth *Rathmann* **CPH 98-3332**
Go in peace and serve the Lord *Hanson* **SCR 120, W&P 46**
Go now in peace *Sleeth* **COK 96**
Go to the world! *Johengen* **G-4395**
Go ye therefore *Cain/Webb* **W&P 49**
Go *Patillo* **GC 454, RS 604**
Go, make disciples *Hanson* **SCR 114, W&P 47**
God be gracious *Kendrick* **HMS12 994**
God be with you *Edwards* **W&P 50**
God beyond all names *Farrell* **GC 491, RS 634, G&P 66**
God has done great things for us *Haugen* **GC 124**
God has done marvelous things *Brokering/Haas* **W&P 51**
God has spoken, bread is broken *Young* **BL, AFP 11-10733**
God is always near *Kemp* **CGA 31**
God is compassionate *Makeever* **DH 46**
God is ever wakeful *Haas* **G-4579**
God is good (All the time) *Chapman* **MAR 186**
God is here *Moen/Overstreet* **HMS12 995**
God is love *Haas* **GC 629**
God is so good *Anonymous* **COK 75, TFF 275**
God mounts his throne to shouts *Kogut* **G-4718**
God mounts his throne *Haugen* **GC 53, RS 80**
God mounts his throne *Inwood* **G&P 208**
God my refuge *Montemayer* **HCW 50**
God of Abraham *Farrell* **GC 391, G&P 450**
God of all mercy *Haas* **RS 232**
God of glory *Hanson* **SCR 89**
God of hosts, bring us back *Furlong* **PS1**
God of love, have mercy *Makeever* **DH 10**
God of the hungry *Soper* **G&P 560**
God of the living *Haas* **RS 232**
God provides a brand new heart *Ylvisaker* **BC**
God sent his Son *Gaither/Gaither* **TFF 93**
God so loved the world *Hanson* **SCR 129**
God so loved the world *Hanson/Murakami* **SCR 18**
God so loved the world *Tate* **VO 27**
God the sculptor of the mountains *Thornburg/Husberg* **TFF 222**
God we praise you *American* **RS 676**
God will make a way *Moen* **HCW 52**
God with us *Kendrick* **HMS5 392**
God without and within *Hanson/Murakami* **SCR 70**
God, be gracious *Kendrick* **HMS12 994**
God, beyond all names *Farrell* **G&P 667, GC 491**
God, here is my life and my will *Young* **BL, AFP 11-10786**
God, in the planning *Bell* **GC 868**
God's love is eternal *Tate* **VO 29**
God's love is for ever! *Smith* **PS2**

Good news *Ethiopian/Olson* **GC 679, RS 797**
Good news, alleluia! *Makeever* **DH 65**
Good people are a light *Inwood* **PS3**
Good soil *Hanson* **SCR 30, W&P 52, WOV 713**
Great is our God *Ylvisaker* **BC**
Great is the Lord *Smith/Smith* **W&P 53, REN 22, MAR 29**
Great is thy faithfulness *Runyan* **WOV 771, REN 249**
Great one in three *Tate/Berrell* **VO 30**
Greater love *Barbour/Barbour* **MAR 30**
Guard my soul *Smith* **PS3**
Guide me, Lord *Hughes* **RS 186**
Guide my feet *Spiritual* **TFF 153**

H

Hallelujah! Praise the Lord *Post* **REN**
Hallelujah! We sing your praises *South African* **TFF 158, WOV 722, RS 692, GC 562**
Happy are they who hope *Dufford* **G&P 167**
Happy are they *Guimont* **RS**
Happy are they *Haas* **GC 18, PCY3, RS 28**
Happy are they *Harbor* **TFF 1**
Happy are they *Porter* **GC 77, G-3026**
Happy are they *Schoenbachler* **STP2**
Happy are those who follow *Cooney* **GC 116**
Harbor of my heart *Warner* **VO 31**
Have thine own way, Lord *Pollard* **TFF 152**
He answers all our needs *Bolduc* **VO 33**
He brings peace *Hanson* **SCR 217**
He came down *Cameroon/Bell* **GC 370, RS 519, TFF 37**
He came down *Haugen* **G-3808**
He came to be baptized *Ylvisaker* **BC**
He has made me glad *Brethorst* **TFF 291, COK 3**
He healed the darkness *Haas* **GC 876**
He is exalted *Paris* **REN 238, HCW 57, W&P 55, VO 32**
He is Jesus *Bolduc* **VO 34**
He is Lord *Smith* **HMS12 998**
He is Lord *Traditional* **SPW**
He shall reign *Chopinsky* **HMS12 999**
He who began a good work in you *Mohr* **W&P 56, HCW 60**
Heal me, O Lord *Eulberg* **TFF 189**
Heal me, O Lord *Moen* **HMS10 828**
Healer of our every ill *Haugen* **WOV 738, GC 882, RS 958**
Healing word *McCoy* **VIN6 82**
Hear me, O God *Tate* **VO 35**
Hear our cry *Kendrick* **HMS12 1001**
Hear the angels *Cain/Kadidlo* **W&P 57**
Heaven and earth *DeShazo/Harvill* **HMS10 829**
Heavenly Father *Park* **VIN7 92**
Hebrew traveling psalm *Ylvisaker* **BC**
Help me, Jesus *Bonnemere* **TFF 224**
Here am I *Batastini* **RS 75**
Here begins the good news *Haugen* **G-4416, SCR 129**
Here I am *Batstone* **MAR 115**
Here I am *Cooney* **GC 49, G&P 204, RS 74**
Here I am, Lord *Schutte* **WOV 752, BC, G&P 542, GC 686, TFF 230, RS 802**
Here I am, O God *Warner* **VO 36**
Here in this place *Haas* **GC 839**
Here is bread *Kendrick* **W&P 58**
Here is love *Lowry* **MAR**
Here is my heart *Nystrom* **HMS13 1070**
Hide me in your holiness *Ragsdale* **MAR 117**
His eye is on the sparrow *Gabriel* **TFF 252**
His love endures forever *Clark* **VIN6 94**
Hold me in life *Huijbers* **GC 599**
Holy child *Makeever* **DH 54**
Holy ground *Davis* **HCW 65, COK 5**
Holy is your name *Haas* **GC 147**
Holy love *Park* **VIN7 107**
Holy love, holy light *Batstone* **MAR 118**
Holy One, in you alone *Makeever* **DH 83**
Holy! Holy! Holy Lord *Ylvisaker* **BC**
Holy, holy *Owens* **W&P 60**
Holy, holy, holy *Cuellar* **W&P 61**
Holy, you are holy *Hanson* **SFL**
Hop on the bus *Underwood* **VIN7 120**
Hosanna to the Son of David *Schutte* **G&P 358**
Hosanna: Song of Mark *Haugen* **G-4416**
Hosea *Norbet* **G&P 471, GC 386, REN 126**
How beautiful upon the mountains *Ylvisaker* **BC**
How blessed *Hampton* **VIN6 106**
How can I keep from singing *Lowry* **RS 733, G&P 616, GC 603, WOV 781**
How glorious is your name *Cooney* **GC 20, RS 32, G-3412**
How good it is *American* **GC 727**
How lovely is your dwelling place *Goebel-Komala* **G-4406**
How lovely is your dwelling place *Joncas* **STP1**
How majestic is your name *Smith* **W&P 66**
How wonderful the three in one *Haugen* **GC 472**

I

I am loved *Gaither/Gaither* **COK 80**
I am the Bread of life *Toolan* **RS 931, GC 828, WOV 702, REN 246**
I am the Good Shepherd *Ylvisaker* **BC**
I am the light of the world *Hayakawa* **G&P 658, GC 510**
I am the living bread *Keesecker* **AFP 11-10684**
I am the resurrection *Ylvisaker* **BC**
I am the vine *Bell* **G-4391**
I am the vine *Hurd* **GC 672, G&P 545**
I Am *Hanson* **SFL**
I believe in Jesus *Nelson* **MAR 121, HCW 71**
I belong to a mighty God *DeShazo* **HMS8 654, MHS 8**
I bend my knees again *Butler/Butler* **VIN8 85**
I can do all things *Baloche/Harris* **HMS11 913**
I can do all things *Smith* **HMS13 1074**
I cannot tell it all *Spiritual/Booth* **G&P 390, OCP 10663**

I come to the cross *Somma/Batstone* **MAR 122**
I come with joy to meet my Lord *American* **GC 806**
I come with joy *Wren/Traditional* **BC**
I could sing of your love forever *Smith* **VIN8 89, HMS13 1075**
I do believe *Ylvisaker* **BC**
I don't belong to me *Hanson* **SCR 152**
I exalt thee *Sanchez* **MAR 123**
I give you thanks *Lindh* **CGA 561**
I have decided to follow Jesus *Traditional* **MAR 198**
I have decided *Liles* **HCW 182**
I have kept the faith *Baloche* **HMS13 1076**
I heard the voice of Jesus say *Bonar/Traditional* **TFF 62**
I know that my redeemer lives *Haas* **GC 854**
I lift up my eyes *Ogden* **PS3**
I long for you *Balhoff/Daigle/Ducote* **GC 63**
I love to be in your presence *Baloche/Kerr* **HCW 75**
I love you, Lord *Klein* **MAR 199, W&P 67, TFF 288**
I place my life *Cooney* **G-3613**
I praise your name *Ylvisaker* **BC**
I put my life in your hands *Haas* **GC 42, RS 61**
I put my life in your hands *Haugen* **GC 43**
I rejoiced when I heard them say *Warner* **VO 41**
I rejoiced *Farrell* **PS1**
I rejoiced *Walker* **PS2**
I saw water *Young* **BL**
I see the Lord *Baloche* **HMS13 1079**
I see the Lord *Falson* **MAR 41**
I see you *Mullins* **CC 90**
I shall not be moved *Spiritual* **TFF 147**
I thank you, Lord *Ylvisaker* **BC**
I turn to you *Cooney* **GC 44**
I turn to you, Lord *Stewart* **RS 64**
I want Jesus to walk with me *Spiritual* **TFF 66, WOV 660**
I want to know you *Evans* **HMS12 1008**
I was glad *Beech* **W&P 68**
I was glad *Haas* **GC 121**
I was on the outside/Song of Mark *Haugen* **G-4416**
I was there to hear your borning cry *Ylvisaker* **BC, W&P 69, WOV 770**
I will always thank the Lord *Soper* **G&P 202**
I will be with you always *Hanson/Murakami* **SCR 118**
I will be with you *Moore* **GC 455, RS 603**
I will bless the Lord *Gouin* **GC 46**
I will bless thee, O Lord *Watanabe* **MAR**
I will bless you, O God *Makeever* **DH 34**
I will bow down and worship *Chambers/Brewster* **HMS13 1081**
I will call upon the Lord *O'Shields* **W&P 70, REN 15**
I will call upon the name of the Lord *Roberts* **TFF 14**
I will celebrate *Baloche* **MAR 43**
I will celebrate *Duvall* **MAR, CEL 66**
I will choose Christ *Booth* **G&P 459, OCP 10592**
I will come and bow down *Nystrom* **HCW 87**
I will delight *Harrah/Schreiner* **W&P 72**
I will enter his gates *Brethorst* **TFF 291**
I will follow *Barbour/Barbour* **MAR**
I will give you peace *Ylvisaker* **BC**
I will never be *Bullock* **HMS11 920**
I will not be shaken *Founds* **MAR 203**
I will not die *Conry* **RS 771, GC 657**
I will offer you my life *Ylvisaker* **BC**
I will praise the Lord *Joncas* **G-3434**
I will praise you Lord *Guimont* **GC 28, RS 41**
I will praise you *Smith* **PS2**
I will praise you, Lord *Inwood* **GC 41, G&P 192**
I will praise you, Lord *Kogut* **G-4718**
I will praise you, Lord *Ridge* **G&P 193**
I will praise your name for ever *Roberts* **RS 192**
I will praise your name *Bolduc* **VO 44**
I will praise your name *Haas* **GC 137, RS 193, PS2**
I will rejoice *Brown* **G&P 674**
I will show God's salvation *Dean* **PS3**
I will sing *Haas* **GC 71, RS 99**
I will sing *Odgen* **PS1**
I will sing, I will sing *Dyer* **GC, W&P 73**
I will walk in the presence of God *Cooney* **GC 109**
I wonder as I wander *Appalachian/Niles* **WOV 642**
I wonder if he knew *Hanson/Murakami* **SCR 196**
I'll be waitin' *Ylvisaker* **BC**
I'll belong to you *Hanson* **SCR 126**
I'll bless the Lord for evermore *Traditional* **BC**
I'll bless the Lord for evermore *Ylvisaker* **BC**
I'm forever grateful *Altrogge* **MAR 44**
I'm going on a journey *Bonnemere* **TFF 115**
I'm not afraid *Ylvisaker* **BC**
I'm so glad Jesus lifted me *Spiritual* **TFF 191, WOV 673**
I've just come from the fountain *Spiritual* **TFF 111, WOV 696, G 802**
I am the Bread of life *Toolan* **WOV 702**
If today you hear God's voice *Haas* **GC 89, RS 129**
If today you hear his voice *Stewart* **RS 128**
If today you hear the voice of God *Bolduc* **VO 45**
If you believe and I believe *Bell* **GC 722, RS 825**
In Christ there is no east or west *Spiritual* **TFF 214**
In Christ, a new creation *Ylvisaker* **BC**
In God alone *Haas* **GC 59, RS 88**
In his days justice will flourish *Joncas* **GC 72**
In his days *Ogden* **PS1**
In love we choose to live *Cotter* **GC 873**
In my life be glorified *Kilpatrick* **SPW**
In the arms of the Shepherd *Weckler* **VO 47**
In the breaking of the bread *Hurd* **G&P 508, GC 841, RS 932**
In the cross of Christ *Haugen* **G-4838**
In the land of the living *Johengen* **GC 38**
In the last days *Makeever* **DH 70**
In the light *Poirier* **VO 48**
In the morning *Houge* **W&P 75**
In the name of the Father *Capers* **TFF 142**

In the presence of the angels *Haas* **PCY3**
In the presence of the angels *Inwood* **PS2, PS3**
In the presence of your people *Chambers* **WOV720**
In the sight of the angels *Guimont* **RS 185**
In the water *Makeever* **DH 68**
In the water *McLean* **WIS 14**
In the wilderness *Ylvisaker* **BC**
In unity and peace *Chepponis* **G-4452**
In your heart there is a voice *McLean* **CCJ, WIS 17**
Increase our faith *Haas* **G-4736**
Indeed, how good is the Lord *Roberts* **TFF 12**
Into the life *McLean* **WIS 11**
Isaiah 49 *Landry* **G&P 711**
It has always been you *Butler/Butler* **VIN6 120**
It is good to give thanks *Dean* **PS3**
It is good *Adler* **CCJ 16**
It won't be long *Makeever* **DH 89**

J

Jehovah *Springer* **VIN6 124**
Jerusalem, my happy home *American* **RS 871, GC 771**
Jesu, Jesu *Ghana* **WOV 765, GC 409**
Jesu, Jesu, fill us with your love *Ghana/Johnston* **G-3000**
Jesus is here right now *Roberts* **RS 930**
Jesus is our king *Prebble* **REN 273**
Jesus lead on *Helming* **VIN8 114**
Jesus reigns *Compton* **MAR 207**
Jesus walked this lonesome valley *Ferguson* **G-3279**
Jesus, amazing *Hanson/Murakami* **SCR 79**
Jesus, be with us now *Haas* **G-4732**
Jesus, child of God *Makeever* **DH 53**
Jesus, child of God *Ylvisaker* **BC**
Jesus, come to us *Haas* **G&P 304**
Jesus, heal us *Haas* **GC 875**
Jesus, help me see *Ylvisaker* **BC**
Jesus, I believe *Batstone* **MAR 130**
Jesus, Jesus *Bullock* **HMS11 923**
Jesus, keep me near the cross *Keesecker* **AFP 11-10744**
Jesus, Lamb of God (All in all) *Jernigan* **W&P 76**
Jesus, lead on *Helming* **VIN8 114**
Jesus, name above all names *Cain* **TFF 268, W&P 77**
Jesus, remember me *Berthier* **W&P 78, RS 770, GC 404, WOV 748**
Jesus, tempted in the desert *Welsh* **RS 548**
Jesus, the Lord *O'Connor* **GC 418, RS 574, G&P 370**
Jesus, the Lord *Paris* **HCW 57**
Jesus, we are gathered *Matsikenyiri* **TFF 140**
Jesus, we want to meet *Oiude* **TFF 145**
Jesus, you are my life *Fry* **MAR**
Jesus, you reign over all *Cook* **MAR 208**
John 3:16 *Lloyd* **MAR**
Join in the dance *Schutte* **G&P 393**
Jonah's song *Williams* **REN 125**
Journey for home *Bolduc* **VO 50**
Journeysong *Hurd* **G&P 581**
Joyfully singing *Balhoff/Ducotte/Daigle* **GC 548**
Just a closer walk with thee *Spiritual* **TFF 253**
Just as Jesus told us *Makeever* **DH 29**
Just like a deer *Joncas* **G&P 205**
Justice shall flourish *Cooney* **G&P 220**

K

Keep me safe, O God *Foley* **GC 23, RS 35**
Keep the faith *Makeever* **DH 98**
King of kings *Batya/Conty* **W&P 80**
King of kings *Dauermann* **REN 268**
King of life *Sadler* **HMS12 1014**
Kyrie eleison *Olson* **W&P 81**

L

Lamb of God *Beech* **WOV 622**
Lamb of God *Paris* **HCW 100, SPW**
Lamb of God *Park* **W&P 83**
Lamb of God, come take away *Makeever* **DH 25**
Lay down that spirit *Mattingly* **VO 52**
Lay hands upon us *Glover* **G-4591**
Lead me, guide me *Akers* **TFF 70**
Lead me, oh lead me *Smith* **HMS13 1085**
Leave your heart with me *Hanson* **SCR 150**
Let all creation sing *Ogden* **PS1**
Let all praise the name of the Lord *Smith* **G-2989**
Let all the earth cry out *Cooney* **G&P 216**
Let all the earth *Haugen* **GC 65, RS 93**
Let all the people praise you *Makeever* **DH 38**
Let all the world sing praises *Falson* **MAR 216**
Let heaven rejoice *Dufford* **G&P 392**
Let it be said of us *Fry* **MAR 217**
Let it rain *Park* **VIN8 126**
Let justice roll like a river *Haugen* **W&P 85, GC 716**
Let my prayer be a fragrant offering *Sappington* **W&P 86**
Let peace fill the earth *Makeever* **DH 90**
Let the fire fall *Mattingly* **VO 53**
Let the fire fall *Misulia* **VO 53**
Let the heavens rejoice *Harbor* **TFF 10**
Let the King of glory come *Joncas* **G&P 299, OCP**
Let the Lord enter! *Ollis* **PS3**
Let the peace of God reign *Zschech* **HMS11 926**
Let the river flow *Evans* **HMS12 1015, VIN6 128**
Let the valleys be raised *Schutte* **G&P 310**
Let the walls fall down *Batstone/Barbour* **MAR 50**
Let there be praise *Tunney* **HCW 211**
Let us go rejoicing *Harbor* **TFF 17**
Let us go rejoicing *Joncas* **GC 120**
Let us go rejoicing *Roberts* **G-4606**
Let us rejoice *Haugen* **GC 114, RS 158**
Let us see, O Lord, your mercy *Smith* **PS1**
Let us talents and tongues employ *Jamaican* **WOV 754, BC**
Let your face shine upon us *Haugen* **RS 30, GC 19**

Let your fire fall *DeShazo/Sadler* **HMS12 1016**
Let your glory fill this place *Graves* **MAR 218**
Let your healing love *Butler* **VIN6 144**
Life in his hands *Hanson* **SCR 10**
Life-giving bread *Manalo* **G-3911**
Lift high the cross *Nicholson* **REN**
Lift up my soul *Hurd* **G&P 302**
Lift up your heads *Fry* **CW 111**
Lift up your heads *Kendrick* **W&P 88**
Lift up your hearts *O'Connor* **G&P 676, RS 691, GC 558, SCR 45**
Light the darkness *McLean* **WIS 22**
Like a deer that longs *Bauman* **RS 77**
Like a deer that longs *Haugen* **G-3261**
Like a little child *Haas* **G-3956**
Like a rose in winter *Hanson/Murakami* **SCR 204**
Like a shepherd *Dufford* **GC 325, G&P 708**
Like a shepherd *Moen/Simpson* **HCW 112**
Listen to the voice of God *Geary* **PS2**
Live in me *Bolduc* **VO 55**
Live in my love *Young* **BL**
Living thanksgiving *Makeever* **DH 99**
Look to the one *Bolduc* **VO 57**
Lord, I lift your name on high *Founds* **W&P 90, MAR 51**
Lord most high *Harris/Sadler* **HMS11 930**
Lord of glory *Manion* **G&P 707**
Lord of heaven *Ashwood* **CCP 23**
Lord today *Ducote* **G&P 338, GC 375**
Lord we pray *Gustafson* **HMS8 668**
Lord, bid your servant go in peace *Wyeth* **RS 874**
Lord, bless your people *Warner* **VO 59**
Lord, come and save us *Haugen* **GC 140**
Lord, come and save us *Kendzia* **G&P 308**
Lord, every nation *Cooney* **G&P 220**
Lord, forgive the wrong *Guimont* **RS 65**
Lord, heal my soul *Guimont* **GC 50**
Lord, how can I repay *Glynn* **PS2**
Lord, I love your commands *Guimont* **GC 117**
Lord, I'm in your hands *Weeks* **MAR 133**
Lord, in your great love *Guimont* **GC 68**
Lord, in your great love *Peloquin* **RS 98**
Lord, it is good *Guimont* **GC 86, RS 124**
Lord, let us see your kindness *Haugen* **GC 79, RS 112**
Lord, listen to your children praying *Medema* **TFF 247, W&P 92, WOV 775**
Lord, listen to your children *Hanson* **SCR 23, WOV 775, W&P 91**
Lord, make us turn to you *Haugen* **GC 75**
Lord, make us turn to you *Smith* **PS1**
Lord, most high *Harris/Sadler* **HMS11 930**
Lord, my strength *Krippaehne* **W&P 93**
Lord, send out your Spirit *Lisicky* **RS 146, GC 101**
Lord, send out your Spirit *Zsigray* **G&P 253**
Lord, we pray *Gustafson* **HMS8 668**
Lord, when your glory appears *Stewart* **GC 25**
Lord, with grateful hearts *Ylvisaker* **BC**
Lord, you are good and forgiving *Dean* **PS3**
Lord, you are good and forgiving *Guimont* **GC 81**
Lord, you are good and forgiving *Smith* **PS3**
Lord, you have the words *Bolduc* **VO 61**
Lord, you have the words *Haas* **GC 27, RS 40**
Lord, you have the words *Haugen* **VO 62**
Lord, you've been our dwelling place *Ylvisaker* **BC**
Lord, your love is eternal *Stewart* **GC 133**
Love is his word *Hutmacher* **RS 750**
Love is never ending *Haugen* **GC 131**
Love you so much *Fragar* **HMS13 1088**
Loving and forgiving *Soper* **G&P 251**

M

Magnificat *Chepponis* **GC 146**
Magnificat *Joncas* **RS 656**
Magnificat *Smith* **PS1**
Magnificat *Ylvisaker* **BC**
Magnify the Lord *Berthier* **RSH 131**
Majesty *Hayford* **W&P 94, MAR 134, REN 63**
Make me a servant *Willard* **REN, W&P 96, MAR 135**
Make my life a candle *Hanson* **SCR 163**
Make your presence known *Barbour* **MAR 221**
Many and great, O God, are your works *Dakota* **WOV 794**
Many are the lightbeams *Haugen* **GC 841**
Maranatha *Schoenbachler* **G&P 29**
Maranatha, alleluia! *Wellicome* **PS1, PS2**
Maranatha, come *O'Brien* **G-4526**
Mark's Sanctus *Ylvisaker* **BC**
Mary's song *Rethmeier* **VIN6 160**
May God bless us in his mercy *Batastini* **RS 95**
May God bless us in his mercy *Guimont* **RS 94, GC 66**
May God bless us in his mercy *Kogut* **G-4718**
May we have peace *Ylvisaker* **BC**
May you run and not be weary *Hanson* **SCR 116, W&P 97**
Meet us here *Marks* **MAR**
Meet us *Rethmeier* **VIN8 136**
Mercy *DeShazo/Sadler* **HMS14**
Mighty is our God *Walker* **HCW 118**
Miriam's song *Barker* **CGA 740**
More like Jesus Christ *McLean* **WIS 28**
More precious than silver *DeShazo* **HCW 122**
Morning has broken *Farjeon/Traditional* **W&P 98**
Most holy one *Willard/Baloche* **MAR 223**
Mourning into dancing *Walker* **CS 125, W&P 99, HCW 125**
Moved by the gospel, let us move *English* **RS 801**
My chosen one *Young* **BL, AFP 11-10753**
My God reigns *Evans* **HMS12 1021**
My God, my God *Haugen* **GC 29, RS 43**
My God, my God *Manion* **G&P 175**
My God, my God *Schiavone* **G&P 177**

My God, my God *Smith* **PS2**
My heart will trust *Morgan* **HMS14**
My heart yearns for thee *Baroni* **HMS12 1022**
My life is in you, Lord *Gardner* **HCW 128**
My Lord will come again *Haas* **GC 769, G-3654**
My Lord, what a morning *Spiritual* **WOV 627, BC**
My peace *Routledge* **MAR 53**
My shepherd is the Lord *Glynn* **PS2**
My shepherd is the Lord *Guiao* **UMP 10/1734U**
My soul does magnify the Lord *Brown* **TFF 168**
My soul in stillness waits *Haugen* **GC 328, RS 495**
My soul is still *Haas* **GC 129**
My soul is thirsting *Joncas* **GC 61, RS 90**

N

Nativity carol *O'Brien* **GC 365, RS 521**
New life again and again *Hanson/Murakami* **SCR 102**
Night of silence *Kantor* **GC 342, RS 523, W&P 101**
Night storm: Song of Mark *Haugen* **G-4416**
No greater love *Joncas* **GC 628**
No greater love *Schoenbahler* **G&P 362**
No greater love *Walker* **MAR 54**
No higher calling *LeBlanc/Gulley* **MAR**
No longer strangers *Ylvisaker* **BC, W&P 102**
No wind at the window *Gaelic/Bell* **RS 876**
Nothing at all but love *Ylvisaker* **BC**
Nothing can come between us *Young* **BL, AFP 11-10848**
Nothing is as wonderful *Underwood* **VIN8 150**
Now God our Father *Dearman/Mills* **W&P 103, CEL 654**
Now in this banquet *Haugen* **W&P 104**
Now let your servant go *Chant* **GC 776**
Now the feast and celebration *Haugen* **WOV 789**
Now the green blade rises *French carol* **GC 444, RS**
Now we raise our thanks to you *Ylvisaker* **BC**
Now we remain *Haas* **GC 594, RS 813, W&P 106**
Now *Cooney* **G-3974**

O

O blessed are those who fear the Lord *Ollis* **PS1**
O God of matchless glory *Duck* **GC 546**
O God, be gracious *Brown* **PS1**
O God, for you I long *Farrell* **G&P 206**
O God, you search me *Farrell* **PS3**
O holy city, seen of John *American* **GC 767**
O how I long to see *Hurd* **G&P 306**
O Jerusalem *Vogt* **LBG**
O Lord let us see your kindness *Harbor* **TFF 8**
O Lord to you *Sadler* **HMS11 937**
O Lord, be my help *Ogden* **PS3**
O Lord, I love the habitation of your house *Bender* **CPH 98-2859**
O Lord, let us see your kindness *Harbor* **TFF 8**
O Lord, my heart is not proud *Rizza* **W&P 109**
O Lord, open my eyes *Ghana* **TFF 134**
O love of God/Amor de Dios *Hurd* **G&P 541**
O loving God *Makeever* **DH 82**
O star of beauty *Glover* **G-4585**
O, mighty cross *Baroni/Chisum* **HCW 136**
O'er the river Jordan *Haas* **G-4689**
Offering *McLean* **WIS 31**
Offering *McLean* **WIS 31**
Oh how he loves you and me *Kaiser* **TFF 82**
Oh Lord, you're beautiful *Green* **MAR 231**
Oh, come, oh, come, Emmanuel *Young* **AFP 11-10891**
Oh, how he loves you and me *Kaiser* **TFF 82**
Oh, let the Son of God enfold you *Wimber* **TFF 105**
Oh, sing to the Lord *Brazilian* **TFF 274, WOV 795**
Oh, when the saints go marching in *Spiritual* **TFF 180**
On Christmas day *Ylvisaker* **BC**
On Christmas night *Hanson/Murakami* **SCR 210**
On eagle's wings *Joncas* **W&P 110, GC 611, G&P 598, RS 740, WOV 779**
On Jordan's bank *Miles* **GC 322**
On that holy mountain *Mattingly* **VO 68**
On the day I called *Cooney* **STP 4**
On the journey to Emmaus *Haugen* **RS 816, G-4278**
On the mountain top *Ylvisaker* **BC**
On the wings of change *Galipeau* **WLP 5209**
Once again *Hanson* **SCS 18**
Once and for all time *Hanson/Murakami* **SCR 200**
One bread we bless and share *Manalo* **G-4362**
One bread, one body *Foley* **W&P 111, TFF 122, WOV 710, G&P 499**
One in the bread *Young* **BL**
One is the body *Cooney* **GC 846**
One Lord *Soper* **G&P**
One *Hanson/Murakami* **SCR 160**
Only by grace *Gustafson* **HCW 140, W&P 112**
Only for your glory *Hanson* **SCR 34**
Only God for me *Harris* **HMS14**
Only this I want *Schutte* **GC 695, G&P 575**
Only you *Baloche/Kerr* **HMS13 1092**
Open our eyes *Keil* **UMP 10/1737U-8**
Open our eyes, Lord *Cull* **MAR 59, TFF 98, W&P 113, REN**
Open our lives to the Word *Makeever* **DH 8**
Open the eyes of my heart *Baloche* **HMS12 1027, HMS13 1093**
Our blessing-cup *Haugen* **RS 155, GC 107, G&P 257**
Our confidence is in the Lord *Richards* **W&P 114**
Our eyes are fixed on the Lord *Guimont* **RS 168, GC 122**
Our eyes are on the Lord *Duffy* **PS3**
Our God is compassion *Cotter* **GC 138**
Our God is here *Haas* **G-5041**
Our God is lifted up *Smith* **SPW**
Our God reigns *Smith* **VO 73**
Our heart *Chisum/Searcy* **HMS13 1094, HCW 143**
Our help comes from the Lord *Joncas* **GC 119**
Our help is in the name *Baroni* **HMS11 938**
Our hope is alive *Ylvisaker* **BC**
Out in the wilderness *Beech* **W&P 115**

Set your heart on the higher gifts *Warner* **VO 80**
Shake up the morning *Bell* **GC 529**
Shall we gather at the river *Lowry* **WOV 690, TFF 179**
Shalom, my good friends *Traditional* **BC**
Share your bread with the hungry *Haas* **G-4734**
Shelter *Lisicky* **G-4426**
Shepherd me, O God *Haugen* **GC 31, RS 756, G-3107**
Shepherd of my soul *Nystrom* **MAR 65**
Shine down on me *O'Brien* **MMP**
Shine on us, Lord *Mattingly* **VO 82**
Shine on us/Now let your servant *Glover* **G-4583**
Shine on us/That Easter day *Glover* **G-4596**
Shine, Jesus, shine *Kendrick* **HCW 155, W&P 123, WOV 651, TFF 64M NAR 238**
Shout for joy *Traditional* **GC 559**
Shout joy to the Lord *d'Inverno* **PS 2**
Shout to God, O faithful people *Ylvisaker* **BC**
Shout to the Lord *Zschech* **HMS10 862, HMS11 947, W&P 124**
Shout with joy *Smith* **PS2**
Show me the path *Haas* **G-4579**
Show me the way *Makeever* **DH 45**
Show me your ways *Fragar* **HMS11 949**
Show us the way *Light/Tate* **VO 83**
Since my mother's womb *Guimont* **RS 100**
Sing a song to the Lord *Lawton* **G-4661**
Sing a song to the Lord *Rushbridge* **PS1**
Sing of Mary, pure and lowly *Traditional* **WOV 634**
Sing out, earth and skies *Haugen* **W&P 126**
Sing to the mountains *Dufford* **RS 590, GC, G&P 673**
Sing unto the Lord *Makeever* **DH 47**
Sing with all the saints in glory *Traditional* **WOV 691, GC 442**
Sing with joy to God *Currie* **RS 109**
Sing with joy to God *Guimont* **GC 76**
Sing, my soul *Traditional* **RSH 129**
Singing praise to God *Haas* **G-5041**
Singing through the water *Hanson/Murakami* **SCR 132**
So you must do *Haugen* **G-4841**
Softly and tenderly Jesus is calling *Thompson* **WOV 734, REN 147**
Someone in need of your love *Makeever* **DH 94**
Somos uno en Cristo *Spanish* **TFF 221**
Song about grace *Ylvisaker* **BC**
Song at the sea *O'Kelly-Fischer* **GC 143, RS 202**
Song of fire and water *Haugen* **GC 154**
Song of longing *Cooney* **GC 51**
Song of the angels *Dufford* **G&P**
Song of the chosen *Cooney* **GC 813**
Song of the Lord's command *Haas* **G-4682**
Song of the mustard seed *Hopson* **G-2239**
Song of the stable *Haas* **GC 364, RS 364**
Song of the three children *Proulx* **G-1863**
Song of three children *Guimont* **GC 150**
Song over the waters *Haugen* **GC 585, RS 855, W&P 127**
Soon and very soon *Crouch* **REN 278, WOV 744, W&P 128, TFF 38**
Sow the word *Zavelli/SJanco* **GC 516**
Speak now, O Lord *Mattingly* **VO 86**
Spirit blowing through creation *Haugen* **GC 462**
Spirit calls, rejoice! *Hanson/Murakami* **SCR 1**
Spirit of the living God *Iverson* **TFF 101, W&P 129**
Spirit of the living God *Makeever* **DH 72**
Spirit of the living God *Sanchez* **HCW 158**
Spirit song *Wimber* **CMH 6, W&P 130, TFF 105**
Spirit-friend *Gonja/Glover* **GC 467, G-4589**
Stand firm *Cameroon/Glover* **G-4593**
Stand in the congregation *Batstone* **W&P 131, MAR 149**
Stand up and give him the praise *DeShazo* **HMS10 867**
Stand up friends *Haas* **GC 478**
Stand up *Carroll* **MAR 240**
Standing on the Lord's side *Ylvisaker* **BC**
Star of David *Murakami* **SCR 206**
Stay here *Taizé* **WOV 667, GC 411, RS 565**
Stay with us *Taizé* **WOV 743**
Step by step *Beaker* **HMS13 1103, W&P 132**
Stir up the love *Ylvisaker* **BC**
Stir up *Makeever* **DH 51**
Streams of living water *Consiglio* **OCP 10898, S&S**
Stretch out your hand *Smith/duPlessis* **MAR 150**
Stretch towards heaven *Smith* **PS1**
Surely goodness and mercy *Peterson/Smith* **CEL 691**
Surely it is God who saves me *Chávez-Melo* **WOV 635**
Surely it is God who saves me *White* **REN 122**
Surely the presence of the Lord *Wolfe* **COK 1**
Swing low, sweet chariot *Spiritual* **TFF 171**

T

Table of plenty *Schutte* **G&P 530**
Table song *Haas* **GC 849**
Take and eat *Joncas* **GC 831, RS 910**
Take of the wonder *Wetzler* **AFP 11-10647**
Take off your shoes *Makeever* **DH 62**
Take up your cross *Traditional* **GC 698**
Take, O, take me as I am *Bell* **G**
Tales of wonder (Creation) *Haugen* **G-3320**
Taste and see *Dean* **RS 72, G&P 200**
Taste and see *Haugen* **RS 70, GC 47**
Taste and see *Hurd* **G&P 199**
Taste and see *Young* **BL, AFP 11-10895**
Teach me how to pray *Hanson/Murakami* **SCR 25**
Teach me, O God *Walker* **PS3**
Teach me, O Lord *Hurd* **G-2715**
Tell what God has done for us *Makeever* **DH 97**
Thank you for the gift *Hanson* **SCR 144**
Thank you, Lord *Park* **VIN8 242**
Thankgiving to the living God *Makeever* **DH 3**
Thanks be to you *Haugen* **WOV 790, RS 708, GC 569**
Thanksgiving to the living God *Makeever* **DH 3**
That boy-child of Mary *Colvin* **TFF 54**

That Christ be known *Schaefer* **W&P 133**
That Easter day with joy *Praetorius* **GC 445, RS 599**
That priceless grace *Ghanaian* **TFF 68**
That we may be filled *Hanson/Murakami* **SCR 182, W&P 134**
The advent herald *Cooney* **G-4972**
The angel Gabriel from heaven came *Basque* **G&P 441, RS**
The aye carol *Bell* **GC 371, RS 525**
The battle belongs to the Lord *Owens/Collins* **SPW**
The blessing cup *Brown* **PS2**
The church song *Beech* **W&P 135**
The cloud's veil *Lawton* **G-4664**
The cross of Jesus *O'Brien* **G-4517**
The cry of the poor *Foley* **RS 69, GC 48, G&P 203**
The day is near *Conry* **GC 768**
The family of the Lord *Hanson* **SCR 39**
The festival psalm *Ylvisaker* **BC**
The fire of your love *Baloche/Kerr* **HMS12 1037**
The first song of Isaiah *White* **REN 122**
The fountain of all life *Haas* **G-5041**
The fullness of the Lord *Ylvisaker* **BC**
The God of all grace *Manalo* **OCP 10510**
The greatest is love *Pote* **CGA 781**
The hand of the Lord *Stewart* **PCY5**
The harvest of justice *Haas* **GC 711**
The heavens are telling *Ylvisaker* **BC**
The Honduras alleluia *Honduran/Glover* **G-4588**
The just will live *Batastini* **RS 33**
The King of glory *Jabusch/Israeli* **W&P 136, REN 267, BC**
The kingdom song *Evans* **HMS12 1040**
The Lamb *Coleman* **TFF 89**
The least of all the saints *Ylvisaker* **BC**
The Lord comes to the earth *Haas/Kodner* **GC 95**
The Lord gave them bread *Guimont* **GC**
The Lord has done great things *Cortez* **G&P 271**
The Lord has done great things *Guimont* **RS 169**
The Lord has done great things *Smith* **PS1**
The Lord has done great things *Stewart* **RS 170**
The Lord is close to the brokenhearted *Brown* **PS1**
The Lord is kind and merciful *Bolduc* **VO 90**
The Lord is kind and merciful *Cotter* **GC 99**
The Lord is kind and merciful *Haugen* **GC 100, RS**
The Lord is king *Guimont* **GC 87**
The Lord is my life and my light *Leftley* **PS2**
The Lord is my light *Haas* **GC 39, RS 57**
The Lord is my portion *Ylvisaker* **BC**
The Lord is my shepherd *Christopherson* **AFP 11-4691**
The Lord is my shepherd *Ollis* **PS2**
The Lord of glory *O'Brien* **G-3778**
The Lord of hosts is with us *Harbor* **TFF 6**
The Lord reigns *Stradwick* **MAR**
The Lord upholds my life *Guimont* **GC 58**
The Lord upholds my life *Haas* **G-3563**
The Lord will bless all people *Haas* **G-4579**
The Lord will bless his people *Guimont* **GC 40**
The Lord will keep me safe & holy *Ylvisaker* **BC**
The Lord's my shepherd *Archer* **G-4645**
The Lord's prayer *West Indian* **REN 180**
The love of God *Tate* **VO 89**
The love of the Lord *Joncas* **GC 702, RS 814**
The name of God *Haas* **RS 152, GC 110**
The name of the Lord *Utterback* **MAR 245**
The night of his betrayal *Ylvisaker* **BC**
The people of God *O'Brien* **GC 653**
The people on your heart *DeShazo/Sadler* **HMS10 869**
The queen stands at your right hand *Kodner* **GC 52**
The queen stands at your right hand *Rees* **PS3**
The river is here *Park* **HMS11 958, CMH 58, VIN6 232**
The seed that falls on good ground *Guimont* **GC 64, RS 92**
The servant song *Gillard* **GC 669**
The Spirit is singing *Hanson/Murakami* **SCR 72**
The spirit of God *Deiss* **GC 458, WLP**
The steadfast love of the Lord *McNeill* **REN 23**
The stranger and the nets *Cooney/Cooney* **VO 92**
The summons *Scottish/Bell* **W&P 137, GC 700**
The tiny child to Bethlehem came *Haugen* **GC 355**
The trees of the field *Dauermann* **REN 302**
The trumpet in the morning *Cooney* **G-4970**
The trumpets sound, the angels sing *Kendrick* **W&P 139**
The vineyard of the Lord *Guimont* **GC 74**
The virgin Mary had a baby boy *West Indian* **TFF 53, GC 345, RS 501**
The wise may bring their learning *Ylvisaker* **BC**
The wondrous day of our God *Haugen* **G-4416**
The word is in your heart *Moore* **GC 518**
There is a balm in Gilead *Spiritual* **WOV 737, TFF 185, RS 764**
There is a longing *Quigley* **G&P 620**
There is a Redeemer *Green* **W&P 140, REN 232**
There was the Word *Makeever* **DH 55**
There's a song *Hanson* **SFL**
There's a sweet, sweet spirit in this place *Akers* **TFF 102**
These things are true of you *Walker* **MAR 248**
They who do justice *Haas* **GC 22**
They'll know we are Christians *Traditional* **CC 94, COK 74**
This bread that we break *Makeever* **DH 30**
This day new light will shine *Beckett* **PS1**
This day was made by the Lord *Walker* **G&P 383**
This is the day *Ganett* **W&P141, TFF 262**
This is the day *Joncas* **RS 576, G&P**
This is the feast of victory *Hillert* **REN 199**
This is the feast of victory *Makeever* **DH 12**
This is the feast of victory *Young* **W&P 142, BL**
This is the gospel of Christ *Brown* **HMS10 870**
This is the time of fulfillment! *Chepponis* **RS 556**
This joyful Eastertide *Dutch* **WOV 676, GC 434**

This kingdom *Bullock* **HMS11 962**
This little light of mine *Spiritual* **TFF 65**
Through our God we shall do valiantly *Garratt* **REN 262**
Throughout all time *Haas* **G-4579**
Thy kingdom come *Cooney* **RS 776, GC 656, G&P 710**
Thy word *Smith/Grant* **TFF 132, W&P 144, CEL 184**
Thy word *Webb* **W&P 143**
'Tis good, Lord, to be here *Speiss* **GC 778**
To God be the glory *Crouch* **TFF 272**
To know you more *Horness* **MAR 76**
To you, O God, I lift up my soul *Hurd* **G&P 302**
To you, O Lord I lift my soul *Roberts* **G-4601**
To you, O Lord *Haas* **PCY9**
To you, O Lord *Haugen* **G-2653, GC 36, RS 53**
To you, O Lord *Soper* **PS1**
To you, O Lord *Thompson* **RS 50**
To you, O Lord, I lift my soul *Roberts* **G-4601**
Today a Saviour has been born *Ollis* **PS1**
Today is born our Savior *Haugen* **GC 91**
Today our Savior is born *Cortez* **G&P 238**
Trading my sorrows *Evans* **HMS14**
Transfiguration *Landry* **G&P 443**
Transform us *Dunstan/Gerike* **RS 881**
Tree of life/Adoramus te *Haugen* **GC 396/397, RS 541/542**
Turn my heart *DeShazo* **HCW 179**
Turn our hearts *Kendrick* **HCW, MAR, HMS10 43, HMS12 1043**
Turn to me *Foley* **G&P 342**
Turn to the Lord in your need *Guimont* **RS 97, GC 69**
Turn your eyes upon Jesus *Lemmel* **COK 55**
Two fishermen *Toolan* **RS 812, GC 688**

U

Ubi caritas et amor *Berthier* **WOV 665, REN 226**
Unless a grain of wheat *Farrell* **G&P 579, GC 697**
Unless you learn *Haugen* **G-4416**
Unto thee, O Lord *Monroe* **CEL 531**
Up from the earth *Cooney* **G&P 386, GC 452, RS 589**

W

Wade in the water *Spiritual* **G&P 456, TFF 114**
Wait for the Lord *Taizé* **GC 332**
Wake from your sleep *Schutte* **G&P 328**
Wake up *Hanson* **SCR 13**
Wake up, sleeper *Ylvisaker* **BC**
Walk across the water *Makeever* **DH 69**
Walk in the land *Mattingly* **VO 94**
Walk in the reign *Cooney* **GC 319**
Washed anew *Keesecker* **AFP 11-10676**
Water from heaven *Hanson/Murakami* **SCR 136**
Waterlife *Hanson* **W&P 145, SCR 129**
Waters of life *Kutscher* **VO 95**
We are an offering *Liles* **W&P 146, HCW 182**
We are called *Haas* **GC 718, RS 820, W&P 147**
We are faithful *Bolduc* **VO 96**
We are God's people *Haas* **GC 97, RS 138**
We are God's work of art *Haugen* **GC 808**
We are his hands *Gersmehl* **COK 85**
We are many parts *Haugen* **GC 733, RS 840**
We are marching in the light of God *South African* **WOV 650, W&P 148, REN 306**
We are members of each other *McLean* **WIS 37**
We are the hope *Tate* **VO 97**
We are the light of the world *Greif* **REN 288**
We bow before his holy name *Ylvisaker* **BC**
We bow down *Paris* **HCW 183, W&P 149, REN 38**
We bring the sacrifice of praise *Dearman* **W&P 150, MAR 251, CEL 213**
We can be lifted up *Hanson* **SCR 105**
We choose the fear of the Lord *Dearman* **MAR 78**
We come to the hungry feast *Makeever* **DH 84, WOV 766**
We come to your feast *Joncas* **GC 850**
We cry out for grace again *Kerr* **HMS12 1045**
We declare your name *Baloche/Baloche* **HMS10 874**
We gather as one *Dinise/Howard* **VO 100**
We have been told *Haas* **GC 699**
We have come into his house *Ballinger* **TFF 136**
We know and believe *Glover* **GC 836**
We long to see your face *Keil* **RS 47**
We love you *Hanson* **SCR 147**
We receive power *Marchonda* **VO 101**
We rejoice in the grace of God *Cook/Cook/Christopher* **MAR**
We say yes *Walker* **MAR 164**
We see the Lord *Pulkingham* **W&P 153, REN 274**
We shall behold him *Rambo* **MAR**
We shall draw water *Inwood* **G&P 288**
We shall not be moved *Ylvisaker* **BC**
We shall not be silent *Conry* **G&P 559**
We shall rise again *Young* **RS 872**
We walk by faith *Haugen* **GC 590, G-2841, RS 723**
We walk by faith *Ylvisaker* **BC**
We were baptized in Christ Jesus *Ylvisaker* **WOV 698**
We who once were dead *Haas* **G-3504**
We will draw near *Nystrom/Harris* **HMS11 966, HMS13**
We will drink the cup *Haas* **GC 709**
We will glorify *Paris* **W&P 154, HCW 187, TFF 281**
We will rise again *Haas* **G&P 603**
We've come to praise you *Grant/Darnall* **MAR 80**
We've come to worship you *Kerr* **HMS10 878**
Welcome the child *Haugen* **G-3803**
Welcome the King *Kendrick* **HMS12 1048**
What a mighty God we serve! *Traditional* **TFF 295**
What a mighty word God gives! *Traditional* **W&P 155**
What feast of love *Barber* **AFP 11-10674**
What feast of love *English* **WOV 701**
What is this place *Huijbers* **G&P 538, RS 892, GC 748**
What shall I render *Douroux* **TFF 239**
What you are *Harris* **HMS14 18**

When I think of the goodness of Jesus *Traditional* **TFF 269**
When Jesus came preaching *Southern Harmony* **RS 773**
When love is found *Traditional* **WOV 749, GC 865**
When the Lord comes *Flowers* **VIN6 262**
When the Lord in glory comes *Moore* **GC 765**
When we eat this bread *Joncas* **G&P 510**
When you call *Makeever* **DH 100**
When you send forth your Spirit *Makeever* **DH 43**
Where two or three *Kendrick* **HMS12 1050**
Where you lead me *DeShetler/Craig* **HMS13 1113**
While we are waiting, come *Cason* **SPW**
Who are we *Makeever* **DH 33**
Who can this be? *Haas* **G-3499**
Who has known *Foley* **G&P 327**
Who shall live on that holy mountain *Ylvisaker* **BC**
Who will stand up? *Soper* **G-4626**
Whom shall I fear? *Evans* **HMS13 1115**
Why so downcast? *Berrios/Brooks/Hamlin* **HCW 191**
Wind of God *Sadler* **HMS13 1116**
Wind of the spirit *Hanson/Murakami* **SCR 18, W&P 157**
With a shepherd's care *Chepponis* **GC 654, RS 738**
With all my heart *Avery* **CC 11**
With all your heart *Makeever* **DH 95**
With joy you shall draw water *Haugen* **GC 148**
With the Lord there is mercy *Haugen* **RS 176, GC 130**
With the Lord there is mercy *Joncas* **RS 174**
With you by my side *Haas* **G-5008**
Within our hearts be born *Joncas* **GC 329**
Without seeing you *Haas* **GC 844**
Women of faith *Harvill/Arterburn* **HMS13 117**
Wonderful Counselor *Yeager* **MAR2 35**
Wonderful, merciful Savior *Rodgers/Wyse* **SPW**
Worthy the Lamb that was slain *Moen* **HCW 192**
Write it on my heart *McLean* **WIS 41**
Write your law upon our hearts *Makeever* **DH91**

Y, Z

You alone *Hanson/Murakami* **SCR 36**
You are God: Te deum *Haugen* **G-5100**
You are God's work of art *Haas* **GC 810**
You are holy *Brown* **HMS10 884**
You are I Am *Evans* **HMS12 1051**
You are mine *Haas* **COK 58, W&P 158, GC 645, RS 762**
You are my all in all *Jernigan* **HMS11 976, MAR, SPW**
You are my child *Ylvisaker* **BC**
You are my God *Delavan* **HCW 196**
You are my help *Ashton* **PS1**
You are my hiding place *Ledner* **MAR 167, W&P 160**
You are my rock *Carpenter* **VIN6 278**
You are my shepherd *Haas* **G-4994**
You are so faithful *LeBlanc/Gulley* **MAR 84**
You are the branches *Joncas* **CGA-755**
You are the Lord of me *Sims* **SCR 76**
You are the potter *Ylvisaker* **BC**
You are the rock of my salvation *Muller* **W&P 161**
You have anointed me *Balhoff/Ducote/Daigle* **G&P 555, GC 676**
You have been given *Kauflin* **HCW 197**
You have been good *Paris* **HCW 198**
You have called us *DeShazo/Nystrom* **HCW 199**
You have come down to the lakeshore *Gabaraín* **WOV 784, RS 817, G&P 580, GC 696**
You have made a home *Cooney* **GC 67**
You have put on Christ *Dean* **G&P 458**
You have put on Christ *Hughes* **GC 245**
You have rescued me *Dufford* **G&P 475**
You only *McCoy* **VIN8 242**
You satisfy the hungry heart *Kreutz* **WOV 711**
You who are thirsty *Ross* **SPW**
You will draw water *Guimont* **RS 204**
You will show me the path of life *Haugen* **GC 24, RS 36**
You, Lord *Hanson* **W&P 162, SCR 142**
You, Lord, have the message of eternal life *Ogden* **PS2**
You're a child of God *Ylvisaker* **BC**
Your constant love *Hanson* **SCR 100**
Your everlasting love *Batstone* **MAR 85**
Your love is finer than life *Haugen* **GC 62**
Your mercy flows *Sutton* **SPW**
Your mercy like rain *Cooney* **GC 330, G-3971**
Your name is praised *Geary* **PS3**
Your song of love *Fabing* **G&P 583**
Your steadfast love *Sandquist* **HCW 200**
Your wonderful name *Haas* **G-5041**
Zion sing *Deiss* **WLP**